WOMEN IN THERAPY
New Psychotherapies for a
Changing Society

Women in Therapy

New Psychotherapies for a Changing Society

Edited by

VIOLET FRANKS, Ph.D.

Adjunct Professor of Psychology, Graduate School
Rutgers University (New Brunswick)

and

VASANTI BURTLE, M.A., Bar-at-Law

BRUNNER/MAZEL Publishers • New York

CONTRIBUTORS

AKHTER AHSEN, Ph.D.
Director, Eidetic Analysis Institute, Yonkers, New York.

GEORGE R. BACH, Ph.D.
Director, Institute of Group Psychotherapy, Los Angeles, California.

JUDITH M. BARDWICK, Ph.D.
Associate Professor, Psychology Department, University of Michigan, Ann Arbor.

AARON T. BECK, M.D.
Professor of Psychiatry, University of Pennsylvania, Philadelphia.

ALBERT ELLIS, Ph.D.
Executive Director, Institute for Advanced Study in Rational Psychotherapy, New York.

BENJAMIN FABRIKANT, Ph.D.
Professor, Department of Psychology, Fairleigh Dickinson University, Teaneck, New Jersey.

IRIS E. GOLDSTEIN FODOR, Ph.D.
Associate Professor, Department of Educational Psychology, New York University

EDITH S. GOMBERG, Ph.D.
Research Psychologist, Veterans Administration Hospital, Ann Arbor, Michigan; Professor, School of Social Work, University of Michigan, Ann Arbor; and Adjunct Professor, Center of Alcohol Studies, Rutgers University, New Brunswick, New Jersey.

RUTH L. GREENBERG
Research Assistant to Dr. Aaron Beck, University of Pennsylvania, Philadelphia.

EPHRAIM M. HOWARD, Ph.D.
Executive Director of the Jewish Community Council of Lower Bucks County and Associate Director of the Institute of Human Ecology and Living Processes, Bucks County, Pennsylvania.

JOYCE L. HOWARD, M.S., M.S.W.
Associate Director of the Institute of Human Ecology and Living Processes, Bucks County, Pennsylvania.

SUZANNE KELLER, Ph.D.
Professor of Sociology, Princeton University, Princeton, New Jersey.

BARBARA KIRSH, M.A.
Sociologist, Institute for Human Development, Educational Testing Service, Princeton, New Jersey.

ARNOLD A. LAZARUS, Ph.D.
Professor and Chairman, Department of Psychology, University College, Rutgers University, New Brunswick, New Jersey.

ESTHER MENAKER, Ph.D.
Adjunct Professor of Psychology, Postdoctoral Training Program, Department of Psychology, Graduate School of Arts and Science, New York University, and psychoanalyst and psychotherapist in private practice.

HUMPHRY OSMOND, M.R.C.P., F.R.C. Psych.
Former Director, Bureau of Research in Neurology and Psychiatry, New Jersey Neuro-Psychiatric Institute, Princeton, New Jersey.

MIRIAM POLSTER, Ph.D.
Co-Director, Gestalt Training Center, San Diego, California.

BERNARD F. RIESS, Ph.D.
Senior Supervising Psychologist and Training Analyst, Postgraduate Center for Mental Health, New York City.

IRADJ SIASSI, M.D.
Associate Professor and Director of Adult Services in the Department of Psychiatry, Rutgers Medical School, New Brunswick, New Jersey.

ANNE STEINMANN, Ph.D.
President and Principal Investigator of Male-Female Role Research, Maferr Foundation, Inc., affiliated with the Research Department of the Postgraduate Center for Mental Health, New York City.

FOREWORD

Women in Therapy: New Psychotherapies for a Changing Society is a valuable collection of original articles that extend far beyond the scope of the title. Today, what it means to be a woman or a man, feminine or masculine, heterosexual or homosexual is rapidly changing—more rapidly than is reflected in the theory and practice of psychotherapies of every persuasion. Dr. Violet Franks and Ms. Vasanti Burtle have recruited an impressive group of innovative psychologists, psychotherapists and sociologists to confront these changing ideas of sex roles.

In one section of the book a variety of therapists, behavioral, analytical, Gestalt, group and others, consider the impact of the new feminism on their practice and thought. Other sections are devoted to the unique aspects of the female depressive, the female phobic, the female alcoholic, the female prisoner, the female homosexual and the female in mental hospitals. Still other parts of this far-ranging collection deal with the history of changing views of sex roles and the biological background of sex and gender.

Although the neglect and distortion of women in and by psychology was a major stimulus for most of the authors, both male and female, the book's contribution is probably equally important for the understanding and helping of men.

Hopefully, this book marks the beginning of a true psychology and sociology of women and the end of the female in psychology as a slightly degraded, slightly inverted, always derivative male.

CHARLES G. GROSS, PH.D.
Professor of Psychology
Princeton University

CONTENTS

ix

PREFACE

It is impossible to face today's world without becoming aware of unprecedented and rapid changes. To appreciate the changing and ever-increasing demands placed upon therapists by women and their families, it is necessary to update our thinking and examine the significant contributions of contemporary therapists in the light of these changes. It is also necessary to look at pertinent research findings as they bear on the role of WOMAN.

Traditionally, and even understandably in a man's world, psychotherapy for women has been viewed from a male vantage point. Ironically, the majority of clients who consult therapists are women and the majority of therapists they consult are men. If therapy is carried out primarily by men in a male-oriented society, then it is tempting—as certain prominent feminists have recently done—to draw the seemingly obvious conclusion that therapy as it now exists fails to take into account the special needs of women. Questioning the validity of this conclusion, we decided that a carefully selected series of papers from a small but distinguished group of experts in the field would be of inestimably greater value than a plethora of assumptions and allegations. To this end, we invited some score of contributors to provide chapters, either individually or in collaboration, and, to our delight, they all accepted. The results are a searching examination of women, their changing roles and identities, their problems, and what happens when they seek professional help. Hopefully, by bringing together such material, we can gain a truer perspective of what is currently going on in the rapidly evolving world of women.

It is no longer necessary to be concerned with arguments about puerile issues such as whether women have "castration complexes," or whether they have "empty space" syndromes, or whether "anatomy is destiny." Like the dodo bird, such polemics become extinct. It is time to examine really vital concerns. Women and their therapists will have to scrutinize the new options and the old roles, and the emerging problems of our changing society. In our search we will find new and constructive directions.

If it is not too presumptuous of us, the goal of this volume is to "raise the consciousness" of our readers, regardless of sex. This can hardly be considered revolutionary for, after all, all books of potential significance have as one of their implicit goals the raising of consciousness. When a book leaves the reader with new knowledge, it changes old clichéed thinking and stereotypes—and this is what consciousness-raising is really about. The women's movement is asking for a reexamination by society at large of the roles and rights of women. Psychotherapists, in their turn—male and female—must reaffirm their recognition that their female clients suffer emotional problems not in a vacuum but in an environment which has conditioned them to think and feel the way they do. These learned constraints provide pressures, frustrations and restrictions which perpetuate poor mental health. It is a "cop out" in this day and age to take refuge in Freudian and other unvalidated assumptions.

One effective method of becoming aware of the value of psychotherapy for women is to draw upon the ideas and experiences of leading therapists and thinkers who are themselves innovators in their field. The authors of the chapters that follow have spent many years either researching or clinically observing human behavior; some have pioneered new therapeutic techniques, others have revised traditional procedures to satisfy contemporary issues. Treating women without becoming aware of these ongoing developments and innovations is like practicing medicine without being aware of the discovery of antibiotics.

Of the many therapies represented in this book, no single approach is necessarily the therapy of choice. It is the unique combination of client needs, the inclinations of the therapist and the demonstrated efficacy of the therapy involved which determine the most effective procedure for the resolution of any particular problem. It is our hope that the present volume will offer many ideas and paradigms for a better understanding between the sexes and a fuller realization of woman's growth and potential both in the public sector and in private life.

We are grateful to the many who have given invaluable aid and support throughout the lengthy engineering of this book. Dr. Norman Adler of the University of Pennsylvania and Dr. Aura E. Star of the Biology Department of Trenton State College gave us helpful suggestions with respect to the technical material which appears in Dr. Bardwick's chapter, and Chérie Diamond carefully and professionally prepared the diagrams. We especially thank Dr. Suzanne Keller of Princeton University who not only contributed the last chapter of the book but gave generously and graciously of her very busy time in the form of both encouragement and helpful suggestions.

We also thank Dr. G. Terence Wilson of Rutgers University for providing the ignition which sparked this project—an essential to a beginning—and Mary Bahr who typed the initial letters which helped get the book started.

If the saying is true that behind the man there is a woman, we also must say that behind the editors of this volume there is a man. This man is Dr. Cyril M. Franks, husband of one of the editors, who contributed lovingly and unstintingly of his time, energy and ideas.

We are pleased to admit and even to emphasize that our efforts in bringing this volume together were completely androgenous. Many men and women are involved. This becomes particularly obvious if we look at our list of contributors, to whom we give our special gratitude. We are indeed fortunate to have had the cooperation of writers, both male and female, with so much foresight, knowledge and competence in their fields! Needless to say, if the credit for the individual contribution goes to the author concerned, the overall responsibility for any omissions and other deficits must be our own.

VIOLET FRANKS
VASANTI BURTLE

Princeton, New Jersey
March 1974

Part I
AN HISTORICAL VIEW

1

CHANGING VIEWS OF WOMEN AND THERAPEUTIC APPROACHES: SOME HISTORICAL CONSIDERATIONS

HUMPHRY OSMOND, VIOLET FRANKS
and VASANTI BURTLE

Since a brief chapter cannot contain that which would properly be the subject of a large book, we can only offer here some hints and indications suggesting the importance of the historical background to current psychiatric treatment for women, as well as to those activities usually subsumed under the general heading of psychotherapy. Even this foreshortened approach has been restricted to Western Europe, not because the experiences of generations of women in other cultures are unimportant, but because the place available and the learning of these authors are inadequate to such a huge task.

EARLY DEVELOPMENT OF PSYCHOTHERAPY FOR WOMEN

There seem to have been three major phases in the development of psychotherapy for women. The first emerged from what Hugh Trevor Roper called the appalling "witchcraft craze" of the 16th and 17th centuries. This was the crowning misfortune of an age of war, schism and pestilence. Because of this craze, large numbers of men, women and children were put to death, often after suffering dreadful tortures. In theory, there was the clear distinction between the witch and the bewitched; the bewitched were the victims of the malice of witches expressed through witchcraft, while witches were those who had made a pact with the devil, selling their immortal souls for immediate advantages. The religious practitioners of the day believed that bewitchment should be treated by exorcism, which included rigorous activities of various kinds not always

3

clearly distinguishable from torture. Those who became witches were in principle excommunicated until they repented but, even after repentance, they were liable to be executed, often by burning, in order to save their souls even at the expense of their mortal bodies. The Inquisitors and their colleagues did not hesitate to employ the most extreme measures for mortifying the offending flesh and terrifying the minds of those who had strayed. Their aim was to insure sincere repentance, no matter what the cost in pain and suffering, so as to save the immortal souls of those who had been duped by Satan.

The witch craze became inextricably muddled with the religious quarrels of the day and, for reasons which are still not wholly clear, most witches were women. Consequently, the furor of the Inquisitors was expended in torturing and burning tens of thousands of these unfortunates. There can be little doubt that many of those who were bewitched and those who were held to be witches suffered from mental illnesses. In 1563, at the height of the witch craze, the enormously courageous Johann Weir published his famous book, *De praestigiis daemonum,* in which he opposed the belief in demons and witches and suggested that many of the witches were mentally ill. His action made it likely that he himself would be accused of witchcraft and so suffer extreme penalties. Although this did not happen, it was more than a century and a half before Weir's humane point of view became gradually accepted. By the mid-eighteenth century, it became unfashionable to burn mad people at the stake. Nevertheless, their condition was not particularly happy. It was not until the end of the 18th and the beginning of the 19th century that reformers like the Tukes, the great Quaker reformers who founded the retreat at York in the 1790's, and their counterparts in North America developed retreats or asylums for those afflicted by madness. It was in this setting that medical attention became focused upon the problem of mental illness in women. Whatever the limitations of diagnosis and treatment during those times, at least the afflicted people were seen as patients and treated medically.

The second series of events which has had such an enormous bearing on women's affairs and which has totally changed their lives has been so successful that, on the whole, we hardly ever think about it. These events had their beginnings with doctors like James Gordon, Thomas Watson, Oliver Wendell Holmes, and the great Semmelweiss; they culminated in Pasteur and Lister with the development of antisepsis and later asepsis. One consequence of this was the rise of the science of bacteriology which has had a great bearing on the health of mothers and children alike. At the same time, the introduction of anesthesia not only wholly altered the scope of surgery but, due to Queen Victoria's prescience and her inspired notion of using her position as Defensor Fidii and head of the Church of England, it became proper for women to have anesthetics in childbirth. Bishops and others had been uncertain about this and quoted biblical texts justifying women's suffering in childbed. Victoria as monarch and mother used her great authority to announce that it was proper for women to have anesthetics to help them bear children without pain and celebrated this by inhaling chloroform at the birth of Prince Leopold.

It is difficult to overestimate the effects of these developments not only upon the physical health of women, but also upon their psychological outlook. At this time, childbearing was a risky business for both mother and child. Many mothers lost a high proportion of those children whom they had conceived and carried with such peril to themselves. In such circumstances, women did not have to be particularly prudish or especially preoccupied with Victorian respectability to be rather less than wholly enthused about sexual relations. For many women it had been the obvious cause of death of their mothers, sisters, and daughters; school friends expected many of their peers to die in childbed. Every pregnancy involved grave dangers. Most of these obstetrical dramas occurred not in the hygienic seclusion of well-run hospitals, but in homes, thus spreading gloom and terror throughout whole families and often communities. So successful has medicine been regarding these matters that it is difficult if not impossible to evoke the atmosphere in which many women approached pregnancy during the pre-bacteriological era. The imaginative can guess what it was like; the unimaginative should look at the record.

It is only during the last 50 years or so that women have begun to reap the full benefits of those great medical advances made in the middle of the nineteenth century. They have also run into problems occasioned by them. Women now live longer and can, on the whole, expect to enjoy better health than men. They do not consider themselves lucky to survive pregnancy, nor do they expect to suffer the loss of many children. Consequently, they are psychologically and socially quite different creatures from their grandmothers and great-grandmothers. Yet, the customs and outlook of the society in which they live are still somewhat attuned to the older ways. One would expect such changes to be a source of stress and strain, and the evidence suggests that they are.

A third great influence on women during the 1860's was the establishment of a profession for women by that extraordinary social reformer,

Florence Nightingale. Before this, for most women, the opportunity for acquiring professional and administrative skills was very limited indeed. It is true that the so-called "oldest profession" had been open to them for centuries and that a certain number of women had availed themselves of it to rise to the highest positions in society, but not all were either able or willing to make use of this particular route to success. It is true that some women, like Eleanor of Aquitaine, Queen Elizabeth I, Catherine the Great and, in a slightly different way, Queen Victoria had been notable and effective figures in their own right, but this was nearly always on the basis of inheritance and not due to their personal capacity to acquire professional skills.

Recognizing both the need for nursing and the need for women to have an appropriate profession, Florence Nightingale provided a slightly sheltered, but absolutely vital field in which women would be able to acquire techniques of management and governing from which for a variety of reasons they had usually been excluded. The occurrence of two World Wars in the first part of the twentieth century made it clear to even the most misogynistic that healthy and capable women raised from generations who did not expect to die in childbed and had not lost many children early in their lives were very different creatures from the stereotype of women who had lived in those early eras when sex, death and procreation went hand in hand—often to the grave. It is against this background of social and medical progress, which made the lives of millions of women less perilous and so more hopeful, that the need for adequate contraception and family limitation, pioneered so courageously by Margaret Sanger, Marie Stopes and others, became self evident.

This then is the unseen context or, perhaps more accurately, the behind-the-scene context against which we believe women's liberation and the interest in that old rag-bag of activities which we now call psychotherapy for women can best be viewed.

But what is so special about women? If one were able to ignore the perils of childbearing, which are probably greatest in urban societies, it would appear that women, on the whole, are physically as healthy as men and not much more liable to psychiatric illnesses either. But in the past it was impossible to ignore the perils of childbirth which not only included death, but psychotic episodes in the puerperium sometimes associated with infection and sometimes due to endocrine reorganization following parturition. During the 19th century, middle class women led restricted and boring lives while lower class women were often drudges, a situation which did not conduce to physical or mental health. Only aristocratic women and those few remarkable creatures who could surmount the obstacles of custom and morality were able to develop their native talents to any great extent. Very few women were well educated, and this was taken to mean by the imperceptive that it was hardly worthwhile wasting education upon those who were naturally frail. The high mortality in early womanhood due to childbearing, the appalling blows suffered by most mothers with the loss of some proportion of their children, combined with the ill health attendant upon inept gynecology and obstetrics, supported those who felt that women could not bear the burden of education when they were already bearing the burden of reproducing the species. While this now sounds like a rather cheap rationalization, 150 years ago or so, it would receive powerful support from anyone who chose to wander around churchyards looking at the inscriptions on the stones. There, one finds the remains of many young mothers and many children under the age of five.

The importance of the reproductive process in women's physical and mental economy has been noted by physicians for centuries. This is hardly surprising in view of the remarkable changes which occur in the uterus during pregnancy and parturition and the physical and psychological disasters which can sometimes accompany and follow this complicated process. Nevertheless, the importance ascribed to the wandering or discontented womb which gave the name to the disorder "hysteria" in women has waxed and waned over many centuries. Benjamin Rush (1743-1813), who was one of the first to write on psychiatry in the U.S.A., did not consider hysteria a uterine condition, but viewed the disease as a token of social distinction among the well born. He did, however, believe that the hysterical condition occurred in women only, though he described something very similar in men using rather different terms. Storer, however, a psychiatrist writing in the 19th century (1871), believed that mental illness in women was more the result of disturbances in their sexual organs than due to changes in their brains. He believed that there was some connection between the female sexual and reproductive organs and the nervous system, which had nothing to do with the brain. He described the "frequent coincidence of uterine crisis or uterine disease with insanity in women" (1972, p. 104). A contemporary, Kellogg (*ibid.*, p. 84), who was of much the same opinion, wrote, "the abnormal mental state of many patients laboring under hysterical menorrhagia, dysmenorrhea, amenorrhea and the affections intimately associated with uterine derangement has long been observed by medical men." Storer quotes the great Dr. John Conolly of Hanwell as noting that "the cases of recent insanity in young women, and especially the cases of puerperal insanity and those arising from lactation were perhaps the first to attract particular attention in reference to the new system." This new system was Conolly's no-restraint.

In her excellent book on hysteria, Ilza Veith (1965) shows that mental disorder was considered sex-related during the 19th century. Indeed, at the beginning of this century, 1909, hysteria was said to affect the female sex almost exclusively, while hypochondriasis affected the male sex almost exclusively. Neurasthenia affected both sexes almost equally. Today, neurasthenia is rarely discussed. Hysteria and hypochondriasis are still retained, though they are no longer sex-related conditions.

Silas Weir Mitchell, the great neurologist-novelist who was thirty years older than Freud and died in 1914 at the age of 85, specialized in the mental disorders of the leisured classes, particularly women. Oddly enough, a self-report written by an influential, though not highly publicized, feminist named Charlotte Perkins Gilman (1935) exists regarding the Mitchell treatment. Mrs. Gilman consulted Dr. Mitchell after the birth of her first and only child early in her marriage, at which time she was suffering from a bout of incapacitating depression. Mitchell was famous for charming his female patients, but he did not succeed with Charlotte Gilman and started on the wrong note by speaking in a rather offhand way about the Beechers, a prominent family with whom she was related. Gilman believed that while Mitchell was well versed in two kinds of "nervous prostration"—that of the businessman exhausted by too much work and the society woman "exhausted by too much play"— her neurosis was beyond him. He recommended the famous rest cure, and she promptly became worse. When the rest cure did not work, she reports in her own words, "By repeated proof that the moment I left home, I began to recover, it seemed right to give up a mistaken marriage." She went on to become a famous writer and orator and lived to a happy old age, though still bothered by recurrent bouts of depression.

She wrote a short story, "The Yellow Wallpaper," in 1891, which was widely read and revealed her own struggle with insanity. She sent a copy of this to Dr. Silas Weir Mitchell "to convince him of the error of his ways" but never received a reply. However, many years later she met someone who was a close friend of Dr. Mitchell and told her that he had changed his treatment of nervous prostration after reading "The Yellow Wallpaper." "If that is a fact, I have not lived in vain," replied Charlotte Perkins Gilman. It seems that this highly intelligent feminist was able to influence a leading psychiatrist of her time and one would like to think that if something of the kind happened today, she would be equally successful. This, of course, occurred before Freud developed psychoanalysis, for "The Yellow Wallpaper" was written in 1891, preceding his first paper "On Hysteria."

FREUD'S THEORY OF FEMALE PATHOLOGY

While it is debatable whether Freud's work can be considered as initiating psychotherapy, what is undeniable is that his development of psychoanalysis in the early 1890's has become the foundation of much of our current psychotherapeutic endeavor, for even those who are opposed to Freud, and there are many of them, cannot state their position without relating it to his psychoanalysis.

Curiously enough, the development of psychoanalysis, particularly in its early days, was concerned almost exclusively with women patients. The sequence of events from Jones (1967) and other sources was as follows. From 1880-1882, Joseph Breuer, a senior colleague of Freud, treated a lady whom he called Anna O. with a form of hypnotic catharsis which she called "chimney sweeping" or "the talking cure." Breuer spent some two years in this endeavor; he ascribed Anna O.'s condition to distress at her father's death and considered that her symptoms were relieved by his treatment. However, Breuer's wife became so jealous of his preoccupation with his young, beautiful and vivacious patient that he had to bring matters to a close. Anna O., herself, then developed a pseudocyesis. According to Jones, Anna then went to the Gross-Enzersdorf Institution some time later and Breuer was of the opinion that she was quite "unhinged." However, in spite of Breuer's gloomy prognosis, she recovered, but not before she had "inflamed the heart" of her psychiatrist. She was a friend of Martha Freud and, by 1892, she had begun a very successful career as a social worker. As we shall discover later in this book, there are several points of view regarding the relationship of Breuer's treatment to her subsequent recovery. This, however, need not detain us here. Breuer told Freud about Anna O. and Freud was fascinated with the case and discussed it over and over again.

At this time, Freud was an assistant in the Department of Neurology and had little opportunity to treat patients; in 1885, he visited Charcot and told him about Anna O. but the great Frenchman was not very interested. On his return from Paris in 1886, Freud, who had been much influenced by Charcot, read papers on hypnotism at the Physiological Club in Vienna. In September of that year, he married Martha Bernays and, on the 15th of October, read a paper on male hysteria which an-noyed Maeynert who had supported him in his visit to Charcot. Maeynert claimed that hysteria couldn't occur among males. However, on the 26th of November, clinical demonstrations supported Freud who was ap-plauded, but—in consequence—he lost Maeynert as a friend and patron. Following his marriage, Freud had to support his wife and the six chil-dren who arrived in about seven years. In his neurological practice, he saw cases of hysteria and, during 1887 and 1888, treated them with hypnosis, massage and electricity combined with suggestion. In 1889, he visited Bernheim in France regarding hypnosis and, on the first of May of that year, began to treat Frau Emmy by the cathartic method for hysteria about which he had first heard seven years earlier from Breuer. By 1892, that is ten years after his meeting with Breuer, he had decided that no neurasthenia occurred without some disturbance of sexual function. In the fall of that year, he treated Fraulein Elizabeth von R. for hysteria by a combination of head-pressing and forced associa-tion. He also treated a Miss Lucy, an English governess, and a girl whom he calls Catherina, aged 18, whom he saw in one interview in the high Alps. In 1893, Breuer and Freud presented their paper, "Psychical Mecha-nisms of Hysterical Phenomena" in which the seduction theory was first announced. In 1895, Breuer and Freud published their studies on hysteria and, on the 14th, 21st, and 28th of October of that year, Freud presented his paper "Uber hysteria" before the Doktor Kollegium. According to Jones, Freud said that Breuer spoke favorably of him publicly but told Freud in a disparaging way, "I don't believe a word of it."

It is important to recognize that, in these four cases which constitute, with the case of Anna O., the famous studies on hysteria, the method used in no way resembles that which we would now consider to be psycho-analytic, for it included hypnotic suggestion, electrical stimulation, mas-sage, baths, rest, forced associations as well as catharsis. Freud seems to have discovered the method he later came to use—free association—from his patient Fraulein Elizabeth von R. in the autumn of 1892. According to Jones, "The patient lying down with closed eyes was asked to concentrate her attention on a particular symptom and tried to recall any memories which might throw light upon its origins. When no progress was made, Freud would press her forehead with his hand and assure her that then some thoughts and memories would indubitably come to her. Sometimes in spite of that, nothing would seem to happen even when the pressure of the hand was repeated. Then, perhaps on the fourth attempt, the patient would bring out the comment, 'I could have told you that the first time, but I didn't think it was what you wanted.' Such experience confirmed his confidence in the device which indeed seemed to him infallible. They also made him give the strict injunction to ignore all censorship and to express every thought, even if they considered it to be irrelevant, unimportant or unpleasant. This was the first step towards the later free-association method."

By March, 1896, Freud had a paper in the *Review Neurologique* on "Traumatic Seduction in Hysteria, etc.," in which he reported 19 fully analyzed cases, all of whom had been seduced. In his paper on the "Etiology of Hysteria and the Seduction Theory" on the second of May of that year, Freud modestly referred to this as "a momentous revelation, the discovery of a caput Nili [source of the Nile] of neuropathology." The great sexologist von Krafft-Ebing, who was to recommend Freud's appointment as a professor some years later, called this "a scientific fairy tale." Freud, however, was undeterred by skepticism and continued to be of the opinion "categorically that the specific cause of all neuroses is some disturbance in the sexual function of the patient. A current one with the actual neurosis and one in the past life with psychoneurosis. More precisely, the cause of hysteria is a passive sexual experience before puberty, i.e., a traumatic seduction. This conclusion was based on thirteen fully-analyzed cases—the age of predilection for the experience was three or four and Freud surmises that one occurring at eight or ten will not lead to neurosis."

In October of 1896, Freud's father died and he said of himself, "Now I feel quite uprooted." In the spring of 1897, he wrote to Fleiss that he was still convinced of the seduction theory. He believed that a large proportion of fathers were involved—that these were not only incestuous, but perverse (i.e., oral and anal); he had noticed symptoms in his brother and several sisters but *not* in himself. He was thus incriminating his recently-deceased father, although it appears that some doubts had crept in. He had had a dream about his niece, Hella, which convinced him of his own incestuous wishes towards his own elder daughter Mathilde, then aged about nine, although not for his younger daughter, Anna, aged four, who, according to the theory, would have been more at risk. He considered that this dream gave him firsthand evidence supporting his theory.

During June and July of that year, his letters to Fleiss report much depression and intellectual paralysis "such as I have never imagined." Jones sees Freud as hovering on the edge of discovery of the oedipus complex and of the "unexpected discovery of his deeply buried hostility to his father." Since he had already accused the recently dead old gentleman of buggering his brothers and sisters, one may ask what was holding him back?

In his letter of the 21st of September to Fleiss, Freud was forced to abandon his seduction theory. As he said of this many years later, "Reality was lost from under my feet." Freud's account of the collapse of the seduction theory was supposedly due to (1) the failure to bring analysis to a proper conclusion scientifically and therapeutically, (2) his astonishment that all his patients' fathers were given to perversity which would then be remarkably common, (3) his "clear perception" that in the unconscious, there is no criterion of reality, (4) the consideration that such memories never emerge in the most severe psychoses. Freud wrote to Fleiss saying, "I have a feeling of victory rather than defeat." Neither he nor Jones could explain this—it seemed at least possible that this was expressing his belief that, if the theory was correct, he was now domiciled with two young ladies who were just about ready for traumatic seduction by him. Freud was hoist with his own petard. His only way out was to destroy his own theory or be confronted with a monstrous situation.

During the next five years, the wreckage of the seduction theory slowly metamorphosed into something entirely different. Daughters who had previously been the focus of their father's unbridled and brutal sexuality from the age of three or four onwards now play a minor and indeed inconsequential role. Sons instead take the center of the psychoanalytic stage and join battle with their overbearing fathers in order to possess their mothers incestuously. In the new drama, the fathers, vexed by their sons' demands, seek to castrate them, and the sons respond with patricide. The seduction theory has vanished and has been replaced by the cornerstone of psychoanalysis, the oedipus complex. The greatest difference between the two theories lay in the fact that, unlike the earlier "caput Nili" of neuropathology which was supposedly based on real events, the new theory was concerned with fantasies, products of the imagination. It thus became incapable of refutation, but this useful quality placed psychoanalysis outside science which has no place for theories which are, in principle, irrefutable. However, at the turn of the century, Freud was probably not aware of this requirement of scientific theories which only became clearly recognized with Popper's work many years later.

What both theories have in common is a preoccupation with incest and an assumption that women are remarkably passive and tractable, the mere objects of male desire.

It took Freud about five years to reconstruct his theory. We can find no evidence that he retracted his earlier dogmatic errors. In a paper in

1898 in which he puts forward his first pronouncement on infantile sexuality, there is no retraction of and no further mention of the seduction theory. From about 1902 onward, it is the oedipal theory which preoccupied Freud most of the time, and it was to this as a dogma that he tried to obtain Jung's oath of allegiance (Jung, 1962). Freud had experienced the collapse of a theory once, and he did not wish to "feel that reality was lost from under my feet again."

He and orthodox Freudians after him came to see the oedipus complex and matters closely relating to it as being the very bedrock of psychoanalytic theory. The part played by women in this development of psychoanalysis does not seem to be large. The main female characteristic which emerged from the Freudian world appears to have been docility combined perhaps with envy that she was not a man. This doubtless did represent fairly well the feelings of many, but by no means all, middle-class women in Vienna in Freud's day, but it would be rash to suppose that this was a universal characteristic of female kind. Freud, however, as we have already noticed, was not one to avoid the most extensive generalizations based on modest data—he was nothing if not a generalizer. He had established his traumatic seduction theory of hysteria in 19 fully-analyzed cases, all of whom he had said he believed had been seduced. In his later years, he frequently discussed the great numbers of cases psychoanalysts had seen, but I have never seen any lists showing the exact number. It goes without saying, of course, that the fully-analyzed cases of 1896 had usually been under treatment a few weeks or a few months at most and would certainly not be described as fully analyzed by his spiritual grandsons and granddaughters today.

Psychoanalysis, founded on the oedipal theory, weathered the major schisms surrounding the defection of Adler, Steckel and Jung between 1910 and 1913 and, what surprised Freud more, perhaps, survived the appalling misfortunes of World War I, when it began to rebuild itself. Following that catastrophe, psychoanalysts began to appear on the scene in some numbers. Quite apart from anything else, the exigencies of the holocaust in which something like ten million young and middle-aged men had been killed had greatly and, as it turned out, irrevocably changed the status of women. Before 1914, feminists and suffragettes were eccentrics.. Before the World War was over, a number of governments who had been reluctant to do so previously decided that women had every right to vote—they had proved it.

ORIGINS OF THE SCHIZOPHRENOGENIC MOTHER

While these great changes do not seem to have affected Freud's view of women greatly, they certainly began to alter women's view of themselves. Melanie Klein developed her child analysis in the 1920's and was invited to the London Institute of Psychoanalysis by Ernest Jones to lecture there. According to Melitta Schmideberg (1971), it appeared that Melanie Klein's intention was to supplant Freud the father by enhancing the importance of motherhood and child development, thus enriching and deepening the scope of psychoanalytic theory which was becoming rather stereotyped by this time. In addition, the practical limitations of psychoanalysis were becoming clearer every day. In Schmideberg's words, "Yet in spite of these achievements there was already some disillusionment. Results of psychoanalytic treatment were felt to be not very satisfactory, and the theoretical discussions which consisted essentially in repeating and elaborating Freud's statements had become boring."

Even before the 1914-1918 war, Freud and his colleagues had doubted whether the psychoses, or narcissistic neuroses as they called them, were treatable by psychoanalysis. By the early 1920's, they were quite sure that they were not. It seems at least possible that Freud was beginning to doubt whether psychoanalysis could treat even the neuroses, and, as he later indicated, his main concern now was to see that psychoanalysis separated itself from medicine and became an independent investigatory science. In his later years, this was to lead to a serious difference of opinion within psychoanalysis which soured Freud's relationship with American psychoanalysis. Freud does not seem to have been greatly concerned about the ultimate therapeutic value of psychoanalysis; Ernest Jones, however, took the matter so seriously that the original play equipment for child analysis is apparently sealed in a special glass case in the London Institute of Psychoanalysis, and he had at least two of his children analyzed by Melanie Klein.

In Kleinian psychopathology, the mother had a central role; she was the target for the early hostility of very young children. Klein believed that the child's superego in its most brutal and punishing aspects derived from attacks against the parent who had witnessed the child's hostility, and thus the child comes to project its own aggression against the parent, who was nearly always the mother, within the framework of his personal superego. Much emphasis was placed on the alternating good and bad aspects of the mother in the child's perception and thus, for the first time, there is clear evidence of a dichotomy in mother as perceived by the child. She can be both wholly good or wholly bad.

It should be noted that Melanie Klein did not suggest that the mothers produced these particular responses, for she believed that children with unusual biological propensities might develop a very distorted view of their mothers.

It is with Karen Horney (1933) that, as with Freud in the seduction theory, parents, particularly the mother, begin to be seen as a noxious influence. While Horney does not ascribe any specific emotional disorders to the influence of maternal prohibitions, her viewpoint became the foundation for much more extreme points of view later on. She says, for instance, "the childhood history of a patient with pronounced perfectionistic trends often shows that she had self-righteous parents who exercised unquestioned authoritative sway over the children, an authority that may have referred by many religious standards or primarily to personal autocratic regime. Often, too, the child suffered much unfair treatment such as parents' preference for other siblings or reproaches for things for which not even the parents or another sibling were to blame; although such unfair treatment may not have exceeded the average, it nevertheless created more than average resentment and indignation because of the disparity between the actual treatment and the parents' pretenses of infallibility. Accusations arising on these grounds could not be expressed because the child was too uncertain of his acceptability."

The emphasis has changed greatly from Klein's perception of the rage-filled and vehement child in the full spate of resentment against his mother, to one in which the child is now seen as the victim of a malignant family constellation. In 1933, Horney described the harmful effects on the child of an unconscious transference towards the son of the sexual feelings which the mother entertains towards her own father. She added that, in such cases, both love and hostility are usually repressed towards the child. Horney continued, "One form in which the conflict between love and hate may consciously come out is in an oversolicitous attitude. Referring to the rivalry between mother and daughter which grows out of a father-fixation, Horney comments, "such a rivalry may show in a general intimidation of the child, efforts to ridicule and belittle her, prevent her from looking attractive and meeting boys, and so on; all this with the secret aim of thwarting the daughter in her female development." Some women are born with strong ties not to their fathers, but to their mothers. Horney claimed that, as a result, they turned away from their femininity and assumed domineering attitudes together with a desire to control the children completely. However, she adds they "may be afraid of them and therefore too lax with them."

Reading the works of Freud, Klein, Horney and the many other psychopathologists, it becomes less and less clear how parents, and particularly mothers, might achieve that golden mean, from which divergencies result in such appalling consequences. One of the difficulties inherent in all these psychopathologically-derived theories is that they make it so difficult, if not impossible, to recognize normality. The path of moral development, which anthropologists and sociologists believe is a broad road trod with comparative ease and safety by most people in most societies, becomes in the hands of psychoanalysts of various persuasions a razor's edge spanning a bottomless pit of catastrophes, upon whose uncertain surface angels would fear to tread. Some psychotherapists become distressed when one observes just how effectively most people cope with these ever-present dangers. Perhaps by hearing about so many and various perils some mothers have had their self-confidence and resilience sapped, rendering them unable to use their natural abilities and thus making them less capable of meeting their very demanding role.

By 1933 then, Melanie Klein's attempt to restore the importance of the mother was resulting in a pre-eminence in vice, rather than virtue. Horney clearly delineates the mother as a transmitter of pathology. Later investigators promoted her to become the major generator of human misfortune. In other words, the incestuous and ravishing ogre-father of Freud was being replaced by an ogress-witch mother not one whit less horrible. By 1931, Harry Stack Sullivan had already formulated his theory regarding the malevolent transformation of personality due to environmental influences. In later studies of the etiology of psychopathology, particular attention was paid to the interaction between patients and their mothers. Mothers' attitudes came to be held responsible for or were assumed to generate pathology in their children. Studies of schizophrenics, for example, not only stressed the influence of the mother, but noted her overprotection or rejection of the child (Kasanin, Knight and Sage, 1934), a rejection which could be either overt or covert (Hadju-Gimes, 1940), resulting from her personal qualities such as aggressiveness, over-anxiety, oversolicitiousness and ambivalence towards her children (Despert, 1942).

Historically, we have now reached World War II in which once again women showed their growing abilities for executive functions of all kinds. In industry, the Armed Services, in politics, they played an increasingly responsible and noteworthy part, often while running their homes under the gravest difficulties such as bombing and rationing. It is therefore a little curious to discover that, by the end of this period, we should find

Frieda Fromm-Reichmann (1948) writing, "The schizophrenic is painfully distrustful and resentful of other people due to the severe warped rejection he encountered in important people in his infancy and childhood—as a rule mainly in a schizophrenogenic mother." Soon after this, Tietze (1949) wrote in her study of schizophrenic patients, "All mothers were overanxious and obsessive—all were domineering—all mothers were found to be restrictive with regard to the libidinal gratification of their children. Most of them were perfectionists and oversolicitous and more dependent on approval by others than the average mother." But Tietze made it easier to convict the schizophrenogenic mother, for she found, "It is the subtly domineering mother who appears to be particularly dangerous to her child—her methods of control are subtle and therefore do not provoke open rebellion as undisguised domination may." One of the difficulties with such subtleties is that they can be seen everywhere, for they may well be in the eye of the beholder, but, by this time, it was open season on mothers, the father having been displaced with a vengeance.

By 1957, Jackson was writing, "Historically the place of psychogenic trauma in etiology appears to be shifting from Freud's original idea of a single traumatic event to the concept of repetitive trauma. The next step would be not who does what to whom, but *how* who does what. Perhaps the next phase will include a study of schizophrenia or schizophrenias as a family-borne disease involving a complicated host-vector recipient cycle that includes much more than can be connoted by the term schizophrenogenic mother. One can even speculate whether schizophrenia as it is known today will exist if parthenogenesis were the usual mode of propagation of the human species or if women were impersonally impregnated and gave birth to infants who were reared by state nurseries in a communal setting."

Jackson does not seem to have read Bowlby's works on the unfortunate effect of such rearing. After such exaltation of the demonic mother, it is something of a comedown to read the review article by George H. Frank (1965). He states:

> Psychologists generally make the assumption that experiences to which the individual is exposed over a period of time lead to the development of learned patterns of behavior. From this, psychologists have reasoned that the experiences the individual has in his early life at home with his family in general, and his mother in particular, are major determinants in the learning of the constellation of behaviors subsumed under the rubric, personality, and, in particular, in the development of psychopathology.
> A review of the research of the past 40 years failed to support this

assumption. No factors were found of the parent-child interaction of schizophrenics, neurotics or those with behavior disorders which could be identified as unique to them or which could be distinguished one root from the other, or any of the groups from the families of controls.

It is difficult to believe that the pillorying of the schizophrenogenic mother which has been achieved by popular press, many novels, radio, television and films has been particularly helpful for raising the self-esteem and improving the self-image of mothers in particular and women in general. Insofar as it can be termed a medical development, since at least some of those involved in the matter were medically qualified, it seems to us that the schizophrenogenic mother should be looked upon as being an iatrogenic disease. Perhaps one of the main goals for psycho-therapies designed to benefit women and to help them fulfill their function in a puzzling and rapidly changing world might be to banish this harmful and poisonous concept. Such banishment can only be at-tained by a more scholarly inquiry into its development than we have been able to do in so brief an article. It seems hardly credible to us that women would wittingly inflict upon themselves the responsibility for causing so grave an illness as schizophrenia on such dubious evidence, but this is not the first time that grave illnesses have been ascribed to dubious and even nonexistent causes. For the best part of a century, an astonishing variety of illnesses were ascribed to masturbation and the lives of several generations of children made quite miserable on this ac-count. Scholarly inquiry has now shown that the origin of this delusion derived from the writings of an 18th-century priest whose views were taken up by a famous French physician, Tissot, and were, with a few honorable exceptions, propagated by other physicians as being part of the conventional wisdom of medicine and scientifically correct; it is humiliat-ing to think that so much misery was inflicted for so little reason. This should stimulate us to rid ourselves of the schizophrenogenic mother whose unnecessary presence we have fastened on ourselves for a quarter of a century. This would benefit a host of those who are currently mothers and large numbers of those who will become mothers. It would seem that women therapists in particular have an especial responsibility in this matter since, ironically, members of their own sex seem to have played such a formidable part in propagating this misleading and damag-ing notion.

We hope too that therapists of both sexes will be alert to the fact that, as with Freud's seductive rapist-father and the schizophrenogenic mother, convenient lay figures which have been derived for the purpose of theory have an inconvenient habit of developing a life of their own. Very few people are really at home with theoretical constructs. Whether such constructs happen to be seducer-fathers, castrating fathers, castrating mothers or schizophrenogenic mothers makes little difference. We have an ineluctable tendency to ascribe these constructs to living people who, like other living people, tend to have weaknesses and frailties. Many parents are not seen at their best when their children have developed some very serious illness even when the doctors are clear about the etiology and are united as to exactly what should be done. In schizophrenia, as in other psychiatric illnesses, this consensus rarely exists, and the parents, already frightened and confused by the disaster which has struck their family, are often seen at their worst. In such circumstances it is not difficult to invest them with the monstrous qualities which Freud and his successors derived to sustain their theories. The fact that those theories were never very convincing to those who were well acquainted with schizophrenia and other psychoses, with many of them now obsolete, has not prevented their being used with cruel bravura to the detriment of patients and parents alike.

THREE MODERN TYPES OF PSYCHOTHERAPY

It may appear that we are implying that psychotherapy should be avoided not only by women but by anyone else; that, however, is not so. What we are suggesting is that this vague and inclusive term requires careful scrutiny both by those who intend to practice it and those who intend to receive its benefits. At one time or another, it has been used to describe everything from such courtesies and considerations as good physicians give their patients to those mind-expanding inspirations which engender a change of life-style and are usually thought to lie in the province of the prophet or guru. This diverse spectrum of activities includes, among other things, Freudian psychoanalysis, encounter groups, primal screaming, Berne's games-playing, Glasser's reality therapy and innumerable permutations and combinations on this enormous theme. It seems to be characteristic of psychotherapists that, however modestly they begin, they usually end by being convinced that their particular method or interpretation is not only better than anyone else's, but has in addition the quality of conferring universal benefits upon all humanity. From time to time, these enthusiasts have even suggested that life itself should be defined in terms of psychotherapy. And then, no doubt, the deity would be described as The Great Therapist.

To account for some of these peculiarities, Miriam Siegler (1973) and one of the authors have suggested that there are at least three kinds of psychotherapy which must be distinguished from each other if we are to avoid an appalling muddle. Though they did not necessarily originate in clinical medicine, for the formal development of this activity owed much to Freud and his associates, all three derive their name from Janet Émile Coué, the father of autosuggestion, and many other physicians, who worked during the last century or so. The very name "psychotherapy" implies some kind of medical activity aimed at treating the mind or soul. This immediately introduced ambiguity, for medicine is seldom concerned with the salvation or philosophy of its patients, but rather with the response of their minds and bodies to treatments intended to cure or alleviate illnesses. Siegler, therefore, suggested that this medically derived activity should be called Psychotherapy I or Medical Psychotherapy. It can then be defined as a form of treatment for people who are in the sick role, which can only be given by a physician or someone supervised by a physician, with the intention of alleviating or curing illnesses by psychological or mental means. This aspect of all treatment has only recently been formalized as psychotherapy, but it has been part of medicine for millennia. It is not confined to psychiatry and never has been. It seems doubtful to us whether, as regards Psychotherapy I, women really have any very special problems except insofar as there is a marked bias in many countries against women physicians. Consequently, most physicians are males, often in their middle and later years, and frequently of a rather conservative disposition. It is therefore likely that women will encounter prejudices during this kind of psychotherapy which may inconvenience, distress and annoy them. If women patients become more vocal regarding these annoyances and as more women enter medicine, such annoyances will be reduced. There seems no reason why medical education should not develop so as to make them very infrequent.

In addition to psychotherapeutic activities dealing immediately with illnesses, there is a second aspect of Psychotherapy I whose goal is to speed recovery from illness, to repair the damage done by it and to prevent recurrences. Even though the physician may do no more than prescribe the particular kind of activity or activities, which may then be given to some other suitable specialist, this remains a medically-directed enterprise. There is an almost exact analogy here with physiotherapy; most physicians who prescribe physiotherapy are far less competent at doing it than those physiotherapists who give the treatments. Nevertheless, physiotherapists accept medical direction, often of a very general kind, because the patients are ill and are in the sick role. It should be noted, however, that many physiotherapists practice quite independently from physicians, particularly in helping athletes of various kinds. Medical psychotherapy in its formal aspects, then, is concerned with the treatment of the psychiatric illnesses whose nature can be specified by psychiatrists, the physicians responsible for treating them. All physicians are expected to be able to recognize and to some extent treat psychiatric problems arising among their patients being treated for medical, surgical and similar conditions. However, there is much more to psychotherapy than this, even though it is doubtful whether most patients today receive the medical psychotherapy which they really require.

Psychotherapy II probably emerged from Psychotherapy I during those years when psychoanalysis was slowly developing training analysis. Various people have claimed the honor of doing this, but these details are less important than the fact that, during the 1920's, Freud and his colleagues began psychoanalyzing people who were not *patients* and, therefore, could not occupy the sick role. These early analysands who were not patients were of two kinds: some were psychoanalysts in training, whether medically qualified or not, and others were creative people who wished to undertake psychoanalysis to increase their insights into life, to acquire greater self-understanding, and to enlarge their general well-being. This role of psychoanalysand is seldom mentioned today, possibly because it is a clumsy word. Siegler and Osmond (1974) have suggested that it be called the "psych" role, since the person concerned is not a patient and, therefore, illness and recovery are not at issue. Psychotherapy II then is a form of educational activity aimed at promoting psychological and social skills in people who are not ill and who do not occupy the sick role. Its goal is to help people to develop their assets and to reduce their liabilities. This kind of therapy includes various forms of psychoanalysis, many kinds of counseling, guidance, behavior therapy, and the teaching of desirable skills which have not yet been acquired, or the refining of those which already exist. It might even include Dale Carnegie courses, Arthur Murray dancing courses, public speaking courses, language courses and other 20th-century versions of the old schools of deportment. It seems most unlikely to us that a medical education is a prerequisite for undertaking this kind of teaching activity.

As Freud became more and more preoccupied with the "psych" role, he became less and less interested in the medical concern of treating patients, which caused considerable disagreement within psychoanalysis itself. During the last 40 years, a great variety of these educational psycho-therapeutic endeavors have developed from which the curious, the ener-getic, the adventurous and dissatisfied may make their choice. There is now a plethora of psychotherapies ranging from classical psychoanalysis, which still continues even though it has become steadily longer with the years, to a great variety of encounter groups with sizes from seven or eight to as many as a hundred whose members undertake their exertions decorously or with abandonment, sometimes completely clothed, at other times entirely nude.

Psychiatrists, like other physicians, naturally have their opinions re-garding the desirability of these activities, but, once it is recognized that they are not part of medicine, then they come to be seen in a very differ-ent light. Surgeons, for instance, probably use a disproportionate amount of their skill upon victims of accidents caused by bobsledding, skydiving, and grand-prix driving. They have done much to encourage the develop-ment of safer equipment, protective clothing, etc., but, so far as we know, they have not attempted to discourage these sports and some surgeons have even become distinguished participants. As yet, very few psychiatrists have been able to recognize Psychotherapy II as a form of education, recreation, or sport and they usually discuss it, often heatedly, as if it were a clandestine treatment, but since Psychotherapy II does not entail giving or accepting the sick role, it can only be considered as treatment if that term is distorted beyond all usefulness.

Psychiatrists as physicians can hardly object to people improving their social, sexual, psychological and managerial manners and this is clearly the intention of those who participate in Psychotherapy II. If this dis-tinction between the two varieties of psychotherapy becomes explicit, we believe that it would then be much easier for women to decide what kinds of Psychotherapy II are particularly helpful to members of their sex at this time when they are assailed by so many problems deriving from the kaleidoscopic changes in a world in flux.

Our studies of psychotherapy suggest that improving illnesses and in-creasing one's psychosocial skills do not exhaust the possibilities of this activity. A small number of psychotherapists are concerned neither with treatment nor with improving various skills; their goal is enlightenment, and they wish to recruit disciples who would opt for their particular form of enlightenment. We have called this Psychotherapy III or En-lightenment Psychotherapy. Those who are enlightened hope to transcend natural limitations and so the candidates for this experience, as a general rule, are thought not to be in need of either Psychotherapy I or Psychotherapy II. Apart from those who, like St. Paul on the road to Damascus, suffer involuntary enlightenment at the hand of God, most seekers find a suitable master or guru who is enlightened, become a disciple, abide by the will of the enlightened person until it "takes," when in some way— still obscure—one is recognized as being a member of the elect. Laing and some others seem to believe that those, to use his terminology, who have been labeled "schizophrenic" are particularly good candidates for enlightenment under his guidance. However, not all masters or gurus who are engaged in the enlightening of others consider that schizophrenia is a valuable first step towards this desired end.

We do not know why these three wholly different activities have become so inextricably muddled during the last 20 years or so but, whether we like it or not, we are faced with the bewildering consequences of a failure to be explicit about matters in which ambiguity must reduce understanding, decrease the chances of benefit, and increase the likelihood of harm. This is not an academic matter. Treatment for illness, receiving an enriching psychosocial education, and being guided towards enlightenment are all worthy enterprises, but those being recruited for any one of them have a right to know which one they are undertaking, and to decide whether they are agreeable to so doing and whether they believe it will meet their needs. Like any delicate useful and expensive tool, psychotherapy must be employed with discrimination and, to obtain the best from it, both its goals and its limitations must be clearly understood.

We hope that this brief survey will put into perspective some of those historical factors which determine not only the varieties of psychotherapy available today, but also the ways in which they are perceived both by those who are skilled in these matters and by those who require their services. Where complicated services are being rendered from one person to another, the results are far more likely to be mutually satisfactory if there is a mutuality and complementarity of expectations. This sometimes happens today, but in our view it would happen much more often if all those involved realized that, for historical reasons, misunderstandings are liable to occur unless those participating in psychotherapy are able to agree from the start upon the nature of the activities to which they are mutually committed. Some of the obstacles to mutual commitment can best be understood in the light of the curious history of psychotherapy which we have sketched here in a manner that is necessarily impressionistic and inadequate. The chapters that are to follow are designed to explore the contemporary status of psychotherapy with respect to the position of women in today's changing society. By trying to understand some of the historical roots, perhaps we can gain better knowledge of current conditions.

REFERENCES

DESPERT, L. Prophylactic aspect of schizophrenia in childhood. *Nervous Child*, 1, 199-231, 1942.

FRANK, G. H. The role of the family in the development of psychopathology. *Psychological Bulletin*, 64, 191-205, 1965.

FROMM-REICHMANN, F. Notes on the development of treatment of schizophrenia by psychoanalytic psychotherapy. *Psychiatry*, 11, 263-273, 1948.

GILMAN, C. P. *The Living of Charlotte Perkins Gilman: An Autobiography.* New York: D. Appleton-Century, Inc., 1935.

HADJU-GIMES, L. Contributions to the etiology of schizophrenia. *Psychoanalytic Review*, 27, 411-438, 1940.

HORNEY, K. Maternal conflicts. *American Journal of Orthopsychiatry*, 4, 175-181, 1933.

JACKSON, D. D. A note on the importance of trauma in the genesis of schizophrenia. *Psychiatry*, 20, 181-184, 1957.

JONES, E. *Life and Work of Sigmund Freud.* London: Pelican Books, 1967.

JUNG, C. G. *Memories, Dreams and Reflections.* New York: Pantheon Books, 1962.

KASANIN, J., KNIGHT, E., & SAGE, P. The parent-child relationship in schizophrenia. *J. of Nervous and Mental Diseases*, 79, 249-263, 1934.

KLEIN, M. *Psychoanalysis of Children.* New York: Norton, 1932.

SCHMIDEBERG, M. A contribution to the history of the psychoanalytic movement in Britain. *British Journal of Psychiatry*, 118, 61-68, 1971.

SIEGLER, M. & OSMOND, H. Notes on orthomolecular psychiatry and psychotherapy. *Journal of Orthomolecular Psychiatry*, 2, 1973.

SIEGLER, M. & OSMOND, H. *Models of Madness; Models of Medicine.* New York: Macmillan (in press).

STORER, H. R. *The Causation, Course and Treatment of Reflex Insanity in Women.* New York: Arno Press and *The New York Times*, 1972. (Originally published by Lee and Shepard, New York, 1871).

SULLIVAN, H. S. Environmental factors in etiology and course under treatment of schizophrenia. *Medical Journal and Record*, 133, 19-22, 1931.

TIETZE, T. A study of mothers of schizophrenic patients. *Psychiatry*, 12, 55-65, 1949.

VEITH, I. *Hysteria: The History of a Disease.* Chicago: University of Chicago Press, 1965.

Part II
BIOLOGICAL AND CULTURAL INFLUENCES

2

THE SEX HORMONES, THE CENTRAL NERVOUS SYSTEM AND AFFECT VARIABILITY IN HUMANS

JUDITH M. BARDWICK

Overall, American psychology, clinical psychology in particular, has looked for explanations of human behavior in terms of people's relationships to other people, people's relationship with the institutions of their society, and people's relationships with intentions or conflicts within their own heads. There has been a lip-service recognition of the importance of physiological factors but there has been no real commitment to understanding and integrating physiological data into theories of normal development or clinical practice.

This is understandable since environmental or social psychological variables are so complex (and not understood) that the impression persists that explanation would be possible if only one were able to understand and measure these parameters well enough. In addition, physiological psychology, usually experimenting with animals, has largely been preoccupied with micro-variables, too far removed and of seemingly little relevance to human personality factors. Thus it has been rather easy to forget that there may be important physiological processes contributing to clinically significant psychological processes.

There are two main reasons for our interest in physiology: first, there is a goal of developing a more inclusive and valid general theoretical explanation for human psychodynamics; second, there is particular interest in trying to explain differences between the sexes. The gonadal steroids have always been implicated in the animal research on sex differences. For mammals some sex differences, notably the establishment of the potential for masculine behaviors, are due to the effect of testosterone upon the central nervous system during a species-specific prenatal or post-natal

27

critical stage. If testosterone is absent during this early critical stage, no matter what the internal or external genitalia are, the animal is behaviorally female. The gonadal steroids have also been clearly implicated as decisive for the development of certain behavior potentials or patterns after puberty.

Studies of steroid effects have been correlational, observing relationships between steroid level and behaviors or other characteristics. Most of the older work with people assayed steroid levels from urine; that was really a measure of steroid metabolites. Since the steroids estrogen, progesterone and testosterone are biochemically very similar, they metabolize to forms of each other (Bardwick, 1971b, pg. 26) and the measurement of *in vivo* levels was intrinsically unreliable. Now, new endocrine measurement techniques using blood plasma and radioactive assays permit a new level of accuracy. As a result there has been a recent explosion of research on the effects of the steroids.

The ultimate goal is to relate steroid levels, their presence or absence, to effects in the central nervous system. In other words, as the *in vivo* steroid levels change, correlative changes in the patterns of affects, behaviors, or sensory processes need to be examined. In the end, the explanation must be rooted in central nervous system physiology as that physiology is influenced by the steroids. The new data allow us to come closer to explaining the correlations as those data relate steroid levels with activity of the neural synapses. The gonadal steroids apparently influence at least some parts of the central nervous system directly because they alter transmitter capacities at the synapses.

The relationship between the endocrines and the central nervous system is not simple. If it were simple the relationship would be obvious and there would not be a basic question of whether there really are significant and direct physiological inputs to psychological states or whether there really are critical physical differences between the sexes that result in some behavioral differences. A simplistic model of steroids and synapses and emotions and behaviors emerges from a review of recent data, but it behooves us to remember that behaviors have many origins, and that an illusion of simplicity may be created by the fact that these data concentrate on only one of many ongoing, interacting physiological systems.

These data concern the ways in which the steroids may affect the central nervous system. That should be an easier question to answer than an inquiry into which behaviors are linked to physiological differences between the sexes, because behavior is a result, an end-process, of many inputs, of which physiology is only one. In other words, the effects of physiological processes, complex as they are, are easier to discern when one concentrates only on those interactions, since behavior has many origins.

STEROID LEVELS

In order to understand the correlational studies that follow, it is necessary to keep in mind the normal hormone fluctuations in women during the menstrual cycle and how those fluctuations are affected when women use oral contraceptives. An extremely simplified description follows. In the first half of the menstrual cycle, after menstruation, from the first to the 14th day, estrogen levels rise, peaking at the 14th day, dip, rise again about the 20th day of the cycle, and fall precipitously at premenstruation. There may be very low levels of progesterone present prior to ovulation, but the level of progesterone increases markedly after ovulation, peaks, like estrogen, near the 20th day of a 28-day cycle, and falls markedly premenstrually. Recent data suggest that women have a surge of testosterone production premenstrually with another surge around ovulation.*

The oral contraceptive works by providing exogenous amounts of the steroids in women. The endocrine system works by negative feedback, which means that when levels of a particular hormone are reached, further production ceases, until the level of that hormone declines. Since the pill provides larger than normal (or non-physiological) dosages of these hormones, women do not produce the hormones themselves and they do not ovulate; but the circulating levels of the hormones are higher than normal, the exact levels being determined by specific pill dosages.

There are two kinds of oral contraceptives, sequential and combination. The sequential pill replicates the normal endocrine sequence in women, providing 15 days of an estrogen pill, followed by 5 days of a pill containing both estrogen and progestin, a synthetic progesterone. This means that the endocrine sequence for those using sequential contraceptives is the same as normal menstruating women but the circulating levels are higher. Women using a combination contraceptive take a pill

---

* Men do not have as complicated a gonadal steroid pattern, but the testosterone cycle in men is not as well understood as the endocrine cycle in women, primarily because men do not have decisive events like menstruation to measure cycles from. The primary steroid in men is the androgen testosterone, the level of testosterone in men is about 10 times that of women, there is a diurnal cycle and there may be a longer cycle of approximately 4 to 6 weeks, but details are not yet known.

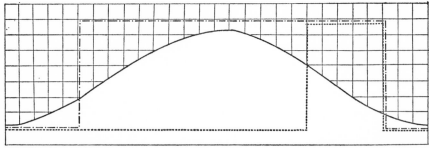

MENSTRUATION   **MIDCYCLE**   **PREMENSTRUATION**

FIGURE 1. *Sequential Pill Hormone Levels and Mood.* Sequentials provide 15 days of of estrogen, five days of estrogen-progestin, paralleling the normal process, but at a much higher hormone level. As a result, moods fluctuate as they do for women who are not taking birth control pills.

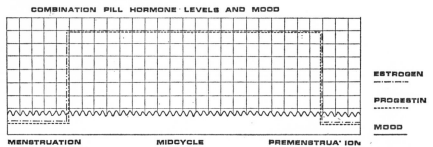

FIGURE 2. *Combination Pill Hormone Levels and Mood.* Combination pills provide a steady, high dose of estrogen and progestin for 20 days. As a result, mood does not vary, but remains at a moderate level of anxiety.

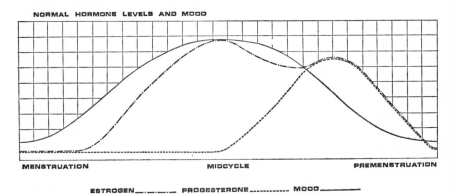

FIGURE 3. *Normal Hormone Levels and Mood.* In the normal menstrual cycle, estrogen peaks at midcycle (ovulation). Both estrogen and progesterone circulate during the second half of the cycle, with the level of both hormones falling off rapidly just prior to menstruation. Moods change with the fluctuating hormone levels—women feel the greatest self-esteem and the least anxiety and hostility at midcycle.

that combines estrogen and progestin for 20 days. This differs significantly from both the pattern and level of a normal menstrual cycle because of the high progestin level during the first half of the cycle.

Correlational Observations

The first study of the relationship between menstrual cycle phases and moods was published in 1942 by Therese Benedek and B. B. Rubenstein. Theirs was an intensive study of the psychoanalytic data of 15 patients in correlation with the menstrual cycle phase which was independently measured, using vaginal smears. They reported that during the first half of the menstrual cycle, as the estrogen level increased, the women were happy, alert, and other- or outward-directed. At midcycle or ovulation, there was a peak in ego integration, which correlates with a peak in estrogen level. After ovulation, along with the increase in progesterone, the women became more narcissistic or inward-directed and passive.* Just before menstruation, when the levels of both estrogen and progesterone fall, they found their subjects tense, aggressive and anxious. If these are observations of an essentially normal phenomenon, based primarily on an endocrine cycle rather than on psychodynamics of women sufficiently anxious to be in psychoanalytic therapy, we should find similar affect phases in a non-clinical population.

There are such studies (Bardwick, 1971a) and we will briefly mention three. Coppen and Kessel (1963) found depression and irritability to be significantly higher at menstruation than at midcycle in their study of 465 women, and they found that the pattern held for normal, neurotic and psychotic women alike. In line with the findings of Benedek and Rubenstein, Natalie Shainess (1961) found that feelings of helplessness, hostility, anxiety, and a yearning for love characterized the premenstrual phase. The tension and irritability were eased at menstruation, but there was often depression along with relief, and that depression could linger until estrogen levels increased. Katherina Dalton's (1964) studies of the pre-menstrual syndrome gave evidence that mood swings were capable of affecting behavior so that almost half of the women who commit suicide, or perpetrate a criminal act, or report sick at work, or are admitted to a psychiatric or medical hospital, are in the four premenstrual or four menstrual days of the cycle. There are, then, many data demonstrating a correlation between the normal endocrine changes during the

---

* We may note that progesterone increases very markedly during pregnancy and one could imagine these affects increasing during pregnancy, but no one has done that research.

menstrual cycle and predictable, normal, emotional states in women. My students and I investigated these relationships in a series of three experiments, with Melville Ivey, Karen Paige, and Merilee Oakes, respectively.

Before discussing these experiments, two methodological comments are necessary since there are studies in which no relationship is found between cycle phase and affect or behavior (Sommer, 1972). This is an area in which the dependent variable used is critical. First, we are looking for changes in state, and most measures are designed to pick up stable qualities and are not sensitive to small, subtle, changes. In addition, measures yield different results depending on whether they tap preconscious processes or more conscious verbal responses. One seems to see the cyclicity of the affect response more clearly in measures which are less self-aware or conscious probably because people perceived themselves as being more consistent than they actually feel or behave, and thus describe themselves as more stable or consistent than they are. It must be remembered that we are dealing with trends of emotional response which are not only usually attributed to some real cause (i.e., I am glad or happy or sad *because* . . .), but are usually so subtle that we are studying their very existence. This means, very literally, that the data in this area are decisively influenced by how you measure what you measure. Second, the data are usually based upon results of group measures. While we believe that there are both normative patterns and significant differences in response between individuals, no one has really looked at the range of responses. Clinically, one sees women who do not seem to be significantly influenced by the menstrual cycle and others who usually experience severe depression, anxiety or rage at premenstruation or menstruation.

We measured affect by scoring spontaneous, taped, 5-minute samples of speech according to Gottschalk and Gleser's Verbal Anxiety Scale. Later we used the same technique to measure hostility. The Gottschalk technique is an explicit coding of the content of phrases which are generated by the subject. The only instructions to the subject are, "Tell me about an event in your life." Thus the choice of the event and the emotional tone of the description are generated by the subject; it is a spontaneous expression of projection by the respondent. The scoring is essentially literal and not interpretive, which means, for example, that when we refer to mutilation anxiety, a subject has described a body injury and it is not our interpretation of a symbolic injury. Since the studies have been described elsewhere, only the essential findings will be described here. In the Ivey study we found that the level of anxiety was very significantly higher at premenstruation than at ovulation when the responses of the same women were measured at both cycle phases over two cycles. Actually these data with normal women were quite parallel with Benedek's data from psychiatric patients. Self-esteem and self-confidence were high at ovulation whereas at premenstruation there was marked anxiety over death, mutilation and separation. These data and those of the next two experiments are group results. It is probable that there are significant ranges of affect shift, individual differences in the amount of content of the emotional lability during the cycle, but we have not looked at the range of individual patterns. These seem to be grossly normal patterns of emotional shifts, but the intensity of emotional shifts and whether or not they affect behavior probably vary significantly from individual to individual.

Since the data are consistent with the idea that the endocrine cycle significantly affects moods, if hostility and anxiety and depression are related to steroid levels, then the cycle should change when women are on the oral contraceptive because the contraceptive changes the steroid levels significantly. Moreover, there should be a difference in the mood cycles of those on combination and sequential pills because the steroid patterns are different. Based on this hypothesis, Paige (1971) studied women using both kinds of pills along with a sample who were not on the oral contraceptive. Paige expected to find that the women using sequential pills would be like non-pill women, with anxiety lowest at midcycle and highest at premenstruation. Women using combination pills, in contrast, were expected to have no significant emotional fluctuations since their hormone levels were essentially stable. We predicted that when endocrine levels are stable, emotions would be too.

The data upheld our expectations. Those women who were not on pills experienced the same kind of significant variations in anxiety and hostility that were found by Ivey. Those subjects using sequential pills had the same kinds of mood cycles that women not on pills experienced. Women using combination oral contraceptives, however, had no significant menstrual cycle effect; there were no significant mood fluctuations for that group. Instead, the levels of anxiety and hostility remained flat throughout the month, though at a consistently high level, as high as nonpill women experienced at menstruation.

Like most of these studies in this area, these were studies of psychological parameters. In the third study, by Oakes, we measured behavior. The behavior we used was the game called Prisoner's Dilemma in which one can play competitively or cooperatively, and we looked for changes in assertiveness or competition and cooperation, as well as mood patterns in women on and off the pill, during the menstrual cycle. In this sample, all women using oral contraceptives were on combination pills. In this study we found that in addition to emotional changes there were behavioral changes. Women on the combination pill were less competitive than were those who were not on the pill. In addition to a flat mood pattern, those on the pill had a flat game-playing pattern—that is, they played the same way at midcycle and at premenstruation. Women who were not on the pill played significantly more competitively at midcycle than they did premenstrually. At premenstruation, women who were not on the pill played like women on the pill did at midcycle and premenstruation. Competitive behavior did not necessarily equate with hostile behavior, but rather seemed to reflect self-esteem and assertiveness, and was associated with a high level of estrogen and no progesterone.

We might note that there was no significant difference between those who were on the pill and those who were not in either the Paige or Oakes study on the attitudinal and demographic variables of education, age, social-class origin, religion, parity, menstrual history, expectations concerning the effects of the pills or predisposition to complain about emotional or physical symptoms. This means that these variables did not account for differences in affect cycles or game-playing patterns. Thus the data support the general hypothesis that women are influenced in some significant ways by the levels of the gonadal hormones.

Silbergeld *et al.* (1971) also compared women who were and were not using oral contraceptives, and found that on Enovid (a combination pill) women reported that they felt less angry, bold, defiant or rebellious. Oakes found that active or assertive qualities seemed to be associated with higher estrogen levels, but only when high estrogen levels were not accompanied by high progesterone levels. You may recall that at midcycle women who are not on pills have markedly high estrogen levels with minimal levels of progesterone. At premenstruation, both endocrines are a low levels. Women on combination pills at midcycle have high levels of both estrogen and progesterone and at premenstruation both endocrines are at low levels. Oakes found that women played the game more competitively at midcycle when they were not on pills and their responses to personality measures were in the same direction: at midcycle, non-pill women, who have high estrogen levels without progesterone, played more competitively and scored on personality measures high in dominance and self-confidence and aggression. When the responses of those on pills were divided by whether the contraceptive was estrogen dominent of progesterone dominant, Oakes found that those women whose pills were estrogen dominant described themselves as higher in aggression, assertiveness and hostility when they were compared with those whose pills were progestin dominant. Those whose pills were progestin dominant scored higher in self-descriptions of deference and nurturance and affiliation.

In the endocrine literature, testosterone seems to be clearly related to levels of hostility or assertiveness or dominance. The affect is not necessarily hostile—it may be assertive or dominant and be experienced by people as a feeling of confidence or esteem. In addition to the effects of socialization, there seems to be a physiological input to the variable of assertiveness or hostility which relates to the level of testosterone. It seems to me possible that characteristic affect differences between midcycle and premenstruation could reflect not only levels of testosterone in women, but also the interactive effect of a high level of both estrogen and testosterone at midcycle, and a high level of testosterone and low levels of both estrogen and progesterone premenstrually. A high midcycle testosterone level in addition to high estrogen might add to the probability of increased assertiveness or competitiveness along with feelings of self-esteem. In contrast, the premenstrual testosterone effect might increase the probability of aggression experienced as hostility.

Gonadal Steroids and MAO

Until very recently we could not go beyond these crude correlations; we could not begin to explain the role of gonadal steroids in the central nervous system, and thus in the regulation of affects and behaviors. Estrogen and progesterone (like reserpine and monoamine oxidase inhibitors) probably influence the central nervous system because they alter monoamine oxidase levels. Monoamine oxidase (MAO) is an enzyme that metabolizes, and thus inactivates, the brain catecholamines. The catecholamines are a category of neurotransmitters at the neural synapses or they are modulators of the synapses. The activity of MAO, which is thought to be the principal inactivator of the catecholamines in the brain, is controlled by the gonadal steroid hormones.

When the neuron is activated and catecholamine is released so that an impulse crosses the synapse, then that amount of the catecholamine must be deactivated. It must be metabolized so that the neuron can go back to its original resting capacity in preparation for refiring. Monoamine oxidase is an agent that causes the catecholamines to metabolize back to their initial state. Therefore, the presence of a high level of MAO means a low level of the catecholamine at the synapse. This is a condition associated with depression. On the other hand, with a high level of estrogen, there is a low level of MAO activity. So some cases of depression respond to estrogen therapy—the increase in estrogen increases the level of catecholamines at the synapse because the increase in estrogen decreases the quantity of MAO or the activity level of MAO. Both testosterone and estrogen appear to affect MAO levels. Klaiber (1967) found that castration of male rats resulted in the absence of testosterone and high levels of MAO. When the animals were given testosterone, their MAO levels fell and their behavioral depression ceased.

High levels of MAO are associated with high levels of depression, and there are some situations or circumstances when high levels of depression are predictable: women on combination pills, women premenstrually, and women at the menopause have significantly high levels of MAO activity and high levels of depression. This is not to say that the origin of the depression would be accounted for solely by the level of MAO. But the depression level is significantly influenced, apparently, by the MAO level and some forms of depression are alleviated by a decrease in MAO activity or level.

Tryptophan is metabolized to serotonin which is another synaptic transmitter. Like the estrogen and testosterone data, low levels of serotonin or low levels of tryptophan are associated with a high level of depression. Serotonin levels are increased by inhibiting MAO which metabolizes serotonin; with increased serotonin there is increased agitation or excitement or euphoria. On the other hand, with a decrease in serotonin, there is depression. The steroids, including those in the oral contraceptives, appear to influence tryptophan, and thus serotonin metabolism.

A change, but especially a decrease, in the level of the neurotransmitters seems to correlate with depression and perhaps with other affects. Depression is found when you have a low level of the biogenic amines—including norepinephrine, serotonin and dopamine. High levels of the biogenic amines (and that probably means an excess of them), including an excess of norepinephrine, serotonin or dopamine, seem to be associated with mania.

Klaiber et al. (1971) examined the plasma MAO activity in the pre- and post-ovulatory phases of the menstrual cycle, in amenorrheic women, in post-menopausal women, and in amenorrheic and post-menopausal women who were treated with estrogen and a progestin. The plasma level of MAO was significantly higher after ovulation compared with pre-ovulation. Depression increases in the second half of the cycle. MAO levels are significantly higher in untreated amenorrheic or post-menopausal women than in women in the post-ovulatory phase of the menstrual cycle. One would thus predict that amenorrheic and post-menopausal women would experience higher depression levels than normal women do, even in the second half of the menstrual cycle.

When the amenorrheic and post-menopausal women were given estrogen, the estrogen significantly reduced MAO activity. The estrogen reduced MAO to levels that were comparable to those of normal menstruating women during the pre-ovulatory half of the cycle. When, however, the women received progestin as well as estrogen, there was a significant increase in MAO activity level over that when they were treated only with estrogen. The MAO level was higher than when estrogen alone was taken, but not as high as it was before treatment when steroid levels would be very low. Women on combination oral contraceptives are on a high dosage of both estrogen and progestin, leading to the prediction that they would experience and maintain a high level of depression throughout the cycle. Paige's data confirmed that hypothesis: when women on sequential pills and non-pill women are in the high estrogen phase of their cycle, depression levels are low; when progesterone (or progestin) levels increase, so does depression. The highest level of depression for non-pill women is at premenstruation when the hormones are at their lowest. Combination pill women maintain an intermediate level of depression, higher than during the estrogen phase, but lower than non-pill women at premenstruation. The depression level therefore seems to correlate very well with levels of plasma MAO.

Klaiber et al. (1971) found there were very significant differences in plasma MAO activity observed across individuals and within any one individual in the various conditions. The great fluctuations in plasma MAO activity within amenorrheic and post-menopausal women were markedly reduced with estrogen therapy. The pre-treatment within-individual variance of these women was 18 and 21 times greater before treatment. The within-individual variance in the plasma MAO level post-ovulation was three times greater than the variance in normal women pre-ovulation. Perhaps one of the variables which increases the probability of negative affects is that women may be responding with anxiety simply because they experience periods of greatly increased affect variability *per se*. That is, if the MAO variability reflects an affect variability, a woman could be upset *because* she is less constant, and therefore less predictable to herself.

Changing hormone states are thus associated with significant alterations in the within-individual variance of the plasma MAO as well as in the mean levels of the plasma MAO. Low levels of plasma MAO and low levels of variability are found pre-ovulation when the blood estradiol levels peak. High levels of plasma MAO are found when plasma progesterone levels are maximum. The plasma MAO levels are very high in syndromes that are associated with low estrogen-amenorrhea and menopause.

The addition of progesterone or progestin appears to offset the effect of estrogen alone. It has been reported that combination oral contraceptives that have both estrogenic and progestenic compounds produce high levels of endometrial MAO activity throughout the cycle. The data infer that women on these combination oral contraceptives are likely to experience markedly high levels of depression throughout the cycle. A pill that uses a synthetic estrogenic compound (mestranol) is associated with low levels of endometrial MAO activity and we would predict low levels of depression for women on this pill throughout the cycle. The MAO activity in plasma and the tissues appears to be sensitive to changes in the gonadal steroids, but how the gonadal steroids effect the MAO activity is not known.

It is postulated that since the biogenic amines are central neurotransmitters, low levels of these biogenic amines are not merely correlated with but may even be a causal factor in a decrease in central nervous activity, which would be observable as depression. It also appears that the bioamine metabolism in the hypothalamus and in other brain areas controls a series of specific releasing and inhibiting factors which are produced in the hypothalamus. These specific releasing and inhibiting factors themselves control the secretion of the anterior pituitary hormones (for example, lutinizing hormone or follicle stimulating hormone). These hormones, those of the anterior pituitary, directly affect the peripheral target organs, including the gonads. The gonads, in turn, produce hormones, including the steroids, which affect not only the target organ but also the activity of the hypothalamus. There is thus a continuous negative feedback system between the hypothalamus, the anterior pituitary and the target organ. In addition, the limbic system and the reticular activating system also influence the hypothalamic-pituitary axis.

The central nervous system, notably the hypothalamic-pituitary relationship, receives input from target organs, and, by a reciprocal negative feedback system, maintains optimal levels, or some levels, of endocrine discharge, and this, in turn, acts to influence both the central nervous system and the target organ. When data demonstrate that the limbic and the reticular activating systems influence the hypothalamic-pituitary axis, then we begin to be able to account for the input of affects, cognition, expectation, sensory input, and so on, as also influencing hypothalamic secretion. Biogenic amine metabolism causes either a change in the level of central nervous system activity or causes a change in the control of the hormones from the anterior pituitary. With a reduction in the catecholamine neurotransmitters in the hypothalamus, which is found in some depressions, there is likely to be a biochemical mechanism involved, influencing the release of the gonadotropines. This could explain why depressed women are very often amenorrheic. The new data are describing interrelationships between the limbic and the reticular systems, affect levels or affect states, and behavior, the bioamine neurotransmitters, the hypothalamic releasing and inhibiting hormones and the secretion of the anterior pituitary hormones.*

ENDOCRINES, COGNITION AND PERCEPTION

The question which this research is ultimately intended to answer is: what are the physiological relationships between the central nervous system, affects and other behaviors? In 1968 Broverman and his associates published a paper about physiologic origins of some generally classic sex differences in styles of cognition.** Broverman related differences between the sexes in cognitive abilities to the relationship between the sympathetic, which is the andrenergic, and the parasympathetic, or cholinergic, nervous systems. Both the sympathetic and the parasympathetic nervous systems are sensitive to the gonadal steroids. According to Broverman the female tendency to excel in over-learned repetitive tasks is facilitated by the activation of the adrenergic nervous system. The male tendency to excel in problem solving and analytic behavior, which requires a suppression of an immediate response, is facilitated by the

---

* This model will surely become more complex as experimental data are generated, because the hormone releasing factors are themselves in systems and the amine neurotransmitters in any system are likely to be competitive in their final effect. In other words, the hypothalamic releasing factors affect some critical point in the hypothalamus and affect the anterior pituitary and then the gonadal system, but there is a serotoninergic system and a dopaminergic system, and an unknown number of systems defined by the prime neurotransmitter in that nervous system.

** Young girls are reported to be superior to boys in such over-learned aspects of verbal behavior as grammar and spelling and girls also tend to speak more clearly and perform better on the usual reading achievement test than do boys. Young girls have also been found to be superior to boys in other cognitive abilities which have significant simple and/or repetitive aspects such as counting or clerical tasks (Maccoby 1966).

cholinergic nervous system which is an inhibiting system. They explained that in the sympathetic system MAO inactivates the neurotransmitter norepinephrine. Estrogen inhibits MAO production. While testosterone does too, it is less effective than estrogen. High levels of norepinephrine, due to high levels of estrogen, will result in high sympathetic system activity in women.

Broverman and his colleagues say that estrogen inhibits the parasympathetic transmitter which is hypothalamic choline acetylase. The parasympathetic system allows for inhibition. Testosterone does not inhibit the parasympathetic transmitter. Thus, the presence of estrogen will inhibit the parasympathetic system because estrogen inhibits that transmitter, but testosterone does not. Therefore, they feel, men can do tasks which require the inhibition of impulses better than women can because parasympathetic system activity is greater in males or, alternatively, is more constant in males.*

Broverman has summarized the views of this team of researchers at this time: they feel that the data from *in vitro* and *in vivo* studies suggest that the steroids testosterone and estrogen affect adrenergic neural processes because they are able to inhibit the activity of the enzyme MAO. MAO affects the functioning of the adrenergic processes because it metabolizes the stores of monoamines in the neural systems. With excessive MAO activity there is an impairment of activity in the adrenergic central nervous system, because the amount of neurotransmitter is too low. Optimal adrenergic functioning would be associated with some relatively low level of MAO activity. (We might parenthetically note that too low a level of MAO leads to increased quantities of false neurotransmitters and actually acts detrimentally. There apparently is some optimal level of MAO which is relatively low rather than high.)

---

* Broverman finds an experiment by John Dawson of particular interest. In the white rat, there are normal sex differences in cognitive abilities, with the female showing a higher level of activity-wheel performance and the male a higher spatial maze learning ability. When Dawson administered the sex hormones of the opposite sex to the rats along with neonatal castration, he found a reversal of the normal sex-based activation-inhibition balance, apparently through the neonatal differentiation of the brain. The effects of the neonatal treatment resulted in changes in the expected direction for both groups of rats on symmetrical maze learning. The masculinization of the female appears to have stimulated inhibitory spatial learning and decreased their activity level as occurs with the normal male rat. Male rats who had been injected with estrogen showed increased activation and depressed inhibition which resulted in poorer spatial learning with more errors. In these data, rats who received steroids of the opposite sex in the neonatal period reversed activation and inhibition behaviors which are sex-linked.

Broverman is saying that behavioral automatization, that is the ability to make rapid, accurate, repetitive responses to familiar stimuli, seems to be dependent on central adrenergic processes. Central adrenergic processes function best with good supplies of norepinephrine. Supplies of norepinephrine are maximum when MAO (which metabolizes the neural stores of norepinephrine) is maintained at a relatively low level of activity. While too high a level of MAO activity will deplete the neural stores of norepinephrine, the gonadal hormones testosterone and estrogen tend to inhibit excessive MAO activity and thus generate good supplies of norepinephrine, enhanced adrenergic functioning and the strong automatization of behavior. In this case women will be superior automatizers to men because estrogen is a more potent inhibitor.*

If affects and cognitive abilities are influenced by steroid, catecholamine and MAO levels, because central nervous system activity has been altered, then other processes should also be influenced by the physiological factors.

Klaiber et al. have found that there is an increase in levels of hypothalamic MAO activity with an ovariectomy in rats and we would expect a decline in the norepinephrine level. There is a decline in behavioral activity following ovariectomy. With an exogenous replacement of estrogen, the hypothalamic MAO activity returns to normal levels and so does the previous high level of activity. The ovariectomy data provide a clear relationship between MAO, presumably norepinephrine and activity level.

Testosterone seems to have similar effects, so that there is a decline in activity in rats when they are castrated, but when testosterone is given to castrated males they are restored to their previous level of activity. Nevertheless, testosterone both in vivo and in vitro seems to be a less potent MAO inhibitor than is estrogen. MAO is inhibited far more by estrogen than it is by testosterone. So one might expect differences between males and females in some particular kinds of activities. If these hypotheses are correct there should be a cyclicity of activity level, as well as of affects, in normal women during the menstrual cycle, and differences between women who are menstruating, pregnant or using oral contraceptives. That research has not yet been done.

Other processes seem to be altered during the menstrual cycle. Moreault

---

* It is possible to hypothesize that females are very much more sensitive to the presence of testosterone than are males simply because they customarily have much lower levels of testosterone. Alternatively, the presence of testosterone during the fetal stage may, quite the reverse, provide the basis for a high sensitivity or response capacity to testosterone in the male. You may note that most researchers believe the latter to be true but the question is not settled.

(1971) studied responses to the Necker Cube during the cycle. The Necker Cube is a perceptual task in which you stare at the cube for 30 seconds and see how many times it reverses. Moreault found that in the second half of the cycle the number of times the cube reverses was significantly greater than during the first half of the cycle.

Vogel *et al.* (1971) and Klaiber *et al.* (in press) report that, in response to photic stimulation, EEG "alpha driving" occurs less in the pre-ovulatory than in the post-ovulatory phase of the menstrual cycle and the "alpha driving" effect is much greater in amenorrheic women than in normal women. When estrogens were given to the amenorrheic women there was a significant shift of the "alpha driving" to normal levels. When anti-adrenergic drugs were given, there was a significant increase in the "alpha driving."

Satinder and Mastronardi (in press) report that the magnitude of auditory figural after-effects varies significantly during the menstrual cycle with a significantly higher magnitude of auditory figural after-effects on day 24 compared with either days 3 or 14. Other studies (Kopell *et al.,* 1969) have found that women tend to estimate a time interval as longer and show a decline in the ability to perceive two flashes which are close together, in the premenstrual phase.

Diamond *et al.* (in press) report that there is a relationship between visual acuity and phase of the menstrual cycle. Visual sensitivity was measured by the ability to detect a test light and that sensitivity was greater at midcycle, tapered off toward menses, and declined abruptly at the beginning of menstruation. After menstruation, visual sensitivity began to increase. There were no significant changes in the visual threshold of men or of women on combination oral contraceptives during the same testing period.

The data thus support the general hypothesis that there are neural changes associated with steroid levels and sensory, perceptual, cognitive, emotional and activity level measures may alter significantly as endocrine levels or combinations alter.

TESTOSTERONE AND AGGRESSION

While we have emphasized data derived from studies of women, if the general hypothesis that steroids directly influence behavior is true, one ought to find comparable data in studies of men. In general, with the exception of verbal aggression, assertiveness, hostility or aggression is more characteristic of males than females. Research, primarily with animals, suggests that the quality has, as one input, the presence or absence or level of testosterone.

Persky *et al.* (1971) correlated psychological measures of aggression and hostility with testosterone levels and production rate in men. They found the production rate of testosterone was significantly correlated with a measure of aggression derived from the Buss-Durkee Hostility Inventory in younger men. This relationship did not hold with older men where age was the principal correlate of the production rate of testosterone. For the younger group a multivariate regression equation was obtained between testosterone production rate and four psychological measures of aggression and hostility which accounted for 82% of the variance in the production rate of testosterone. The lack of significance among the older men would seem to be due to the fact that plasma testosterone levels and testosterone production rate are about half as large in older men as in younger men.*

There are trait measures of hostility and state measures. Persky believes that the trait measure of hostility was associated with the production rate of testosterone while the state measure was associated with the plasma level of testosterone. This suggests that the capacity to experience aggressive feelings as reflected in their self-report trait measure is associated with the ability of the male gonad to produce testosterone. The manifest expression of hostile feelings which was reflected in the state self-report measure, is, Persky believes, associated with the circulating hormone level. Feelings of hostility and aggression seemed to be important determinants of testosterone production in young men. Recalling the negative feedback loops of the endocrine and central nervous systems, it seems likely that the level of testosterone could be high because of the affect and that an affect could be more likely because of the level of testosterone.

Kreuz and Rose (1972) studied plasma testosterone levels, levels of fighting and of verbal aggression in prison and in records of past criminal behavior in 21 young male prisoners. There were no significant correlations between testosterone levels and fighting behavior in prison. It should be noted that the plasma testosterone levels in the prisoner group were not significantly different from levels which have been observed in other groups of young men. That is, many men who have no criminal

---

* David Gutmann's psychoanalytic studies of TAT responses indicate a significant fall-off in aggression, hostility, assertiveness, and feelings of personal mastery in older men, in diverse cultures. This decline begins in late middle age when there is also a decline in testosterone production.

history and do not commit violent acts have plasma testosterone levels as high as those of the prisoners who committed aggressive crimes in adolescence. Of course we do not have measures of the plasma testosterone levels of those violent men when they were adolescents—it is possible that they could have been deviantly high.

In this study it was found that the 10 prisoners whose adolescent histories included the more violent and aggressive crimes had a significantly higher level of testosterone than the 11 prisoners whose histories were not violent. The authors suggest the hypothesis that "In individuals predisposed to antisocial behavior by virtue of familial and social factors, increasing levels of testosterone during adolescence serve to precipitate such behavior. Thus, it is suggested that testosterone acts in a permissive fashion for the appearance of forms of aggression such as antisocial behavior. More specifically, testosterone may serve to stimulate increased activity, drive or assertiveness, and in certain individuals this may be utilized in antisocial, aggressive acts."

Kolodny *et al.* (1971) studied levels of plasma testosterone and semen analysis and the degree of homosexuality in males. They studied 30 male homosexual students between the ages of 18 and 24, interviewed them and classified them according to the degree of homosexuality. They gave their subjects physical exams, determined the plasma testosterone level, did an analysis of semen and took buccal smears. The results of the physical exam and the buccal smear were all normal. The plasma testosterone level of the homosexuals was compared with the levels of a control group of 50 heterosexual males between the ages of 17-24. These plasma testosterone levels in the homosexual were significantly below the control group mean of 689mg per 100 milliliters for the homosexuals who were either exclusively homosexual or almost exclusively homosexual. An analysis of variance also showed that there was a significant difference, at the $p = .01$ level, in the sperm counts according to the degree of homosexuality. The correlation of sperm count and plasma testosterone concentration was $r = .7$.

Homosexuals can be categorized on a scale from those who are rarely homosexual to those who are exclusively homosexual, on a range from 1-6, where 6 is exclusively homosexual. The plasma testosterone levels of groups 2, 3 and 4 were 775, 681, and 569 and these values were not significantly different from the control group mean.* But the means for

* In the Masters and Johnson laboratory they have found that the normal range of adult male testosterone concentrations in plasma has been established as between 400-1,000 mg. per 100 milliliter. And the mean was 684 plus or minus 148 as the

groups 5 and 6, that is the two most exclusively homosexual groups were 372 and 264 which are significantly different from the control levels at less than the .01 level of significance. In addition, the semen of the almost exclusively homosexual male had either marked low spermatazoa counts or very impaired motility, although they all were in excellent health. Further investigation of endocrine variance in homosexuals may clarify whether the relationship of low testosterone levels and exclusive homosexuality in males is due to a primary pathogenesis or is a secondary hypothalamic response to human homosexual orientation.

That is a question very much like that raised in relationship to aggression—in this case it is whether a low level of testosterone may be a causative factor of almost exclusively homosexual choice or whether an almost exclusively homosexual choice results in low sperm count and low plasma testosterone levels.* This evidence of endocrine dysfunction is actually rather difficult to explain and one could not say whether this defect is testicular, pituitary, or hypothalamic. In the older endocrine literature, endocrine abnormalities were not found in the great majority of homosexuals and there is no data to support the idea that endocrine dysfunction is a major factor in the pathogenesis of male homosexuality. In fact it is possible that these low levels of plasma testosterone are the secondary result of a primary homosexual orientation which was psychosocial in origin with a depressive reaction relayed through the hypothalamus from the higher cortical centers. But again there are insufficient data to evaluate this hypothesis.

There are behaviors that do not need hormonal stimulation and there are other behaviors that do. So one must not only be careful of a generalization between species but must be careful to distinguish between kinds of behaviors which appear to depend upon or be significantly influenced by prenatal levels of steroids and pubertal levels of steroids. If, as in many other sex-related tendencies, the full maturation of a behavior requires a pubertal endocrine surge in addition to some fetal effect, it makes it more difficult to discern the earlier tendency before the definite adult behavior. It is likely that different behaviors have different time

---

standard deviation. The normal range of adult female plasma testosterone values is 25-125 mg per 100 milliliters with the mean of 74 plus or minus 25. We find then that the male has something on the order of 10 times as much plasma testosterone as does the female.

* Bernstein & Rose (1972) have reported positive correlations between male hormone levels and aggressive behavior in rhesus monkeys. Males with the highest testosterone levels were also socially dominant. They are now experimenting to see whether the hormone level determines aggression or the reverse.

sequences and different relationships in time to steroid levels. In addition, it is probable that behaviors themselves affect the hypothalamic-pituitary axis because behaviors appear to affect the central nervous system structurally or permanently.*

THE EFFECT OF BEHAVIOR UPON PHYSIOLOGY

Overwhelmingly, research has investigated the effect of physiological states upon behavior. If you remove endocrines, what happens? If you replace endocrines, how does behavior differ? The implication here is that relationship is only one way, that physiology affects the nervous system and therefore behavior. If that were true, behavior would, I think, be far more predictable.

It seems much more likely, however, that in addition to physiological effects upon behavior, behaviors and affects will themselves influence the central nervous system. The model of central nervous system interaction would tend to support such a general idea so that input from the environment affects the central nervous system: the central nervous system has sub-sets of systems which are designed to be particularly responsive to particular kinds of input; and these, in turn—particularly through the hypothalamic-pituitary axis which is also influenced by the lower centers —will directly affect further functioning of the organism through the endocrine system. Will behavior enter the feedback loop and will the capacity of the organism, at the physiologic level, be permanently affected by previous behaviors? Do particular kinds of behaviors or emotions or perceptions act on the central nervous system so as to induce a permanent change in that system or other systems? Will this structuralization increase the probability of the system's continuing to operate in the ways which were elicited in the first place? There are two recent reports which imply that if one were to look for structural changes in the central nervous system it is highly possible that they could be found.

Rosenzweig, Bennett, and Diamond (1972) reported differences between the brains of rats from the same litter who experienced three different conditions: standard lab cages, impoverished cages where the rat was

---

* These data have the possible implication of more physiological input on "CNS wiring" than we usually acknowledge. Although it is inevitably and obviously true that behaviors are socialized, one has the feeling that many behaviors are generated by the organism and are *then* responded to—and this means that, to some extent, some are not elicited by the environment but the environment provides some reasonably normal stimulus input that the physiologically-developmentally normal organism is equipped to respond to. One such example is language; perhaps there are more and some are distributed differently, in terms of frequency, between the sexes.

alone, and cages with enriched playthings where they also had playmates. They report that experience affects the level of the enzyme acetylcolinesterase which metabolizes the neurotransmitter acetylcholine. Experience was also found to influence the weight of the brain samples—rats who had had an enriched experience had a greater cortical weight and thickness, a greater total activity of acetylcolinesterase, but less activity of the enzyme per unit of tissue weight. Experience did not change the number of nerve cells to any degree in the occipital cortex, but it produced larger cell bodies and nuclei. The most consistent effect of experience was a change in the ratio of the weight of the cortex to the rest of the brain. The cortex increased in weight quite readily, whereas the weight of the rest of the brain changed little. There was an increase in dendritic spines—that is projections of the dendrite at the synapse in rats who have had enriched environments—and there was an increase in the size of the synaptic junction. The effect of experience seems to be increased synaptic contact, especially marked in those who have had enriched experiences. Formal training in rats, that is in things like running a maze or pressing a lever, produces changes in brain anatomy and chemistry, but the type of training seems to determine the kind of changes. Formal training produces smaller changes and different patterns of change from differences in environmental experiences. We might hypothesize that those specific formal training effects would be less than the effects of enriched environments in which there would be a multiplicity of inputs of various kinds of experience, and therefore, insofar as experience affects the brain or any other part of the nervous system, the greater the breadth of experiential input the greater the physiologic change.

Lewy and Seiden (1971) reported that rats performing a lever pressing response for water in an operant conditioning situation, when they were compared with control groups, showed an increase in brain norepinephrine metabolism. Previous work has showed changes in behavior as a function of norepinephrine metabolism. In this study they demonstrated that behavior itself can modify norepinephrine metabolism. And they conclude "behavior itself can affect brain chemistry, thereby changing the chemical substrate on which the drug acts." In other words, insofar as behavior causes neural change, combining data from both the Rosenzweig and the Lewy and Seiden studies one might predict that, at the very least, experience or use effects structural change at the synapse, together with a chemical change, so that the amount of neurotransmitter which is available has changed. Insofar as this effect has structuralized, it will become a permanent change.

These recent data continue to support the idea of the significance of physiological variables in the development of and evocation of moods and sensory-perceptual responses and activity levels and other behaviors in animals and in people. There are differences between sexes and there are differences within either sex. The complexity of human behavior has obvious inputs of both physiology and socialization. It is an inadequate and futile question in general to ever ask either-or. The physiologic variables are themselves emerging not only as critically important but as enormously complex. As the model continues to fill in, we find that socialization, or experience, or behavior, or affect may influence the physiology of the organism. Conversely, we find that the behavior, the affects, and anticipations of the organism may be influenced by the physiology of that organism. Thus, we are in an extraordinarily complex interactive model which further data will clarify. That clarification is likely, it seems to me, to reveal even further complexity. But, I am optimistic in believing that when we understand the relationships very well then the broad tendencies, the significant variables, will begin to emerge relatively simplistically because that is what usually happens when you understand phenomena.

REFERENCES

BARDWICK, J. M. Psychopharmacology and sex; psychological responses associated with the use of oral contraceptives. Paper presented at the Fifth World Congress of Psychiatry, Mexico City, Nov.-Dec., 1971a.

BARDWICK, J. M. *Psychology of Women.* New York: Harper & Row, 1971b.

BENEDEK, T. & RUBENSTEIN, B. B. The sexual cycle in women: The relation between ovarian function and psychodynamic processes. *Psychonomic Medicine Monographs,* 3, Nos. 1 & 2, vii-307, 1942.

BERNSTEIN, I. & ROSE, R. Notes reported in *Behavior Today,* 2, No. 9, 2, Feb. 28, 1972.

BROVERMAN, D. M., KLAIBER, E. L., KOBAYASHI, Y., & VOGEL, W. Roles of activation and inhibition in sex differences in cognitive abilities. *Psychological Review,* 75, 23-50, 1968.

BROVERMAN, D. M., CLARKSON, F. E., KLAIBER, E. L., & VOGEL, W. The ability to automatize: A function basic to learning and performance. In Christine Kris (Ed.), *Learning Disabilities: Multidisciplinary Approaches to Identification, Diagnosis and Remedial Education,* to be published by the Macmillan Co.

COPPEN, A. & KESSEL, N. Menstruation and personality. *British Journal of Psychiatry,* 109, 711-721, 1963.

DALTON, K. *The Premenstrual Syndrome.* Springfield, Ill.: C. C Thomas, 1964.

DAWSON, J. Effects of neonatal sex hormone reversal on sex differences in cognitive abilities in the white rat, preprint.

DIAMOND, M., DIAMOND, A. L., & MAST, M. Visual sensitivity and sexual arousal levels during the menstrual cycle, in press.

GOTTSCHALK, L. A. & GLESER, G. D. *The Measurement of Psychological States through the Content Analysis of Verbal Behavior.* Berkeley: University of California Press, 1969.

IVEY, M. E. & BARDWICK, J. M. Patterns of affective fluctuation in the menstrual cycle. *Psychosomatic Medicine*, 30, 336-345, 1968.

JAFFE, R. B., PEREZ-PALACIOS, K., & SERRA, G. The reproductive cycle in women. In D. Lednicer (Ed.), *Contraception: The Chemical Control of Fertility*. New York: Marcel Dekker, Inc., 1969, 1-22.

KLAIBER, E. L., BROVERMAN, D. M., & KOBAYASHI, Y. The automatization cognitive style, androgens and monoamine oxidase. *Psychopharmacologia*, 11, 320-336, 1967.

KLAIBER, E. L., KOBAYASHI, Y., BROVERMAN, D. M., VOGEL, W., & MORIARTY, D. Effects of estrogen therapy on plasma MAO activity and EEG driving responses of depressed women. *American Journal of Psychiatry*, in press.

KLAIBER, E. L., KOBAYASHI, Y., BROVERMAN, D. M., & HALL, F. Plasma monoamine oxidase in regularly menstruating women and in amenorrheic women receiving cyclic treatment with estrogens and a progestin. *Journal of Clinical Endocrinology and Metabolism*, 33, 1971.

KOLODNY, R. C., MASTERS, W. H., HENRY, J., & TORO, G. Plasma testosterone and semen analysis in male homosexuals. *New England Journal of Medicine*, 285, 1170-1174, 1971.

KOPELL, B. S., LUNDE, D., CLAYTON, R. B., & MOOSE, R. H. Variations in some measures of arousal during the menstrual cycle. *Journal of Nervous & Mental Disease*, 148, 180-187, 1969.

KREUZ, L. E. & ROSE, R. J. Assessment of aggressive behavior and plasma testosterone in a young criminal population. *Psychosomatic Medicine*, 34, 1972.

LEVINE, S. N. & MULLINS, R. F., JR. Hormonal influences on brain organization in infant rats. *Science*, 152, 1585-1592, 1966.

LEWY, A. J. & SEIDEN, L. S. Operant behavior changes norepinephrine metabolism in rat brain. *Science*, 175, 454-456, 1971.

MACCOBY, E. E. Sex differences in intellectual functioning. In E. Maccoby (Ed.), *The Development of Sex Differences*. Stanford, Calif.: Stanford University Press, 1966.

MOREAULT, D. Self-esteem and the menstrual cycle. Unpublished Honors Thesis, University of Michigan, 1971.

OAKES, M. Pills, periods, and personality. Unpublished Doctoral Dissertation, University of Michigan, 1970.

PAIGE, K. E. The effects of oral contraceptives on affective fluctuations associated with menstrual cycle. *Psychosomatic Medicine*, 33, 1971.

PERSKY, H., SMITH, K. D., & BASU, G. K. Relation of psychologic measures of aggression and hostility to testosterone production in man. *Psychosomatic Medicine*, 33, 265-277, 1971.

ROSENZWEIG, M. R., BENNETT, E. L., & DIAMOND, M. C. Brain changes in response to experience. *Scientific American*, 22-29, 1972.

SATINDER, K. P. & MASTRONARDI, L. M. Sex differences in auditory figural after-effects as a function of the phase of the menstrual cycle (In press).

SHAINESS, N. A re-evaluation of some aspects of femininity through a study of menstruation: A preliminary report. *Comprehensive Psychiatry*, 2, 20-26, 1961.

SILBERGELD, S., BRAST, N., & NOBLE, E. P. The menstrual cycle: A double-blind study of symptoms, mood and behavior, and biochemical variables using Enovid and Placebo. *Psychosomatic Medicine*, 33, 411-428, 1971.

SOMMER, B. Menstrual cycle changes and intellectual performance. *Psychosomatic Medicine*, 34, 1972.

VERNIKOS-DANELLIS, J. Effect of hormones on the central nervous system. In S. Levine (Ed.), *Hormones and Behavior*. New York: Academic Press, 1972, 11-63.

VOGEL, W., BROVERMAN, D. M., & KLAIBER, E. L. EEG responses in regularly menstruating women and in amenorrheic women treated with ovarian hormones. *Science*, 172, 388-391, 1971.

3

CULTURAL VALUES, FEMALE ROLE EXPECTANCIES AND THERAPEUTIC GOALS: RESEARCH AND INTERPRETATION

ANNE STEINMANN

A great deal of confusion and even more controversy exist regarding the changing status of women. As women all over the world have become more educated and exposed to opportunities, they have begun to alter their traditional expectations and demand equal rights in society with men. Conflicts have arisen between men and women over the changes in women's goals and values (particularly as they threaten the power and privileges of men) and the ways in which these changes affect the individual woman and society at large. This chapter will present data from 20 years of empirical research into the role perceptions of men and women, and the disparities between them that produce stress and confusion.

If one examines briefly the evolution and history of the traditional role that women are re-evaluating, their claims of past injustices and demands for real equality seem more than a little justified.

For early man, the first business of life was survival, both of the individual and of the species, and men and women took on equal, but very different, responsibilities to insure that survival. Masculinity and femininity came to be identified with the division of labor that originally had been very practically determined on the basis of biological considerations—physical strength, and childbearing functions, for example. Marriage, in one form or another, evolved to assure that the division of labor and responsibility remained fairly equal, but equality in human relationships is difficult to maintain.

51

As woman became dependent on man for the support of her children, man began to take his choice of responsibilities. Eventually, by taking steps to institutionalize the role he had chosen and the authority that derived from his physical strength and biological independence, he was also able to institutionalize woman's relative lack of strength and her dependence, and arrive ultimately at the conclusion that women were inferior and therefore deserved their inferior status.

The intellectual and scientific advances of the last two centuries, however, have reduced the problem of survival to one of controlling man's aggressive drives and preventing him from destroying himself with his new, and potentially lethal, technological prowess. The roles and activities for each sex that were developed in the first stages of mankind's evolution are no longer necessary for survival, and the concepts of masculine and feminine values that were distilled from those early roles are now open to question and revision.

It is women, understandably, who are doing the questioning and taking a decidedly non-passive and unsubmissive stand in demanding redress of their grievances, and changes in the roles assigned to them. Before proceeding, however, with an analysis of the sex-role revolution, it is necessary to understand the polarization of sex-related values in our society.

CULTURAL VALUES

The traditional concept of the feminine role is one in which the woman conceives of herself as the "other," the counterpart of the man and children in her life. She realizes herself indirectly by fostering their fulfillment. She performs a nurturing role. Her achievement is to help others achieve. Her distinguishing feature is that she fulfills herself by proxy. This woman is a *passive* woman.

The *liberal* concept of the female role is that concept held by the woman who embraces a self-achieving orientation. She strives to fulfill herself directly by realizing her own potentialities. She performs an achieving role. Her distinguishing feature is that she seeks fulfillment through her own accomplishments. This new woman is an *active* woman.

Very little hard data have been collected that reveal where women in general place themselves in regard to the traditional and liberal concepts of the female role, or that show what they really want from life and what they think men want them to be and to have. In addition, the small body of empirical research that exists on women and their role confusion has failed to be very helpful in promoting communication and understanding between men and women in conflict, because it has not explored the attitudes and problems of men in this brave new world of changing roles.

In an attempt to fill this void, the author has been engaged for the last 20 years in research on the female role. For the past 10 years, with Dr. David J. Fox as collaborator and partner, the research has expanded to a study of the male role as well as the female role (Steinmann and Fox, 1974). The intention was, and still is, to conduct research oriented toward a clearer understanding between men and women with regard to their own self-perceptions, a clearer understanding of how each man and woman relates to and interacts with members of the opposite sex, and, finally, a clearer understanding of the social roles of men and women. In addition, we hoped to report and analyze conflicts and problems women face because they are women and men face because they are men.

The remainder of the chapter will describe the research into female cultural values, role perceptions, and expectancies in general, including data obtained on male attitudes to these questions. Findings from the research will be discussed, and conclusions will be drawn as to the most effective methods of achieving therapeutic goals which benefit both sexes, goals which will narrow the disparity in understanding between men and women and enable them to achieve mutual respect and accommodation. As illustrations, two specific cases of therapy will be described in detail.

The research was begun with the assumption that advances in technology and the sciences, together with the development of effective contraceptive measures, have released contemporary women around the world from the constrictions of the home, and enabled them to become more concerned with their own self-achievement and activity outside the family constellation, to engage in professional and vocational careers never before open to them. In most cultures, however, traditional values continue to serve as barriers to women who want to express themselves in ways formerly reserved for men. It appeared, then, that women worldwide might experience conflicts in trying to fulfill themselves as people, while at the same time attempting to play the more traditional "feminine" role demanded of them by their societies and their husbands. The intention in undertaking the research was to obtain empirical data on the perception of the female role in terms of two basic questions raised by the foregoing observation: First, how do women view themselves, considering themselves as they are, as they would like to be, and as they think men would like them to be; and second, how do men see their ideal woman.

Two hypotheses reflecting these questions were formulated: one, that despite differences in socioeconomic class, ethnic or racial background, level of education, occupational or professional status, women universally share a desire to combine self-realization with the more traditional nurturant roles bestowed on them in part by their biology, and that they share a perceived conflict between the activity and independence they would like and the passivity and dependence men want them to exhibit. The second hypothesis was that men verbalize a level of activity they desire for women not significantly different from the level of activity women say they wish for themselves (Steinmann, 1963).

PROCEDURE

Description of Research

The two hypotheses have been tested, during 20 years of empirical research, on over 20,000 subjects (approx. 14,000 women and 7,000 men) from many parts of the United States, as well as other countries, including Argentina, Peru, Mexico, Germany, Czechoslovakia, Brazil, Israel, England, France, Greece, Finland, Iran, India, Philippines, Poland, Turkey and Japan.

In the United States, men and women questioned ranged in age from 17 to 70 years, though most were concentrated in the 28 to 48 age range. The largest occupational groups were teachers, physicians, attorneys, artists, scientists, and people in business. Among the women investigated, there were groups composed of those who called themselves housewives, although among other groups quite a few described themselves as "physician-housewife," "teacher-housewife," etc.

Thousands of graduate and undergraduate students were studied from different types of colleges and universities, including a suburban college close to a large metropolitan area, public colleges with and without strong academic pressures, and an expensive private college for women.

Professionals and students queried were black as well as white, although other groups in the United States were almost all white (Steinmann and Fox, 1970). The European samples were Caucasian, and the South American samples were comprised of an unspecified racial and ethnic mixture. All samples represent a reasonable cross section of the better-educated segments of their populations, and most might be called, under a very broad definition of the term, middle class. It was decided to test middle class subjects with some degree of education, both because the instrument used in the research requires literacy, and because it was felt that lower middle, middle, and upper middle class women would have opportunities for self-realization if they chose to pursue them. In addition it seemed, from superficial evidence, that education, particularly higher education, has widened the disparity of role concept between men and women (Steinmann and Fox, 1969a).

The instrument used for this study was the MAFERR Inventory of Feminine Values.* The inventory** consists of 34 statements, each of which expresses a particular value or value judgment related to women's activities and satisfactions. The respondent indicates the strength of her or his agreement or disagreement with each statement on a five-point scale, ranging from "strongly agree" to "strongly disagree," through the midpoint of "I have no opinion."

Seventeen of the 34 items are considered to provide a respondent with the opportunity to delineate a family-oriented woman who sees her own satisfactions coming second after those of her husband and family, and who sees her family responsibilities as taking precedence over any potential personal occupational activity. The other 17 items delineate a self-achieving woman who considers her own satisfactions equally important to those of husband and family, and who wishes to have opportunities to realize any latent ability or talent. The score on the Inventory represents the difference in strength of agreement with the 17 family and 17 self-achieving items. A respondent who took equal but opposite positions on each set of items would have a score of zero; a respondent who consistently took diametrically opposite positions on the item groups would have a score of minus 68 if she always took the strongest possible family-oriented position, and a score of plus 68 if she always took the strongest possible self-achieving position. Scores between zero and plus 68 thus represent intermediate degrees of a self-achieving orientation, and scores between 0 and minus 68 represent intermediate degrees of family-orientation.

The split-half reliability of the Inventory, correlated through the Spearman-Brown procedure, is .81. The items have face validity in that they are statements with generally accepted connotations, but they have also been submitted for validation to seven judges, who agreed on the nature of the categorization as family or self-oriented. Finally, the items

---

* Listed in "A Sourcebook for Mental Health Measurements," Human Interaction Research Institute, L.A., California, 1973. And, *Tests in Print, II,* Ed. Oskar B. Buros, Highland Park, New Jersey (in press).

** Originally devised by Alexandra Botwin, Ph.D.

were considered non-threatening in that they were in the form of impersonal clichés.

Three forms of the Inventory were used in the research with females. First, subjects were asked to respond to the items in terms of how they themselves felt. They were given the same 34 items in scrambled order and asked to respond as they thought their ideal woman would. The third time, with the items again scrambled, they were asked to respond as they thought a man's ideal woman would respond. In the initial research, men responded to only one form of the MAFERR Inventory of Feminine Values, the form asking the respondents to answer as they thought their ideal woman would.

The items on the Inventory can be divided into five categories, or clusters. The first category includes statements such as *"I am energetic in the development and expression of my ideas,"* or *"When I am doing something with a group of people, I often seem to be drifting into a position of leadership."* These and others like them are concerned with the personal and social characteristics of women. A second group of items concerns the interrelationships between husbands and wives. This group includes items such as *"I would like to marry a man I could really look up to,"* or *"I would rather not marry than sacrifice some of my essential beliefs and needs in order to adjust to another person."* A third area is concerned with motherhood, such as the item, *"I will have achieved the main goal of my life if I rear normal, well-adjusted children."* The fourth group of items concerns the interrelationship of work and family responsibilities for women, including such items as *"I believe the personal ambitions of a woman should be subordinated to the family as a group."* The fifth group involves a woman's self-realization, e.g., *"I would like to create or accomplish something which would be recognized by everybody."*

It was felt that a woman's responses to these statements would place her somewhere on a continuum between the extremes of feminine attitudes in all of these areas. At one extreme would be the woman who considers her role and function in life wholly in terms of serving her husband and children. This woman would derive her satisfactions from the achievements and accomplishments of her family, from her role in facilitating and encouraging their accomplishments and from the smooth accomplishment of her own family responsibilities. If this woman were asked whether marriage and children take precedence over everything else in her life, she would say, "Yes, they do." And if she were asked whether the "main goal in her life is to raise normal well-adjusted children," she would also say, "Yes." But if we asked whether a married woman should crave personal success or be satisfied with the accomplishments of her husband and children, her answer would be that personal success is unnecessary, that her needs for gratification would be met by her husband and children. The "others before self" pattern of this extremely family-oriented woman would carry over into her social relationships as well, and so she would see herself as concerned with the feelings of others, and as a listener rather than a talker, a follower rather than a leader.

At the other extreme would be the woman who sees herself primarily as a fully-functioning person in her own right and who believes that her needs and desires are as important as those of her husband and children. While she might accept household responsibilities, her primary satisfactions would come from the utilization of her abilities and talents in situations beyond the family. This woman would say "No," when asked if normal, well-adjusted children represent the main goal in her life. Marriage and children would not take precedence over everything else in her life. Moreover, she would not be satisfied with the achievements of her husband and children but would want her own personal success; she would want to "create or accomplish something which would be recognized." This extremely self-oriented woman would not only believe that as a capable person she has a duty to be active, but if she had to choose, she might prefer to be famous than have the affection of one man. This woman, too, would generalize her approach and attitudes, and so, when questioned about her relationships with people other than her husband, she would say that in social situations she is a talker rather than a listener, a leader rather than a follower, and argues with people who try to assert their authority over her.

Of course, few women would place themselves at either extreme, but it was felt that by administering the Inventory to so many different women in so many different cultures over a period of years, it would be possible to derive from their responses something more than just a generalized impression of what women really think of themselves, and what they would like to be, and what they think men would like them to be. Far too many researchers, it seemed, assumed certain attitudes and beliefs on the part of women, or projected their own attitudes and beliefs, without sufficient evidence to back them up, or simply made sweeping claims based on small and convenient samples of opinion. This research was designed to test significant samples and gather concrete evidence. A table exhibiting such evidence from cross-cultural samples is found at the end of the chapter (Table 6). It is a statistical report on one set of data and will be described later (see also Steinmann, 1973a). Other tables, where suitable, are inserted in the text.

Wherever the Inventory was administered, the results were extraordinarily consistent. All over the world, the same pattern emerged, a pattern that showed little variation among different age groups, ethnic groups and educational groups. The pattern, simply stated, was that the vast majority of women perceived themselves as more or less balanced between self and family orientations. Furthermore, when these same women were asked to describe their ideal woman, there was a similar consistency of response. While some of them described their ideal woman as slightly more active and outgoing than they believed themselves to be, most saw their ideal as slightly more family-oriented than they themselves were. The basic quality of this ideal woman, then, was one of relative balance between the extremes of activity and passivity (as was the most common self-perception of the subjects), with a slight tilt towards family orientation.

A dramatic shift occurred, however, when women were asked what man's ideal woman was like. In sample after sample the same answer came back: women believed that men wanted a woman who was strongly oriented to her family, who was relatively passive and submissive in social and personal situations, and who clearly saw her role as wife and mother taking precedence over any possible activity as an individual outside the family. This family-oriented ideal that our female respondents attributed to men was as true of the female physician or businesswoman as of the housewife. And it characterized the college undergraduate in the United States as accurately as it did her counterpart in Greece, Japan or Argentina (Steinmann and Fox, 1966a, 1969b). The implication of these responses was clear—women were saying they were pretty much as they would like to be, but they are not at all what they thought men wanted. There was a consistent conflict in women's minds as to what their role should be, a feeling that in order to please their men they would have to be untrue to themselves.

It was at this point that the need for research into men's attitudes on the subject became apparent. The MAFERR Inventory of Feminine Values was again used, this time in a form called Man's Ideal Woman. Samples of male subjects which were as similar as possible to the female samples in profession, age, socioeconomic status and nationality were given the Inventory and asked to respond as they thought their ideal woman would do. The results were fascinating. Men consistently portrayed as their ideal a woman who was balanced between family orientation and self-orientation. In other words, the men's ideal woman was almost exactly the same woman that women said they actually were. She was nothing like the passive, family-oriented, home-centered ideal the female samples had attributed to men.

These results strongly indicate that men and women, cross-culturally and over a period of 20 years, profess agreement as to the proper role for women, but have failed utterly to communicate this agreement to each other. Men, in answering the MAFERR Inventory, claim to want just as much self-realization for women as women want for themselves, if not, in some cases, more. But women don't believe it (Steinmann and Fox, 1966b).

INTERPRETATION AND FURTHER RESEARCH

All this gives rise to some intriguing questions. Is one to conclude that communication and understanding between the sexes have broken down as drastically as the foregoing results indicate? Or are there perhaps other explanations for the discrepancy between men's and women's ideal woman? Four modes of interpretation of the research data suggest themselves:

First, both men and women thought they were telling the truth and our results reflected a serious lack of communication between them.

Second, women were projecting what *they* really felt and wanted onto men.

Third, men were talking a current liberal stereotype of woman and might neither believe nor behave as they talked, the changing role of women confusing their male expectations of the female role and perhaps forcing them into hypocrisy, either conscious or unconscious.

Fourth, when men expressed a liberal concept of the female role, they were exposing an ambience which might or might not be the result of their own use of projection and their unwillingness to accept an active role in a complex society which seems to be technology-dominated and in the throes of the breakup of sexual stereotypes.

These interpretations needed further exploration to determine which, if any, might be the answer to the puzzle. A new program of research was begun into decision-making and family interaction, and in addition it was decided to examine the personal characteristics each sex values in the other.

Procedure

Three new instruments were developed for this study. The first, a Decision-Making Survey, offered the respondent 22 common family decisions
ranging from recurring decisions, like where to go on an evening out, to
decisions which may occur no more than once or twice in a lifetime, like
what living arrangements to make for an aging parent. Respondents were
given five choices: they could indicate that the decision should be completely the husband's, primarily the husband's, equally shared by husband
and wife, primarily the wife's or completely the wife's. In addition to
determining how this decision "should" be made, they were asked how
they thought it was made today by people like themselves.

The decisions studied can be grouped into three areas: *economic decisions,* such as buying an unnecessary dress, moving to a more costly
apartment, or deciding how to spend money received as a gift; *social or
recreational decisions,* such as what to do on an evening out, or what the
husband or wife should do with spare time; *family life decisions,* like
deciding on the sexual pattern of the marriage, whether to have a baby,
or whether the husband should change occupations.

In the pilot phase of this study, four forms of the Decision-Making Survey were used. Respondents were asked about the same 22 decisions in
terms of different combinations of the wife working or not and there
being children or not. The initial data indicated that only one variable
produced different results—whether or not the wife worked. The presence
or absence of children had no significant effect on the response pattern,
either in general, or in terms of specific decisions, and so, in the major
survey, involving about 1,000 respondents, only two forms of the instrument were used. First, subjects answered in terms of a hypothetical couple
in which the husband provided good financial support and the wife did
not work, and then they responded to the same decision situations, in
scrambled order, in terms of a couple in which the wife worked because
the husband did not earn enough to enable them to do all that they
would want.

The second instrument was called the Situational Survey. In this one,
respondents were asked to indicate how both the husband and wife would
think and act in different family situations, such as the husband coming
home and finding dinner not ready because his working wife had been
delayed at her job. The Situational Survey is a free-response instrument,
in contrast to the checklist format of the Decision-Making Survey, so
content analysis was used to categorize the responses to the different
situations.

The third instrument involved an Inventory of Personal Characteristics which men and women consider important in each other, in terms of prospective husbands and wives and after 15 years of marriage. It used an objective ranking procedure.

The reliability of each of these instruments was evaluated through the test-retest procedure and, for each instrument, more than 90 percent of the subjects gave responses of the same nature after a lapse of several weeks. There is obviously no more than face validity to the instrument in the sense that we must assume that the situations pose realistic choices for the respondents and that their consistent responses represent how they believe people would think and act in these situations. All three instruments were administered at one data collection: first, the Decision-Making Survey, then the Situational Survey, and last, the Personal Characteristics Inventory.

In analyzing the results, first, of the Decision-Making Survey, a general finding was revealed. Except in the case of clearly individual decisions (how to vote, what to do with spare time), both men and women felt that marital decisions involving both husband and wife should be shared. In fact, women appear to have *greater decision-making responsibility than they want*. It is as though men have backed away from their responsibilities, saying to the woman, "O.K., girls, this is your emancipation; you make the decisions." This finding appears to validate the earlier interpretation that women project onto men their own desire to be more family-oriented.

The Situational Survey explored whether men and women felt there was a discrepancy between what men thought or felt, and what they actually said in situations with potential for conflict arising from the wife's independent activity. Four such situations were described to the subjects (men and women) and they were asked to indicate what the man in the situation would say. The purpose was to determine whether the subjects felt that men were verbalizing support for a high level of independent functioning for women, while not actually desiring this independence. The results provided two important generalizations:

1. The men took a generally liberal position on this survey, accepting the wife's independent activity in each situation. This seems to support the earlier interpretation that men saw an ideal woman as being balanced between the extra-family and intra-family orientations.

2. When men did take a liberal position, a large majority of the women did not believe they were sincere, suggesting, perhaps, that women are reacting to a perceived reality that is virtually invariable—no matter

what men say, women must still take ultimate responsibility for home and children *before* they are free to engage in independent activity.

The third and final stage of the survey concerned personal characteristics valued by men and women of the opposite sex in a variety of circumstances and settings. This phase of the research had three purposes: to test the current strength of some stereotypes about women in general and working women in particular; to estimate the perception of equality of opportunity for women; to learn about the personal characteristics most valued in one sex by the other, prior to marriage and fifteen years after marriage. The results of this study are too complex to present in full at this time, but the most important findings are summarized:

1. About half the men and women continue to believe that women best express intelligence intuitively, and more women hold this view than men.

2. A majority of both sexes disagreed with the notion that men do not like intelligent women, with the men showing higher incidence of disagreement than women.

3. A majority of both sexes felt that when out with men, women often speak less intelligently than they are capable of doing. They did not say why this is so if men supposedly like intelligent women.

4. Both men and women felt that men should take the responsibility for speaking for the husband and wife in public when the couple agree on the issue under discussion.

5. A majority of both sexes felt that equal opportunities for women have resulted in equal intellectual achievement, with the greater agreement expressed by men. However, both men and women felt that women are not interested in intellectual achievement (Steinmann and Fox, 1969c).

The results of these new studies reinforce the findings of the earlier research: women want to live their lives according to a set of values that includes self-realization as well as wife- and motherhood, but do not believe that men accept their personal aspirations (Steinmann, 1969). Again, men in this new research consistently express the same perceptions of women's needs and abiilties that women have of themselves. The communication gap may result in part from the fact that men and women say they believe in one thing, while living their lives according to different values, based on what they think the opposite sex wants them to be.

The second phase of the research, while still not conclusive, appears to support the first of the four possible interpretations of the original study based on the Inventories of Feminine Values: both men and women thought they were telling the truth and the discrepancy between what men said they wanted in a woman and what women expected them to say reflected a serious lack of communication between them. Assumptions are made by each sex regarding the other's attitudes toward appropriate sex roles without any direct discussion between them on the subject. It is possible, then, that men and women are often fighting an imaginary enemy in the battle of the sexes, and that if they could only be made to understand each other more clearly, some of the skirmishes might be avoided.

While it is true, as stated, that the results of both phases of the research were so consistent as to be boring, there was one notable exception—a sample whose responses to the MAFERR Inventory of Feminine Values were in the same direction as the responses of the other samples, but differed greatly in degree, and perhaps therefore in significance. It seems valuable, at this point, to describe this sample in some detail, in the interest of pointing out a trend in female sex-role perception that the authors feel may grow more pronounced in the future.

In 1970, the MAFERR Inventory of Feminine Values was administered to a group of feminist women, members of an association for women in the field of psychology. These women had had superior educations, with attendant expectations of job and status reward which our system promises to the well-educated. In addition, their exposure to the intellectual and professional aims of the establishment had given them an awareness and insight into the cracks in the system. This group of women had observed that the rewards promised them by their conditioning are meted out arbitrarily and not always on the basis of merit. (This of course is true for men as well, but not as consistently as it is for women.)

Using the MAFERR Inventory, it was possible to study this group of self-achieving women with regard to their perception of self, ideal woman, and man's ideal woman, and to compare them to other groups of women who had been tested with the same instruments. Further, since this study was one of the first to concentrate on the feminist movement in the 1970's, in terms of self-concept and men's concept of women, it was hoped the results might enhance understanding of educated, self-oriented women and perhaps serve as a mechanism for social change in the future.

The sample for this study consisted of 54 women who responded to the three forms of the Inventory mailed to 96 women listed as members of the association, an avowedly feminist professional organization. The mean age of the respondents was 34, and it was found that 52 had a graduate education, while the remaining two were currently enrolled as seniors in college.

Fifty-two women replied to the question of interpersonal relationships with men that had been included to measure this particular variable. Fifty-two percent were presently married, 19 percent were either divorced or separated, an additional 17 percent indicated they had a few close male friends, and the other 12 percent were involved in a relationship with one man. In response to a question relating to the dominant parent in their own childhood, about half answered "father" and half "mother." In examining parents' educational level it was found that over 25 percent of the women had mothers who had a higher educational level than the fathers. This suggests a relationship between a mother's education and the self-achievement orientation of her daughter.

A final variable examined concerned the length of time these women had participated in the feminist or women's rights movement. For the 46 women responding to this question, the mean time of active involvement was only one and a half years. Most women also indicated that they had been philosophically involved for a much longer period of time, but that their activity in structured organizations (NOW, etc.) had been quite recent. This finding adds validity to the earlier assumption made by Friedan (1963), that many women are unhappy with their stereotyped role in the home and covertly desire to broaden their horizons. The continuing growth of women's liberation groups throughout the country further suggests that women are now openly admitting to themselves, as well as to others, their strong feelings of frustration with traditional roles assigned to them by society.

As revealed in the scores of the first form of the Inventory (self-perception), these women considered themselves to be extremely self-achieving, and therefore rejecting of traditional stereotypic behavior expected of women by the society at large. Item analysis showed that they primarily resented stereotypic role behaviors related to marriage and the family. They were not willing to put themselves in the background and settle for the achievements of the men in their lives; they were more concerned with their personal growth and self-actualization. A national composite of 762 women compiled previously by the MAFERR Foundation provided an interesting comparison with the sample of the feminist women. The mean score on self-perception for the national sample was $+3.05$, while the mean score of the professional women was $+28.9$. The data show that while the composite sample of women was attempting to combine, in harmony, both self and family roles, the feminist women are not interested in domesticity or traditional roles related to family functioning.

Regarding the concept of ideal woman, it was found that the present

TABLE 1

Means and Standard Deviation of Woman's Concept of Self (A),
Ideal Woman (B), and Man's Ideal Woman (C)

FEMALE PSYCHOLOGISTS AND THE MAFERR NATIONAL
FEMALE SAMPLE[1]

Group	Number	A		B		C	
		X	SD	X	SD	X	SD
Female Psychologists	54	+28.9	9.6	+32.2	11.1	—24.8	21.3
MAFERR National Female Sample	762	+ 3.05	9.09	— .26	12.56	—19.35	15.58

1. See "Self- and Ideal Sex-Role Perceptions of Men and Women and Their Ideal Perceptions of Each Other" (Steinmann and Fox, 1969a).

sample of activist women perceived their ideal woman to be slightly *more achieving* than they perceived themselves. However, the similarity of means for the concept of self and ideal woman (+28.9 to +32.2) suggested that the activist women were behaving in ways they approved. Again, the ideal of +32.2 was in striking contrast to the national composite ideal of —.26. The national composite woman perceived her ideal as *more passive* than she perceived herself.

An item analysis yielded some interesting findings related to this concept of ideal woman. For example, the national sample agreed with the statement that "encouragement is a wife's greatest contribution to her husband" and saw its ideal woman as "being capable of putting herself in the background," whereas the feminist women did not.

The professionals had a mean score of —24.8 for the concept of man's ideal woman. The standard deviation of 21.3 indicated the great variety of attitudes existing among this select group of women. Although this sample, as a group, felt that man's ideal woman was more passive than did the national composite (—19.35), the standard deviation was quite large for both groups. The present sample, however, had a discrepancy score of 54 points between its mean perception of self and its mean perception of man's ideal woman, three times as great as the discrepancy score of only 18 points demonstrated by the national sample. The data bring into sharp focus the extreme conflict of self-achieving women in terms of how they see themselves, compared to how they think men want them to be (Table 1).

So a major finding of this study was that whereas most women in previous samples presented self-concepts combining family and self-achieving orientations, the sample of professional feminist women tended

Table 2

Means and Standard Deviations of Man's Concept of Ideal Woman
(BB), and Man's Concept of Woman's Ideal Woman (G)

MALE PSYCHOLOGISTS AND THE MAFERR NATIONAL
MALE SAMPLE[1]

Group	Number	BB X	SD	G X	SD
Male Psychologists	51	+14.2	10.4	+13.9	9.9
MAFERR National Male Sample	423	+ 1.02	12.25	—	—

1. See "Self and Ideal Sex-Role Perceptions of Men and Women and Their Ideal Perceptions of Each Other" (Steinmann and Fox, 1969a).

to reject traditional roles associated with marriage and the family, and to emphasize instead the primary importance of self-realization and activities outside the home. This latter attitude may reflect the system's failure to fulfill the promises of women's education, which seem to assure the possibility of combining home and career. Taken together, the results of *this* study, compared with those of the national composite, suggest the depth of conflict and confusion in educated feminist women (Steinmann and Rappaport, 1970).

The researchers decided at this point to measure male psychologists for their perceptions of an ideal woman. They were asked to respond to the items, first, as their ideal woman would and, second, as they felt women's ideal woman would answer. Of the 51 male psychologists completing both forms, it was found that most said they desired a self-achieving woman (+14.2), not at all like the woman that the feminist women had predicted. As to their concept of woman's ideal woman, the psychologists again indicated a self-achieving woman (+13.9), though only half as achieving as the women perceived themselves and their ideal woman (Steinmann, 1972a).

Discrepancies in male-female role expectancies for professional men and women in psychology appear to run along the same lines as those of most men and women in our society, but this sample of male psychologists perceived their ideal woman as more self-achieving than the national composite of males, which expressed a mean of +1.02. So that while the present study supports earlier findings regarding female role perception among women in general, it also illustrates the severity of the conflict for these professional women. These women were acting in accord with their own activist ideas toward role behaviors, but not in accord with the familial orientation they perceived men to desire in women. And while the male psychologists stated that they wanted a self-achieving, creative woman, it is vital to underscore the fact that there exists a large discrepancy between the female psychologists' concept of women's active role, and the males' concept of women's active role (Table 2).

Further, to validate our conclusions, we offer a detailed analysis of the table found at the end of the chapter. It describes the responses to the MAFERR Inventory of Subjects from ten selected samples: three from the United States, two from Czechoslovakia, four from Brazil, and one from England. Ages of the subjects ranged from the late teens to the middle sixties, although the majority were under forty. Otherwise the samples conform to our earlier general descriptions of subjects as to race, education, etc. It was decided to consider the overall pattern of data from these samples, which represent diverse geographical areas, to obtain insight into cross-cultural perceptions of woman's role by males and females. These data were collected and analyzed within the last five years and up to the present time. An examination of the table reveals the following:

On Woman's Self-Concept (Form A)

In all countries, the undergraduates have a self-concept that is self-achieving ($+3.2$ for the U.S.; $+6.2$ for Brazil; and $+4.7$ in England). Professional women have a self-concept which is much more self-achieving ($+28.9$ for the U.S.; $+11.4$ for Czechoslovakia; and $+6.8$ for Brazil). The working class sample for the United States, and the non-professionals and teachers in Brazil seem to have a more passive or home-oriented concept. It is interesting to note that the working class in Czechoslovakia has a strong self-achieving concept. We will discuss this later.

On the Concept of Woman's Own Ideal (Form B)

Again, it is interesting to note that, among the professionals, the ideal is either very close to the self-concept or more self-achieving than the self-concept. The ideal of the other groups is slightly more home-oriented but still quite close to the self-concept.

On Woman's Concept of Man's Ideal Woman (Form C)

In all samples women indicate that they believe man's ideal woman to be passive, putting her personal growth and development second to her role in the home and family; while man's concept of his ideal woman was in fact very different. Woman's concept of man's ideal woman (C) then, is seen as passive and man's concept of his ideal woman (BB) is seen as more active, actually balanced, for the most part, between home orientation and self-achievement.

These discrepancies are seen more dramatically in the undergraduates and professionals from the United States and the professionals from Czechoslovakia and Brazil. The women's mean score on Form C (Woman's Concept of Man's Ideal Woman) among U.S. undergraduates was —15.1, while the mean "ideal woman" among male undergraduates (Form BB) was +1.5. The mean on Form C for woman professionals in the United States was —23.8 and men professionals rated their ideal woman at +14.6—an even greater disparity in ideal woman perceptions. The means for the Czech professional women on Form C was almost as passive (—14.7) as the Czech professional men's ideal woman was active (+13.6). In Brazil the mean for professional women on Form C was —14.2, about the same as that of the Czech professional women, but the mean ideal woman score of +4.9 for the Brazilian professional men was not as active as that of the Czech men.

Discrepancies in other samples are not as drastic as those in the highly educated groups, but there are some comparisons. Working class samples of women from the United States rated man's ideal woman at a passive —9.7, while the men actually rated her slightly active at a mean of +2.2. In Czechoslovakia, the working class women rated the man's ideal woman at —13.5 while the mean ideal woman of the men was +2.9. The means of the men in both of these countries were very similar, while the means of the women were quite different. As opposed to the working class of the United States and Czechoslovakia, the non-professionals in Brazil agree that the ideal of the men is on the passive side: the women's rating is —6.0 and the men's is —2.2. The mean scores for the undergraduates from England also point out differences in opinion, with the mean for women's view of man's ideal woman a passive —17.8, and the mean for men's actual view an active +2. These scores parallel the scores of the U.S. undergraduates (—15.1 for women and +1.5 for men). British and American undergraduate women sampled thus think men want a more passive woman than do the undergraduates in Brazil (their rating is —6.4), but the means for men undergraduates' concepts of their ideal woman in these three countries are quite similar (+2.2 in the U.S.; +1.2 in Brazil; and +.2 in England). The scores are not high, but they are all on the plus side.

The greatest disparity is seen in concepts of role among the professionals in all countries. The mean for the professionals in the U.S. on woman's own ideal was +32.2, while women's concept of man's ideal was —23.8; the mean ideal self for women professionals in Czechoslovakia was +10.1, while their mean rating of man's ideal was —14.7; and in Brazil the mean for women's own ideal was +10.2, and for her concept of man's view, —14.2. The disparity is seen in other categories, but to a lesser degree. Working class female respondents in the U.S. rated their ideal at +.4 and the man's ideal at —9.7. The working class Czech women rated their ideal at +8.3 but felt that men would rate their ideal at —13.5.

Undergraduates in England also followed the emerging trend. The women rated their ideal at an active +3.8, while their perception of man's ideal was rated at —17.8. The only aberrant results in the comparison of these two forms (C and BB) was in the non-professionals in Brazil. Both the women's ideal (—1.0) and their concept of the man's ideal (—6.0) were on the passive side, but again their concept of man's ideal was significantly more passive than the men's ideal.

It is clear from these results that all samples of women believe that their men want a more passive and non-assertive woman than the men themselves claim to desire. The greatest discrepancy is between United States professional women and men (—23.8 as against +14.6); the discrepancy between the sexes' concept of man's ideal woman is nearly as great for the Czechs (—14.7 as against +13.6). In Brazil, however, the discrepancy is not as noticeable. Professional men here still desire a woman who is more active (+4.9) than the woman think they want (—14.2) but their ideal is not as active as the ideal of the U.S. and Czech men.

A final comment on the Czech women. One interpretation of their strong self-achieving self-concept might very well be that these women need a strong self-concept in order to live in their difficult society. This was corroborated in interviews with these women in Prague. The MAFERR Inventory scores of the professional women in particular indicate their expectation of freedom to pursue active professional lives, and possibly relieve the burden of too many jobs and responsibilities (Steinmann, 1973a).

In summary, then, it can be stated unequivocally that the original hypotheses are true. The length and breadth of the research described prove, first, that women around the world, from cultures where industrialization, urbanization and universal education occur, share a conscious desire to combine self-actualization with family orientation, but they feel strongly that men are not eager for them to fulfill themselves too far away from the home. In general, women feel that they *are* the balanced people they want to be, but that they *are not* the homebodies men want them to be. So there is a *conflict* existing within women as to what their proper role should be. Should they attempt to be what they want to be, and risk masculine disapproval, or should they play it safe and succumb to the age-old stereotype?

Second, the research has shown, as posited, that men *say* they want the same combination of roles for women that women want for themselves, that is, they want women to combine family interests with interests outside the home. But women don't believe them. Here there exists a tremendous discrepancy, once again, between women's perceptions of what men desire for them, and men's *stated* expectancies in terms of women's roles.

Several possible explanations of the discrepancy, which leads in large measure to the conflict in women, have been discussed here, and it is safe to conclude that all are responsible, singly or in combination, for the lack of understanding between men and women. One conclusion, however, is inescapable—men and women are not *communicating* with each other about the problem. In addition, it is clear that the more education women have, the higher their aspirations for themselves, the wider the gap in communication, understanding and, it might be added, trust, between them and men in general. For these women, the Reality Principle looms large: the work they have been educated for is often not available to them, and if it is, they are usually paid less than men are for it; and if they should wish to have a family, they must either put aside their careers or take on the back-breaking burden of full responsibility for both. For no matter how liberal men may sound on the subject of self-realization for women, few are willing actually to share responsibility for home and family with a working wife.

THERAPEUTIC GOALS

The discrepancies between role concepts of women and men, consistently found in the research described, point up the differences in values and the hollowness of the present role expectancies of both sexes, and the resultant need for therapeutic goals which will help men and women examine and understand their own motives and goals, and break down the barriers to communication between them. The MAFERR Inventory of Feminine Values proved valuable in identifying areas of conflict and confusion, not only as trends in the general population, but in the individual patient as well. In addition, the Inventory served as a helpful guide in checking therapeutic progress. After identifying inner conflicts and stresses due to sex-role ambiguities and confusion, and working through them in therapy, the Inventory was readministered to measure growth and change. Here an evaluation of the cluster responses, as described at the beginning of the chapter, was helpful.

To illustrate the application of the MAFERR Inventory to individual and couple therapy, two case studies are presented.

The first case involves a young woman who was in individual therapy from June, 1967 to June, 1972. Jill was a 17-year-old high school student in New York City when she was referred for therapy. She disliked school and had few close friends. Her presenting problem was a basic insecurity which seemed to stem from a lack of acceptance of self and a compulsive desire to create a new self-image. This insecurity was traced directly to her rejection of her active and outgoing mother and her identification with a passive father. At the start of therapy, Jill revealed a need to protect her father from the wrath of the overpowering and hostile mother. Upon further investigation, it was found that these family conflicts led Jill to feel somewhat apprehensive and uncertain about her future role as a woman. She feared that she, too, would assume many of the qualities she detested so much in her own mother. Jill was tested with the MAFERR Inventory of Feminine Values at the beginning of therapy, with the following results:

On the self-perception form, Jill saw herself as an extremely independent, assertive and self-achieving woman ($+42$). Her ideal woman (-13) was completely opposite to her self-perception. She felt that a woman should be passive, submissive, and totally concerned with family. The discrepancy between her self-perception and her ideal woman was astounding (55 points). This was a particularly significant finding, for it clearly revealed Jill's intrapsychic quandary. Would she develop into the hostile and aggressive person she resented, or would she be able to shift her orientation, as she desired, to be a more passive and submissive individual? The image of her mother was always with her despite the fact that she rejected this image for herself.

A major goal throughout therapy was to re-examine Jill's stereotypes and to point out the fallacies in her cognitive processes. Jill, with much effort, came to accept some of her aggressive tendencies as part of her own self while realizing that she was not, in fact, doomed to be exactly like her mother. In therapy, the positive as well as the negative aspects of

TABLE 3

Jill Pre-Post Scores on MIFV

Form	June '67	June '72	Change
Self Perception	+42	+44	+ 2
Ideal Woman	—13	+49	+62
Man's Ideal Woman	—30	— 9	+21

her mother's personality were explored. Jill realized that her complete rejection of her mother was unfair and there were definite positive aspects in her role identification. As therapy progressed, Jill came to accept herself while learning how to control and redirect her undesirable patterns of behavior.

Whereas in 1967 Jill felt her future role demanded a compliance with traditional female values (—13), in 1972 she expressed a new and liberated ideal (+49). For now Jill wants to remain the way she is, an active and self-achieving woman who is concerned about her development as a human being as well as a daughter and, perhaps eventually, a wife.

It is important to note that Jill's concept of her ideal woman changed 62 points on the Inventory of Feminine Values, while her self-concept changed only 2 points. What does this indicate? Quite clearly, Jill has changed her attitudes and values. She no longer feels the compulsion to conform to traditional role behaviors, nor is she fearful of becoming a duplicate of the horror she originally perceived her mother to be. She is free to be comfortable with what she is and is not suffering, as she once did, because of her failure to play a narrowly defined role—a role projected by our society at large.

Note a second important aspect of change in Jill's responses to the Inventory. In 1967 she indicated that men would desire an extremely passive and domestic woman (—30 on the Man's Ideal Woman form), but her feelings were drastically different in 1972 (—9). One might assume that, through a therapeutic intervention and of course her own reactions to a changing environment, Jill has become much more realistic and more in touch with the world. Her perception of what men really expect in a woman has changed significantly by 21 points. She now feels that men desire a woman who is more well-balanced between self-achievement and family interests, and not one who is extremely submissive (Steinmann, 1972b). (See Table 3.)

In evaluating the benefits of the MAFERR Inventory of Feminine Values, in this case of individual therapy, the therapist found that the

Inventory revealed a role conflict existing within the patient. More important, it zeroed in on some specific areas of the conflict. The course of therapy was defined a little more clearly, and the specific areas of confusion were dealt with intensively. At different stages in therapy the Inventory was readministered to measure change and progress. It is, of course, hardly necessary to point out that the MAFERR Inventory is only a tool to aid therapy. The crux of the patient's improved functioning is his or her own self-understanding and consequent behavior modification.

The MAFERR Inventory of Feminine Values has proved useful in couple and family therapy, often with the addition of a nearly-identical Inventory of Masculine Values. Space limitations prohibit a detailed description of the latter, but its purposes are very similar to those of the Female Inventory: to measure a man's perceptions of himself relative to family and work and how he balances and combines the two; to determine how his ideal man would rate career and home interests in relative importance; and to see what he thinks women want in an ideal man—a husband more interested in his home than his work; a hard-driving, ambitious businessman or professional; or some combination of the two. It is enough to say here that men, as revealed by the Inventory of Masculine Values, are often just as confused in their self-concepts as women, and when men and women seek therapy together to improve or salvage their interpersonal relationships, the Inventories are helpful as diagnostic tools.

It is apparent to many therapists working in the field of family therapy that men and women in conflict are often quite unaware of the sources of the trouble, or they blame their problems on superficial and relatively minor incompatibilities because they are unable or unwilling to look deeper into themselves for the real causes. The MAFERR Inventories seemed to provide clear, objective evidence of fundamental differences which the couple, with the help of a therapist, can then address. Here again, as in individual therapy, the Inventories are only tools, but tools which can save a great deal of time and provide valuable insights for couples in therapy. The following case study is an example of the effective use of the MAFERR Inventories in the therapy of a couple experiencing marital difficulties.

Mr. and Mrs. James, the husband 46 years of age, and the wife 35, entered therapy after four years of marriage. Mr. James was seen twice a week, Mrs. James once a week, and both together twice a week for just over six months. Both of them had been previously married and divorced. Mr. James had three sons, 17, 15 and 13. Mrs. James had three children,

TABLE 4

Mrs. James' Pre-Post Scores on MIFV

Form	October '71	June '72	Change
Self-Perception	− 2	+ 6	+8
Ideal Woman	+18	+17	−1
Man's Ideal Woman	− 5	− 8	−3
Woman's Ideal Man	+ 1	+10	+9

two girls ages 14 and 8, and a son aged 12, at the time of the first meeting. The major presenting problem was their failure in interaction with the children from previous marriages. The youngest child of Mrs. James lived with her and her new husband. The other two lived with their father and his new wife. These two children were hostile toward their mother and her new husband.

Mr. and Mrs. James were given the MAFERR Inventories of Feminine and Masculine Values early in therapy, and some underlying areas of real stress were revealed.

Mrs. James, like Jill, had a very large discrepancy between her self-perception (−2) and her concept of her ideal woman (+18), an indication that while she perceived herself as balanced between self-achieving and family interests, her ideal woman was significantly more self-achieving than her self-concept. Interestingly, her concept of man's ideal woman (−5) was not significantly different from her own self-perception (−2).

Mrs. James and the therapist discussed the Inventory scores, and in the course of therapy she came to understand the importance and the sources of the discrepancy between her self-perception and her ideal concept. Of her own accord, Mrs. James, who had had only two years of college before her first marriage, decided to complete her education and was accepted at a prestigious college near her home. When she was tested on the Inventory after the eight months of therapy, none of her scores had changed significantly except her self-perception, which had risen eight points, from −2 to +6. Her concept of man's ideal woman had dropped only three points (from −5 to −8), which suggests that her problems were rooted in her own ambiguities regarding the female role and not in what she felt men expected of her (Table 4).

In the opinion of the therapist, examination and discussion of the Inventory scores provided a shortcut to action for Mrs. James in the realization of her ideal concept. As therapy progressed, she learned to accept the strength of her ideal concept and the importance of fulfilling

TABLE 5

Mr. James' Pre-Post Scores on MIMV

Form	October '71	June '72	Change
Self-Perception	+ 8	+ 5	— 3
Ideal Man	— 4	+ 7	+11
Woman's Ideal Man	—16	—26	—10
Man's Ideal Woman	—10	— 8	+ 2

her own potential as a human being in order to free herself to meet her family responsibilities without resentment. Her relationship with her husband and their respective children improved.

Mr. James began therapy with a discrepancy between self (+8) and ideal (—4) perceptions. His ideal concept of a man was more family-oriented than his self-perception; he considered himself a failure in terms of his role as a father and husband. In addition, his concept of what women want in men was —16, another expectation he felt he was failing to meet. In reality, Mrs. James indicated that her ideal man would have a score of +10, *more* career-oriented than her husband perceived himself to be. The lack of communication between the two was underscored for the therapist by the difference between what Mrs. James wanted in a man and what Mr. James thought she wanted—a total difference of 26 points. Interestingly, while Mr. James' ideal man became more self-achieving after the eight months of therapy (+7), his concept of his wife's ideal man became more home-oriented (—26). This confusion contributed to Mr. James' feelings of inadequacy in his role as husband and father (Table 5).

While the thrust of the therapy was to concentrate on the husband-wife relationship, significant emphasis was placed on what it takes to be an adequate and successful parent. The trauma of the divorces had caused both Mr. and Mrs. James to feel ineffectual and guilty in their performance as parents. An examination of the Inventory cluster pattern on Women's Attitudes Toward Motherhood/Men's Attitudes Toward Fatherhood was useful in pinpointing similarities and differences in their feelings.

At the start of therapy, analysis of the clusters on the Inventories had shown that the James' primary area of discrepancy was in attitudes toward parenthood—they disagreed on all five items. At the conclusion of therapy, they were more congruent with one another because of their greater willingness to compromise their beliefs in this important area. As communication and understanding on these points increased, they both reported more satisfaction with themselves and improved interaction with their children. The analysis of the cluster patterns on the original Inventory scores had led the therapist to focus on the James' attitudes, beliefs and perceptions regarding effective childrearing practices, with some hard evidence as a starting point, and the results were gratifying (Steinmann, 1972b).

This case illustrates that in marital therapy, just as in individual therapy, the husband and wife must become aware of each one's underlying difficulties before he or she can work with self-acceptance and reciprocal growth. The MAFERR Inventories are useful in gathering information that can help pinpoint the roots of the conflicts.

To return, however, to the problem of sex-role conflict in women: if for one reason or another, a woman is forced to suppress her need for self-expression, she will experience a loss of self-esteem, she will become less effectual in all spheres of her life. This is true for all women, but it is particularly severe for the educated woman and even more severe for the highly educated woman who, in the process of her education, was given high aspirations for personal success in the world of business or the professions.

For a woman to obtain gratification in her life and to sustain a high opinion of herself, she must continually develop deep reservoirs of intellectual and spiritual strength, as well as ways to use and express herself, to gain respect and admiration in the society of adults. Therapists must encourage this development, but in order to do so they must be aware of their own attitudes and feelings about women's roles. We know that bias exists in many people. Is the therapist free of bias, stemming from his or her concept of sex role? Only when one is free of bias can one be helpful to the woman who comes for help with problems related to sex-role confusion. This chapter has concentrated on women, but men too are subject to the preconceptions of a therapist, affirmative or negative.

One study proving there are therapists who are biased was completed recently at Worcester State Hospital, Massachusetts by Inge and Donald Broverman, with Paul Rosenkrantz, Susan Vogel and Frank Clarkson. They developed a sex-role questionnaire with over a hundred polar items, one pole being stereotypic male and the other stereotypic female. The Brovermans divided a group of clinical professionals into thirds and asked one group to mark the questionnaire to describe a mentally healthy adult. A second group marked the form to described a mentally healthy male adult, and a third defined a mentally healthy female adult. However, these subjects might have responded to the more personal MAFERR Inventories, the important point is that in this study they were responding objectively, as professionals.

The mental health therapists reinforced the standard sexual stereotypes of the society. They assigned the same characteristics to a mentally healthy adult and a mentally healthy male adult, but a mentally healthy female, unlike the male, was seen as passive, emotional, dependent, uncompetitive, non-objective, submissive and easily influenced. To quote the Brovermans, this characterization of a mentally healthy female "seems a most unusual way of describing any mature, healthy individual." The Brovermans, and others, interpret this sort of finding as relating directly to the Freudian or neo-Freudian training of the therapists (Steinmann, 1973b).

However, it is most important to emphasize that when therapists discriminate, they do so not as Freudians or neo-Freudians, but as the kind of people they are, as male and female people who have not been thoroughly analyzed and who do not understand their own projections. To blame it all on Freud is unjust as well as inaccurate. To sacrifice objectivity to emotionalism in interpreting Freud does nothing to further the goal of understanding the needs and abilities of women.

There is a mistaken notion among some people, deriving from the classic Freudian theories of sexuality, that many Freudian analysts equate femininity with passivity. This thinking does not fit the facts. *Activity* in the development of the girl was stressed by many of Freud's interpreters. A woman is not all passive. She is no more all vagina than a man is all penis. Certainly motherhood is not passive. It is significant to note that while Freud sharply differentiated girls' characteristics from boys', he understood that there are a great many feminine aspects in males and a great many masculine aspects in females. These characteristics are distributed in various amounts. It would therefore be expected that there are individual differences in responses depending upon the degree of masculinity in women, and vice versa.

All of Freud's major interpreters (mostly women) state emphatically that a woman should realize her masculine potential—thrusting self-achievement and self-accomplishing fulfillment—in order to be a full person. If Mrs. Portnoy had done that, Philip Roth would not have had to write *Portnoy's Complaint*. In fact, the widely-held opinion that Freud had a negative attitude toward women is difficult to reconcile with the fact that he inspired and was inspired by intellectual women. By encouraging women to participate professionally, he actually demonstrated his own feeling that women are not intellectually inferior to men. What he identified was woman's *feeling* of inferiority, but he insisted that by exercising their masculine thrust, women could rid themselves of their own inferior feelings, and also demonstrate to men their intellectual equality.

All this is by way of suggesting that when a therapist, male or female, cites Freudian theory to support a passive definition of femininity, he or she may be exhibiting an unresolved conflict and using it to influence therapy. Just as some therapists discriminate against blacks, poor people, middle class or rich people, others discriminate against members of the opposite, or even the same, sex.

If, for instance, a male therapist feels that woman's place is in the home, because that is where he likes his wife to be, he will use Freud to bolster his own righteous, if self-serving, opinion that women should not reject their femininity (a statement that means all things to all men and women). On the other hand, a Women's Lib spokeswoman will use an anti-Freud position to bolster her contention that most male and even female therapists can't treat women because of the "Freudian" male supremacy stereotype built into the mental health model.

Many who practice psychotherapy are aware that many married (and single) women have extremely low self-concepts and severe feelings of inadequacy resulting from stereotypical and discriminatory practices. Discrimination relating to employment, status, wage-earning, and exploration of intellectual abilities and expectations has caused women deep frustrations and emotional hardships. Certainly it is not the role of the therapist to use distortions of psychic principles to deepen women's frustrations. Therapists, male and female, who blithely accept a cultural stereotype when they tell women to accept their "femininity," and reject completely the concept of woman as a whole person, a person with masculine and feminine attributes, only add to the cultural confusion.

Finally, in terms of therapeutic goals, when a therapist discovers sex-role confusion in patients, it is his task to uncover in the course of therapy the real sources of the confusion. If a young, educated woman indicates she believes men do not want her to realize her intellectual potential to the extent that she wants to, is she perhaps saying that she herself is divided on the question? Does she want very much to fulfill traditional "feminine" expectations, but hide the fact from herself and project it as an attitude onto men? Or, on the other hand, is she in fact achievement-oriented and facing a real conflict because of her perception of man's ideal woman?

In couple therapy, if the man indicates that he wants the woman to fulfill herself outside the home just as much as she does, and she does not believe him, part of the problem may lie in the definition of "fulfill herself"; he means she should be president of the PTA, while she wants to be president of an advertising agency.

In other words, while diagnostic tools such as the MAFERR Inventories and others have provided much-needed hard data on male/female sex-role perceptions, and are proving invaluable as diagnostic tools in casework, the burden is still on the therapist to help his patient trace the *real* sources of his or her problem and reconcile his or her conflict in terms of sexual identity. In this regard, it is impossible to over-emphasize the necessity for the therapist to discard stereotypic attitudes and approach each case with a full acceptance of the wide range of appropriate roles for both men and women in today's world.

CONCLUSION

In these changing times, women are quite legitimately questioning traditional concepts of femininity and trying to find ways to express themselves intellectually and creatively, without sacrificing their important and rewarding roles as lovers, wives and mothers. Without in any way underrating the problem women face, however, it is vital to remember that men as well as women in our society suffer severe ambiguity in defining their "appropriate" roles. They are living at a time when every gain for women is paralleled by a corresponding loss of male sexual dominance, freedom, power, job opportunities, and status. Traditionally, to be male was to be active, to be a good provider, to have authority, and to make decisions at home and abroad. Sexually, man was master. He was a doer, a thinker, the axis on which the rest of the world revolved.

The society which engendered and utilized that kind of masculine behavior has changed. Men, like women, now face a dilemma: how can a male be true to his own physical and psychological needs while allowing the females with whom he interacts maximum freedom to develop their own potential? Moreover, how can he maintain a sense of individual worth and find opportunities for creative expression in an increasingly mechanized and depersonalized world?

This dilemma is one that must be resolved by men and women working together to change static and stereotyped attitudes about male and female roles that no longer benefit them. In this transitional age of sex-role identification, nothing will be gained by making men (or women) out as

TABLE 6

Cross-Cultural Concepts of Female and Male Attitudes Toward Feminine Role[1]

Means & Standard Deviations of Woman's Concept of Self (A), Ideal Woman (B), and Man's Ideal Woman (C)

Means & Standard Deviation of Man's Concept of His Ideal Woman (BB)

Country & Category[2]	Total Sample(N)	FEMALE FORMS						MALE FORMS		
		A		B		C		Total Sample(N)	BB	
		X	SD	X	SD	X	SD		X	SD
United States										
Undergraduates	285*	+3.2	11.34	+2.7	14.19	−15.1	13.49	182	+1.5	12.91
Professionals**	54	+28.9	9.63	+32.2	11.13	−23.8	21.30	54	+14.6	10.42
Working Class-Clerks	31	−1.2	9.98	+.4	9.10	−9.7	13.24	34	+2.2	15.29
Czechoslovakia[3]										
Professionals	32	+11.4	9.21	+10.1	9.85	−14.7	16.11	45	+18.6	10.34
Working Class	33	+9.4	7.52	+8.3	9.73	−13.5	9.52	30	+2.9	8.95
Brazil[3]										
Undergraduates	100	+6.2	13.69	+5.8	11.03	−6.4	17.09	100	+1.2	12.65
Professionals	58	+6.8	14.61	+10.2	12.81	−14.2	22.71	91	+4.9	15.04
Non-Professionals	78	−4.1	18.61	−1.0	13.90	−6.0	15.83	68	−2.2	12.62
Teachers	78	−1.3	10.46	+.9	13.84	−10.1	17.25	***		
England[3]										
Undergraduates	43	+4.7	8.23	+3.8	14.09	−17.8	12.36	36	+.2	12.19
Total	792							640		

* 206 for Form B

** Psychologists

*** No males sample

1 Maferr Inventory of Feminine Values Used

2 These data were all collected in the period 1968-1973.

3 The following people collaborated on foreign studies: *Czechoslovakia*—Dr. Karl Pech; *Brazil*—Professor Edith Ramos; *England*—Dr. Jane Hilowitz.

the enemy. Men must certainly recognize, once and for all, that the power structure of the male-female relationship is changing, and they must revise their attitudes and behavior, yield and divide their power, and free themselves to engage in new areas of activity and expression and to enjoy relationships with women rooted in equality, love and mutual respect.

Women, in their turn, must acknowledge that men face problems no less perplexing than their own, and join with men in an effort to understand each other as they try to understand themselves. They must also expect that a multiplicity of goals will bring conflicts unless they are very sure of their priorities, or can reorder their priorities at various times of their lives.

In time, social institutions that reinforce worn-out sexual stereotypes will be changed and young men and women will reach maturity secure in the knowledge of the many role options available to them and of the possibility of relationships not limited by unnecessary and artificial boundaries. But for now, both men and women must open new lines of communication that will help them solve their mutual problems and develop new ways of relating far richer than any they have experienced before.

REFERENCES

BROVERMAN, INGE, ET AL. Sex-role stereotypes: A current appraisal. *Journal of Social Issues*, Vol. 28, No. 2, pp. 59-78, 1972.

FRIEDAN, BETTY. *The Feminine Mystique.* New York: Norton, 1963.

STEINMANN, A. & Fox, D. J. *The Male Dilemma.* New York: Jason Aronson, 1974.

STEINMANN, A. A study of the concept of the feminine role in fifty-one middle class American families. *Genetic Psychology Monographs*, 67, 275-352, 1963.

STEINMANN, A. The ambivalent woman. *New Generation*, Vol. 51, No. 4, 29-32, Fall, 1969.

STEINMANN, A. Perceptions of the feminine role among male psychologists. *International Mental Health Research Newsletter*, Vol. XIV, No. 1, p. 6, Spring 1972a.

STEINMANN, A. Studies in male-female role identification. Presented at the Third Annual Meeting of the Society of Psychotherapy Research, Nashville, Tennessee, June 15-17, 1972b.

STEINMANN, A. Cross cultural concepts of masculine and feminine roles. Presented A.P.A. Division of Psychotherapy, Midyear Convention, Division 29, Freeport, Grand Bahama Island, Feb. 28-Mar. 4, 1973a.

STEINMANN, A. Sex role bias in psychotherapy. *International Mental Health Research Newsletter*, Vol. XV, No. 2, 8-12, Summer, 1973b.

STEINMANN, A. & Fox, D. J. Male-female perceptions of the feminine role in England, France, Greece, Japan, Turkey & the United States. A cross-cultural study. *International Mental Health Research Newsletter*, Vol. VII, No. 4, 7-16, Winter 1966a.

STEINMANN, A. & Fox, D. J. Male-female perceptions of the female role in the United States. *Journal of Psychology*, Vol. 64, 265-276, 1966b.

STEINMANN, A. & FOX, D. J. Self and ideal sex-role perceptions of men and women and their ideal perceptions of each other. In *New Directions in Mental Health*. New York: Grune & Stratton, pp. 232-243, 1969a.

STEINMANN, A. & FOX, D. J. Specific areas of agreement and conflict in women's self-perception and the perception of men's ideal women in two South American urban communities and an urban community in the United States. *The Journal of Marriage & the Family*, Vol. 31, No. 2, 1969b.

STEINMANN, A. & FOX, D. J. Decision-making and the contrast between thought and behavior in sex-role interaction. In *New Directions in Mental Health*. New York: Grune & Stratton, 1969c.

STEINMANN, A. & FOX, D. J. Attitudes toward women's family role among black and white undergraduates. *The Family Coordinator*, 363-368, October 1970.

STEINMANN, A. & RAPPAPORT, A. Self achieving vs. family orientation of "professional-liberated" women. (Perceptions of female sex roles among members of association of women psychologists.) Presented at the 78th Annual Convention of the American Psychological Association, Miami Beach, Florida, Sept. 3-7, 1970.

4

THE PSYCHOTHERAPIST AND THE FEMALE PATIENT: PERCEPTIONS, MISPERCEPTIONS AND CHANGE

BENJAMIN FABRIKANT

INTRODUCTION

A review of frequently used texts in courses on counselling and psychotherapy shows little or no distinction between males and females as patients in either diagnosis, treatment procedures, or goals. There has been some attention to whether the individual should be considered a "patient" or "client," but not the fact of the person as a "male" or a "female." A further review of the indexes of books on the teaching of psychotherapy shows an interesting lack of entries under either "women" or "females" as patients or clients. For the past century, the implicit assumption seems to have been that the male and female patient is an interchangeable individual and that the single term is sufficient to indicate both. Perhaps this also reflects the thinking of the major theoreticians and practitioners, namely that there is essentially no difference in how the therapist responds to the sex of a patient.

There has been exploration of the relative advantages of the patient having a male or a female therapist, depending on the parental figure considered to be the focus of the difficulty. The assumption made seems to be that the sex of the patient is less important than the sex of the therapist. The therapist of choice for young children was usually a female on the assumption that the mother figure is more important to the child in the early years. Later in childhood and particularly for the male child, the male therapist becomes more important. The explanation was that the male child needed a male model with whom to identify.

A review of the material published by some of the major sources of articles on psychotherapy (*Psychotherapy-Theory, Research and Practice* since 1966, *Psychology Today* since 1968, and *Ms* magazine since its inception) has brought to light very little experimental work on the perceptions of the female patient by either male or female therapists, and concomitantly little on the effects of these perceptions on the process, goals, or results of psychotherapy. In 1952, Fiedler and Senior stated that the patient was very sensitive to the therapists' feelings about themselves as well as about the patient. In 1971, Barbara Stevens wrote:

> But the patients psych out therapists too and fairly rapidly. How therapists feel about themselves, how they relate to others, what kind of behavior makes them uncomfortable or they approve of are readily seen by the patients. Moreover, they provide extensive clues for deciphering the therapist's values and beliefs about women.

Freud has been held responsible for a major portion of the difficulties experienced by women as patients. There has been a profusion of articles and expositions in the past few years stating, in strong terms, that Freud's early ideas of the female role, and his overall view of the psychology of women, have had much to do with the plight of the female and the difficulties of the female as a patient in psychotherapy. The thesis is that the therapist (seen as the male analyst) pushed the female (as well as the male) patient in the directions dictated by psychoanalytic theory. The women contend that these ideas have done much to downgrade women and the importance of the female role (cf. Gilman, 1971, Stevens, 1971, Greer, 1970, Bengis, 1972, West, 1972, Roche Report, 1971, Roiphe, 1972, Cummings, 1972, McDonald, 1972). Several key books, including the 1972 *Abstracts of the Standard Edition of the Complete Psychological Works of Sigmund Freud* have no entry on women as patients. There are a number of entries pertaining to the understanding of the psychology of women, but nothing about what this means, in a very real and pragmatic sense, to the individual therapist and female patient in terms of psychoanalytic goals. The following appears in the Strachey translation of the *Complete Introductory Lectures on Psychoanalysis*, published in 1966:

> I have promised to tell you of a few more psychological peculiarities of mature femininity, as we come across them in analytic observation. We do not lay claim to more than average validity for these assertions; nor is it always easy to distinguish what should be ascribed to the influence of the sexual function and what to social breeding.

In her article on women psychoanalysts and women's liberation, Roiphe also discusses some of the misperceptions and misinterpretations of the relationship between biology and psychology as it affects both men and women in our society. In 1971, Kronsky wrote: "I know of only two serious articles which discuss the icplications of femininity for psychotherapy, and neither of them deals specifically with questions of technique."

At this point, three years later, there are perhaps half a dozen published articles which are seriously concerned with the same question. One refers to specific techniques (Rice and Rice, 1973) and another (unpublished) to modifications of current approaches which lend themselves to the feminist viewpoint (Fodor, 1972). Kronsky adopts the psychoanalytic viewpoint, with some modifications, in discussing techniques for the management of assertiveness in female patients. Presenting several case studies and then generalizing to the more positive aspects of the feminist therapist for female patients, she concludes that "It may well be that the feminist oriented psychotherapist will have to be a woman herself."

Objecting strongly to the approach used by Kronsky, Fodor prefers behavior modification. First, she interprets the patient's symptoms in feminist terms and then, in a number of case studies, she shows how behavioral methods might be applied in such instances. There may be some questions as to her interpretations of the meaning of the symptoms, but her results indicate a possible approach to a feminist-oriented therapy.

Rice and Rice's (1973) recent and thorough review of the implications of the women's liberation movement for psychotherapy focuses on the predominance of the male therapist in both the psychological and psychiatric professions. They also reiterate the fact that the older female therapists were trained in the male dominated training programs and so are molded in the male model.

In a personal communication, Rice (1973) agrees that the older group of both male and female therapists does follow a more traditional approach in their perception of female patients' sex role expectations (Fabrikant et al., 1973).

Without presenting specific data, Rice and Rice discuss the past, current and possible future roles of women as therapists and as "different" patients. They feel that the male therapist is threatened in his traditionally perceived role as the authority/expert and father figure. Any challenge to this is met with strong resistance by a male therapist. They propose training the newer therapists in the areas of sex differences and the newer knowledge of the psychology of women. They also feel that the therapists should be more aware of alternative life-styles and sex roles, and take the initiative as direct agents of social change. They do not accept the passive analytic or client-centered approach, which they feel simply reinforces the older patterns of male-female behavior. For them, a possible approach to therapy for women would be a group with male and female co-therapists as leaders.

In her article on the problems of the professional women therapists, Fabian (1972) indicates that the female psychotherapists are outside the mainstream of the close relationships between and among psychotherapists. Women are perceived not so much as colleagues in the total sense but as interlopers. This occurs during both the training period as well as on a staff level. Her comments are comparable to the reports of female medical and dental students. It would be interesting to investigate the possible effects of this experience on the female (as therapist, physician or dentist) and on her perceptions and behavior towards female and male patients (as well as towards colleagues) later on in her career.

Krakauer (1973), writing for *Ms* magazine, also discusses the problems of a female patient looking for a therapist who is not in the traditional mold and who is feminist oriented. A possible source, she suggests, is a feminist referral source, where this exists, or experiences of friends who have been in therapy. Either of these might be less effective away from metropolitan areas. With Kronsky, she agrees that a women therapist may be more attuned to the newer attitudes that are developing in women's roles. But this, of course, is still speculative and open to investigation.

Jackson (1972), reviewing a series of studies discussed elsewhere in this chapter, comes to the conclusion, "Traits ascribed to women are in general more negative than those ascribed to men. . . . Masculine traits . . . are perceived as socially desirable and reflecting better adjustment and competence."

The general consensus seems to be that, although most patients seeking treatment are women, they seem to prefer men to women as their therapists. Jackson, not unreasonably, feels that the sex of the therapist may be an important factor in the treatment process. Since the female role is downgraded in our society, to be assigned to a female therapist is to be given "second best." This may have serious negative effects on the therapist-patient interaction. She further elaborates on the possible negative effects of seeing a female therapist in both female and male patients. She states:

> It seems clear that the therapeutic process is affected by both the race and sex of the therapist. When these are present, the content of therapy may be changed, the appearance of certain phenomena may be accelerated, and the way issues are presently modified. Issues re-

lated to these factors continue throughout therapy, but certain facets must be dealt with immediately if an effective alliance is to take place.

The Roche Report presents a series of brief interviews with different prominent psychiatrists. It is of interest that, of the male therapists, Scher and Grosz find that women's liberation has no influence on their female patients, whereas Frank finds some favorable aspects. The long interviews with Turkel (female) and Frank (male), focusing on the possible effects of the women's liberation movement on their patients are more positive. Turkel says:

> Every time there's an article about women's lib in the *New York Times* or the *New Yorker*, I get repercussions from most of my female patients. . . . I have yet to have a male patient mention women's lib. I think the movement has scared the hell out of some of them.

Cummings (1972) interviewed a number of practicing male and female psychotherapists. Their viewpoints concerning women's liberation were somewhat more moderate than those of the Roche Report. Both male and female therapists indicated favorable aspects of the effects of the women's liberation movement on female patients and women in general, whether patient or not.

McDonald (1972) and the Rejoinder in "Letters to the Editor" (*Center Magazine* 1972) form a unit. Reviewing much of the literature on psychoanalytic theory, presented by both believers and critics, he attempts to present a balanced point of view, indicating the strengths and weaknesses in both camps. His success, or lack of it, may be judged from two of the letters of rejoinder. Charlotte Klein writes:

> To the editors: Huzzah! Mr. McDonald deserves a reverberating cheer for what I consider to be a remarkable overview and analysis of the women's liberation movement.

This is strongly countered by Siew-Haw Beh, who says:

> To the editors: "The Liberation of Women" should be subtitled "A Man's Way of Leading Women Backward." The article by Donald McDonald is subjectively eclectic in a way that leads to greater confusion and ambiguity while important issues are skirted, clouded or avoided.

Siew-Haw Beh emphasizes an important factor found in many of the articles pertaining to therapy and its relationship to the feminist movement. The larger group of women in therapy are 1) white, 2) educated, 3) middle class, 4 housewives/mothers, 5) or working as a necessity rather than choice. Little attention is paid to the working mother from the lower class family, daughters from these lower class families (many, if not most, of the studies of attitudes involved college students), and women from deprived families. These groups seem to be outside both the mainstream of the women's liberation movement and from consideration as therapy patients.

Roiphe interviews Helen Deutsch, who presents the traditional Freudian psychoanalytic viewpoint. In response to Roiphe's question, "Why do you suppose the new feminine militants dislike Freud and psychoanalysis?" Deutsch replies, "Only because they misunderstand, and because Freud emphasized the difference between the sexes."

In Dr. Deutsch's book (1944) on female sexuality, she writes, "The awakening of the vagina to full sexual functioning is entirely dependent on the man's activity and this absence of spontaneous vaginal activity constitutes the psychological background of feminine passivity."

Roiphe, emphasizing that it would be as wrong for women to deny their biological functions as it would be for men to deny theirs, concludes, ". . . That my spirit, my intellect cannot be divorced from my intimate bodily functions and that it will do only harm to deny them. . . . If Greer, Millett et al., ever take a break at the barricades and review the troops, they will find volunteers from all over, some of whom have been fighting in their own way for 70 years."

Gilman, in his strong article against psychoanalysis, states:

> At bottom, feminist anger against Freud stems from the fact that he reinforced the idea of biological determinism at the very moment when technology was becoming capable of eliminating or radically curtailing such coercion.

He concludes:

> . . . and remarked, playing the devil's advocate, that there was no way to disprove Freud's theory that women had been biologically shortchanged. She nodded, then said: "Well, if it were true that we were created inferior, then we'd have a right to cry out against nature, or God, or whatever. As it is, Freud sets himself up as nature's interpreter, so we've got every right to cry out against him."

Gilman might have pointed out that this might well be so, if Freud had actually set himself up as nature's interpreter.

The article by Bem (1970) starts with material from the Bible and the morning prayer of the Orthodox Jew. These all indicate that the woman was born for the man, and the male gives thanks that he was born neither gentile, slave, nor woman. In the Koran, men are said to be superior to women as a God-given fact. Bem holds that the ideology stated in these prayers and writings is still very much with us, but in a "nonconscious" manner. We pay lip service to an egalitarian philosophy, and behave in a sexist way. Phyllis Chesler (1971) summarizes the Broverman work, and, from her research and clinical work, presents the following conclusions:

1. For a number of reasons, women "go crazy" more often than men, and this craziness is more likely to be self destructive than other-destructive. . . .
2. Most female "neuroses" are a result of societal demands and discrimination rather than the supposed mental illness of the individual. . . .
3. The therapist-patient relationship reinforces a system of beliefs and attitudes that is psychologically damaging to the patient and psychologically rewarding to the doctors. . . .

She feels that:

It is difficult for me to make practical suggestions for improving treatment as long as it keeps its present form and structure. . . . How can a woman learn to value being female from a therapist who devalues and misunderstands that sex. . . .
. . . She cannot. It therefore seems to me that some far-reaching changes will have to take place both in the attitudes of clinicians and in the nature of the therapy they dispense.

Her 1972 book (Chesler, 1972b) presents the case even more strongly—only a woman therapist who herself is a feminist can understand and help a woman patient. She concludes by saying, "Therapists, far from letting women out, have been adding more locks. We can no longer expect them to set women free."

A significant article by Broverman, Vogel, Broverman, Clarkson, and Rosenkrantz (1972) summarizes the available material on sex role stereotypes as follows:

Our research demonstrates the contemporary existence of clearly defined sex role stereotypes for men and women contrary to the phenomenon of "unisex" currently touted in the media. Women are perceived as relatively less competent, less independent, less objective, and less logical than men. Men are perceived as lacking interpersonal sensitivity, warmth, and expressiveness in comparison to women. Moreover, stereotypically masculine traits are more often perceived to be desirable than are the stereotypically feminine characteristics. Most importantly, both men and women incorporate both the positive and negative traits of the appropriate stereotype in their self-concepts.

As Chesler, Broverman, *et al.*, and Fabrikant have found, clinicians also accept these stereotypes and no major differences have been found so far between male and female therapists' perceptions of these sex role stereotypes.

CURRENT FINDINGS

In collaboration with several female research associates, the writer undertook a series of research projects, two of which have been completed (Fabrikant *et al.*, 1973 and the current material). The first study is essentially a replication of some of the work done by Broverman *et al.* (1970, 1972) with more focus on the background, training, and attitudes of the therapist, plus analysis of the personal and attitudinal questions.

As a group, the psychotherapists' responses to many of the questions indicated a somewhat more liberal view than that reported in the studies of Chesler, and Broverman. For example, both male and female psychotherapists agreed that:

1. Women need not be married to have a full life.
2. Marriage should be run as a co-equal partnership.
3. Women cannot be completely satisfied or fulfilled in only the wife/mother role.
4. Woman's sexual satisfaction is a necessary part of marriage. A small number of female therapists felt that the woman should be essentially a passive partner in the sexual relationship.
5. A woman can experience a fulfilling sexual relationship with someone other than her husband.
6. A woman should exercise the freedom to choose life roles other than those of marriage and a family.

When discussing women as patients, rather than as members of the general population, both male and female therapists agreed that the female patient should be less dependent on her husband financially and socially, but not sexually. The double standard still seems to be in effect as applied to the female patient.

The female therapists feel that there is a difference in goals for the female patient based on the sex of the therapist. The male therapist felt that the sex of the therapist was less important in goal setting than the ability of the therapist *per se.*

With Jackson, Rice, and Chesler, female therapists feel that the female therapist is more effective with female patients than is the male therapist. A large number of male therapists stated that they felt that female therapists were more effective than males, regardless of therapist orientation or type of patient.

All of the therapists were asked to respond to an adjective check list describing Sex Role Characteristics as applied to either the male or female. These characteristics, or traits, are comparable to the lists found in the earlier studies. This was done to see if the more liberal quality in response to the questions held constant. The analysis of the words on the list indicated the following choices:

There was statistically significant agreement between the male and female therapists in describing the male as:

> aggressive, assertive, bold, breadwinner, chivalrous, crude, independent, virile.

Male therapists added the following in their descriptions of the male:

> achiever, animalistic, attacker, competent, intellectual, omnipotent, powerful, rational.

Female therapists did not agree with the above, but added:

> exploiter, ruthless, strong, unemotional, victor.

In describing the female, both male and female therapists agreed on the following:

> chatterer, decorative, dependent, dizzy, domestic, fearful, flighty, fragile, generous, irrational, nurturing, overemotional, passive, subordinate, temperamental, virtuous.

Male therapists added:

> manipulative, perplexing

Female therapists added:

> devoted, empathic, gentle, kind, sentimental, slave, yielding.

As a further comparison with some of the other studies, the words were grouped with respect to the positive and negative values placed on them by society. The male therapists rated 70% of the female words as negative as contrasted to rating 71% of the male words as positive. Female therapists were very close, rating 68% of the female words as negative, and 67% of the male words as positive.

Essentially then, the perceptions of male and female sex role characteristics found in the present study parallel those indicated in other studies. The results also seem to belie a number of the more liberal attitudes presented by the male and female therapists in the earlier part of this study.

Earlier in this chapter, Stevens' point was noted that patients readily picked up the therapists' actual values and perceptions during the process of therapy. Fifty therapists, 25 male and 25 female, were asked to respond to both a list of questions and a shortened list of words describing the sex role traits. Rather than the previously used forced choice method on the words, we allowed them some freedom in rating the intensity of each word as it applied to either or both the male and female. We received replies from twice as many male therapists as female. We asked each therapist to ask both a male and female patient to complete the same forms as the therapist, as well as additional questions as to *how the therapist came across to the patient,* and to return them to the investigators without discussion with the therapist. We received twice as many responses from female patients as male. It is interesting to note that although we began with the same number of males and females in each sub-group, there was a marked difference in the number of each who completed and returned the material.

To attempt to overcome the objections to some of the other studies, we included therapists in a broad age range, drawn from clinics, private practice, community agencies, feminist groups, traditional university training and clinic settings. Thirty-one therapists responded (12 female, 19 male), and 50 patients (33 female and 17 male). The male therapists apparently were somewhat more willing to respond than were the female therapists. At the same time, perhaps the female patients felt that they understood their therapists and were consequently less defensive. The total sample size in each sub-group is small. The responders were not grouped into "therapists" or "patients" but viewed as female or male, patient or therapist, respectively.

The questions covered the following areas:

TABLE 1

Backgrounds of Psychotherapists

	Male	Female
N	19	12
Age	36	37*
Married	16	8*
Years Married	12	14
Divorced or Separated	1	4*
Major Decisions when younger		
Father	47%	33%
Mother	21%	17%
Joint	32%	50%
Parents living together	95%	83%

* significant

For the therapist to respond to:

1. Background of the therapist.
2. Training, supervision and experience as a therapist.
3. Therapist's current marital status and sex role attitudes.
4. Views of marriage and female sex role in general.
5. Role of women as patients in therapy.
6. The effectiveness of the therapist as a function of the sex of the therapist.

For the patient to respond to:

1. Background of the patient.
2. Experience as a patient.
3. Patient's current marital status and his/her perceptions of therapist's sex role attitudes.
4. Perception of therapist's views of marriage and sex role in general.
5. Perception of therapist's view of the role of women as patients in therapy.
6. Perception of therapist's view on the effectiveness of the therapist as a function of the sex of the therapist.

Both groups were also asked to respond to the words in the Adjective Check List according to how these words related to male or female traits. The therapists were asked to give their *own* responses, while the patients were asked to do this according to how they perceived the therapist rating of the same word.

Table 1 shows that the current therapists are about 10 years younger than those in the first study (Fabrikant *et al.,* 1973). The male therapists

Table 2

Training, Supervision and Experience of Psychotherapists

	Male	Female
N	19	12
Doctorate	15	3*
Orientation		
Analytic	70%	60%
Other	30%	40%
Currently in therapy	2	6*
Sex of Therapist	65% male	82% male+
Years in Therapy	1.8	3.5*
Years in Practice	16	8

* significant
+ including those who had been in therapy in the past

have fewer broken marriages, but have not been married quite as long. The male therapists also have a history of more intact family units when younger. The mother was more important in decision-making for the female therapists which may have resulted in the female being seen as stronger in those families. The results of other studies that there is a positive relationship between the status of the parents' marriage and one's own hold for psychotherapists as well as for the general public.

There is a major difference in the educational background, according to data included in Table 2. Males have continued to the doctorate or postdoctoral level five times as frequently. A possible explanation is that the male went directly through to complete his education and then into practice. The female did not begin her professional work until almost a decade later, or at about 30 years of age. They were either in other jobs, or had gone directly into marriage from college.

A younger group of therapists would be expected to be less influenced by analytic concepts and lean more towards either an eclectic or less traditional approach and theory (behavioral, experiential, humanist, etc.). The results indicate that the analytic and neo-analytic orientations have maintained a strong attraction for those therapists responding in this study.

Previous studies indicate that females are in therapy more frequently and for a longer period of time. Both of these findings are further supported by the experience of the psychotherapists themselves. Fewer males have been or are currently in therapy; they also spend less time in therapy. The female therapist, apparently despite her more liberated style, sought out a male therapist even more frequently than did the

TABLE 3

Current Marital Status of Psychotherapists

	Male	Female
N	19	12
Married	16	8*
Marriage is		
Moderately satisfactory		
to satisfactory	93%	75%*
Unsatisfactory	0%	25%*
Number of children	1+	2+
Major decisions made:		
Jointly	94%	58%*

* significant

males. This may have something to do with the availability of female therapists, or with their own personal needs.

Both male and female therapists report very few childless families (see Table 3). The female therapists report that over half of their families have three or more children. Female therapists also report more of the extremes of satisfaction and dissatisfaction in their marriages than do the males. This might well tie in to the higher frequency of divorce and separation among the female therapists. The female therapist is more likely to express her negative feelings about the marriage and take action rather than remaining passive and "making the best of it." Since a number of the female therapists are either divorced or separated, they have no one with whom to share the decision-making process. However, the very high percentage of male therapists who state that decisions are made on a joint basis may not be a reflection of reality, but more of expectation.

Table 4 indicates that the female patient in this study is slightly younger, has fewer years of formal education, is less often married, with more children in the family. She is also more frequently single and has a higher incidence of divorce. There are three separations among the male patients, but no divorces. When younger, the father made the decisions for the family of the female patients more frequently. This might indicate the development of a stronger male image for the female than for the male patient. However, this does not mean the development of a positive view of the male, only that the male figure was a stronger individual in a direct sense.

While the difference in the choice of the sex of the therapist is not

TABLE 4

Backgrounds of Patients

	Male	Female
N	17	33*
Age	30	28
Education—College	93%	50%*
Married	12 (70%)	17 (51%)*
Single	2	7*
Divorced or separated	3 (separated)	8 (divorced)*
Families with no children	50%	30%
Major decisions when younger		
Father	24%	37%
Mother	35%	34%
Joint	35%	28%
Parents living together	100%	90%

* significant

TABLE 5

Psychotherapy Experiences of Patients

	Male	Female
N	17	33
Sex of therapist—male	80%	67%
Length of time in therapy	2.3 years	5.7 years*
Number of therapists	1.3	1.4

* significant

significant (Table 5), it does differ markedly from the sex choices of the therapists themselves, and might reflect a trend where the female patient increasingly selects a female therapist. This does not agree with a later finding that female patients do not consider the sex of the therapist as an important variable in therapeutic effectiveness. Perhaps their choices indicate their feelings more strongly than does the verbalized material. The female patients report that they have been in therapy over twice as long as the male patients. Combining this with a similar finding for the therapists themselves as patients, the overall results most strongly support the feminist viewpoint that females in therapy are victimized by a social structure and therapeutic philosophy which keeps them dependent for as long as possible. There is no rationale for a continuation of this practice, and psychotherapists of all persuasions must re-examine their philosophy, practices, and goals in the light of these findings.

TABLE 6

Current Marital Status of Patients

	Male	Female
N	17	33
Married	70%	51%
Satisfied with marriage	60%	60%
Dissatisfied with marriage	25%	25%
Decisions		
Self	25%	45%
Joint	75%	45%

* significant

The higher number of female patients making decisions by themselves, as shown in Table 6, is a reflection of the number of single and divorced female patients and not of a life-style. Over half of each group seems to be satisfied with their marriages, which might lead one to believe that a disturbed marriage is not what brought the individuals into therapy.

Female patients state that they enter therapy with complaints of dissatisfaction with home life, followed in frequency by dissatisfaction with job or career. Male patients agree with the first, emphasizing conflicts with the wife as central. This is in direct contradiction with the reports in Table 6. The males report dissatisfaction with job or career as an infrequent reason for entering therapy. Women enter therapy with initial complaints of dissatisfaction with either the role of wife/mother, or conflict between this role and the strong desire for their own life-style, which might include a career. This is reported by both the female therapists and the female patients themselves. A pertinent finding is that no group reports dissatisfaction with "self" as sufficient to energize one to seek therapy. There must be a very specific reason that is either socially or personally acceptable before therapy is acceptable.

In the following, the attitudes of the therapists are contrasted with the patients' reports of how they perceived the therapists' attitudes during the process of therapy. The task presented to the patients was a difficult one. There are the complexities introduced by the therapists' selection of the patients, as well as the patients' own transference and relationship needs.

Psychotherapists and Patients—Marriage and the Female Role

Male and female therapists agree that neither men nor women need be married to experience a full and satisfying life. The individual should be free to select roles other than those related to marriage and a family. Male and female patients report that this attitude is what they felt from the therapists.

Male and female therapists also felt that, if one is married, then the marriage should be a partnership. This attitude is conveyed more to the male than to the female patient. The female patient reports that the therapist's attitude is that the male should dominate the marital relationship.

The following differences appear related more to sex gender rather than to a perception and reflection of therapists' views and attitudes. Male therapists and male patients agree that the majority of women can be satisfied and fulfilled by the wife/mother role. Female therapists and female patients sharply and significantly disagree with this contention. There may be a conflict here between a report of the attitudes of the general population and the response to one's own subjective needs. There is a similar male versus female difference for the response to who should make the decision on abortion. The female therapists and female patients state most strongly that the woman should make the decision. Male therapists and male patients suggest a joint decision is more acceptable to them.

Male therapists and male patients state that a male can be satisfied and fulfilled in being a husband and father. However, the female therapists and female patients report, very strongly, that they do not see the male as satisfied in these roles. Here, the females are probably more perceptive than the males who may be giving an "expected" response in terms of *their* perceptions of the purposes of therapy and the newer male roles in society. On the question of abortion, the female view reflects the stand of the feminists who consider the male as irrelevant in the decision process, except insofar as he is the physician.

Sex gender differences are also reflected in the fact that female therapists and female patients state that bringing up children is unequivocally the mother's responsibility. Male therapists and male patients state, just as strongly, that this should be a joint responsibility. This may well be a source of much family friction. The woman may feel that she is being imposed upon in having the responsibility forced upon her by the male's abdication of his role with the children. Then, when she accepts the responsibility, the male claims that she is usurping a joint role to herself. The women, therefore, may be deciding to take this responsibility directly, without the difficulties imposed by the vagaries of unconscious choices.

Male therapists and male patients remain strongly traditional in that the male is the provider of the major portion of a family's income. Female therapists and female patients verbalize the newer viewpoint among many women, the major portion of the income may come from either adult, or the female, or both.

The above presents a mixture of traditional viewpoints held by both sexes as well as differences, particularly in the female, in the direction of increasing equality and freedom. The males have yet to clarify some of the conflicts between their expressed attitudes and their behavior.

The area of sex attitudes and activity is a very important one in the psychotherapeutic process. The deepest and strongest expression of feelings revolves around this area of life. The results described below indicate the difficulties that therapists of both sexes have in changing attitudes, as well as some indications that a beginning has been made.

Male and female therapists agree that sexual satisfaction is an important part of life and marriage for both the female and the male. Either sex can experience a fulfilling sexual relationship with someone other than the spouse. The therapists also state that the female need not be the passive partner in the sexual relationship (in contrast to early analytic thinking). These attitudes are so perceived by both male and female patients as indicated in their responses. However, there are some important inconsistencies as well. The responses to the questions on sex, as indicated in Table 7, are illuminative.

Questions:

1. Should the same standards of sexual behavior apply to both sexes?
2. Should the husband be totally dependent on his wife for sexual satisfaction?
3. Should the husband and wife have other sexual partners?
4. Should the wife be totally dependent on the husband for sexual satisfaction?

Answers:

TABLE 7

Marriage and the Female Role—Sex

| | Therapists | | Patients | |
	Male	Female	Male	Female
N	19	12	17	33
1. yes	95%	92%	75%*	82%*
2. yes	53%	44%	33%	42%
3. yes	35%	33%	39%	48%*
4. yes	50%	54%	46%	70%*

* significant

TABLE 8

Female as Patient

	Therapists		Patients	
Agree with statement:	Male	Female	Male	Female
N	19	12	17	33
Female free to select life-style	100%	100%	100%	97%
Female less dependent on male socially	74%	92%	86%	87%
Male less dependent on female socially	78%	90%	47% *	77% *
Female financially independent of husband	38%	56%	47%	61% *

* significant

The patients, particularly the males, do not hold that the therapists really believe in a single standard of sexual behavior for marital partners despite the therapists' verbalizations to that effect. As indicated (Table 7), the therapists state that husbands and wives may have sexual partners other than the spouse. However, what seems to be reflected is the attitude that the wife should be more dependent on her husband for sexual satisfaction than the husband on the wife. The female patients also indicate that the double standard comes through to them very strongly from the therapists. Perhaps the therapists are saying that the patients of both sexes (or everyone) should be more free sexually, but not as free as they, the therapist, verbalize. Listen to them, agree with them, just don't go ahead and do it!

The Role of the Female as Patient in Psychotherapy

The therapists' attitude is that the goal for a female patient in therapy is to select her own life-style. However, there is the finding, reported earlier, that male therapists and male patients felt that the female can be satisfied and fulfilled in the wife/mother role, which contradicts the data in Table 8. Perhaps one of the reasons for the contradiction is the wording of the question. When one is asked whether a female should be free to define her own role and life, the reply is "yes!" When the question is worded in terms of fulfillment in the wife/mother role, the males reply with the traditional view, and the females with a more liberal one.

Male and female therapists both agree that females should be less dependent on males—boyfriends or husbands—socially. However, the therapists' attitude that the male should be less dependent on the female socially is reflected accurately by female patients, but not by the male

TABLE 9

Roles, Goals and Effectiveness

Agree with statement:	Therapists		Patients	
	Male	Female	Male	Female
Male and female therapists differ in goals for male and female patients	33%	46%	18%*	44%*
Male therapists encourage female patients to follow role of wife/mother	33%	60%*	8%*	27%*
Male therapists encourage male patients to be assertive and dominant	39%	50%	8%*	27%*

* significant

patients. The male patients report a need for a continuing dependence on the female for social relationships. A possible explanation is that the male patient may have interpreted this as an option where males turn to other males, thereby raising the possibility of either a passive or a homosexual relationship which might be very disturbing to many of these male patients. Even if they do not interpret this in this way, the fact that a new role option is opened for an individual by a therapist does not mean that the patient is ready to accept this. There is the feeling that one must attempt new roles in order to satisfy the therapist, even if one is afraid to do so. If one misperceives and does not see the option, then there is no felt need to comply.

Therapy

Male therapists and male patients state that male and female therapists do not differ in their goals for male and female patients (see Table 9). Female therapists and female patients disagree with this. However, when the specific areas are delineated, male and female patients report that the female therapists do not seem to be as objective as they might be. The male therapists state that they neither encourage nor limit their female patients to the traditional wife/mother passive female role nor do they particularly encourage their male patients to be primarily assertive and dominant. The female therapists disagree and state that the male patients do both. On these, both the male and female patients indicate that the attitude of the male therapists prevail and that the female therapists may be reporting a bias, not a reality. To extrapolate, the widely held feminist view that the male therapists perpetuate male dominance and female passivity is not supported by these results.

TABLE 10

Sex of Therapist

		Therapists		Patients	
		Male	Male	Female	Female
N		19	12	17	33
Sex of the therapist is an important factor in effectiveness in psychotherapy	YES	16%	30%	73%*	44%

The Effectiveness of the Therapist as a Function of the Sex of the Therapist

While the therapists differ, the difference is not significant (Table 10). However, the patients report that there is a very strong impression, particularly from the male patients, that, again, the male therapists may be verbalizing an expected attitude rather than accurately reporting the transmitted one. While male therapists state that they do not consider the sex of the therapist as an important factor in effectiveness, the patients and the female therapists report a different view.

In a later question relating therapeutic effectiveness based solely on the sex of the therapist, the therapists and patients agreed that female therapists do not view themselves as more effective with female patients solely as a function of being a sister female. This result questions some of the earlier statements of some feminists that only female therapists are able to work effectively with female patients. Effectiveness may be more a result of ability and sensitivity rather than gender.

Sex Role Characteristics

The therapists were asked to evaluate each word as descriptive of either the male and/or female sex role and the intensity, mild, moderate, or strong, they ascribe to the word. The words that did not differentiate significantly in the first study were omitted, and the remaining 49 words were used in the present study. The patients were asked to indicate the male and female therapists' choices as reflected to them during the therapeutic process. One concern was that the therapists might rate the majority of words as equally applicable to both the male and female. The patients, perceiving this, if it did occur, would then also report the words in the same way. This would leave us with little to interpret in a meaningful way. Table 11 shows that this did not occur. We can, therefore, continue with an analysis of the choices.

TABLE 11

Distribution of Choices

| | Therapists | | Patients | |
	Male	Female	Male	Female
M	18	14	16	22
F	13	15	16	11
Equally Applicable	18	19	17	16
No response	0	1	0	0
N	49	49	49	49

Male and female therapists selected the following characteristics as equally applicable to males and females in society: animalistic, dependent, devoted, hesitant, intellectual, manipulative, temperamental, virtuous, wise. The patients reported that this was also how they perceived the therapists' choices.

Previous studies listed animalistic, intellectual and wise as male, with the others as female characteristics. These results represent something of a change. The shift of characteristics seems to have gone in both directions. Several of the positive characteristics have gone from male to equal, and some of the negative ones from female to equal.

The next group was reported by the therapists as male characteristics and agreed to by the patients: bold, faithful, independent, kind, loving, omnipotent, victor, virile.

There were differences in degree, with the therapists reporting stronger intensity, with the patients stating that often a milder or moderate intensity is what they perceived. On "virile," the patients reflected the therapists' attitude of this as strongly male. In other studies, "faithful," "kind," and "loving" were considered female characteristics. The change in perception of these very positive characteristics from female to male might be contrasted with those selected by therapists as female characteristics, and reflected as so by the patients: castrating (strong intensity), chatterer, decorative (mild intensity), dizzy, fragile, generous.

Of these six characteristics, only one, "generous," would be considered as a positive attribute. In keeping with this, male therapists and male patients selected the characteristic "attacker" as female, while the female therapists and female patients see "attacker" as male. Earlier studies reported "attacker" to be perceived as a male characteristic by both therapists and the general population. This is another shift, and might be further explored in view of the more aggressive stance of women today.

TABLE 12

Gender Characteristics of Adjectives

	Therapists		Patients	
	Male	Female	Male	Female
breadwinner	M	M	=	=
chivalrous	M	M	=	=
compassionate	=	=	F	F
flighty	M	M	F	F
irrational	=	=	F	F
passive	=	=	F	F
powerful	=	=	F	F

Perhaps "non-passive," "assertive" and "attacking" are perceived differently by males and females in our society

In previous studies, "compassionate," "irrational," "passive" and "flighty" were seen as female characteristics, while "powerful," "breadwinner," and "chivalrous" were seen as male. Here (see Table 12), the therapists appear to see themselves as more liberal, to the point that they perceive "flighty" as male. However, the patients do not agree with the therapists' statements of their own perceptions. It may be that the patients here are responding more in terms of the general population stereotypes as well as to their own personal needs ("powerful" perceived as feminine) rather than being as objective as they seem to have been with other sex role characteristics. Of course, it may also be that the therapists are against presenting verbalized changes, which have not appeared as part of the therapeutic interaction. In that sense, the patients are more objective than the therapists. This is grist for further exploration of this and additional data to see what "clusters" of role characteristics are elicited.

The data presented in Table 13 are difficult to interpret. For each role characteristic, three of the four groups agree on the direction of choice, with the fourth group in disagreement. With some, the patients seem to be reflecting the therapists, in others, themselves. A reliability study might produce some interesting results, except that a repeated study would find the patients and therapists at a different point in therapy, and comparisons might be inconclusive.

The therapists view the female as the exploiter in our society, not the male. In the same light, the therapists also see the female as assertive. The remaining characteristics are viewed either stereotypically or as equally applicable. In keeping with other indications, the female patients seem

TABLE 13

Further Gender Characteristics

	Therapists		Patients	
	Male	Female	Male	Female
assertive	F***	F***	F*	M*
authoritarian	M	F***	F****	F***
devoted	=	F*	=	=
exploiter	F*	F*	F*	M**
fearful	=	=	F	=
nurturing	=	=	=	M**
rational	M	=	M	M
slave	=	F*	F**	F**
subordinate	=	F*	=	=
unemotional	M	=	M	M

* indicates level of significance, ranging from * for low significance to **** for very high significance (.05 to .001).

to be responding to their own needs in response to nurturing. Again, the therapists see either sex as nurturant, and not as the usual female role. One question to be followed up would center around the therapists' perceptions of the female as castrating, exploitative, and assertive. The female therapists add authoritarian to this essentially negative picture. A sharply polar view of the female comes out of this with subordinate, slave, fragile, and decorative as the opposite pole.

To explore the problem of values in sex role characteristics, a positive or negative value was assigned to each characteristic. The direction was developed out of the contextual use of the characteristic in the literature and in other studies already cited. As examples, castrating, crude, and fearful would be negative, and faithful, bold and kind would be positive. The distribution for each of the four sub-groups is presented in Table 14.

The results indicate that everyone, therapist and patient alike, still has many stereotypes. Male characteristics are seen as positive, female as strongly negative.

The results of this study do not present as clear a picture of one-sided bias as reported in the earlier studies cited. The results are complex, confusing, and often contradictory. At the risk of being perceived as an idealist, or a male Uncle Tom, the writer feels that the responses to the questions indicate a more liberal attitude towards females in both male and female therapists. The evidence also points to this newer attitude as transmitted to, and perceived by, their male and female patients. On the basis of this, the reported strongly negative feelings against current psy-

TABLE 14

Direction of Values

| | Therapists | | Patients | |
	Male	Female	Male	Female
Male characteristics—positive	83%	86%	81%	82%
Female characteristics—positive	31%	33%	31%	9%*

* significant

choanalytic therapists as perpetuators of male chauvinism are open to question. The majority of male and female therapists in this study consider themselves as analytically oriented. Thus, it may be that the younger male or female analytic therapist is not as tradition-bound as has been so forcibly stated in the feminist literature. This is not to deny that, in a number of areas (for example, sex, income, and responsibility for children), choices continue to be made on a sex gender, male versus female basis rather than in terms of therapist attitudes.

There is some discrepancy between the responses to the questions and the results of the Adjective List which points to a need for further clarification and continuing exploration of changing ideas and attitudes. Some of the more traditionally viewed male characteristics are no longer seen as uniquely male. A number of the traditional female characteristics are perceived as equally applicable to both sexes and/or to males. Some of the differences between therapists' attitudes and patients' perceptions may also be a result of anxiety concerning new role options. Although therapists are more open to change, patients may not be ready to exercise the newer roles and thus may "misperceive" the therapists' attitudes. Where the option is not perceived, there is no demand to try out the new option.

Still a very important problem is that male role characteristics are still seen as positive and female characteristics as negative. This agrees with the Broverman studies in their conclusion that women, in accepting the prevailing "feminine" view of themselves, find themselves labeled "neurotic." These females would find it very difficult to see themselves as mentally and emotionally "healthy." However, the results of this study, if consistent with those found in future studies, indicate that there are changes. The female can be perceived by therapists, by themselves, and eventually by society at large as healthy in sharing equally with males without the need to shift the males to an extreme pole.

REFERENCES

ANTHONY, N. *Letter to a Psychiatrist*. Pittsburgh: Know, 1972.

BENGIS, I. *Combat in the Erogenous Zone*. New York: Knopf, 1972.

BEM, S. & BEM, D. We're all nonconscious sexists. *Psychology Today*, 22, Nov. 1970.

BRODSKY, A. M. *Feminist Therapist Roster*. Pittsburgh: Know, 1972.

BROVERMAN, I. K., BROVERMAN, D. M., CLARKSON, F. E., ROSENKRANTZ, P. S., & VOGEL, S. R. Sex role stereotypes and clinical judgments of mental health. *Journal of Consulting and Clinical Psychology*, 34, 1-7, 1970.

BROVERMAN, I. K., VOGEL, S. R., BROVERMAN, D. M., CLARKSON, F. E., & ROSENKRANTZ, P. S. Sex-role stereotypes: A current appraisal. *The Journal of Social Issues*, 28, 58-78, 1972.

CHEEK, F. A serendipitous finding: Sex role and schizophrenia. *Journal of Abnormal and Social Psychology*, 69, pp. 392-400, 1964.

CHESLER, P. *Marriage and Psychotherapy*. Pittsburgh: Know, 1972a.

CHESLER, P. *Women and Madness*. New York: Doubleday, 1972b.

CHESLER, P. The sensuous psychiatrists. *New York Magazine*, June 19, 1972, 52-61.

CHESLER, P. Men drive women crazy. *Psychology Today*, 18, July 1971.

COLEMAN, J. & BROEN, W. *Abnormal Psychology and Modern Life*. 4th edition. Homewood, Ill.: Scott, Foresman and Co., 1972.

CUDLIPP, E. *Understanding Women's Liberation*. New York: Paperback Library, 1971.

CUMMINGS, L. What psychiatrists say about women's liberation. *Family Weekly*, 4, July 2, 1972.

DE BEAUVOIR, S. *The Second Sex*. New York: Bantam Books, 1952.

DEUTSCH, H. *The Psychology of Women: A Psychoanalytic Interpretation*. New York: Grune and Stratton, 1944.

EKSTEIN, R. & WALLERSTEIN, R. *The Teaching and Learning of Psychotherapy*. New York: Basic Books, 1958.

FABIAN, J. The hazards of being a professional woman. *Professional Psychology*, 3, 324-326, 1972.

FABRIKANT, B., LANDAU, D., & ROLLENHAGEN, J. Perceived female sex role attributes and psychotherapists sex role expectations for female patients. *New Jersey Psychologist*, 23, 13-16, 1973.

Feminists call psychiatry sick. *Bergen Record*, 5, June 9, 1972.

FENICHEL, O. *The Psychoanalytic Theory of Neurosis*. New York: Norton, 1945.

FIEDLER, F. E. & SENIOR, K. Exploratory study of unconscious feeling reactions in 15 patient-therapist pairs. *J. of Abnormal and Social Psychology*, 47, 446-453, 1952.

FODOR, I. Sex role conflict and symptom formation in women: Can behavior therapy help? Unpublished manuscript, 1972.

Follow-up: The liberation of women. *The Center Magazine*, 4, 13, July 1972.

FORD, D., & URBAN, H. *Systems of Psychotherapy. A Comparative Study*. New York: Wiley, 1967.

FRANKS, C. M. (Ed.). *Behavior Therapy: Appraisal and Status*. New York: McGraw-Hill, 1969.

FRIED, E. *Active-Passive: The Crucial Psychological Dimension*. New York: Harper & Row, 1970.

FRIEDAN, B. *The Feminine Mystique*. New York: Dell, 1963.

FREUD, S. *The Complete Introductory Lectures on Psychoanalysis*. New York: Norton, 1966.

FROMM-REICHMANN, F. *Principles of Intensive Psychotherapy*. Chicago: University of Chicago Press, 1950.

GILMAN, R. The femlib case against Sigmund Freud. *New York Times Magazine*, Jan. 31, 1971, 10-47.

GORNICK, V. Towards a definition of the female sensibility. *Village Voice*, 21, May 31, 1973.

GOUCH, H. A cross-cultural analysis of the CPI femininity scale. *Journal of Consulting Psychology*, 30, 136-141, 1966.

GREER, G. *The Female Eunuch.* New York: McGraw-Hill, 1970.

GUERNEY, B. *Psychotherapeutic Agents: New Roles for Nonprofessional Parents and Teachers.* New York: Holt, Rinehart & Winston, 1969.

GUMP, J. Sex role attitudes and psychological well being. *Journal of Social Issues*, 28, 79-92, 1972.

HALLECK, S. *The Politics of Therapy.* New York: Harper and Row, 1971.

HARDING, M. E. *Women's Mysteries Ancient and Modern.* New York: Bantam Books, 1971.

HARTMAN, S. *Princess Valium Meets Shrinkthink: Sexism in Psychiatry.* Pittsburgh: Know, 1972.

HEIDE, W. S. *Reality and Challenge of the Double Standard in Mental Health and Society.* Pittsburgh: Know, 1972.

HEINE, R. *Psychotherapy.* Englewood Cliffs, N. J.: Prentice-Hall, 1971.

HILL, N. (Ed.). *The Violent Women.* New York: Popular Library, 1971.

JACKSON, A. Problems experienced by female therapists in establishing an alliance. Paper presented at APA Hawaii, September 2, 1972.

KAYTON, R. & BILLER, H. Sex role development and psychopathology in adult males. *Journal of Consulting and Clinical Psychology*, 38, 208-210, 1972.

KAZICKAS, J. Women are asking: Is therapy couched in chauvinism? *The Sunday Record*, 3, May 13, 1973.

KOMAROUSKY, M. Functional analysis of sex roles. *Sociological Review*, 15, 508-516, 1950.

KOMISAR, L. The new feminism. *Saturday Review*, 27-30, February 21, 1970.

KRAKAUER, A. A good therapist is hard to find. *Ms Magazine*, 2, 23, 1973.

KRONSKY, B. Feminism and psychotherapy. *Journal of Contemporary Psychotherapy*, 3, 89-98, 1971.

LEWIS, M. Parents and children: Sex role development, *School Review*, 80, 230-239, 1972.

MADDI, S. On women—The couch as rack. *Saturday Review*, 61, Dec. 23, 1973.

McCLELLAND, D. C. & WATT, N. F. Sex role alienation in schizophrenia. *Journal of Abnormal Psychology*, 73, 3, 1968.

McDONALD, D. The liberation of women. *Center Magazine*, 5, 24-42, May 1972.

McKEE, J. & SHERRIFFS, A. Men's and women's beliefs, ideals and self concepts. *American Journal of Sociology*, 64 ,356-363, 1959.

MENNINGER, K. *The Theory of Psychoanalytic Technique.* New York: Harper and Row, 1958.

OBERNDORF, C. *A History of Psychoanalysis in America.* New York: Harper and Row, 1953.

REEVES, N. *Womankind Beyond the Stereotypes.* New York: Aldine-Atherton, 1971.

RICE, J. Personal communication, April 25, 1973.

RICE, J. & RICE, D. Implications of the women's liberation movement for psychotherapy. *American Journal of Psychiatry*, 130, 191-196, 1973.

RICKLES, N. K. The angry woman syndrome. *Archives of General Psychiatry*, 24, pp. 91-94, 1971.

ROBERTS, R .(Ed.). *The Unwed Mother.* New York: Harper and Row, 1966.

ROCHE REPORT. Women's lib: What is its impact on female and male psychology? *Roche Report: Frontiers of Psychiatry*, 11, 1, 1971.

ROIPHE, A. What women psychoanalysts say about women's liberation. *New York Times Magazine*, 10, February 13, 1973.

ROSENKRANTZ, P. S., BEE, H., VOGEL, S. R., BROVERMAN, I. K., & BROVERMAN, D. M. Sex role stereotypes and self concepts in college students. *Journal of Consulting and Clinical Psychology*, 32, 287-295, 1968.

ROTHGEB, C. (Ed.). *Abstracts of the Standard Edition of Complete Psychological Works of Sigmund Freud*. Washington: U.S. Department of Health, Education and Welfare, 1971.

SAHAKIAN, W. (Ed.). *Psychotherapy and Counseling*. Chicago: Rand McNally, 1969.

SARNOFF, I. *Testing Freudian Concepts: As Experimental Social Approaches*. New York: Springer, 1971.

SHAPIRO, E. T. Women who want to be women. *The Woman Physician*, 20, 399-413,

SHERFEY, M. J. The evolution and nature of female sexuality in relation to psychoanalytic theory. *Journal of the American Psychoanalytic Association*, 14, 28-128, 1966.

SPENCE, J. & HELMURICH, R. Attitudes towards women scale: An objective instrument to measure attitudes towards the rights and roles of women in contemporary society. *Selected Documents in Psychology*. APA Journal Supplement Abstract Service #153, 1972.

STEVENS, B. The psychotherapist and women's liberation. *Social Work*, 11, 12-18, 1971.

TEMERLIN, M. K. Suggestion effects in psychiatric diagnosis. *Journal of Nervous and Mental Disease*, 147, 349-353, 1968.

TENNOV, D. Feminism, psychotherapy and professionalism. *Journal of Contemporary Psychotherapy*, 5, 2-11, 1973.

TORREY, J. *Psychoanalysis: A Feminist Revision*. Pittsburgh: Know, 1972.

VILAR, E. *The Manipulated Man*. New York: Farrar, Straus and Giroux, 1972.

WEST, A. G. A woman's liberation or exploding the fairy princess myth. *Reflections*, 7, 20-32, 1972.

WOLFF, C. *Love Between Women*. New York: Harper and Row, 1972.

ZUCKER, H. *Problems of Psychotherapy*. New York: The Free Press, 1967.

Part III

FOUR APPROACHES TO PROBLEMATIC BEHAVIORS

5

COGNITIVE THERAPY WITH DEPRESSED WOMEN

AARON T. BECK and RUTH L. GREENBERG

Recently it has been argued that women, by virtue of sex role definitions, face a daily routine that is more repetitious, frustrating, emotionally exhausting, and narrow in scope than that of their masculine counterparts. In other words, it is said, the social roles allotted most women—their subservient posture as secretaries, nurses, and assistants and especially those duties that attend housewifery and motherhood in the current American social scheme—are inherently depressing.

Although enormous methodological problems are involved in assessing the prevalence of mental illness in any form, available statistics seem to confirm the common impression that more women than men suffer from depression. According to Roth (1959), the incidence of depression may be as high as 8% of women, compared to 4% of men. Were the many male depressions that go "masked" by physical symptoms to be uncovered, the discrepancy between male and female rates for depression would undoubtedly diminish. Nevertheless, the large numbers of women who seek help for affective disorders indicate that depression in women is a health problem of some magnitude.

Depression is a puzzling and even paradoxical disorder. An acknowledged beauty, suffering from depression, may beg for plastic surgery in the belief that she is ugly; an accomplished musician may conclude that her talent is worthless. Severely depressed patients may seek punishment, humiliation, and death despite outward signs of achievement and social success. Yet, unless suicide intervenes, the chances for the depressed patient's recovery are excellent, and complete remission of an episode of depression occurs in 70-95% of cases, although recurrences are common (Beck, 1972a). The interpretation of these phenomena is surrounded by

113

controversy. Whether depression is an exaggeration of a normal low mood or qualitatively different from a normal mood, whether depression is a "reaction" or a disease, biological or psychological in origin—these issues are still unresolved.

The symptoms of depression can be divided into emotional, cognitive, motivational, and behavioral manifestations. The emotional (affective) manifestations include the characteristic dejected mood: the depressed woman may describe her feelings as sad, lonely, or bored, or in somatic terms ("a lump in my throat"). Further, she may express negative feelings about herself specifically, ranging from mild disappointment in herself to outright self-hatred. She may complain that she no longer enjoys things as she used to, and that her emotional involvement with others has diminished. She is likely to cry a lot and have lost her sense of humor.

The depressed woman may be apathetic about caring for her home and other responsibilities; she has ceased to gain satisfaction from these activities. At first, she may respond to this loss of interest in ordinary responsibilities by increasing her participation in recreational activities. Saul (1947) attributed this change to an upset in the "give-get" balance in depression. When a young woman marries and bears children, for example, she may find herself emotionally depleted after a time by her constant giving in response to the demands of home and family, while she receives relatively little in return. A mildly depressed woman may compensate for this loss by indulging in passive recreational activities, but in more severe depression, even these fail to gratify her.

Women are also vulnerable to feelings of depression later on in life, when children grow up and move away from home. When a woman devotes the majority of her time and energy to her home and family, she looks forward to her children's adulthood as a time when she can begin to derive pleasure from them after her investment of years of work and concern. Yet as they become more adult, they become more independent of her ministrations and look outside the family for stimulation, leaving a gap in her life which she is unprepared to fill. When the children finally do leave the house, she may be overwhelmed by feelings of uselessness and apathy—the "empty nest" syndrome.

The emotional component in depression is accompanied by cognitive factors. These include a low self-evaluation—the patient's tendency to see herself as deficient in attributes that are important to her: health, beauty, intelligence, achievement. She may complain that she is deprived of love or suffers from poverty; she is likely to be concerned with her personal appearance, believing it has degenerated since the onset of her illness. Secondly, she has negative expectations about the future; she believes she will never be well and that her present difficult circumstances will continue to worsen. Third, the depressed person has an egocentric notion of causality, and believes she herself is to blame for everything that goes wrong around her. She measures herself according to rigid standards and is highly self-critical when she fails to meet them. In addition, she finds herself unable to make decisions; she believes she will choose badly and would rather avoid responsibility and commitment.

Indecisiveness is related not only to the cognitive but to the motivational change in depression. The depressed patient's motivations are strikingly regressive in nature. Whereas the patient may have been, before her illness, a highly efficient wife, mother, or professional, she may now be unable to mobilize herself even to eat or take medication. She sees everyday tasks as immense burdens and longs to be free of them; she may even seek death as a means of escape. She yearns to be helped and guided and cared for.

Appetite loss, sleep disturbance, libido loss, and fatigability are the common physical symptoms of depression. Interestingly, fatigability correlates more highly with pessimism and lack of satisfaction than with the other physical symptoms (Beck, 1972a). Delusions and hallucinations may be present. Finally, the depressed patient's activity level may be either retarded or agitated.

THEORIES

Many recent theoreticians of depression have emphasized the depressed person's helplessness and low self-esteem, and his sense of hopelessness and loss. Bibring (1953) defined depression as "the emotional expression (indication) of a state of helplessness and powerlessness of the ego." Expanding Freud's concept of intrapsychic loss in melancholia, Gaylin (1968) wrote that "depression can be precipitated by the loss or removal of *anything* that the individual overvalues in terms of his security." Depressed patients report that they have lost status, self-esteem, or gratifying interpersonal relationships (see Breed, 1967). In short, the depressed person sees himself as unable to cope with his present and future difficulties. Further, he believes that his present unhappy circumstances will continue indefinitely. Sarwer-Foner (1966) noted that depressed patients share a belief

... that their depressed state will continue indefinitely and never end. ... [The] patient himself is all too often unable to pinpoint or verbally present [this delusion] ... to the physician as psychotherapeutic "material. ..." It is rather overwhelmingly natural (i.e., ego syntonic) to his depressed state because he is unaware of any ability to cope with or change what is for him, an accepted fact. ... Along with this hopelessness, one sees very clearly their helplessness. There is nothing that they can do through their own efforts to restore their inner organs, alter their own destructiveness or remedy a degraded, worthless, empty inner state, one so impoverished that they can do nothing well. ...

The depressed patient, in other words, sees himself as suffering from an insoluble problem. Bjerg's finding (1967) that 81% of the suicide notes he studied "seemed to refer to the person's seeing himself as having a desire (other than suicidal) which could not, cannot, or will not be fulfilled" constitutes independent support for the "insoluble problem" formulation of depression (Beck, 1972b).

With this conception of depressive illness in mind, one is tempted to postulate, as feminists have done, a kinship between the subjective feelings of helplessness in depression and the objective helplessness and powerlessness of women in American society, when compared to the prestige of men in male-oriented professional and business worlds. On reading Bibring's assertion that "everything that lowers or paralyzes the ego's self-esteem without changing the narcissistically important aims represents a condition of depression," it is easy to picture the educated young woman still nourishing plans of graduate school and career but faced in reality with low status tasks of housekeeping and child-raising and submissive attention to her husband's needs. Such a woman may in fact have suffered the losses of status,* self-esteem, and gratifying interpersonal relationships which have been associated with depression.

Alluding to Freud's analogy between grief and melancholia, Phyllis Chesler (1972), a feminist clinical psychologist, writes that women are always in mourning for what they never had—namely, a positive conception of their own possibilities. This line of reasoning implies that women, since early in history subject to the whims of biology and the male ego and confined to roles of low and servile status, share an attitude of resignation with which the hopelessness of depressed women can easily be equated. Chesler believes that the symptomatology of depression is merely an intensification of traits which normal socialization processes

---

* At least legally, marriage itself can be a downward status step for women (see Jessie Bernard, *The Future of Marriage,* p. 39).

induce in women: passivity, dependence, self-deprecation, self-sacrifice, naiveté, fearfulness, failure.* Depression, Chesler contends, is a woman's "style" of responding to stress just as schizophrenia, with its overt hostility and aggression, is a masculine "style." Chesler implies that not only the types of psychological disorders from which women suffer but the prevalence of these disorders among women are related to sex-role factors. If mental illness is, by definition, a departure from expected social roles, then women, offered a narrower range of roles than men, will more often suffer from mental illness.**

Sociologist Jessie Bernard (1972) has argued that depression, among other problems of women, can be attributed to the "bad deal" they get in marriage. She cites, for example, Genevieve Knupfer's finding that "more married than unmarried women tend to be bothered by feelings of depression, unhappy most of the time . . . sometimes feeling they are about to go to pieces. . . ." Bernard notes that many married women, especially women with children, are isolated in private homes in homogeneous suburban areas, often at great distances from family and old friends, and that these conditions are particularly trying to college graduates accustomed to the beehive activity of dormitory life. Isolation itself, she points out, can produce brooding, erratic judgments, and a sense of powerlessness. Bernard contends further, with reference to findings by Knupfer, Cheraskin and Ringdorf, Ross, and others, that marriage makes women increasingly helpless, submissive and conservative, demands more adjustments on the part of wives than of husbands, and "neuters" women sexually. Energetic, self-motivated young women with their own opinions and ambitions succumb to a traditional model of wifely behavior which requires domesticity, modesty, sexual inconspicuousness and fidelity, and a gradual merger of the wife's aspirations with those of her husband. This sacrifice of identity, Bernard suggests, must be related to the many psychological disabilities that afflict married women. It is interesting to note the many ways in which Bernard's point of view is consonant with Chesler's. The modesty, submissiveness, and sexual conservatism which society expects of a married woman correspond to the depressive's low self-esteem, dependence, and libido loss.

If, as Chesler and other feminists assert, depression is a normal response to rigid, exploitative sex-role definitions in a male-dominated, authori-

---

* In this connection, Chesler cites Alfred Friedman's finding that depressed women are even less verbally hostile and aggressive than nondepressed women.

** For a powerful critique of Chesler's work, see Barbara Harrison's review of her book, *Women and Madness*, in *The Nation*, January 22, 1973, pp. 117-119.

tarian society, then the role of psychotherapy may be limited to encouraging revolutionary sympathies in individual patients. However, alternative schools of thought on depression give rise to more optimistic views of psychotherapy. The behavioral school sees the depressed patient as lacking important sources of positive reinforcement because of environmental change (e.g., the death of a friend) or personal inadequacy. If depression is "a function of inadequate or insufficient reinforcers," then therapy can ameliorate the condition by providing a different reinforcement schedule or helping the patient to utilize whatever sources of reinforcement are available (Lazarus, 1968). Lewinsohn, Shaffer, and Libet (1969) have suggested that depression may result from a lack of social skill; they found that depressed patients both elicit and emit fewer actions than nondepressed controls, that the messages they emit are shorter, that the timing of these messages is "off," and that depressed persons interact with an increasingly limited number of people. These authors conclude that effective therapy will positively reinforce social skills and constructive activities and negatively reinforce depressive activities, e.g., complaining.

A second theory of depression from which specific therapeutic techniques have derived is the cognitive model. Cognitive theory (Beck 1972a) assigns a primary role to the cognitive manifestations of depression in contrast to traditional views which hold that all other symptoms are secondary to a basic emotional disturbance. Beck found in clinical studies that depressed patients tended to perceive their experiences in an idiosyncratic way (Beck, 1963). In recollecting dreams and early memories and in projective tests, depressed patients saw themselves as deprived, frustrated, humiliated, rejected, or punished—"losers." Depressed patients also held indiscriminately negative views of the outside world and of the future. This constellation of negative perceptions of the self, the world, and the future Beck labeled "the cognitive triad." The emotional, motivational, and behavioral changes in depression can be seen to flow directly from the depressed patient's perception that he is worthless, the world barren and calamitous, and the future bleak no matter what he might do to try to improve it.

In addition to the systematic bias in the content of the cognitions, Beck found typical errors in the form of cognitions. These errors include *arbitrary inference,* in which a conclusion is drawn despite inadequate or contrary evidence; *overgeneralization,* or the process of drawing broad generalizations on the basis of a single incident; *magnification* of the importance of a particular event; *selective abstraction,* or focusing on a single detail rather than the whole context of a situation; and *cognitive deficiency*, which refers to disregard for important aspects of life situations, such as the long-range consequences of drinking or overeating. These typical distortions may affect the patient's judgment concerning only circumscribed areas of experience, especially those relating to his own abilities or prospects.

Beck theorized on the basis of these observations and a growing body of clinical research that, as depression develops, a primitive or immature cognitive organization, akin to Freud's "primary process," preempts more mature or "secondary process" thinking. The primitive schemas are absolute rather than relative, dichotomous rather than graduated, global rather than discriminative. In Beck's model, affect is intimately linked to cognition (Beck, 1972b). Between an event and an individual's emotional reaction to it, a cognition or "automatic thought" intervenes which dictates the resulting affect. When this thought represents an inaccurate or distorted appraisal of the event, the affect will be inappropriate or extreme. For example, when a friend fails to meet him on time for lunch, the depressed patient may infer that the friend no longer cares for him, and overgeneralize to the conclusion that he has lost all his friends. As a consequence, he feels sad. Beck argues that the affect itself has stimulus properties, that is, carrying the example further, the depressed person will see his sadness as evidence confirming his original perception: "I'm feeling sad, so I must be badly off." When this downward spiral of cognition and affect is set in motion, the motivational system is also affected. Believing herself unable to perform a specific household task, for example, a depressed woman became dysphoric. After identifying her feeling of sadness, she avoided working on the grounds that she felt too bad and would consequently do a bad job. Finally, this perception was linked by association to generalized cognitive schemata regarding her own worthlessness and inferiority.

PERSPECTIVES

Cognitive therapy, an outgrowth of the theory sketched above, refers to a body of techniques that either directly or indirectly alter the depressed cognitions. A detailed discussion of these techniques follows in a later section. Here, however, it will be interesting to note that cognitive theory offers a unique perspective on the problems of women as described by writers such as Chesler and Bernard. In order to explain the prevalence of depression in women, we suggest, it is not necessary to determine whether or not women in contemporary America are objectively oppressed. It would suffice to show that women tend to *see themselves* as needfully dependent, helpless, repressed. Jessie Bernard reports a telling experiment by David Olson. Olson asked young couples expecting babies

> . . . such questions as these: Which one of them would decide whether to buy insurance for the newborn child? Which one would decide the husband's part in diaper changing? . . . When there were differences in the answers each gave individually on the questionnaire, he set up a situation in which together they had to arrive at a decision in his laboratory. He could then compare the results in the simulated situation. He found . . . that *husbands perceived themselves as having more power than they actually had in the laboratory "reality," and wives perceived that they had less.* Thus, whereas three-fourths (73 percent) of the husbands overestimated their power in decision making, 70 per cent of the wives underestimated theirs.

If, as Olson's experiment suggests, women have a culturally induced tendency to *see themselves* as powerless (that is, if women persist in interpreting individual events in terms of their own helplessness and powerlessness rather than selecting from an uncensored set of interpretations)—then, according to cognitive theory, they will respond repeatedly with depressed affect. Whether or not the original perception of powerlessness was founded on objective fact, the resulting dysphoria will be interpreted as evidence confirming that perception. Thus, women may be more definitively bound by internalized cultural expectations than by specific obstacles to their happiness and success.

Carrying these associations a step further into the realm of pure speculation, we might consider psychologist Martin Seligman's analogy between the effects of learned helplessness in dogs and reactive depression in man (Seligman, in press). Dogs subjected to uncontrollable shock demonstrate passivity in the face of trauma and difficulty in learning that responding produces relief—symptoms analogous to the motivational deficits in human depression. According to Seligman, it was not trauma *per se* "that produced failure to escape, but having learned that no response at all can control trauma." Many female children are taught that their personal worth and survival depend not on effective responding to life situations but on physical beauty and appeal to men—that is, that they have no *direct* control over the circumstances of their lives. Throughout adolescence they are subjected not to physical shock, but to parental and institutional supervision that both restricts their alternatives and shelters them from the consequences of any disapproved alternatives they do choose to pursue. Perhaps women, like dogs who have learned that their own behavior is unrelated to their subsequent welfare, lose their ability to respond effectively and to learn that responding produces relief.

Many women who have experienced depression personally or in friends and relatives are surprised to learn that the psychotherapeutic marketplace now offers approaches to depression that are less demanding of time and money than are the therapies with which the layman is most often familiar. One of these alternatives is behavior therapy, which derives from principles of learning theory. The behavior therapist attacks depression by changing the patient's behaviors in order to increase the level of positive reinforcement she receives. Lewinsohn (1972) noted that behavioral methods for treating depressed patients fall into five categories: 1) Increasing the patient's activity level. Hospital staff may insist that a depressed patient perform menial tasks. Or the therapist may make use of the Premack Principle, according to which high frequency behaviors such as smoking may be used to reinforce low frequency behaviors; in other words, the therapist permits the patient to take a cigarette only when she has, for example, expressed a self-confident thought (Homme). Or he may have the patient keep a record of her activities. 2) Identifying potential reinforcers. This technique consists essentially of finding out what the person likes to do, then getting her to do it more often. 3) Inducing affects which are incompatible with depression, such as amusement or affection. 4) Enhancing the patient's instrumental skill, i.e., training him to deal effectively with his environment so that he is able to elicit a greater degree of positive reinforcement, such as with assertive training or social skill training. Many depressed people have trouble expressing interest or affection for others and so receive little in return. When a depressed patient is deprived of a potentially reinforcing activity such as social interaction because it arouses fear, the therapist may use systematic desensitization to control the fear response. Similarly, Hannie and Adams (1973) used "implosive therapy" in the treatment of agitated depression. Group therapy may be used to provide feedback on the patient's interpersonal behavior and its consequences and to develop new patterns of responding to other people. 5) Increasing drive level, such as with behavioral deprivation, e.g., subjecting the patient to a period of bed rest which makes him more sensitive to incoming stimuli (Lazarus).

Lewinsohn's own method involves extensive observation of the patient and his family in the patient's home. The initial phase of treatment consists of a two-week diagnostic period in which base-level data on the patient's activities and interpersonal interactions are accumulated. The patient is required to fill out mood ratings and monitor his activity level. According to Lewinsohn, this intensive involvement with the patient at the beginning of treatment provides a high level of positive reinforcement needed to reverse the patient's worsening condition. At the end of this period, when the accumulated data permit the therapist to make inferences regarding the relationships among the patient's activities, interpersonal conduct, and mood, the "behavioral diagnosis" is explained to the patient, treatment goals are agreed upon, and treatment procedures outlined. For example, in one case the therapist told the patient that,

> We wanted to make her talk about her numerous concerns . . . contingent upon her increasing her activity level; that we were going to use a rather complicated procedure involving a green light, etc., in such a way that she could only talk about her depression when the green light was on, etc.

From the outset, a three-month time limit is set for therapy. In this framework the patient and therapist find it necessary to set realistic goals and tend to make efforts to achieve these goals within the allotted time.

Behavioral treatment encourages the patient to make use of available reinforcers and uncover new sources of reinforcement. Lewinsohn and Graf (see Lewinsohn, 1972), using base-level data derived from daily mood ratings and activity schedules, had a computer select ten activities most highly correlated with the patient's good moods, and granted the patient increased therapy time in proportion to the amount of time spent in these pleasant activities. When a therapist finds the depressed mood to be related to patterns of interpersonal behavior which minimize the amount of positive reinforcement the patient receives in social situations, the therapist's observations and recommendations can be instrumental in altering these contacts. Many depressed patients rarely initiate social contacts and as a result become isolated; some need to be made aware that their contact with others is hostile or critical. Lewinsohn has even equipped patients in group therapy with earphones so that the therapist could provide "instant reinforcement." Depression may follow the loss of a single particularly satisfying form of reinforcement, e.g., when a dedicated student is forced to leave school because of pregnancy. In these cases, the therapist may simply find a way to "reinstate" the reinforcer (Gathercole, 1972), such as by arranging for the new mother to take a college course.

An important element in the behavior therapist's repertoire is the technique of "shaping" performance behaviors (or "graded task assignment") (see Burgess, 1969). Depressed patients who have trouble completing even very simple tasks may be successfully treated with this technique. As described by Gathercole (1972), the therapist breaks down a target behavior into small steps, and praises the patient for performing the first, simplest steps, no matter how remote from the actual target behavior they may be; he then successively praises the patient's completion of the more complicated steps, until a normal level of activity is restored. An "auxiliary therapist," such as a spouse or friend, may be trained to provide this kind of positive reinforcement outside of the consultation hour. Similarly, a spouse may be trained to modify his hostile or critical responses to the patient.

Jackson (1972) presents an interesting rationale for treating depression by means of self-reinforcement, particularly with patients who lack friends or relatives who could cooperate in providing positive reinforcement for adaptive behaviors. In this system, the patient actively involves himself in observing his own behavior in the problem areas, selects a final "target" behavior and a reinforcer, and defines specific behavioral goals; he arranges to administer the reinforcer in the event that he performs satisfactorily. The patient then performs the task and evaluates his performance in relation to the standards he has set. Finally, he administers positive reinforcement to himself when he judges that he has met his goal.

Jackson cites the case of a 22-year-old housewife whose depressed feelings were related to her inability to evaluate positively or reward herself for anything she did. The only positive reinforcement she received "came from her surroundings, this being infrequent and neutralized by self-devaluating statements. It turned out that, over time, compliments became a discriminative stimulus for self-criticism." This woman chose housework as the most important activity to monitor; for a number of days she kept records of her activities, moods, and the number of rewards she gave herself for housekeeping, "such as 'praising yourself, doing something you like, or feeling contented as a consequence for doing housework.'" She was then helped to define specific, attainable goals for each chore and instructed to "reinforce herself positively contingent upon her evaluation of her activity." At first, in order to make these operations more concrete, she was given a box of poker chips and told to dispense up to 10 of them to herself, according to how many she thought she deserved.

A somewhat different approach to behavior therapy is "motor psychotherapy," described by Barnard and Banks (1967). In motor psychotherapy, the therapist functions as a role model who demonstrates to the patient safe, effective ways to express aggression. In general, the therapist attempts to elicit aggressive behavior on a graduated scale, beginning with activities such as tossing a ball back and forth, then throwing it harder and harder. He may then request that the patient yell "Ho!" as he throws the ball.

COGNITIVE THERAPY

Like the behavior therapist and in contrast to practitioners in the psychoanalytic tradition, the cognitive therapist actively involves himself in the psychiatric interview in order to formulate the problem, define goals, and devise specific operations to deal with each problem area. He is concerned with the overt symptom or behavior rather than the origin of symptoms in early experiences or unconscious conflicts, and so can complete a course of therapy in a relatively short time. Unlike the behavior therapist, however, he formulates the presenting symptoms in terms of basic misconceptions and thought patterns which become apparent as the patient reports her spontaneous thoughts and experiences. He trains the patient to become more aware of her "automatic thoughts" and chooses from a wide range of therapeutic techniques which can alter the maladaptive cognitions (Beck, 1970a). Because cognitive therapy deals with conscious experience and takes the patient's thoughts at face value, the patient can easily comprehend the therapist's interpretation of her difficulties and the nature of the therapy to be used; she is encouraged to dispute his formulations rather than defer to "authority." The therapist becomes a collaborator rather than a god-figure. He allies himself with the patient against the depressive symptoms that afflict her.

The mildly or moderately neurotic patient is most often only marginally aware of the idiosyncratic cognitions which underlie her emotional and behavioral problems (Beck, 1972a). When reporting her experiences, the untrained patient will often report that a specific event was followed by an unpleasant affect. For example, a woman may report that she (a) saw an old boyfriend and then (b) felt sad. Typically, the untrained patient cannot understand why the external stimulus (a) should have produced the affect (b). At the therapist's guidance, however, she is able to identify the intervening variable, i.e., the cognition. In this case, the patient may have thought to herself, "He will see that I am no longer as attractive as I used to be," or "He will reject me." This "reminder" of her "lost" youth and attractiveness makes her feel sad. Although the patient may be highly attractive to all eyes but her own, the idiosyncratic cognition appears completely plausible to her and seems to arise involuntarily, as if by reflex. For this reason, it is often useful to teach a patient to monitor her thoughts over a period of time. A housewife who sought help because of global feelings of depression, apathy, and inertia was instructed to pay close attention to her thoughts from the time she awoke in the morning, throughout the day; as soon as she began to feel blue, she was to try to discern what was "going through her mind" at the time, and to keep a record of her observations. After a day or two she realized that whenever she began her household chores she would think, "I'm an incompetent housekeeper, I'll never be able to get this done." When she had avoided working for an hour or two, she would chide herself again.

Simply learning to recognize idiosyncratic thoughts may temper the depressed mood, but the patient must learn further to "distance" herself emotionally from her thoughts, that is, to view them objectively, with the critical perspective that will enable her to judge whether they are realistic or justified. Even patients who are unusually discerning when evaluating subjects of little personal concern may not question the validity of their perceptions of their own worth or effectiveness; they may need to be reminded that "thinking does not make it so." When the patient begins to subject her perceptions to "reality testing," the downward spiral of cognition and affect can be arrested. At this point, the therapist may train the patient to recognize specific distortions and deficiencies in her thinking (see the discussion of cognitive theory above). For example, a patient who reacts to a single, isolated failure with the thought, "I'm incompetent at everything I do," can identify this cognition as an instance of overgeneralization and substitute a more balanced view of her capabilities. A woman who assumes that her friends no longer care about her when no one telephones for a day or two realizes, when she "objectifies" and scrutinizes her thinking process, that Mary has been ill and Joan out of town; she has learned to weigh the evidence on which her spontaneous conclusions are based, and consider alternative explanations. Another patient was overly absorbed in the negative aspects of her life. When she was required to write down and report back positive experiences, she recognized her selective attention to the negative.

A depressed patient may profit by stating explicitly why a particular cognition is inaccurate or unjustified. One depressed woman, whose activity level was somewhat retarded, feared that she would be unable to prepare dinner. When she verbalized to herself, "I've done this many times before and there is no reason that I should be unable to now," she was able to complete the meal.

A second approach of the cognitive therapist is to call to the patient's attention stereotyped themes that pervade her thinking. The "automatic thoughts" which constitute the patient's immediate reaction to an event may be in fact a kind of cognitive shorthand for elaborate ideas, deeply rooted in past experiences. Thus, the therapist may observe that the patient sees in many diverse situations evidence of her own inferiority, inadequacy, deprivation, or guilt. He can then demonstrate to the patient that these ideas are actually distortions of reality. A woman who reported that she had "made a fool of herself" at a job interview recognized that this assessment reflected not her actual performance but her tendency to see herself as a subject of humiliation. However, rather than accept the therapist's interpretation as the "final word," the patient is urged to check and recheck his formulation against her own experiences. By continually evaluating new experiences and feedback from past events, she works with the therapist toward her own understanding of the mechanisms which produce distress. In this way, the patient acquires skill in meeting new difficulties as they arise.

Thirdly, the therapist may observe that the patient holds certain misconceptions, prejudices, and even superstitions which need to be exposed and evaluated. In one case, a physician suffered from intense feelings of depression when her research contributions failed to win her recognition. In therapy, she was able to recognize that she held a set of interlocking premises, such as, "If I fail to become famous, my work and life are meaningless. Recognition is the only gratification I can achieve." The therapist demonstrated that other areas of her life, such as her family, were rich sources of gratification and that recognition had not in fact provided much satisfaction in the past. Subjecting her basic premises to a process of validation helped her to stop worrying about recognition and to get more enjoyment out of her work.

Sometimes the idiosyncratic cognitions take a pictorial rather than a verbal form. A college instructor, for example, had a visual image of herself stuttering and becoming confused during her class. The therapist suggested that she imagine herself conducting the class with ease; when she had done so, she felt more optimistic and was in fact able to teach with more confidence. Pictorial fantasies may be valuable clues to the content of a particular problem. A woman who felt depressed following a dinner party with close friends told the therapist that she had a spontaneous fantasy during the evening in which her husband left the party with another woman. She had felt a deep sense of loss, as if the fantasied event had actually occurred. When recounting her experience, however, she came to see that she had a deep-seated belief that she was inferior to other women and that her husband knew this and would eventually leave her. When she was helped to check her belief against objective evidence, she had to admit that she was, in fact, unusually accomplished and attractive and had an exceptionally devoted husband; with this recognition, the depressed feelings lifted.

The cognitive therapist may encourage a patient to repeat such fantasies a number of times. Experience has shown that the fantasy tends to become more realistic with each repetition or that the emotional reaction may become less unpleasant although the content does not. In some cases, the therapist may induce fantasies. When a patient is depressed over a particular situation, he may have the patient imagine the situation a year or several years from the present. A woman who was depressed because her child required a minor operation was relieved when she pictured him in a year, playful and happy and without disability (Beck, 1970b).

In addition to these fundamentally intellectual methods for changing the depressed cognitions, the cognitive therapist may use behavioral techniques, such as the graded task assignment. When a depressed housewife, for example, is unable to function in the home, the therapist may give her a series of tasks of increasing difficulty to perform, at which she has a good chance of succeeding. At first she may be required only to make the beds, then to cook a meal, and so on. When she has clearly succeeded at a task, however simple, her lethargy decreases and she is motivated to try more.

The appropriateness of this technique in treating depression has been underscored by recent experimental work. Loeb, Beck, and Diggory (1971) found that depressed patients are uniquely sensitive to experiences of success and failure. Although depressed and nondepressed patients performed equally well on a series of card-sorting tasks, the depressed patients were significantly more pessimistic about their ability to complete the task than non-depressed patients, and evaluated their performance as significantly poorer than did the nondepressed patients. However, after a success, depressed patients were more optimistic, and showed higher levels of aspiration and better performance than depressed patients who had failed. Interestingly, the reverse was true for the non-depressed group—these patients performed better after failure than after success.

Since the various phenomena of depression are closely intertwined, change in any one area can be expected to produce improvement in others. For this reason, the therapist may select specific, narrowly defined "targets" for intervention, such as the patient's passivity or loss of motivation. A young woman, for example, was admitted to the hospital with a typical cluster of depressed symptoms—severely depressed mood, negative self-evaluation, loss of interest and gratification. She insisted that although in the past she had enjoyed reading among other activities, she could no longer read, nor would she get any satisfaction from anything else that she might try. Focusing on her loss of interest, it was possible to get her started at reading again by helping her to locate a short, short story and listening while she began to read it aloud. A short time after this initial, modest success, she had completed the story and was reading a novel; her lethargy and depressed mood had lifted, at least temporarily. She was then able to see that she had not actually lost her ability to enjoy things and was willing to try other activities as well.

Self-criticism and self-loathing may be effective "target areas" for the therapist. Dr. Jay Efran (1973) notes that, under certain circumstances, the patient may find relief in expressing the sentiment of feeling sorry for herself. When accompanied by tears, such statements may be beneficial, Efran writes, because they help the patient to view himself tragically, that is, with true sympathy. Genuine pity for oneself is an antidote to self-hatred. Similarly, display of laughter and/or anger may also provide temporary escape from feelings of self-revulsion.

In some cases, experiential factors alone are adequate to produce attitude change. The warmth of a sympathetic psychotherapist of whatever persuasion or interpersonal exchange in an encounter group is a powerful experience that may indirectly counter depressed cognitions. Thus, the cognitive therapist is alert to the possibilities inherent in introducing a patient to volunteer work, employment, or consciousness-raising groups. It should be noted that during episodes of severe depression, cognitive therapy may be used chiefly in conjunction with supportive therapy, which offers the patient reassurance, ventilation of her problems through discussion with a sympathetic outsider, guidance in dealing with specific problems and in making beneficial changes in her environment (Beck, 1972a). During the postdepressed period, however, the patient's attention can be directed toward the basic premises and patterns of inference that underlie the depressed moods.

CONCLUSION

So hard is the fortune of poor womankind—
They are always objected, always confined;
They are controlled by their parents until
*   they are made wives,*
And slaves for their husbands the rest of
*   their lives.*

The Wagoner's Lad, Traditional Folk Ballad,
in Leach (1955)

It is indubitably true that women have been offered, throughout history, only the narrowest range of alternatives in choosing their life-styles. Rarely has a woman had the opportunity to direct her own life, to realize her personal conception of happiness and fulfillment. Recently, however, the attitude that marriage and motherhood in the conventional mode are the only proper goals for a young woman has been relaxed. The possibilities for change inherent in current attitudes go far beyond what has already become incarnate in social habit and legal actuality. But women, both as a group and as individuals, will go nowhere unless a critical decision is reached—that is, despite socialization and precedent, to accept responsibility for their lives, goals, families, careers, and psychological symptoms without falling back on the easy excuses of masculine preference, social appearances, difficult times and circumstances. The girl in the folk song undoubtedly suffered from manipulation and abuse, yet it is likely that her modern counterpart would emerge, at middle age, widowed or separated and unobligated by family ties, still ruled by habits of mind that reduce even this new freedom to a new level of enslavement. She may feel victimized by a fear of death and aging, by her children's indifference, by financial insecurity or anxiety about new jobs and living arrangements. The fundamental challenge remains what it has been all along—to master and command trying circumstances and thereby transform them into an acceptable and even rewarding way of life.

Women are in fact no more predisposed to suffer from depression than are men. What distinguishes male from female depression is simply that the events which typically "trigger" depressions tend to be sex-typed. While a man is more likely to become depressed at critical junctures in his career or business life, women tend to experience these crises after childbirth, when children leave home, during marital turmoil. Knowing that these and other crises will have to be negotiated in the future, young women will do well to concentrate on preventing future depressions by cultivating habits of self-respect and self-reliance and by leading a balanced life, participating in a variety of activities rather than depending on family ties alone for emotional and intellectual sustenance. In other words, women must at last accept as their own the fully human goals of survival, productivity, and enjoyment, rather than the limited goals of serving men and deriving vicarious satisfaction from their accomplishments. In their subordinate posture, women are vulnerable and continually on the defensive, overvalue looks, health, youth and other undependable assets, and panic when they think them threatened. Finally, by restricting their attention to the "feminine" sphere in the age of supertechnology and the "global village," women sacrifice a sense of the objective reality that exists beyond domestic confines.

It is hard to dispute the contention that our culture tends to view women as ineffectual, dependent, and overly emotional, and troubled or depressed women as pathetic or manipulative. No doubt the fact that the culture confirms her negative self-evaluations is an added obstacle to the woman who becomes depressed. Yet women can re-educate themselves to recognize these prejudices for what they are—attitudes that may rule masses of people, but need in no way affect an individual's estimate of her own worth. When depression progresses to the clinical stage, professional help can make it possible for the depressed woman to weather the crisis and lay the groundwork for more effective responding in the future.

REFERENCES

BARNARD, G. W. & BANKS, S. H. Motor psychotherapy: A method for ego enhancement. *Mental Hygiene*, 51, 604-611, 1967.

BECK, A. T. Thinking and depression: I. Idiosyncratic content and cognitive distortions. *Archives of General Psychiatry*, 9, 324-333, 1963.

BECK, A. T. Cognitive therapy: Nature and relation to behavior therapy. *Behavior Therapy*, 1, 184-200, 1970. (a)

BECK, A. T. Role of fantasies in psychotherapy and psychopathology. *Journal of Nervous and Mental Disease*, 150, 3-17, 1970. (b)

BECK, A. T. *Depression: Causes and Treatment*. Philadelphia: University of Pennsylvania Press, 1972. (a)

BECK, A. T. The phenomena of depression: A synthesis. In D. Offer, and D. X. Freedman (Eds.), *Modern Psychiatry and Clinical Research: Essays in Honor of Roy R. Grinker, Sr.* New York: Basic Books, 1972. (b)

BERNARD, J. *The Future of Marriage*. New York: World, 1972.

Bibring, E. The mechanism of depression. In P. Greenacre (Ed.), *Affective Disorders.* New York: International Universities Press, 1953.

Bjerg, K. The suicidal life space: Attempts at a reconstruction from suicide notes. In E. S. Schneidman (Ed.), *Essays in Self-Destruction.* New York: Science House, 1967.

Breed, W. Suicide and loss in social interaction. In E. S. Schneidman (Ed.), *Essays in Self-Destruction.* New York: Science House, 1967.

Burgess, E. P. The modification of depressive behaviors. In R. D. Rubin and C. M. Franks (Eds.), *Advances in Behavior Therapy.* New York: Academic Press, 1969.

Chesler, P. *Women and Madness.* Garden City, New York: Doubleday, 1972.

Efran, J. S. Self-criticism and psychotherapeutic exchanges. Mimeographed paper, 1973.

Gathercole, C. E. Modification of depressed behavior. Paper presented to a conference at Burton Manor organized by University of Liverpool, Department of Psychiatry, June 3, 1972.

Gaylin, W. *The Meaning of Despair: Psychoanalytic Contributions to the Understanding of Depression.* New York: Science House, 1968.

Hannie, T. J. & Adams, H. E. The effects of implosive therapy in the treatment of agitated depressions. Mimeographed paper, 1973.

Jackson, B. Treatment of depression by self-reinforcement. *Behavior Therapy,* 3, 298-307, 1972.

Lazarus, A. Learning theory and the treatment of depression. *Behavior Research and Therapy,* 6, 83-89, 1968.

Leach, M. (Ed.). *The Ballad Book.* New York: A. S. Barnes and Co., 1955.

Lewinsohn, P. M. Clinical and theoretical aspects of depression. Paper presented at the Georgia Symposium in Experimental Clinical Psychology, 1972.

Lewinsohn, P., Shaffer, M., & Libet, J. A behavioral approach to depression. Paper presented to the American Psychological Association, Miami Beach, Florida, 1969.

Loeb, A., Beck, A. T., & Diggory, J. Differential effects of success and failure on depressed and nondepressed patients. *Journal of Nervous and Mental Disease,* 152, 106-114, 1971.

Roth, M. The phenomenology of depressive states. *Canadian Psychiatric Association Journal,* 4 (Supplement), S32-S54, 1959.

Sarwer-Foner, G. J.: A psychoanalytic note on a specific delusion of time in psychotic depression. *Canadian Psychiatric Association Journal,* 11 (Supplement), S221-S228, 1966.

Saul, L. J. *Emotional Maturity.* Philadelphia: Lippincott, 1947.

Seligman, M. E. P. Depression and learned helplessness. In R. J. Friedman, and M. M. Katz (Eds.), *The Psychology of Depression: Contemporary Theory and Research* (in press).

6

THE PHOBIC SYNDROME IN WOMEN: IMPLICATIONS FOR TREATMENT

IRIS GOLDSTEIN FODOR

PROLOGUE

Adult woman's alternatives to autonomy in relationships are obedience, flight or phobia.

Obedience

> Thy husband is thy lord, thy life, thy keeper,
> Thy head, thy sovereign, one that cares for thee
> And for thy maintenance commits his body
> To painful labor both by sea and land,
> To watch the night in storms, the day in cold,
> While thou liest warm at home, secure and safe
> And craves no other tribute at thy hands
> But love, fair looks and true obedience.

> Kate (*The Taming of the Shrew*)
> WILLIAM SHAKESPEARE

Flight

> Helmer [to Nora]: . . . lean on me; I will advise you and direct you. I should not be a man if this womanly helplessness did not just give you a double attractiveness in my eyes . . .
> Nora: Goodbye.

> *A Doll's House*
> HENRIK IBSEN

Phobia

> Woman age 41 . . . the patient was chronically anxious and feared death or sudden illness if she went out on the street, on trains, in cars,

132

or to the theatre or church. She had reached a point at which she could not perform any of her duties and was helpless. Her husband had to remain home with her and even then she continued to be frightened.

The Phobic Syndrome
TERHUNE (1949)

Miss K. . . . 23-year-old university graduate . . . apprehensive of walking outside unaccompanied lest she should fall . . . range of activity gradually became more and more circumscribed. At one stage she would walk in the street only if her mother held her arm; later she entirely refused to leave the house and by the time I saw her, she was practically bedridden, apart from very tense wall-hugging journeys between her bed and a couch in the drawing room.

WOLPE (1958), p. 174

INTRODUCTION

This paper will explore the hypothesis that phobic symptoms, particularly that of agoraphobia in women, and their associated syndrome—super-helplessness and dependency—appear related to sex role conflict. Stereotypically, women are viewed as emotional, submissive, excitable, passive, house-oriented, not at all adventurous and showing a strong need for security and dependency (Broverman, 1970). Many women have been trained for adulthood as child women. Under the realistic stresses of adult life and marriage these "stereotypic" emotional, passive, helpless women become anxious, wish to flee, dream of being more independent or of rescue or escape. For some the emotional stress is too great and phobia provides another solution. Thus, they cling to their childish fears or return to them under the realistic stress of the adult role or conflict, sinking further into an exaggerated version of the stereotypic feminine role, becoming dependent on those around them and avoiding autonomy, initiative or assertiveness. This route is available for women since their socialization experience has not prepared them to be mature adults. Documentation of the way girls and women are presented in the media, particularly children's books, will be utilized to demonstrate the relationship between fearfulness and dependency in girls and women and societal social conditioning which provides the fertile ground for the development of phobia in adulthood.

Psychoanalytic and behavioral theories will be reviewed to aid in understanding more deeply the origins of the phobic syndrome and its interaction with cultural conditioning. The question is how to treat this syndrome and help women master fears and become more independent. A behavioral treatment stressing interpersonal factors and sex role conflict resolution will be proposed.

THE PHOBIC SYNDROME

Definition

The diagnostic classification manual of the American Psychiatric Association (1968) places phobia under psychoneurotic disorders.

Marks (1969), following work of Terhune (1949), Laughlin (1954), Errera (1962) and Andrews (1966), in his comprehensive work on fear and phobias defines phobia as

> . . . a special form of fear originating from the Greek word Phobis meaning flight, panic-fear, terror which is 1) out of proportion to demands of the situation, 2) cannot be explained or reasoned away, 3) is beyond voluntary control and 4) leads to avoidance of the feared situation (p. 3).

Incidence and Classification

Agras *et al.* (1969) surveyed an entire Vermont community and found the incidence of phobia to be 6.3 per 1,000, while in a clinic population (which reflects only those seeking help) the incidence of phobia is about 2-3% in the United States and England (Marks, 1969, 1970).

Marks categorizes the phobias of adulthood into two categories. Those in Class I are phobias of external stimuli which comprise four subgroups: a) agoraphobia, b) social phobia, c) animal phobia, and d) miscellaneous specific phobia. Those in Class II are phobias of internal stimuli and include a) illness phobias and b) obsessive phobias. There is general agreement about the phobias described in category I. However, there is controversy about whether obsessive states are true phobias. Since the majority of phobic case descriptions as well as the majority of cases in Marks' sample of psychiatric patients (85%) falls into category I and since this group contains the phobic categories most prevalent in women, we shall limit our discussion to the phobias in this group.

Table I is adapted from Marks (1969) and presents data on frequency, sex incidence, onset age, phobic situation and response to treatment of the four subgroups in Class I, the phobias of external stimuli. The data come from three main sources: Marks' clinical sample; case reports and research from the literature; and epidemiological surveys.

TABLE 1

Class I: Phobias of External Stimuli (adapted from Marks, 1969)

	Animal Phobia*	Agoraphobia**	Social Phobia***	Miscellaneous Specific Phobias****
Frequency	rare	common	not uncommon	not uncommon
Sex incidence	95% women	75% women (in expanded sample, 84% women, Hawkes, 1970)	60% women	50% women
Onset age	early childhood	15-35	15-30	anytime from early childhood to old age
Phobic situation	monosymptomatic phobia of single animal species with little generalization	multiple going out alone, shopping, traveling, closed spaces, social situations, much generalization; multiple generalized anxiety, panic attacks, dizziness, depression (includes claustrophobia)	restricted to social activities, e.g., eating, drinking or writing in company	restricted to specific locus: heights, thunder, darkness, travel, closed spaces, driving, etc.
Response to treatment	good	variable: poor in patients with multiple panic attacks and obsessions	quite good	quite good; may need prolonged treatment

* Marks, Table 3.3, p. 107.
** Marks, Table 3.6, p. 110.
*** Marks, Table 3.9, p. 113.
**** Marks, Table 3.10, p. 114.

When we examine these data it would appear that animal phobia and agoraphobia are the phobias of women, while social and specific phobias appear more equally in men and women. Do women admit more fears when surveyed or come for help for phobia more often? These possibilities exist but would not explain the differential sex ratios for the various phobic symptoms.

Agoraphobia

Agoraphobia has received the most attention in both the psychoanalytic and behavioral literature (Marks, 1970, reports that agoraphobics account for half of all patients with phobic disorders). Often when research is conducted with phobic patients, the bulk of the sample are agoraphobics. Marks presents additional data on agoraphobics (75% of whom were female in his sample) from nine other published studies involving over 700 patients (see Table 2).

When we examine Table 2 we see that, on the average, 84% of the cases are female (range 64-100%). They have an average age of onset in the mid-twenties; 89% are married. Marks describes the personalities as typically dependent, anxious and shy. The families are reported to be stable, overprotective and close. It is found in all geographic areas and across all socioeconomic classes.

Marks (1969) summarizes the main features of the syndrome in agoraphobia in discussing the results of a nationwide English "Open Door Survey" of 2000 agoraphobics. The main classes are 1) *fears of going out*— street, movies, shops, etc.; 2) *closed spaces*—such as elevators; 3) *travel*— trains, buses, subway, ships, planes; 4) *fear of bridges or tunnels* (really special cases of 1 and 2, it appears). The fears he reports could occur in different combinations and could be associated with generalized anxiety, panic attacks, depressions, etc.

Phobias and Dependency

Andrews (1966) provides an extensive review of the literature on phobia (mainly child phobics and adult agoraphobic case descriptions from the psychoanalytic and behavioral literature) presenting strong evidence for the phobic symptoms as co-existing with personality patterns of dependency and avoidance. In childhood cases where parents' behaviors are able to be observed, parental overprotection is the rule. Andrews believes that phobics experience "early interpersonal familial learning situations in which the avoidant-dependent pattern . . . is an adaptive role for the

TABLE 2

Comparative Features of Published Series of Phobias

(Marks, 1969, p. 125)

	Terhune (1949, 1961)	Friedman (1950)	Tucker (1956)	Roth (1959)	Bignold (1960)	Errera & Coleman (1963)	Warburton (1963)	Klein (1964)	Roberts (1964)	Marks & Gelder (1965, 1966)	Sim & Houghton (1966)	Snaith (1963)
Main symptoms	Phobias	Travel phobia	Agora-phobia	Phobic anxiety deperson-alisation	Agora-phobia	Phobias	Agora-phobia	Agora-phobia	Agora-phobia	Agora-phobia	Phobic anxiety	Agora-phobia
Number of patients	86	50	100	135	10	19	53	32	41	84	191	27
% incidence in psychiatric practice	2·5	—	—	—	—	2·8	—	—	—	†2-3	—	—
% female	67	64	89	70	100	74	89	81	*100	89	51	63
% married	85	—	74	—	100	94	—	—	*100	73	—	—
Mean age at treatment	20-40	17-53	28	36	37	31	37	34	20-40	32	36	38
Mean onset age	young adult life	9-42	—	20-40	33	—	—	—	—	24	30	—
Premorbid personality	"soft" passive anxious	—	dependent	dependent anxious shy	—	—	—	50% dependent	anxious	mixed	—	—
Home background	stable	stable	—	stable	—	—	—	—	—	stable	—	—

* artefact through deliberate selection
† Hare (1965)
— not given

child (p. 462)." Andrews cites Wolpe's (1958) case described in prologue as one of his many examples to illustrate this parental overprotectiveness and its relation to phobia:

> An only child . . . she had been incredibly overprotected by her mother who insisted on standing perpetually in attendance on her. She was permitted to do almost nothing for herself, forbidden to play games lest she get hurt and even her final year at high school was daily escorted over the few hundred yards to and from the gates of the school by her mother who carried her school books for her (p. 174).

Going beyond Andrews' examples, one is indeed struck by similar examples in the phobic literature. Deutsch (1929) described a mother-fixation (p. 52): ". . . in the anamnesis the mother said the patient could never bear her to be away and that really, ever since her daughter's birth, she had been a slave to her."

Terhune (1949), who surveys 86 phobic patients, says (p. 163), "The phobic person is one who has been overprotected, brought up soft . . . occurs in infantile persons. It is a process of regression to childhood dependence on omnipotent adults for protection."

He cites the following cases:

> Woman, dependent on mother, who develops phobia upon mother's death [p. 166]; woman, age 27, "spoonfed" [p. 166]; man, 57, brought up in luxury, overprotected [p. 167].

Other examples include Friedman (1950):

> Mother took care of all her needs. Patient wanted to live with mother after her marriage [p. 267];

Marks (1970), 17-year-old agoraphobic:

> She was dominated all her life by her mother [p. 544];

Sperling (in press):

> Mrs. A craved her mother's approval and had overidealized her . . . became very submissive and close to her mother, competing with father and other men for her mother's attention [p. 11].

Phobias and Avoidance Reactions

Andrews makes a claim that the other side of dependency is the "pattern of avoidance, particularly of activities which involve independent, self-assertive handling of the difficult fear-arousing situations" (p. 459).

There appear to be at least two aspects of this avoidance reaction. One is a tendency to avoid assertion, particularly of angry feelings (Andrews says phobics believe closeness and assertion are incompatible), and the other is to avoid learning how to cope with and master feared (as well as other) situations which hinder the development of competence.

There are numerous examples in the literature about the lack of assertion in phobic states, again with analysts and behaviorists providing similar descriptions. In the Wolpe (1958) case cited previously, "she found her mother's solicitude and interference very irritating (p. 175)," and she did nothing about it. Goldstein (1970), in discussing an agoraphobic, says (p. 306), "When her mother imposes upon her in any way, she feels obligated to comply, which sometimes means doing really troublesome things. It makes her angry, but she is not able to resist."

Sperling (in press), who has analyzed phobic mother-child pairs, talks of parents of phobics as "highly intolerant of any expression of anger on the part of the child. Mrs. A. could never fight or explode openly. . . . She envied those who could be aggressive and express themselves freely" (p. 13).

Husbands as well as parents elicit similar avoidance of angry feelings and assertion. Symonds (1971), in discussing three phobic cases, says:

> The phobias were one of the ways to handle repressed feelings, immobilize them, prevent them from any act which might be interpreted as aggressive or self-assertive; in fact, it was a statement to be very contrary since it made them helpless and harmless; she speaks of Mrs. A.'s husband, who told her repeatedly she was an aggressive, castrating woman and all their difficulties were because of her. They did not argue . . . she accepted his accusations. . . . These women never complain openly about their husbands (pp. 146-148).

Wolpe and Lazarus (1966), in discussing a patient with a "fear of being closed in and an urge to escape while engaging in conversations," talk of an inhibited woman who upon making the first averse remark about her husband "pried open long-suppressed anger and frustration at his absolute domination over every one of her activities" (p. 94).

While the phobic symptoms—particularly those of agoraphobia, where the patient cannot cope with the outside world but remains housebound —lead to the avoidance of assertive response, active competence and mastery, of equal importance is the wish to have others do things for one, be around for support and cater to one's helpless state. Thus, Friedman (1950) cites a female phobic who "feared responsibilities of marriage"

(p. 266), demonstrating a wish to avoid adult status and remain with her mother. Terhune (1949) describes a case in which, "She was desirous of position and the good things in life but made no effort to acquire them." Later this patient married. In another case (p. 166), "She had never tried very hard to do anything and never had to." Sperling (in press) relates a dream in patient A (p. 15): "She could not walk again. She was being driven around in a car, like a baby in a carriage."

Andrews (1966) concludes his extensive review in this area by saying that he has never heard of a phobic who has been described as "self-assertive, independent or fearless" (p. 461).

Research Evidence

Some recent research correlates these clinical impressions. Dixon *et al.* (1957), using a Fear Survey Scale on a phobic population, found that phobic symptoms tend to occur together, falling into two clusters. One cluster consistent with Class I phobias contained items involving the threat of separation, helplessness and loneliness.*

Palmer (1972) studied phobic patients using the Fear Survey Scale and Rotter's locus of control scales, finding that fearfulness is associated with an external locus of control of reinforcement. Palmer argues (p. 2) that by virtue of the parents' roles as the primary dispensers of reinforcement throughout childhood, the avoidant-dependent pattern has "been learned by the phobic as the most effective way of adapting to his early family relationships."

Seligman (1973) describes experimental research on "learned helplessness"—where persons' actions have no effect on life—which produced symptoms of depression, passivity and lack of aggression.

One must conclude that the pattern of parental reinforcement, childhood learning and socialization experience may provide the clues to our understanding of the phobic symptoms and their associated personality traits in women, particularly the propensity to develop agoraphobia—the most constricting of all the phobic symptoms.

SOCIALIZATION, SEX ROLE STEREOTYPING AND PHOBIA

There appear to be similarities between aspects of the phobic syndrome —the extreme superhelplessness, avoidance of mastery experiences, competition, and lack of assertiveness—and descriptions of stereotypic femi-

---

* The other cluster related to Class II phobias (fear of physical injury) and Dixon labeled them "castration fears."

nine behavior. For example, when mental health professionals were asked to rate traits of a healthy male, healthy female and healthy adult, they said that the healthy female

> differs from the healthy male by being more submissive, less independent, less adventurous, more easily influenced, less aggressive . . . less competitive, more excitable in minor crises, having feelings more easily hurt, more emotional, more conceited about their appearance, less objective and disliking math and science. This constellation seems a most unusual way of describing any mature, healthy individual (Broverman, 1970, pp. 4-5).

The clinicians' attitudes reflect the beliefs of the larger society where different expectations exist for males and females and where from birth onwards a social sex role curriculum is prescribed.

> For boys . . . great things are in store for him. The demands placed upon him at once highly imply a high evaluation . . . the child is persuaded that more is demanded of boys because they are superior; to give him courage for the difficult path he must follow, pride in his manhood . . . a second weaning, less brutal and more gradual than the first, withdraws the mother's body from the child's embraces . . . the boys . . . are little by little denied the kisses and caresses they have been used to. As for the little girl, she continues to be cajoled, she is allowed to cling to her mother's skirts, her father takes her on his knee and strokes her hair . . . her tears and caprices are viewed indulgently (S. de Beauvoir, 1953, pp. 252-253).

Scientific research supports this statement. Thus, Block (1973) reviews the literature and describes his own data from longitudinal and cross cultural research:

> For males, socialization tends to enhance experimental options . . . for women socialization process tends to reinforce the nurturant, docile, submissive and conservative aspects of the traditionally defined female role and discourage personal qualities conventionally defined as masculine: self-assertiveness, achievement orientation and independence (p. 525).

Socialization: Dependency and Competence

All infants start off dependent and this early dependency is reinforced by the parents. Somewhere in the second year of life a shift occurs, the child must give up the dependent state and become more active and autonomous and the parent must reinforce independent behavior while extinguishing dependent behavior. Mahler (1972) talks about the separation-individuation process, while Erikson (1963) speaks of this as the stage of autonomy vs. shame and doubt. After gaining trust in the mother and the environment he actively explores the environment and begins to assert his autonomy. However, a conflict occurs because he is now revolting against his previously enjoyed dependency. Erikson's next stage (initiative vs. guilt) is discovering goals.

Developmental psychologists have concerned themselves with how this shift from dependency to autonomy occurs. Research studies support the view that girls are reinforced for continued dependency, while boys are reinforced for autonomy. Thus, while female infants are actually reported to be sturdier than male infants, parents think of them and respond to them as more fragile. Overhelpful behavior is more frequently given to girls and parents appear to be more invested in and responsive to their son's achievement-oriented behaviors (Mischel, 1970, Maccoby and Masters, 1970).

Hoffman (1972) summarizes the findings in this area as follows:

> a) since the little girl has less encouragement for independence b) more parental protectiveness c) cognitive and social pressure for establishing an identity separate from the mother and d) less mother-child conflict which highlights this separation, she engages in less independent exploration of her environment . . . continues to be dependent upon adults for solving her problems and needs her affectionate ties with adults (p. 147).

Furthermore, when we examine data on the few girls who are rated competent and who achieve, we find they are often said to receive more "maternal rejection" (which might be defined as absence of "smother love") as well as discipline similar to that received by boys (with the father taking an active role in this process) so that independence and competence are rewarded.

The Media and Sex Role Stereotyping

Parental differential sex role expectations are further enhanced by the schools and media advertising, books, films and television where boys and men and girls and women are most often portrayed in stereotypic extremes. Bandura *et al.* (1969) have intensively investigated the potent effect of TV and film role models on children's behavior. How such role models could influence sex role identification is suggested by Kohlberg (1966):

> We shall postulate the following five mechanisms by which the development of sex-role concepts leads directly to the development of masculine-feminine values: 1) The tendency to schematize interests and respond to new interests that are consistent with old ones 2) The tendency to make value judgments consistent with a self-conceptual identity 3) The tendency for prestige, competence, or goodness values to be closely and intrinsically associated with sex-role stereotypes, e.g., the association of masculinity with values of strength and power 4) The tendency to view basic conformity to one's own role as moral, as part of conformity to a general socio-moral order 5) The tendency to imitate or model persons who are valued because of prestige and competence, and who are perceived as like the self (p. 11).

The media certainly furnish prestige models for imitation, suggest sex-linked interests and support goodness and conformity notions. One example of the potent effect of advertising and pressure for sales personnel toward channeling of interest is reflected in findings by Lyon (1972) that "in 30 hours of Christmastime observation in a toy department, no field worker reported a single scientific toy bought for a girl" (p. 57).

Children's Readers

To understand more fully the pervasive and exaggerated sex role stereotypes presented in the media, we shall examine the growing research on children's readers.

A NOW task force (*Dick and Jane as Victims,* 1972) conducted a survey of 134 elementary school readers from 14 different well-known publishers in use in several New Jersey suburban school systems. The major findings are presented in Table 3. Jacklin and Mischel (1973) report similar results.

The NOW task force also have an excellent slide presentation to illustrate their findings. Generally, boys are shown doing brave, adventurous, even superhuman feats (riding alligators or shooting buffalos) while girls are most often behind fences, windows, immobilized, watching. (In the pictures, the girls appear to have agoraphobia.) The boys' faces are alive, their bodies active; the girls' faces are dead, sad, and even their bodies are rigid with their hands held tightly to the body or behind their back.

The dialogue is equal to the pictures. Examples from the readers are as follows (*Dick and Jane as Victims,* 1972, pp. 42-47):

"Look at her, mother, just look at her. She is just a girl. She gives up."

... helplessness swept over her like a sickening wave.

. . . Wilbur (Wright) laughed, "Whoever heard of anyone's mother building a sled."

"We don't want to play with girls," said Jeff. "They'd be too easy to beat."

"It's easy . . . even I can do it . . . and you know how stupid I am" [said by a girl].

"Oh no," I said. "It is no secret. We are willing to share our great thoughts with mankind. However, you happen to be a girl." Smart Annabelle flipped her eyelashes at me. "Come on, Albert," she said. But Albert stood still. "Excuse me," he said. "I think I will stay and learn to build an Electrothinker."

"My Sally has fallen into the water," the little girl tells Dick. "Can't you save her?"

"I can't, I can't." Amy was crying. "It won't push. Oh, Stuey, get me out. It's so dark in here."

He felt a tear coming into his eyes, but he brushed it away with his hands. Boys eight years old don't cry.

TABLE 3

Sex Roles in Children's Readers*

	Frequency of Themes	
Active Mastery Themes	Boys	Girls
Ingenuity, cleverness	131	33
Industry, problem-solving	169	47
Strength, bravery, heroism	143	36
Routine helpfulness	53	68
Elective or creative helpfulness	54	19
Apprenticeship, acquisition of skills, coming of age	151	53
Earning, acquisition, unearned rewards	87	18
Adventure, exploration, imaginative play	216	68
Second Sex Themes		
Passivity and pseudo-dependence	19	119
Altruism	55	22
Goal constriction and rehearsal for domesticity	50	166
Incompetence, mishaps	51	60
Victimization and humiliation of the opposite sex	7	68

P. 54, *Dick and Jane as Victims* (1972).

Children's Readers and Fearfulness

Linked to the portrayal of girls as helpless and incompetent is a further stereotypic notion that girls are also fearful. Girls express fears three times more often than boys. Furthermore, adult women are also viewed as fearful and in need of protection by their sons. Examples are as follows (pp. 42-47):

> Cries of fright came from the women and children around her.

> "Oh, Raymond, boys are much braver than girls."

> "Do not be afraid, Mother," said Jack, "I will do what I can."

> Sam led, and Helen went after him. Helen held his hand in a hard grip. She was timid in the darkness . . . Helen fell and Sam helped her get up.

> "Eek! a dog!" squeaked a lady with a bag of apples. "Go away, doggie, go away."

> Mrs. Allen shuddered. To think her boy killed such a creature made her a bit proud, but also just a little bit faint.

> Babs was not happy. The dog was so big he scared her. She knew that he was Teddy's dog. She did so want a little dog.

> "No," said Pam. "The water is too deep. Grandma wouldn't like it. Some big boys are swimming out there. Let's ask them to get it."

> Roger's mother wept, afraid that her son would be eaten. But Roger was a brave boy.

The most frequent theme for boys is daring, overcoming fear through suppression or perseverance, while girls' fearfulness or inadequacies further enhance the boys' image of success. Thus, little boys master fear by contrasting themselves with little girls and labeling their behavior good. The task force report states:

> Boys struggle with and subdue fears of horses, heights, crawly things, the dark and even a buffalo stampede. One boy overcomes his fear of horses and rides on it in an emergency. When two little girls stand on chairs and shriek for their younger brother to rescue them from a frog it is in the best feminine tradition (p. 23).

Research on Children's Fears

The media do not accurately portray children as they actually are, since boys and girls are both fearful, although there is lack of agreement about the relative frequency or fear reported for both sexes in the literature. MacFarlane *et al.* (1954), reporting on children's fear as part of the Berkeley longitudinal growth study, found that numbers and types of fears change with age. Specific fears were reported at least once by 90% of the children. While there were no overall differences in the frequency of fears for boys and girls, at different ages there were differences. For boys the peak was at age 3½ where 56% of the boys reported fears, while, for girls, the peak occurred at age 3, where 67% of the girls reported most fears. There was another peak for both sexes at age 11 (40%), after which there is a drop-off, with boys' fears declining more than girls. (At age 13, 21% of the girls and 4% of the boys remain fearful.) While Jersild (1946), Angelinio *et al.* (1956) and Lapouse and Monk (1959) do find sex differences, these differences are slight and may reflect exposure to the media.

Of interest is the finding of a peak of fearfulness (primarily fear of animals—age 3 to 3⅓) at about the time the child is being pressured to become more autonomous from the mother and family. Is fear a human reaction to the stress of separation? Sperling (in press) suggests such a link, viewing, "phobic manifestation as an indication of problems in separating and establishing a necessary degree of age-adequate independent functioning" (p. 8).

Furthermore, while boys' fears appeared to extinguish at adolescence, 21% of the adolescent girls in MacFarlane's sample were still fearful. Since animal phobias are the common problem of childhood and since the phobic frequency data suggests that these phobias in adulthood are almost exclusively female cases (Marks, 1969, reports 95% of animal phobics are women), it would appear that these phobias are residues of earlier fears and may reflect different socialization pressures for boys and girls. Hoffman (1972), in reviewing the research on mastery of fears, says that mastery exploration can alleviate fear but girls are not reinforced for this type of mastery. The pressures on boys may have their tolls in other ways. Many more boys are taken to child guidance clinics—perhaps the casualties of the pressure to adapt the stereotypic masculine image. (The ratio of boys to girls seen at child guidance clinics varies from 3:1 to 10:1, depending on the study (Bentzen, 1963)).

Adolescence, Sex Role Stereotyping and Fearfulness

Adolescence is viewed by Erikson (1963) and others as a time to develop an identity. Yet, as we have seen, girls are actually encouraged to remain dependent and fearful and to "identify" with or model stereotypic adult females who are viewed as less desirable, competent and healthy. As Broverman (1970) suggests (p. 6), "women have a conflict over whether to exhibit the positive traits considered desirable for men and adults and have femininity questioned or to behave in prescribed feminine manner and accept second-class adult status."

S. de Beauvoir (1953) comments on the adolescent girl's state as follows:

> It is a most unfortunate condition to be in, to feel oneself passive and dependent at the age of hope and ambition, at the age when the will to live and to make a place in the world is running strong. At just this conquering age, woman learns that for her there is to be no conquest, that she must disown herself, that her future depends upon man's good pleasure. On the social as well as the sexual level new aspirations awake in her, only to remain unsatisfied; all her eagerness for action, whether physical or spiritual, is instantly thwarted. It is understandable that she can hardly regain her equilibrium (p. 337).

Adolescence can be viewed as a time when women have to make a choice—how dependent or independent they will be. Terhune's (1949) view of phobia has relevance here: Phobias arise in young adults when an "apprehensive, dependent, immature person is trying to realize his ambitions and become an independent successful member of society" (p. 163).

Social Phobias and Adolescent Strivings

Most social phobias begin in adolescence and may reflect such stress. The fact that males and females are more equally represented in this category (60% female, Marks, 1969) suggests the stress inherent in coping felt by both sexes. Most social phobias involve specific situations (giving talks in public, talking to and meeting people at parties, etc.) and relate to evaluative anxiety. These young people are forging out in new areas. The women in particular have little previous reinforcement history to guide them for this type of mastery and few independent familial female models to copy. Palmer (1972) has shown that phobics especially look toward the environment for reinforcement clues. Often the extra stress comes from rebellion against the family's values. In some families mild independence in females is equated with rebellion by the mothers. Hence, the phobics show greater concern with getting approval from others, since they are giving up familial reinforcers in the family. In women particularly, social phobias appear in this author's experience when dependent women are struggling to overcome maternal and societal pressures to remain within stereotypic roles. For example, one patient developed severe speech anxiety in college around the time she had to tell her parents she no longer wished to become a nun like her older sister. Outwardly, these patients appear independent (they may live away from families, work, etc.), but they are typically shy and non-assertive; the phobias represent a holding on to their frightened little-girl roles, suggesting a lack of integration of the sex role polarities. However, since they are actively struggling—unlike agoraphobics, who appear to give up—their prognosis is quite favorable.

Adolescence and Marriage

Most girls handle adolescent stress by abdication. Even those girls who were achieving become concerned with their femininity and withdraw from active competition and mastery, substituting instead romantic notions of finding the right man who will do these things and take care of them. Grades go down, girls lose interest in math and science and prepare for marriage: "She will free herself from the parental home, from her mother's hold, she will open up her future, not by active conquest, but by delivering herself passive and docile into the hands of a new master" (S. de Beauvoir, 1953, pp. 307-308).

Phobias After Marriage

There is little in the media to prepare women for the mature, adult, independent female role, a woman who can be more than a wife or mother. The media emphasize the romantic nature of marriage and motherhood and do not prepare women for the realistic competent responsibilities of marriage or train them in maintaining autonomy within a relationship. Adult women more and more are becoming dissatisfied with their role. Lucy Stone's (1855) statement is still applicable today: "In education, marriage, in everything, disappointment is the lot of women" (p. 75). Many more women are behaving like Nora in Ibsen's *A Doll's House,* as evidenced by the high divorce rate (approaching one out of two to three marriages); even more are running for psychotherapy (women outnumber men as outpatients by three to two, according to Dohrenwend and Dohrenwend, 1969) and some either never grow up, essentially remaining at home, or in extreme cases (like Wolpe's (1958) young college graduate who couldn't even walk) sink into phobic states. Some who marry choose domineering men who treat them like children, while others who appeared independent before marriage slip back into the stereotypic feminine role afterwards. Under the stress of the marriage relationship, some married women who appear to have accepted the dependent wife role develop agoraphobia, which could be viewed as an exaggeration of the stereotypic feminine role.

Marks' (1969) sample (see Table 1) would suggest that agoraphobia develops on the average five years after marriage in women with dependent personality patterns. One might suppose that this is a time when a woman might feel most trapped in the marriage (particularly with young children to care for) and feel the stress of autonomous needs.* Marks (1969), in discussing the open door sample of agoraphobias, 89% of whom were women, reports that 20% worked, 20% were content to remain at home, and 58% were housewives who wanted to work but did not and this last group has the most severe phobias.

Symonds (1971), in a paper entitled "Phobias after Marriage: Woman's Declaration of Dependence," says:

> For many years I have been interested in a specific clinical problem which occurs when a young woman, who was apparently independent, self-sufficient and capable, changes after marriage and develops phobias or other signs of constriction of self. These changes invariably cause her to become excessively dependent and helpless . . . she becomes fearful of traveling . . . to be alone even for a moment. She usually can no longer drive a car herself . . . in less dramatic cases she becomes fearful of making any decisions or of taking any responsibility on her own. She clings to her husband for constant support, apparently changing from a capable "strong" person into a classically helpless female (p. 144).

Sperling (in press), another psychoanalyst, describes a similar pattern in a patient with both colitis and agoraphobia:

> Mrs. A. expressed feeling like a "caged animal" but one that needed to be caged or she would go wild and hurt others and herself. . . . She felt trapped in her marriage as she had felt herself trapped with her mother. She could not leave her husband because "I am his whole life," as she could not leave her mother who had been her whole life. . . . While Mrs. A. had left her mother, she had devalued her as an object in reality but she had not resolved her dependent relationship with her. Instead she transferred this relationship to her husband. Analysis revealed that she envied any woman who could divorce her husband and live alone or remarry (p. 11).

---

* We assume the average age of marriage is 20.

Other case examples include the following: Friedman (1950):

> . . . female, 33, unable to travel, did not consider herself happily married and constantly thought of her former boyfriend . . . if it were not for children would have left husband (p. 266).

In another case, Friedman (1950) says:

> Phobia developed following marriage to man selected by mother served as means of antagonism against her mother who forced her to marry a man whom she did not love (p. 271).

Wolpe (1970), discussing an agoraphobic:

> The relationship of her phobia to certain unsatisfactory features of her mariage was soon apparent . . . essential to establish emotional freedom to leave the marriage if necessary to overcome the conditioned basis of the agoraphobic symptomology (p. 299).

Wolpe, in discussing three agoraphobic women in a case discussion with Goldstein (1970), says of the agoraphobia:

> . . . a kind of trapped feeling being experienced by the patient . . . a very large percentage of the patients are female and married, and the symptoms develop concurrently with feelings of wanting to break or violate the strictures of the marriage contract (p. 305).

Seidenberg (1972) discusses a case of "existential agoraphobia" in a young wife and mother, linking the onset of the symptoms to the contrast in life between the woman, who feels that life is set and nothing will happen, and her brother, who has just begun to achieve in the world.

INTERPERSONAL VIEW OF PHOBIA

As we see, there is remarkable similarity of case descriptions in the agoraphobic literature provided by psychoanalysts and behaviorists. It would appear that trapped-ness in marriage may be related to a propensity to develop agoraphobia. While marriage is the stereotypic trapped-ness situation for young women in our culture to be in, it may not be the marriage *per se* but the interpersonal trapped-ness, particularly the feelings of being dominated with no outlet for assertion, that is responsible for agoraphobia.* Thus, while women in our society are most often put into this position and the stereotypic feminine role encourages submissive traits, one could become involved in similar interpersonal situations in a lesbian relationship or in a situation involving any two people.** or two conflicting role expectations. It is the pressure from the environment (particularly from the significant reinforcers there).

Andrews (1966), in evaluating Friedman's (1950) cases, says (p. 460), "For many the phobia was a way out of a difficult situation in which two or more people were exerting equally dominating but conflicting pressures on the patient, parents vs. husband, and the other alternative would have been open defiance of someone."

(We might also interpret this pressure perhaps as coming from the wish to be different from the way the husband or parents or society expects one to be. In that situation, one's own feelings are not allowed free expression.) For women, the struggles typically take the form of sex role conflict for, as Kohlberg (1966) has suggested, it is morally wrong to deviate from one's sex role stereotype. One way of handling this

---

* Symonds (1971) provides a psychoanalytic view of the development of agoraphobia in a young woman who was dominated by her husband which illustrates the complex interpersonal factors. "Travel-phobia occurred about 8 years ago when she and her husband were on a tour. She recalled the details of this with great difficulty only after many years of treatment. The essential factor was that Mrs. M. had insisted on the trip over her husband's reluctance. To her this represented a very aggressive act, and when he expressed some dissatisfaction with the trip, she remembers only a mild feeling that he was dampening her enthusiasm. The next day, she was frightened of the plane they took and the remainder of the trip was a nightmare. Insisting on the trip in the first place had a special significance to Mrs. M. It was one of the only times that she can remember where she persisted in actualizing a very personal desire of hers. She had always yearned to travel and especially looked forward to this after getting married. The awareness that her husband did not share her enthusiasm was catastrophic for her" (p. 148).

** If one is to accept agoraphobia as a married, female symptom, we still have to account for the 14-25% of the male cases. This author has worked with two male agoraphobics whose personality patterns fit the dependent-avoidant pattern described previously. One young man from a close family developed the phobia soon after marriage when he was forced to give up plans to go to college to enter the family business after the father's death. His mother then came to live with the newlyweds. The travel phobia developed while waiting for the subway to take him from the disliked job to the unpleasant situation at home. The second young man was a college senior who was emotionally and economically dependent on his widower father with whom he lived. The phobia developed when the father remarried and the father stopped supporting him, exerting pressure for him to go out on his own. At that time, he woke up one morning in a panic state about leaving the house and traveling. In both of these men, the phobia postponed entry into an independent career and they remained tied to their parent until the symptoms extinguished with behavioral treatment.

pressure to be more "masculine," that is, independent, assertive, autonomous, competent, achieving, is to conform even more to the stereotypic role if the stress is too great (the consequences of making a move are dangerous, anxiety-provoking, etc.). Agoraphobia leaves one even more helpless, dependent and submissive. Furthermore, the symptom has the secondary effect of keeping one that way. Women can't flee if they fear flying. It also allows for some expression of the anger even indirectly since it prevents the husbands from taking the trips too and demands of them extra sacrifices.

Lazarus (1970) also comments on the complexities of the marriage relationship in phobics. He speaks of

> Wives . . . who deliberately or inadvertently develop agoraphobic symptoms in order to punish or "imprison" their husband, or other side of coin agoraphobics whose extreme dependency rests mainly on their tacit acquiescence to someone's implicit demand to limit their own range of free movement, thus bolstering the faltering "strength" of the now needed escort or protector (p. 409).

The struggle in the marriage is often a re-enactment of the childhood separation experience, with the spouse taking the place of the parent. However, it is different because men presumably struggle themselves with their "masculine" stereotypic image, which often makes them strong and brave in contrast to the helpless, incompetent women (as the beginning patterns portrayed in the children's readers). Hence, woman's struggle for autonomy in marriage is particularly threatening to the husband's own sexual identity struggle. Furthermore, while in the early separation from the family there was a marriage to escape to, this time, like Ibsen's Nora, the possibility of walking into a void is frightening. For women unhappy in this type of marriage, fantasies of romantic escape with another man may prevent a phobia (although many of the cases in the literature, particularly those of Friedman (1950), report such wishes). In some women, then, this trapped feeling leads to phobia.

The big question is how to treat phobia.

TREATMENT APPROACHES

There are two major treatment approaches to phobia, the psychoanalytic and the behavioral, evolving from two divergent theoretical backgrounds. We shall look at the theory and literature of these two schools to try to evolve a treatment approach most suited to women, based on the preceding understanding of phobia.

Psychoanalytic Theory of Phobia

There are many conflicting, confusing discussions of phobia in the psychoanalytic literature. Basic to the psychoanalytic understanding of phobia are the points discussed by Fenichel (1945), one of the major interpreters of traditional psychoanalytic theory:

1) What a person fears, he unconsciously wishes for (p. 196).
2) . . . threat that causes temptation to be feared is castration or loss of love [others call this separation anxiety (p. 196)].
3) Temptation is either of a warded-off impulse or a punishment for an unconscious impulse or both (p. 169).
4) Projection and displacement are major defenses. Attempt to escape from an internal dangerous impulse by avoiding a specific external condition which represents the impulse is the most frequent type of displacement (p. 199).
5) There is regression to childhood . . . tries to regain favorable situation where external protection is available (p. 206).

To illustrate these points Fenichel cites the following as a typical explanation for agoraphobia:

> The anxiety attacks of a female patient with agoraphobia and crowd phobia have the unconscious definite purpose of making her appear weak and helpless to all passers-by. Analysis showed the unconscious motive of her exhibitionism was a deep-seated hostility, originally directed toward her mother, then deflected onto herself. "Everybody look!" her anxiety seemed to proclaim, "My mother let me come into this world in this helpless condition without a penis" (p. 200).

What can one say about such an interpretation! (See Greer (1971), Millet (1969), Firestone (1970), among others, for critique of the psychoanalytic theory of women.) One has to ask, however, if this model could be useful for understanding women if we posit a different type of conflict (a role conflict) other than the sexist Freudian one Fenichel espouses. The following is an attempt to reword his ideas to make for testable premises using sex role conflict issues previously discussed within an interpersonal framework.

1) Women may fear being autonomous and independent, but wish for the same as well.
2) Threat is loss of external reinforcements: loss of love of husband or parent or world; also loss of economic support.
3) Suppressed independent, assertive strivings represent temptations. Women have been conditioned to feel guilty if they deviate from

the stereotypic role and exhibit behavior that has been labeled "unfeminine."

4) Avoidant responses have been major way of handling conflict. There is a symbolic association between feared stimulus and suppressed strivings. They can represent the wish to flee (fear of trains, etc.) or avoidance of situations that remind one of current trapped-ness (e.g., claustrophobia, fear of elevators, enclosures, etc.), or both.

5) By being phobic, woman avoids independent adult role, becomes dependent, childlike again. Interpersonal message following Leary (1957) is "I am a distressed, weak, unhappy person in need of your help and direction" (pp. 294-296). The family and husband reinforce this dependency since they prefer her to be phobic and tied to them rather than free, independent and well.

If the above revisions of psychoanalytic theory could help in analysis, are there clues in the literature about how psychoanalysis or psychoanalytically oriented psychotherapy could help phobic women?

Psychoanalysis, Therapy and Phobia

Psychoanalytic theory, which stresses the transference relationship, might provide phobics with an opportunity to grow up, this time under the guidance of a parent who will encourage role exploration, independence and self-assertion. Yet, when one examines the published psychoanalytic literature, there is an overabundance of interpretive material and relatively little detailed analysis of the transference relationship that might provide a guide for feminist analysts to promote change and growth.

Hence Ivey (1959) talks of the role of the therapist in treating a phobic as "providing a strong ego ideal from which the patient could gain support through identification to facilitate the maturing process" (p. 48) without providing explicit instruction *how* this is to be accomplished.

Friedman (1959) provides more detail, but is equally obscure in his discussion of the treatment of phobia in his article in the *American Handbook of Psychiatry*:

> As soon as the transference situation appeared propitious, the patient was requested to come alone. She complied readily, but had to telephone me before each session in order to assure herself that I was expecting her. After a few months she became able even to go unaccompanied to her place of work, although she still had to call me very frequently to feel secure. Her evident dependency needs and defensive devices, as well as the strong hostility underlying her de-

pendency, could then be analyzed in the light of the transference situation. It thus transpired that the phone calls served to reassure the patient that the wishes against the analyst as a transference object had not materialized.

Hence, while the presumed underlying cause was uncovered, it is unclear how this analysis promotes growth.

Many analysts encourage assertion within the analytic situation, particularly using the transference situation as a beginning experience for the patient in self-assertion. However, again there is an absence of explicit detail.

Symonds (1971), who is aware of the sex role conflict issues, discusses the treatment of about a dozen phobic women with dependency conflicts who completely submit to their husband's domination and who are non-assertive as follows:

My patients all had some confusion and uncertainty about their femininity and saw marriage as a confirmation of their feminine identity. This proved they were really women. They were willing, in fact eager, to avoid any evidence of self-assertion . . . since they consider such impulses as masculine . . . too aggressive . . . now become involved with men, they tended to suppress all their assertive impulses for fear it would endanger their much needed partnership. Treatment for these patients is painstakingly slow and prolonged. Underlying the anger, the frustration . . . is a profound resignation . . . marriage has represented the only acceptable way to have significance (p. 150).

. . . these women are caught in a chronic, unresolved conflict of a profound nature which paralyzes them and it may take years of analysis before they develop enough of a sense of self to handle their life effectively. However, unless they do it themselves, it won't work out (p. 146).

In therapy with such patients I focus on themselves . . . not on the marriage or the husbands. Slowly and painstakingly they discover islands in themselves which they have ignored, discarded and minimized. Gradually, they acquire enough feeling of self to make their needs known to their husbands, to stand behind themselves, not abandon themselves (p. 152).

How one gets these patients to be more self-assertive or to develop these islands is unclear from the published presentation.

Friedman (1950) discusses "short term therapy"* with 50 travel-phobics,

---

* He considers 123 visits in 23 months short therapy.

stressing direct interpretation of the underlying conflict. He reports a third of the patients recovered and a third mildly improved.*

> After the dynamics of the case were worked through many patients failed to recover. They agreed with the interpretation but stated they were too frightened to take the steps indicated by the therapist. Persuasion and suggestion as well as working through a positive transference were necessary for successful therapy (p. 269).

Evaluation

The published psychoanalytic and psychoanalytically oriented psychotherapy cases have a surplus of analytic interpretation often far afield from the reported observations. The process of analysis (which is rarely described) where one examines from all perspectives one's feelings, thoughts, perceptions, dreams, etc., about the phobia could, for example, be considered a form of consciousness raising, if done with a feminist therapist who could provide a basis for cognitive restructuring. The transference aspects of the analysis would also appear to be useful if there were detailed descriptions on how it worked, as well as some verifiable research. Additionally, the interpersonal emphasis of Sullivan (1949) and his followers, who have not generally dealt with phobias in their writings, might also be helpful. Generally, psychoanalysis is not available for most phobics. Even Symonds agrees that "it is prolonged treatment, often with partial success" (p. 152); one must add that it is expensive and useful mostly to verbal, more intellectual patients.

Contemporary psychoanalysts and therapists might better help phobics if they followed Freud's (1919) original directive which necessitated a departure from standard analytic practice:

> One can hardly ever master a phobia if one waits till the patient lets the analyst influence him to give it up . . . one succeeds only when one can induce them through the influence of the analysis to . . . go about alone and to struggle with their anxiety while they make the attempt.

Behavior Therapy

Which epitaph shall be mine?

> She couldn't try
> for fear she'd die;

---

* Weiss (1964) talks of resistance of agoraphobics to treatment, speaks of analyzing cases for 10-15 years with hardly any improvement.

She never tried
and so she died.

or

She couldn't try
for fear she'd die
But once she tried,
her fears, they died.

—FRIEDMAN (1959)

Etiology of Phobia: A Behavioral View

Behavior therapists view symptoms as maladaptive behaviors that are learned. Lazarus (1966) accounts for phobic states as arising from "1) a classically conditioned autonomic disturbance . . . 2) instrumental conditioning in the form of a habit of avoiding the CS (conditioned stimulus) . . . [in case of agoraphobia] third category: social reinforcement for engaging in the instrumental avoidance behavior" (p. 96). Using this model, how might we account for the high preponderance of agoraphobic symptoms in young married women?

1. *Autonomic conditioning.* Wolpe (1958) views phobia as relating to "situations which evoke high intensities of anxiety" (p. 78) and cites the following agoraphobic case, illustrating the autonomic conditioning aspects of phobia:

> Very unhappy. I was always in a state of complete exhaustion trying to take care of the two children and not wanting to really, I guess . . . wanted to get pregnant because it would be some sort of fulfillment . . . then when I had the children didn't know what to do with them . . . completely exhausted . . . resented my life. . . . One day when foodshopping . . . felt as if I wanted to erupt . . . I wanted to scream but didn't. A few days later, I went into Center City to meet my mother and sister and all of a sudden I began to feel very funny. And I told them I had to leave and that was the day I tried to walk home from the bus and I couldn't walk . . . (p. 302).

Wolpe then makes a connection between the feeling that is associated with the beginning of the phobia to one described as a little girl when she lost her mother in a store: ". . . this is the same feeling I have now when I am left in a store alone" (p. 302). Wolpe (1958) also believes one can get a

> . . . similar spread of anxiety to new stimuli based upon "symbolism." For example, a woman of 20 came for the treatment of claustro-

phobia of two years standing. The onset of this turned out to be related to a marriage in which she felt "caught" like a rat in a trap. Many years earlier she had a fearful experience in a confined space, and this had led to slight uneasiness in such places as elevators. Her marital situation now generated a chronic undertone of "shut in" feeling, with which the physical enclosement of elevators now summated to produce a substantial fear reaction (p. 99).

2. *Avoidance behavior.* The phobia constitutes the avoidance behaviors: the first patient fears going out of the house, the second elevators. Wolpe (1958) accounts for the avoidance behavior as follows: ". . . the prospect of taking the action that would lead out of the situation simply adds new anxiety to that which already exists and this is what inhibits action" (p. 80).

Lazarus (1966) views the conflict as one of "avoidance-avoidance . . . if she ventures out alone, she is beset by anxiety; if she avoids anxiety, she is faced with social isolation" (p. 97). (One must add that she is also faced with a dull life.)

3. *Social reinforcement.* Following the view of agoraphobia presented earlier, women are reinforced for their avoidant behavior, since it is consistent with the stereotypic feminine role. Since women's place "is in the home," a woman who avoids leaving the house isn't so abhorrent. However, the avoidant behavior has other properties in that the dependent, helpless behaviors associated with the phobic syndrome are also reinforced. Bandura (1969), citing examples of Levy's overprotected children, states that

> . . . interpersonal difficulties are most likely to arise under conditions where a person has developed a narrow range of social responses which periodically force reinforcing actions from others through aversive control (e.g., . . . helplessness, . . . suffering and distress and other modes of responding that command attention (p. 48).

Lazarus (1966) stresses the reinforcement of agoraphobia:

> It is presumably impossible to become an agoraphobic without the aid of someone who will submit to the inevitable demands imposed upon them by the sufferer . . . depends upon interpersonal as well as intrapersonal variables both for its origin and maintenance (p. 97).

If agoraphobia in women develops from a conditioned autonomic reaction to the stress of trapped-ness in a relationship following a lifelong history of societal reinforcement for stereotypic female behavior, then how might behavioral treatment help such a woman to resolve her avoidance-avoidance conflict (between dependent and independent strivings) and help break the familial reinforcement pattern that maintains the phobia? Essentially, such treatment would help women by providing a structure to learn new ways of behaving, to try out new roles to aid in role integration and provide different contingencies of reinforcement—this time for mastery and competence.

Behavior Therapy Techniques: Desensitization

Wolpe (1958) developed the standard treatment for phobia based on the "reciprocal inhibition principle":

> If a response inhibitory of anxiety can be made to occur in the presence of anxiety-evoking stimuli it will weaken the bond between these stimuli and the anxiety [Wolpe and Lazarus, 1966, p. 12].

This procedure of systematic desensitization (which is a form of counter conditioning) employs a relaxation procedure to enable the patient to learn an alternative, incompatible response to the conditioned anxiety-producing stimuli. The typical relaxation procedure modeled after Jacobson (1938) stresses muscle tension and relaxation. Once the patient can relax, she is presented with the threatening scenes in a graduated fashion (called a hierarchy) so she now associates these previously feared stimuli with relaxation instead of anxiety. To further enhance the extinction of the avoidance response, *in vivo* (real life) practice is usually carried out in conjunction with the desensitization procedure. In many respects, this treatment could be viewed as training in how to cope with and face fears and unpleasant physical sensations, rather than avoiding them (Goldfried, 1971).

One of the major theoretical differences between behavior therapy and psychoanalysis centers on the "symptom substitution" issue. Psychoanalysts view symptoms as outer manifestations of internal conflict and take a negative view of behavioral techniques which stress removal of symptoms. Generally, current research confirms desensitization as an effective treatment, particularly when compared with conventional psychotherapy. Furthermore, when follow-up research is conducted, symptom substitution is not found; rather there is instead more general improvement extending to other areas of the patient's life (Wolpe, 1958, Lazarus, 1963, Bandura, 1969).

TREATMENT MODEL FOR AGORAPHOBIA USING BEHAVIOR THERAPY

The Role of the Therapist

Andrews (1966) states that

> in conducting therapy with phobics it is necessary first to "accept
> the patient's gambit," that is the therapist must establish himself in
> the directive-nurturant role which is normally "pulled" from others
> by the phobic's symptoms and other demonstrations of helplessness
> . . . having established himself in the helpful guiding role . . . the
> therapist must begin to use this relationship as leverage to urge the
> patient to venture out of safety and confront fear-arousing situations.
> The therapist does not reduce his support, but quite clearly indicates
> confidence in the patient and rather directly urges him to take steps
> toward self-reliance (p. 45).

While psychoanalysts stress the importance of the transference relationship, behavior therapists for the most part do not stress relationship
variables. In fact, the therapist could be a film strip, tape recorder or
computer. However, in working with agoraphobic women, one must agree
with Andrews on the importance of the therapeutic relationship.

At first, the phobic will become very dependent on her therapist. The
relaxation procedure often encourages dependency. She also requires
help in hierarchy construction and careful planning of her *in vivo* experiences. However, as therapy progresses, more and more responsibility
for planning the therapy is placed with the patients. Relaxation tapes
are taken home, more homework assignments are given, more stringent
in vivo procedures are to be carried out, etc. Often the patient becomes
upset and discouraged when she realizes she actively has to work on her
problems. She may become increasingly demanding, complaining about
the physical sensations accompanying the phobia, asking for more relaxation sessions, etc. The therapist must resist catering to her dependency at
these times, pointing out to her what she is doing, as well as providing
reinforcement (in form of extra attention from the therapist, phone calls,
praise, smiles, applause, checks on chart, etc.), contingent, following Agras
et al. (1968), on the increasing development of initiative and autonomy.

Behavioral Diagnosis

Treatment begins with a behavioral diagnosis (Wolpe, 1970) based on a
focused, detailed history of the phobic patterns which often provides an
entry into the more generalized problem, e.g., the inability of the
phobic to oppose parents or husband.

As part of the behavioral diagnosis, the patient is asked to record phobic occurrences during the week, what was done to overcome the fears, when the patients gave in, etc., and what were the antecedent conditions that set them off or consequences of fearful behavior (that presumably maintain them). These homework assignments are particularly useful to enable women to see interaction between their fears and the familial reinforcement patterns.

Treatment of the Phobic Symptom—Desensitization

Most phobic patients enjoy learning to relax. They view it as "coping" behavior to enable them to deal with anxiety and discomfort that are so much a part of their life. With simple monosymptomatic phobias, desensitization of the presenting phobia following relaxation training could be conducted as follows:

> Ms. C was an unmarried 40-year-old editorial assistant who lived at home with her mother and rarely dated. She came into treatment in a state of urgency about an elevator phobia because she was job-hunting and it was impossible to be interviewed for a position in the city without riding an elevator. She felt ridiculous answering want ads for desirable jobs to inquire first of all, "What floor is it on?" . . . In treating Ms. C we worked up a typical hierarchy for the elevator phobia, starting with elevators in low buildings with operators and proceeding to express automatic elevators in tall buildings. As we desensitized her to items high on the hierarchy (most fearful), she was encouraged to try *in vivo* trials for low items (less fearful). At first I was able to accompany her, at other times she went with friends, and finally alone, usually calling me to receive praise and encouragement for her efforts (Fodor, 1974).

Expanded Desensitization

Not all agoraphobics respond well to such simple desensitization (Marks and Gelder, 1965). Wolpe and Lazarus (1966) talk of such a case who failed at conventional desensitization for her symptom of "being closed in" in conversations because the surface symptom masked suppressed rage at her husband, which was the more generalized problem. Lazarus (1966) presents further criticism of the unidimensional procedures, arguing for a "broad-spectrum behavior therapy: If lasting improvement is to be achieved, treatment must eliminate the primary conditioned responses which frequently underlie the higher-order maladaptive responses of which the patient may complain" (p. 95).

Thus, with a patient like Ms. C we could stop therapy at the surface desensitization. Her basic "claustrophobic life-style" would not have changed, although she was now more mobile and less anxious in the city. In expanded treatment, we desensitized her to the more general fear (become independent, sexual, going up in the world)*—in other words, doing the more "stereotypic" male things. This is not as easy as it looks, for it involves many hierarchies and the desensitization procedure can be tedious (for the therapist) in such cases.** Hence, with Ms. C we moved from the surface concerns with claustrophobia to situations that were more basic separation-individuation concerns. The process of generalized hierarchy construction often brings out important features that have been suppressed; at times the patient achieves "insight" into the associations between certain stimuli and her fears and anxieties. Often, the process provides a basis for cognitive restructuring as well. With Ms. C, while the first set of treatments took six weeks, the expanded treatment continued for the rest of the year (on a once-a-week basis). Assertive responses were also used (see Chapter 9 by A. Lazarus in this book). Ms. C was able to make significant changes in her own life, expanded her social life and became more of an autonomous woman.

Feather and Rhoads (1972) utilize a similar procedure which they call "psychodynamic behavior therapy." However, their procedures go beyond the patient's own verbalization, incorporating interpretive material (often of a psychoanalytic nature) into their hierarchies.

Behavior Rehearsal

Extinguishing the phobic symptom is not the prime goal of treatment; rather treatment aims to alter a dependent, avoidant life-style. Behavior rehearsal is another technique useful in developing new ways of behaving.

In one case, Ms. T, a severe agoraphobic, typically began her sessions complaining about her husband's mistreatment of her and reciting her weekly suffering. She was asked to keep a behavioral record of their interactions. When we studied the record, the following pattern emerged. He appeared to handle her superdependency and chronic complaining most of the time by avoiding home—finding an excuse to work late, etc.

---

* Hierarchies included moving from mother's house (answering ads, looking at apartments, telling mother she was moving, guilt-inducing scenes on mother's part, assertion with mother, etc.). Following the move, hierarchies dealt with aspects of her social life, fear of men, sex, etc.

** Susskind (1970) proposes an idealized self-image variant of desensitization that is helpful in such cases.

When he walked in the door, his wife immediately accused him of taking a client out to her favorite restaurant (she could go out accompanied), denying her pleasure, not caring. Thus the husband would then try to make up for his lack of attention; by catering to his wife at these times he reinforced complaining and dependency. We worked on alternatives to sitting at home alone waiting for him to arrive. We planned projects and relaxation procedures which helped to avoid build-up of anxiety which generated the hurt or rejected feelings. Then we dealt with alternative ways of greeting him, showing an interest in his life and talking about positive things she had done during the day. The husband started to come home more often and began taking a greater interest in Ms. T and her therapy. This procedure was a first step in helping Ms. T become less dependent on her husband and more of a person in her own right.

Group Therapy

Since agoraphobic women appear to have problems similar to many other contemporary women who are struggling with trapped feelings in a marriage relationship, group treatment with an emphasis on the discussion of woman's role and on setting goal or life plans is also indicated. Most agoraphobics lead very conventional lives; they often are neither well educated nor into women's lib and are unlikely to go into consciousness-raising groups. Group treatment as an auxiliary to individual desensitization is helpful since the group can provide additional reinforcements for change as well as help in dealing with some of the realistic issues involved in achieving autonomy (e.g., economic dependency on men). Also, assertive techniques can be demonstrated and tried out in the group. In the group, women are encouraged to pursue outside interests, work, earn money to pay for their own treatment, etc. Books such as Greer (1971), Friedan (1963) and de Beauvoir (1953) are assigned or discussed.

Modeling

Bandura (1969) has demonstrated that phobics will approach a feared object, following exposure to a model who can cope. Variants of the modeling procedure include models who are initially fearful but master the feared stimulus, as well as "coping" models who rationally talk themselves out of their fears. A female therapist who is comfortable with her own identity is most helpful in enabling these women who have avoided being independent, assertive initiators to see how such a woman is able to be happy and still "feminine." If you see women in your own home, let them see you relate to your husband or the man in the house; let them watch you interact with your children. It is important for them to observe an economically independent, autonomous female person. If they are being seen by a male, he should let them know about the women in his life, his wife, children and how he values their non-stereotypic traits.

In group, one should also bring in other women to take part in the group, particularly independent women from different social backgrounds; otherwise the therapist with her advanced degrees becomes like a movie star who is too far removed from the patient. Also it is good to show the patient how to master one's own fears (e.g., of driving, separating, etc.).

Work with a male model or co-therapist is also essential since it is important for women to get positive feedback from their expanded role repertoire from men as well as women. Otherwise, they may behave independently with women and still be dependent with men.

Work with Families

Lazarus (1966) views the family as playing a vital role in sustaining and maintaining the agoraphobic's behavior, stating that "one is unlikely to achieve lasting therapeutic change without treating them concurrently" (p. 97). For example, Ms. T's husband should work closely with her and the therapist to plan altered contingencies of reinforcement. In working with families, one often has to work with the mother as well as the husband, since she has problems letting go. This might involve group treatment, perhaps even consciousness-raising groups. Also important to keep in mind is that most agoraphobics are also mothers; Marks (1969) and others report a relationship between mother's and child's fears. The daughters of agoraphobics not only have the usual societal social conditioning but a phobic model to imitate as well. Work with the patient around freeing the next generation of female children is most essential.

OTHER PHOBIC CONDITIONS

Many other attitudinal fear reactions seen in women could also be treated as a phobia. Recently the author has been seeing several severely obese young women who substitute a preoccupation with eating for living. These women appear to have a fear of thinness. They are overprotected young women who hide under their layers of fat to avoid being autonomous, grown up and adult. Since their problems with autonomy, usually with their mothers, are similar to that of their agoraphobic sisters, they might benefit from a similar treatment approach. This author

(Fodor, 1974) described a similar approach for a severe work block in a woman artist which masked a larger problem relating to fear of success.

We dealt with the fear of success by constructing a hierarchy of all possible outcomes to success, e.g., a showing at a gallery, a favorable review in the *New York Times,* husband's faculty colleagues congratulating her while her husband looks on, on lecture tour, etc. After completing relaxation training and the desensitization process, the patient could work without anxiety and completed enough paintings to have a local showing. Instead of associating work output with anxiety, Mrs. A, through treatment, developed a new set of contingencies. Working now became associated with good feelings of independence and creativity which were further reinforced by Mrs. A's husband and friends in real life. Mrs. A was now able to accept recognition for her own work without feeling that she was being less feminine, for femininity was now redefined as including work and success for her.

CONCLUSION

Woman's biggest problem is overcoming dependency. Somehow, even most independent women hang on to a few phobic symptoms (often fear of driving or flying) as a last remnant of dependency.* Women and men both must be able to integrate dependent and independent sides of themselves. One way community programs may further help women is to provide clinics to help them outgrow their childhood fears by short term desensitization programs that have proven so effective (Bandura, 1969, Marks, 1969). No longer will women have to put up with ridicule or sexist interpretations of the last residues of childish fears,** but instead could feel like a recent participant in an experiment on extinction of snake phobia, who wrote in a personal communication: "What I experienced [in addition to extinguishing a fear response to snakes] was a feeling of self-confidence which transferred and generalized into many other areas of my life . . . as a stimulus for many of the growth changes that have since occurred."

Generally, by following Kohlberg's (1966) view of how roles are learned, behavior therapy helps women to facilitate sex role integration by

---

* Some seemingly independent women are afraid of riding bikes, skating or skiing. Since they have only recently learned to stand on their own feet they fear what they can't control.

** Feldman (1949): "Women who fear mice are disclosing phallic acceptance of the mouse. They fear sexual attack and are afraid the mouse will run into their genitalia."

1) Providing appropriate techniques (such as desensitization, assertive training, etc.) for the extinction of old roles or the expansion and learning of new ones.

2) Challenging the "morality" of conforming to sex role stereotyping and altering the reinforcement contingencies so that prestige, competence or goodness can now be associated with new or expanded interests and role behavior.

3) Presenting non-stereotypic female therapists for the patient to model; enabling the patient to experience approval from both male and female therapists for expanded role repertoires.

4) Helping to develop new interests and behaviors that do not bear a label of "masculine" or "feminine" but are sought because an autonomous person now has goals.

REFERENCES

AGRAS, S., LEITENBERG, H., & BARLOW, D. Social reinforcement in the modification of agoraphobia. *Archives of General Psychiatry*, 19, 423-427, 1968.

AGRAS, S., SYLVESTER, D., & OLIVEAU, D. The epidemiology of common fears and phobias. *Comprehensive Psychiatry*, 10, 2, 151-156, 1969.

ANDREWS, J. D. Psychotherapy of phobias. *Psychological Bulletin*, 66, 455-480, 1966.

ANGELINO, H., DOLLINS, J., & MECH, E. Trends in the fears and worries of school children as related to socio-economic status and age. *Journal of Genetic Psychology*, 89, 263-276, 1956.

BANDURA, A. *Principles of Behavior Modification.* New York: Holt, Rinehart and Winston, 1969.

BENTZEN, F. Sex ratios in learning and behavior disorders. *American Journal of Orthopsychiatry*, 33, 92-98, 1963.

BLOCK, J. H. Conceptions of sex role: Some cross-cultural and longitudinal perspectives. *American Psychologist*, 28, 6, 512-526, June, 1973.

BROVERMAN, K., BROVERMAN, D., CLARKSON, F., ROSENKRANZ, P., & VOGEL, S. Sex role stereotypes and clinical judgments of mental health. *Journal of Consulting and Clinical Psychology*, 34, 1, 1-7, 1970.

Committee on Nomenclature and Statistics of the American Psychiatric Association. *Diagnostic and Statistical Manual: Mental Disorders.* Washington, D. C.: American Psychiatric Association, DSM-II, 1968.

DE BEAUVOIR, S. *The Second Sex.* Bantam Edition, translated by H. H. Parshley. New York: Alfred Knopf, 1953.

DEUTSCH, H. The genesis of agoraphobia. *International Journal of Psychoanalysis*, 10, 51-59, 1929.

DIXON, J., DE MONCHAUX, C., & SANDLER, J. Patterns of anxiety: The phobias. *British Journal of Medical Psychology*, 30, 34-40, 1957.

DOHRENWEND, B. & DOHRENWEND, B. *Social Status and Psychological Disorders.* New York: John Wiley, 1969.

ERIKSON, E. *Childhood and Society.* (2nd ed.) New York: Norton, 1963.

ERRERA, P. Some historical aspects of the concept of phobia. *The Psychiatric Quarterly*, 36, 325-326, 1962.

FEATHER, B. & RHOADS, J. Psychodynamic behavior therapy: II. Clinical aspects. *Archives of General Psychiatry*, 26, 502-511, 1972.

FELDMAN, S. Fear of mice. *Psychoanalytic Quarterly*, 18, 227-230, 1949.

FENICHEL, O. *The Psychoanalytic Theory of Neurosis.* New York: Norton, 1945.

FIRESTONE, S. *The Dialectic of Sex: The Case for Feminist Revolution.* New York: Bantam, 1970.

FODOR, I. Sex role conflict and symptom formation in women: Can behavior therapy help? *Psychotherapy: Theory, Research, Practice,* 2, 1, 1974.

FREUD, S. Turnings in the world of psychoanalytic therapy. *Collected Papers,* Vol. II. London: Hogarth Press, 1919, pp. 399-400.

FRIEDAN, B. *The Feminine Mystique.* New York: Dell, 1963.

FRIEDMAN, J. H. Short term psychotherapy of "phobia of travel." *American Journal of Psychotherapy,* 4, 259-278, 1950.

FRIEDMAN, P. The phobias. In S. Arieti (Ed.), *American Handbook of Psychiatry,* Vol. I. New York: Basic Books, 1959, pp. 292-306.

GOLDFRIED, M. Systematic desensitization as training in self control. *Journal of Consulting and Clinical Psychology,* 37, 2, 228-234, 1971.

GOLDSTEIN, A. Case conference: Some aspects of agoraphobia. *Journal of Behavior Therapy and Experimental Psychiatry,* 1, 305-313, 1970.

GREER, G. *The Female Eunuch.* New York: Bantam, 1971.

HOFFMAN, L. Early childhood experiences and women's achievement motives. *Journal of Social Issues,* 28, 2, 129-155, 1972.

IBSEN, H. A doll's house. Translated by R. Farguharson Sharp. *Four Great Plays by Ibsen.* New York: Bantam, 1959.

IVEY, E. Recent advances in the psychiatric diagnosis and treatment of phobia. *American Journal of Psychotherapy,* 13, 35-50, 1959.

JACKLIN, C. & MISCHEL, H. As the twig is bent: Sex role stereotyping in early readers. *School Psychology Digest,* 2, 3, 1973.

JACOBSON, E. *Progressive Relaxation.* Chicago, Ill.: U. of Chicago Press, 1938.

JERSILD, A. T. Emotional development. In L. Carmichael (Ed.), *Manual of Child Psychology.* John Wiley and Sons, 1946.

KOHLBERG, L. A cognitive-developmental analysis of children's sex-role concepts and attitudes. In F. Maccoby (Ed.), *The Development of Sex Differences.* Stanford, Cal.: Stanford University Press, 1966, pp. 82-173.

LAPOUSE, R. & MONK, M. Fears and worries in a representative sample of children. *American Journal of Orthopsychiatry,* 24, 803-818, 1959.

LAUGHLIN, H. P. Fears and phobias. *Medical Annals of District of Columbia,* 23, 441-448, 1954.

LAZARUS, A. The results of behavior therapy in 126 cases of severe neurosis. *Behavior Research Therapy,* 1, 69-79, 1963.

LAZARUS, A. Broad-spectrum behavior therapy and the treatment of agoraphobia. *Behavior Research Therapy,* 4, 95-97, 1966.

LAZARUS, A. Review of I. Marks, *Fear and Phobias. Behavior Therapy,* 1, 409-410, 1970.

LEARY, T. *Interpersonal Diagnosis of Personality.* New York: Ronald Press, 1957.

LYON, N. A report on children's toys and socialization of sex roles. *Ms,* December 1972, 57-58.

MACCOBY, E. & MASTERS, J. Attachment and dependency. In P. Mussen (Ed.), *Carmichael's Manual of Child Psychology,* Vol. 2. New York: John Wiley, 1970.

MACFARLANE, J., ALLEN, L., & HONZIK, M. *A Developmental Study of the Behavior Problems of Normal Children.* Berkeley: University of California Press, 1954.

MAHLER, M. On the first three subphases of the separation-individuation process. *International Journal of Psychoanalysis,* 53, 3, 333-338, 1972.

MARKS, I. M. & GELDER, M. G. A controlled retrospective study of behavior therapy in phobic patients. *British Journal of Psychiatry,* 111, 561-573, 1965.

MARKS, I. *Fears and Phobias.* New York: Academic Press, 1969.

MARKS, I. Agoraphobic syndrome: Phobic anxiety state. *Archives of General Psychiatry,* 23, 538-553, 1970.

MILLET, K. *Sexual Politics.* New York: Avon Books, 1969.

MISCHEL, W. Sex-typing and socialization. *Carmichael's Manual of Child Psychology,* Vol. II. Edited by P. Mussen. New York: John Wiley, 1970, pp. 3-72.

PALMER, R. Relationship of fearfulness to locus of control of reinforcement and perceived parental behavior. In R. Rubin, H. Fensternheim, J. Henderson, and L. Ullman (Eds.), *Advances in Behavior Therapy.* New York: Academic Press, 1972, pp. 1-6.

SEIDENBERG, R. The trauma of eventlessness. *The Psychoanalytic Review,* 59, 1, 95-109, 1972.

SELIGMAN, M. Fall into helplessness. *Psychology Today,* 7, 1, 43-48, June 1973.

SPERLING, M. Somatic symptomology in phobia: Clinical and theoretical aspects. *Psychoanalytic Forum,* forthcoming.

STONE, L. Disappointment is the lot of women. In L. Tanner (Ed.), *Voices from Women's Liberation.* New York: Signet, 1970.

SULLIVAN, H. S. Psychiatry: Introduction to the study of interpersonal relations. In P. Mullahy (Ed.), *A Study of Interpersonal Relations.* New York: Hermitage Press, 1949.

SUSSKIND, D. The idealized self-image (ISI): A technique in confidence training. *Behavior Therapy,* 1, 538-541, 1970.

SYMONDS, A. Phobias after marriage: Women's declaration of dependence. *The American Journal of Psychoanalysis,* 31, 144-152, 1971.

TERHUNE, W. The phobic syndrome: A study of 86 patients with phobic reactions. *Archives Neurological Psychiatry,* 62, 162-172, 1949.

WEISS, E. Psychodynamic formulation of agoraphobia. *The Psychoanalytic Forum,* 1, 4, 378-386, 1966.

WOLPE, J. *Psychotherapy by Reciprocal Inhibition.* Stanford, Connecticut: Stanford University Press, 1958.

WOLPE, J. Identifying the antecedents of an agoraphobic reaction: A transcript. *Journal of Behavior Therapy and Experimental Psychiatry,* 1, 299-304, 1970.

WOLPE, J. & LAZARUS, A. *Behavior Therapy Techniques.* New York: Pergamon Press, 1966.

Women on Words and Images, *Dick and Jane as Victims: Sex Role Stereotyping in Children's Readers.* Princeton, New Jersey: Author, 1972.

7
WOMEN AND ALCOHOLISM

EDITH S. GOMBERG

DRINKING

Alcoholism is defined in terms of deviance from accepted social customs relating to drinking, so it is best to begin with some information about the social drinking of American women. In the United States and in most other countries and cultures, more men than women engage in social drinking. Said another way, there are more women abstainers than there are men abstainers; the main supporters of the temperance movement during the late 19th and early 20th centuries were women.

The gap between the sexes seems to be narrowing, however. A survey done shortly after World War II (Riley and Marden, 1947) indicated that there had been a sharp rise in the number of women drinking from 1940 to 1946, and, "the gap between men and women, particularly under 50, is smaller than it was 6 years ago" (p. 267). That change may have been related to World War II but the percentage of American women who drink socially continues to rise. The most recent survey (Calahan, Cislin, and Crossley, 1969) indicated that where the percentage of American men who drink rose from 75% to 77% over the last quarter century, the percentage for American women rose from 56% to 60%, an increase twice as large as for men. Each percentage point represents approximately one million people.

An interesting analysis of some novels, written between 1900 and 1904, and some written between 1946 and 1950, in terms of references to drinking situations, shows some relevant changes (Pfautz, 1962). In almost half the drinking situations described in the earlier novels, it is a man drinking alone. In the later novels, this percentage has dropped considerably. Drinking has become much more frequently a heterosexual social activity: drinking in "mixed groups" occurs in 12% of references in Victorian novels but this has shifted to almost 40% by the mid-20th

169

century. Women drinking with other women shifted from .4% of references to 1.5%—while remaining a small percentage, it has tripled. It is difficult to remember back to a standard where advertisers were constrained about showing women in liquor advertisements: they now appear with men, drinking with other women, and even drinking alone.

Social drinking by women also varies with age and social class. The percentage of all drinkers is highest at ages 21 to 39, and then declines. Classifying drinkers as infrequent, light, moderate, and heavy (Calahan *et al.*, 1969), recent surveyors found the highest percentage of heavy drinkers for both men and women to be in the age group 45 to 49. As far as social class differences go, the myth of universal lower class debauchery has dissolved in the statistics. The less money in a social class, the fewer the drinkers. Lawrence and Maxwell (1962) presented figures which indicated clearly that the women and men of lower income groups tend to be social drinkers less frequently. And again, the most recent survey (Cahalan *et al.*, 1969) shows clearly that the lower the "index of social position," the smaller the percentage of women who drink. Eliza Doolittle is somewhat misleading in her statement, that "gin was mother's milk to me," if she purports to speak for lower class women in general.

DRUNKENNESS

What about drunkenness? Although there is a more permissive attitude in American society about women's social drinking and about such drinking in mixed groups and in public places, there is very little change from attitudes of disgust and scorn toward female intoxication. Where male intoxication is viewed with indifference, amusement, often with pity, drunken behavior is taboo for women. The universality of this attitude is such that both sexes and all social classes show the same negative attitude (Lawrence and Maxwell, 1962). There is clearly a double standard. Knupfer (1964) asked respondents in a survey what they thought of a man and of a woman who have had too much to drink, and "it is 'typical' of both sexes to think it worse for a woman to drink too much" (p. 153). Women alcoholics themselves, a particularly vulnerable group, express disgust and rejection of female intoxication (Curlee, 1967).

Why does a society which is increasingly permissive toward women engaging in social drinking set limits of acceptability at female intoxication? This is an important question because it generalizes to alcoholic women and, there, attitudes of disgust and irritation may become more hidden because alcoholism is "a sickness," and one is supposed to be sympathetic to sick people.

In her discussion of female drinking patterns, Knupfer (1964) sees the rejection of female intoxication as involving two aspects, one relating to the division of labor between the sexes and the other relating to loss of customary sexual restraints and inhibitions. In her work role, a woman's efficiency in using household appliances may not be markedly lowered by her alcoholic intake. Many women are, presumably, "plateau drinkers," and housework itself does not require a very high level of skill. The aspect of women's work which *is* impaired by her alcohol intake is, "the quality of sensitivity to the needs of others" (p. 157), i.e., her role as wife, mother, daughter, sister, housekeeper, nursemaid, etc. This is also the viewpoint of Child, Barry and Bacon (1965) who state, in a cross cultural study of sex differences in drinking customs:

> It seems reasonable to expect that most societies would limit drinking and drunkenness in women more than in men. Under the generally prevailing conditions of human life, temporary incapacity of a woman is more threatening than is temporary incapacity of a man. For example, care of a field can be postponed for a day, but care of a child cannot. The general social role of the sexes makes drunkenness more threatening in women than in men (p. 60).

Knupfer's second point, the link made by the respondents of women's intoxication to the loss of customary sexual restraints, raises an old, unanswered question about the relationship between drinking and sexual behavior. Historically, from earliest Biblical injunctions and Roman law, women's drinking and sexual "irregularities" are linked (McKinlay, 1959). It is a fact of life that women are able to participate or at least be sexually available even when drinking heavily whereas men are likely to be rendered impotent by large amounts of alcohol. However, the concern and anxiety expressed by many of Knupfer's subjects about violations of approved standards of sexual restraint is clearly a double standard. The issue of alcohol-and-sexual-behavior is really two issues, one of knowledge, one of attitudes. We do not actually know that women who become drunk or who are alcoholic are more likely to engage in sexual behavior. There are some pretty lurid case histories (Karpman, 1948) but when physicians are asked about the sexual behavior of their alcoholic women patients (Johnson, 1965), they disagree among themselves, some reporting "loose sexual morals" and others saying "no." Popular attitudes however, are clearly negative; whatever the actual facts, attitudes toward women's drunkenness are negative and there is strong popular belief that female drunkenness and loose sexual behavior are associated.

The intense disapproval of female drunkenness places a constraint on women against heavy drinking and, in Knupfer's view, this confers some "cultural protection" against alcoholism.

ALCOHOLISM

Recent analyses of epidemiological data show clearly that when we consider the functional mental disorders, psychoses and neuroses, by whatever measure, more women than men show such disorders (Gove and Tudor, 1973). However when we consider the disorders of deviant behavior such as alcoholism, delinquency, and narcotics addiction, the ratio goes the other way, and this differential holds true for other countries (Edwards, Hensman and Peto, 1972). We are now faced with a critical question often raised in discussions of alcoholism in women: since it occurs less frequently among women and since they must break through constraints and "cultural protections" to a greater extent than their male counterparts, is the alcoholic woman "sicker" or "much more abnormal" (Karpman, 1948) than the alcoholic man? Physicians apparently believe she is (Johnson, 1965). There is some evidence to support this: one study of indices of deviance from normative standards suggests that women alcoholics, as adolescents, are more deviant from other female adolescents than men alcoholics, as adolescents, are deviant from other young men (Jones, 1968; Jones, 1971). But as we shall see, reports of good or bad prognosis for women patients, as compared with male alcoholic patients, vary widely and present contradictory results. It is our contention that this question of "sicker" or "much more abnormal" is not a useful one What "sicker" or "poor prognosis" usually means is that we do not yet know the best and most effective way to help patients with this particular disorder, hence our failure rate. But it may also mean that we do not like that patient and that disorder. Some of this has been displayed in the professional view of heroin addiction. Such addiction was viewed as having very poor prognosis but we know now, from our experience with young men in Vietnam and returned to the United States, that prognosis has much to do with the circumstances and setting of the drug abuse.

There is a value judgment implicit in clinical description of women psychiatric patients as bad patients or at least worse than male patients. There are studies which report women psychiatric patients to be noisier, more excitable and belligerent, but there are other reports which describe women as adapting to the role of patient much better than men do (see Gomberg, in press, for discussion).

Ellinwood, Smith, and Vaillant (1966) state unambiguously that their clinical impression of women addicts and their comparative data did not agree:

> In a narcotics hospital the manner of female addict presentation appears quite different from her male counterpart. The females are considerably more attention-seeking, are more erratic and frequent medical clinics more often with severe complaints of non-organic origin. Not infrequently, females appear to be psychotic or borderline psychotic. These and other impressions prompted this study. Interestingly, however, the data revealed much more uniformity between male and female addicts than clinical impression had led us to believe (p. 37).

It is a cliché to say that women alcoholics are worse, i.e., worse behaving patients with poor prognosis. Yet there is no clear evidence that either of these definitions of worseness holds up in comparisons with male alcoholics.

Early History

In describing the history and dynamics of women alcoholics, we will not be speaking of women in low income groups or women who have gotten into difficulty with the law. There are a number of studies about women problem drinkers in penological institutions (Lisansky, 1957, Myerson, 1959, Cramer and Blacker, 1963, Cramer and Blacker, 1966, Mayer and Green, 1967), and about drinking problems of delinquent girls (Widseth, 1971, Widseth and Mayer, 1971). There is virtually no information available about the problem drinking of black women and other minority group women. We are reporting and summarizing a literature which is based primarily on white, middle class, white collar, married or formerly married women. There have been a number of literature reviews (Lisansky, 1957, Schuckit, 1972, Lindbeck, 1972, Gomberg, in press), and our discussion is derived primarily from the clinical literature.

If we consider loss of a parent during childhood, psychiatric illness in the family of origin, or alcoholism in the family, the histories of women who become alcoholic show such disruptive and traumatic events to a greater extent than a normal population and to a greater extent than male alcoholics (Gomberg, in press). There is a caveat. This kind of family history of disruptive events and psychopathology characterizes many other psychodiagnostic groups. Robins (1966) reports strong similarities in the childhood histories of alcoholic, hysterical, and sociopathic patients. That these early trauma take their toll is clinically evident later in life in the lack of trust, manifested as conflict over dependency, and in the isolation and frustration and anger of the alcoholic woman patient.

There is only one longitudinal study which gives us some picture of the alcoholic woman as adolescent (Jones, 1971). Although the sample is small, the description of personality and behavior fits well with what we see later clinically. Jones' subjects were persons who participated in the Oakland Growth Study in California and they are now in their late forties. According to their responses in an interview, the women subjects were divided into abstainers, light, moderate or heavy drinkers, and problem drinkers; these categories refer to their current, adult alcohol usage.

The future problem drinker, as a youngster, has experienced adolescence as a severe crisis period. The future problem drinkers are, ". . . judged to be submissive as youngsters, rebellious as adults." Jones presents a case summary sketch, typical of those who later become problem drinkers:

> At 15, life is full of adolescent self-doubt and confusion. She fears and rejects life, is distrustful of people, follows a religion which accentuates judgment and punishment. She escapes into ultrafemininity. This protective coloration will keep her going through the mating season but very likely she will recognize the emptiness and impotence in later years (pp. 67-68).

Parenthetically as a provocative thought, it should be noted that Holzberg (1963) found schizophrenic women strikingly different from schizophrenic men and normal men and women in "the severity of moral judgment" and "the tendency toward extreme moral judgments." Jones' problem drinkers tended toward religions which "accentuate judgment and punishment."

Jones points up many areas of similarity between those adolescents who later became abstainers and those who became problem drinkers as adults, but the girls who are abstainers later in life are, as adolescents, more responsible, conventional, consistent, ethical, and emotionally controlled, and ". . . they are also able to accept a dependency relationship at an age when this may be a determining ingredient for mental health."

What emerges, then, is a history of early emotional deprivation, and a picture of a submissive, passively resentful girl undergoing a stormy adolescence, showing some signs of difficulty in impulse control, fearful of dependency relationships and trying to solve her problems with super-femininity.

Sexual Role

There are three different areas which will be discussed under sexual role: physiological phenomena; sex role identity; marriage, children, and sexual adjustment.

Physiological phenomena. There is a long-standing debate whether alcoholic bouts are or are not triggered by premenstrual tension. Like the studied relationship between the menstrual cycle and suicide (Wetzel and McClure, 1972), the results are confusing and contradictory. It appears that the discomforts of the premenstrual period do add to the stresses (Belfer, Shader, Carroll and Harmatz, 1971), but there is also a tendency among alcoholic women to look for specific reasons for precipitants to rationalize the fact of their drinking. Whether women's drinking bouts are triggered off more readily by a crisis situation, whether they are more vulnerable than men to social environmental stresses, or whether they feel a need to justify their drinking, we are not certain. But premenstrual tension, while it adds a source of stress, can hardly be considered a major etiological factor.

There is apparently a relationship between a high incidence of gynecological-obstetrical problems like infertility, miscarriages, hysterectomy, etc., on the one hand and alcoholism on the other (Kinsey, 1966, Wilsnack, 1972). It is not clear which comes first. Kinsey (1966) indicates that many of his subjects were into problem drinking *before* their gynecological-obstetrical problems occurred, and Curlee (1970) found approximately the same sequence. It is also possible that there is a common pattern of traits or characteristics shared by women who manifest gynecological-obstetrical problems and by alcoholic women. Research on women with psychosomatic complaints relating to menstruation and pregnancy suggests that they may be described in terms of conflict over dependency, passive behavior, subtle manifestations of aggression, etc. (Bardwick, 1971, Howells, 1972)—i.e., strikingly similar to a trait description of women with alcohol problems. A significant research question could be examined in studying these two groups of women with gynecological-obstetrical problems, those who are alcoholic and those who are not: what are the factors which determine ultimate symptom choice in fairly similar groups?

There is a strong relationship between depression and alcoholism among women (Schuckit, Pitts, Reich, King and Winokur, 1969, Schuckit, 1972); the relationship between feminine physiological events like menstruation, emotional states like depression, and alcoholism, have yet to be worked out.

Sex role identity. The assumption has been that alcoholic women were behaving in a *masculine* way, i.e., drinking, but the findings are that alcoholic women do *not* reject femininity but rather tend to overemphasize and overvalue the wife-mother role. When *conscious* femininity is involved and attitudes toward sex role are expressed overtly, alcoholic women emphasize their femininity and maternal feelings (Kinsey, 1966, Wilsnack, 1972). They do not differ from a control group on femininity scores of the California Psychological Inventory (Belfer *et al.,* 1971).

But there is conflict and ambivalence. Both Parker (1972) and Wilsnack (1973), measuring conscious and less conscious attitudes, found that, while on a conscious level there is "overidentification" (Parker's term) or "hyperfemininity" (Wilsnack's term), *unconscious* measures show less femininity and more masculinity than control groups. (This has not been measured in the pre-alcoholic state except in Jones' (1971) study where presumably conscious attitudes are described as "ultrafemininity.") The woman who is now an alcoholic is not a truly "hyperfeminine" person; at least she has not made this mode of adaptation work for her. She is conflicted and ambivalent about being a woman, she still protests her femininity while the more assertive, aggressive aspects of her personality are denied, just below the surface.

Marriage, children, and sexual adjustment. Women who become alcoholic marry to the same extent as the general population and although we do have a subgroup of lonely, single, unmarried drinkers, there are far fewer of them than of the married or formerly married. The divorce rate is higher than the general population (Fort, 1949, Lisansky, 1957, Rosenbaum, 1958, Kinsey, 1966); this is also true of male alcoholics.

The potential for trouble lies partly in the women's expectations. Women who later become alcoholic apparently have an intense need for love and reassurance relating to the deprivations of childhood, but coupled with this is difficulty in accepting dependency relationships. She has problems with trust but looks to marriage and a man for ultimate fulfillment. More often than not, "marriage is . . . a painful, disappointing experience" (Lindbeck, 1972). Blane (1968) describes her as a woman who has developed out of the frustrations of childhood very strong dependency needs, and ". . . an aggressive insistence that her needs be fulfilled." Alcohol serves a multiple of purposes: escape, expression of anger, revenge, and a sense that here is one source of pleasure that can be controlled and turned to at will.

Many women who have alcohol problems drink with their husbands who also have alcohol problems and there is some evidence that transmission from husband to wife of symptomatic drinking is not uncommon; however, it rarely works in the other direction (Lisansky, 1957, Rosenbaum, 1958, Wanberg and Knapp, 1970, Jacob and Lavoie, 1971). This transmission from husband to wife has also been noted in narcotic addicted couples (O'Donnell, Besteman and Jones, 1966). The nonalcoholic husband of a problem drinking woman reacts in a variety of ways—protectively, unforgivingly, with denial, with anger, etc. We know little about husbands' responses but we do know that marital problems seem to be the central issue that drives alcoholic women to seek help with their drinking (Sclare, 1970).

There seems to be a great absorption and emotional involvement in the mothering role. There is, as we noted, a high incidence of problems like miscarriage, infertility, and hysterectomy among women who develop alcohol problems. There is also a good deal of concern about mothering; this was noted by Lisansky (1957), and it has been noted by many clinicians who agree that one of the worst threats that can be made is the label of unfit mother and the children taken away from her. Fort's (1949) observation of her women subjects in Alcoholics Anonymous is relevant:

> Severity cannot be measured by the same standards as in men—less brawls, job loss, etc., but social discrimination against the children, especially against the daughter . . . is to the woman alcoholic a great shock while it may not even be noticed by an alcoholic father.

Wilsnack's (1973) recent study reports that when alcoholic women subjects are asked how many children they would have liked to have had, the average was 4.15 children, significantly more than the 2.94 reported by control subjects.

There is far more talk about the promiscuity of women with drinking problems than there is evidence. Lack of sexual interest is probably far more common than promiscuity. Many women alcoholics drink at home, alone or with husbands, and while infidelity and promiscuity undoubtedly occur, they are not inevitable concomitants of female alcoholism. The amount of extracurricular heterosexual activity may be related to social class, locale of drinking and drinking partners; common law marriages and prostitution occur more frequently in a prison population, for example, than they do in an outpatient population. It is interesting to note that physicians disagree among themselves when asked about the sexual activity of women patients with drinking problems:

> There was disagreement as to the woman alcoholic's moral code. Some felt that she had loose sexual morals, had more psychosexual conflict such as homosexuality, and was more likely to get into social difficulties. Others felt that the married women kept good contact with their families. They stated that within the family, they seldom stray away as the male alcoholic has a tendency to do (Johnson, 1965, p. 350).

It is hardly surprising to find that the problem of female alcoholism revolves around female sex role and the emotional problems generated by difficulties in making the role work. The combination of early deprivations, problems of trust, conflicts over dependency, concealed anger, and difficulties in impulse control is a dangerous one.

Patterns of Alcoholism

In general, women who become problem drinkers get started a little later than men but present themselves to treatment facilities at approximately the same mean age. This "telescoping" has sometimes been used as an argument that alcoholism in women is a more virulent disease process. Such an argument ignores the differentials in adolescent drinking customs, in the machismo role of alcohol for young men, in the division of labor between the sexes which puts the young married woman more often than not at home and the young married man in a more social and visible position at work. There are quite adequate explanations of the difference in age of onset in terms of different sex norms surrounding drinking without resorting to the "much worse" explanation.

There is also evidence that women cite a *reason* for the onset of problem drinking more than men do. Such precipitants have been extended, in various researches, to cover virtually any and all life stresses, specific traumatic events, long-standing sources of unhappiness, and personality traits; thus, loss of a loved person, an operation, marital conflict, loneliness, feelings of inadequacy are all cited as *reasons* given by alcoholic women for drinking. One cannot say whether women are more likely to cite such precipitants because they feel more need to justify or explain or rationalize their alcoholism. One aspect of this which has been ignored is its relationship to process and reactive mental disorders: process disorders have gradual onsets and no apparent precipitating stress, whereas reactive disorders have more sudden onset with stress acting as precipitant. Reactive disorders presumably have better prognosis. If women, more than men alcoholics, tend to be *reactive* alcoholics, onset being more abrupt and precipitating stress often present, why has this not been taken as a sign of better prognosis?

One consistent and logical finding is that women tend to drink at home and alone much more often than men do (Wood and Duffy, 1964, Johnson, DeVries and Houghton, 1966, Wanberg and Knapp, 1970, Jacob and Lavoie, 1971), and they are described as "hidden drinkers" (Lindbeck, 1972) or "secret drinkers" (Pemberton, 1967). Since they drink more often at home, alone and with others, they are less frequently arrested than men, but getting into trouble with the law relates to social class status and to how public the drinking is. Our middle class woman alcoholic is certainly more protected in one sense because her drinking is not so visible but the question has been raised whether middle class women are not more punished *within the family* and lower income women *outside the family* (Fort, 1949)—it is a question worth investigation.

At any rate, women alcoholics drink at home more because they, like other women, are at home more. We do not really know whether women who are working outside the home present more or less or the same amount of alcoholism as those who stay at home. Women with careers who become alcoholic and who manifest such alcoholism at work are not likely to be objects of sympathy and it is a reasonable guess that they are less tolerated at work than men with alcohol problems. Many of the career women who had problems with drinking, whom I have known clinically, exercised sufficient control to confine drinking to evening and weekends and several of them destroyed their careers when this control broke down. There are probably company personnel files containing relevant information but there are no published reports on working women and alcohol problems.

The frequency of alcoholism and drinking problems among the husbands of alcoholic women is high—in one study, four times as frequent for the husbands of women patients than for the wives of men patients (Lisansky, 1957). In a large sample of alcoholic patients at a mental health center, men alcoholics reported that they were *not* apt to drink with their wives, while women alcoholics significantly more often do drink with their husbands (Wanberg and Knapp, 1970). Women are at home more and women alcoholics more often drink at home so they are more likely to be drinking alone or with husband.

The trend of the evidence is that women alcoholics will use drugs other than alcohol more than will men alcoholics (Curlee, 1970, Horn and Wanberg, 1971). This is true in the United States; several British studies did not turn up differences between men and women alcoholics on this score (Sclare, 1970, Rathod and Thomson, 1971). Whether this relates to the British male to female ratio of alcoholism which is approximately 3 to 1, compared to the U.S. ratio of 5 or 6 to 1, is unclear; British and American attitudes toward drug usage differ, too. The greater usage of drugs by women than by men alcoholics in the U.S. would appear to be related to two points. First, women in general in the U.S. use drugs more and one recent survey shows "not employed housewives" as the occupational group with the largest percentage of users of barbiturates, antidepressants, diet pills, relaxants, minor tranquilizers and other seda-tive/hypnotic drugs (Differential Drug Use Within the New York State Labor Force, 1971). Second, there seems to be a tendency for physicians to prescribe mood-modifying drugs more readily for women patients in general. This has been demonstrated in Britain and in Canada (Cooper-stock, 1971) and there is every reason to believe that it is true in the United States. Whether women are more prone to generalized substance dependencies than are men is an unresolved research question. There is evidence that before the passage of the Harrison act in 1914, the major American user of opiates was the housewife.

ASPECTS OF PSYCHOTHERAPY

It may be useful to think of women who have drinking problems as presenting primary or secondary alcoholism. In primary alcoholism, the abuse of alcohol is the *central* symptomatic feature though medical and interpersonal consequences have aggravated the difficulties. In secondary alcoholism, there is a diagnosable antecedent condition, usually depres-sion, and alcohol is used as a way of coping. Perhaps it is best of all to think of alcoholism as described by Knight (1937) as, ". . . an attempt at cure, that is, an attempt at some solution of the emotional conflict. . . . Any type of neurotic conflict which may be present." Whatever the dynamics are, we may ask what drives a woman with drinking problems to seek help and, so far as we know, the main trouble area which moti-vates her into treatment is familial and interpersonal (Sclare, 1970,

Edwards, Hensman and Peto, 1972). Men will look for help most often because of trouble at work, women because of trouble at home. This suggests some emphases for psychotherapeutic work with alcoholic women.

We begin with analysis of the strengths and liabilities in the woman herself and in her social environment. The familial situation should be evaluated for potentially supportive persons. Conjoint therapy seems a useful approach. Pemberton (1967), observing successes and failures among the woman alcoholics treated, notes that women living alone (widowed, separated, divorced) made comparatively poor response but,

> When progress after discharge was discussed with the successful females, it was quite striking that all had succeeded in modifying the structure of their familial group and had established for themselves a personally satisfying role within it (Pemberton, 1967, p. 371).

Most successful therapeutic interventions would appear to be family rather than individual patient efforts.

Second, for those married women alcoholics who have children, dealing with the problems these children may manifest is not only therapeutic for the women and the children, it may be a kind of long-run prevention operation. The children of a mother with drinking problems will be themselves vulnerable to alcoholism and working with them should be a major priority. Women with drinking problems are often disturbed and very guilty about the difficulties their children encounter and this is a handle, anxiety-loaded and painful but often effective, for therapeutic intervention.

There are a number of organized groups which may be of help. Alcoholics Anonymous and its subsidiary organizations for relatives of alcoholics are available, as well as other groups like Parents without Partners. For some, participation in a group of people with similar concerns is helpful. We assume that a woman alcoholic who is receiving psychotherapy has had complete medical examination and that her medical problems, related or unrelated to her drinking, are being treated. While some prescribed drug treatment may help in the total therapeutic plan, a very conservative approach seems wisest.

Several research studies suggest that group therapy is more effective with male patients and that women alcoholic patients (perhaps all women patients?) are less responsive to group therapy and look for individualized, one-to-one relationships (Pemberton, 1967, Curlee, 1971). When group therapy is used, it is a good guess that smaller and mixed groups would be better, although whether women will do better in groups of women or in mixed groups or in very small or somewhat larger groups has not been systematically studied. This, however, depends very much on the setting, the therapist, and the woman patient's individual history and needs.

One of the most critical areas for the psychotherapist to explore is the question of the function alcohol serves for the patient. The enormous enchantment of alcohol is in the multiplicity of purposes which it serves. Alcohol, when it is used in social drinking kept within acceptable limits, has some pleasurable effects. It helps one to relax and enjoy social gatherings, it is used for celebration, and if one has doubts about its positive and pleasurable aspects, one should try the experiment of a period of abstinence. Alcohol is the first drug substance of choice in American social life and in most other countries as well and almost all drinking is social. But alcoholism is *not* social drinking, it is an abusive use of a substance which is taken in controlled, more acceptable ways by others. What leads the problem drinker to abuse of alcohol? We speculate—we know that alcohol dims the hard edges of reality and escape from painful feelings, at least momentarily, is provided. When she drinks, the alcoholic woman also irritates the people around her, and she can therefore, in one act, express hostility and anger others and at the same time punish herself with her self-abasing drunken behavior. Furthermore, the bout and its consequences help her justify continued drinking because others reject her for it and she is now into a circle of drinking, rejection by others, and continued drinking. Perhaps most important of all, the drinking gives her a feeling of control and mastery over her life. She is disappointed and frustrated in love relationships and people do not meet her needs on demand but the bottle offers warmth and pleasure and a kind of companionship *when she wants it*. In this sense, women's problem drinking is a kind of autoerotic activity. Finally, alcohol serves to "enhance feelings of womanliness" (Wilsnack, 1972), and it is more than likely that, frustrated in her daydreams of happiness with a man and a home and children, she fantasies girlish daydreams while she drinks.

It is this multiplicity of reinforcing effects which makes alcohol so dangerous a drug for some individuals who carry into adolescence and adult life a particular complex of problems surrounding sexual role, aggression, impulse control and dependency. There may be a physiochemical predisposition which is carried by some individuals and not by others, but there is no strong evidence of that so it seems best to view alcoholism as a psychosocial problem, as a form of deviant behavior which is adopted by some because it serves their particular needs.

A final word on treatment—we have no research evidence about the relative efficacy of different therapeutic modalities. It is my own impression that the major issue is not whether one uses behavior modification, deep psychotherapy, reeducation, conditioned reflex therapy, or alternatives. First, the strengths of the patient, her life situation and social environment seem more critical in determining outcome. There are probably patients who will do better with one treatment technique than another but we know little about making this determination, so the major determinant of outcome at this time seems to me largely independent of the treatment modality used. Second, in a deviance disorder like alcoholism, the attitude (conscious and unconscious) of the therapist toward women and toward alcoholics and the enthusiasm and interest of the therapist seem far more related to outcome than the technique used. In sum, the assets of the patient and the concern of the therapist are, I believe, the major determinants of effectiveness, not the treatment modality used.

PROGNOSIS

The question of prognosis for women alcoholics was raised in an early review by Lisansky (1957). One point of view was that women alcoholics were "much more abnormal" (Karpman, 1948) than men alcoholics either because they were more poorly adjusted to social norms or because they were more repressed than men. It followed from this that women patients were more difficult to treat. However, this early review raised several questions about pre-alcoholic personality problems and different normative behavior for the sexes and how this related to prognosis, and it made the point that,

> As a rule, women alcoholics, like men, are not seen in clinics or hospitals until the drinking problem has gone on for some years. It is likely that the social consequences of the drinking problem, i.e., family break-up, job dismissal, rejection by friends and associates, and general social disapproval, are greater for the woman alcoholic who is known as such. The woman patient who appears at a clinic or hospital after years of uncontrolled drinking could therefore conceivably be a more disturbed individual than her male counterpart as a *result* of her alcoholism and its socially punishing consequences, and not because she was initially, in her pre-alcoholic personality, a more disturbed individual (Lisansky, 1957, p. 590).

There are several research reports which comment on prognosis of women alcoholics. Davies, Shepherd and Myers (1956) comment that sex of the patient "had no prognostic significance." Of the 50 alcoholic patients they studied, 11 were women and of these 11, six fell into the best prognostic group "although women alcoholics are often stated to fare worse than men." Fox and Smith's (1959) report of treatment of 251 patients, 37 of them women, indicates *better* prognosis for women patients:

> A larger percentage of the women than of the men . . . responded favorably. . . . Seventy-five patients (26 per cent of the men and 51 per cent of the women) followed through the program and showed good progress. . . . Twenty-two patients (8 per cent of the men and 11 per cent of the women) followed the program irregularly but made some progress.

Glatt (1961) found a higher percentage of recovered and improved patients among male than among female alcoholics, approximately two-thirds of the men showing improvement as compared to half of the women. Pemberton's (1967) figures for improvement are more modest in general, although here again better prognosis for male patients is reported: 46% of the men were counted as "successful" in treatment as against 20% of the women patients. Finally, Curlee's (1970) report of private hospital patients shows more chronicity, "having been in and out of therapy repeatedly," among women patients than among men.

The picture is by no means clear. But it seems reasonable to conclude that there are some factors involved in prognosis which are different for the two sexes, and some which transcend sex differences. Factors like marital stability and intactness of the family, and certain patterns of drinking, e.g., intermittent as opposed to steady drinking, may be relevant for both sexes; work record may be a more relevant prognostic indicator for men, relationships and concern about children for women. It is a complex judgment involving as it does a patient's strengths, life situation and motivation for seeking help. The sex of the therapist is not unrelated to outcome either; it may be coincidence that the one study which reports more favorable response with women patients is by two professional women therapists.

THE WIVES OF ALCOHOLIC MEN

Since we are talking of women and alcoholism, there is another group of women who are deeply affected by alcohol abuse and problem drinking; these are the wives of men who are alcoholic. Much has been written on the subject. Interestingly enough, there has never been a single research report on the husbands of alcoholic women although there has been a great deal, popular and otherwise, written about the alcoholic women themselves.

A recent article (Edwards, Harvey and Whitehead, 1973) reviews the literature about wives of alcoholics. The reviewers describe three images of alcoholics' wives: first, she is an aggressive woman who marries an alcoholic so that she may dominate; second, she is a woman whose personality and behavior fluctuate with the different stresses in the various stages of family life with an alcoholic; third, she is a woman who may or may not have been maladjusted before marriage and who may or may not react to the stresses of her marriage with personality dysfunction. The first image, subjected to experimental studies, has found no evidence to support it. The second image, response to stress, has been validated insofar as there is evidence that the personalities of the wives do change with changes in the husband's involvement with alcohol. A derivative viewpoint of the first image was that wives would decompensate as their husbands became abstinent because their control would be threatened, but research reports indicate that wives tended to *improve,* not deteriorate, when husbands stopped drinking. Current research suggests that the wives of alcoholics are ". . . essentially normal personalities of different types," presumably indistinguishable from any sample of women undergoing some stress.

That it should have taken three decades to arrive at this view makes one wonder. The image of alcoholics' wives as aggressive and domineering women was popular at the same time that clinical psychiatric literature was replete with descriptions of the domineering mother and passive father who so frequently made up the early family history of psychiatric patients. The talk of Momism and the negative picture of alcoholic wives would seem to be part of a period in which clinicians wrote of bad mothers and bad wives as the dynamic forces of psychopathology.

But that is only part of the truth. The fact is that family patterns have undergone change, that sexual roles seem to be shifting, that families are more matriarchal and less patriarchal than they were half a century ago. We really are uncertain about the consequences of these changes and how they affect mental disorders. The families of alcoholics are part of a larger society in which these changes are occurring and how this relates to the dealings of husbands and wives in the families where the husband is alcoholic, we can only speculate.

SUMMARY

A point of view which has been prevalent describes the alcoholic woman as "much sicker" than her male counterpart. There is evidence of more disruption in early family life and more deviance in adolescence among women alcoholics than among men. It is inexorably logical that women, breaking through stronger taboos and more cultural restraints, are probably more deviant than men who develop alcohol problems. Nonetheless, we have not been able to separate out the consequences of alcoholism and the difficulties compounded by the drinking from what preceded the onset of alcoholism when patients present themselves. We really do not know to what extent failures in therapy are due to the greater deviance of alcoholic women, the conscious and unconscious attitudes of therapists toward alcoholic women, and/or the punitive consequences of the woman's drinking which have left her even more distrustful and difficult to reach than before.

The picture we get of the middle class, white, married woman in her 30's and 40's is one where early problems of childhood and adolescence have created a situation in which her needs for affection and support and reassurance are intense but her coping mechanisms are not good. Dependency and trust are problems for her and she looks to marriage and the traditional female role as her solution. She overbuys the feminine role but it does not seem to work out for her. Drinking almost always begins in social situations but alcohol turns out to have magical powers in that it serves many purposes for her simultaneously: oblivion, revenge, control, self-destruction. Most of the women we have seen clinically drink at home, more or less secretively, and this increases the isolation. The woman problem drinker is depressed, frustrated, angry. So she continues drinking.

The most effective motivator in looking for help seems to be trouble within the family, deep concerns about the woman's relationship with her husband and/or her children. If the marriage and family are intact, her chances are better because there are quite clear indications from the research literature that the greater the extent to which one is able to rehabilitate family life, including the woman's role in it, the better her chances of terminating her alcoholism.

We have virtually no information about women problem drinkers who are black, poor, or Lesbian. Studies of women who are careerists, with or without families, and who become alcoholic are rare; there are some autobiographies of women in the entertainment world who have had alcohol problems like Lillian Roth or Diana Barrymore and an occasional account by women executives who have been alcoholic (e.g., Kent, 1967). There are a few studies which discuss the older woman alcoholic, the widowed or "empty nest" drinker (Curlee, 1969). There are several studies of problem drinkers among women prisoners; most striking is their extreme isolation and the absolute dearth of anyone to take some emotional responsibility for them. A striking difference observed between more respectable outpatient clinic women alcoholics and women problem drinkers in a correctional state farm was the almost universal absence of *anyone* concerned about those in the latter group and the women prisoners' fantasies of loving, waiting mothers (Lisansky, 1957).

The problem in female alcoholism, as in other psychological disorders, is not so much a problem of double standard applied to diagnosis and therapy, but rather a problem of neglect. Virtually all psychiatric, psychological and sociological theory about alcoholism has been about men; the problem is perhaps too much of a single standard rather than a double one. Theory and practice has been derived from men's lives and men's experience and it has been assumed that this could be generalized to women, that there was little need for modification of theory and practice based on sex difference. At this moment, one of our major problems is the extent to which we can indeed generalize from male experience in the field of alcohol usage and alcohol problems. There is a sizable amount of anthropological data that show drinking customs in almost all societies to differ for men and women. Do alcohol problems differ, too, in etiology, dynamics, clinical manifestations and effective therapies? We have been discussing the differences but we should not get carried away by these differences and overlook the commonality of unhappiness, inadequate coping mechanisms and the attractions of alcohol which characterize the alcoholic, male or female.

REFERENCES

BARDWICK, J. M. *Psychology of Women.* New York: Harper and Row, 1971.

BELFER, M. L., SHADER, R. I., CARROLL, M., & HARMATZ, J. S. Alcoholism in women. *Archives of General Psychiatry*, 25, 540-544, 1971.

BLANE, H. T. *The Personality of the Alcoholic: Guises of Dependency.* New York: Harper and Row, 1968.

CALAHAN, D., CISLIN, I. H., & CROSSLEY, H. M. *American Drinking Practices: A National Study of Drinking Behavior and Attitudes.* New Haven: College and University Press, 1969.

CHILD, I. L., BARRY, H., III, & BACON, M. K. Sex differences: A cross-cultural study of drinking, *Quarterly Journal of Studies on Alcohol*, Supplement no. 3, 69-61, 1965.

COOPERSTOCK, R. Sex differences in the use of mood-modifying drugs: An explanatory model. *Journal of Health and Social Behavior,* 12, 238-244, 1971.

CRAMER, M. J. & BLACKER, E. "Early" and "late" problem drinkers among female prisoners. *Journal of Health and Human Behavior,* 4, 282-290, 1963.

CRAMER, M. J. & BLACKER, E. Social class and drinking experience of female drunkenness offenders. *Journal of Health and Human Behavior,* 7, 276-283, 1966.

CURLEE, J. Alcoholic women: Some considerations for further research. *Bulletin of the Menninger Clinic,* 31, 154-163, 1967.

CURLEE, J. Alcoholism and the "empty nest." *Bulletin of the Menninger Clinic,* 33, 165-171, 1969.

CURLEE, J. A comparison of male and female patients at an alcoholic treatment center. *The Journal of Psychology,* 74, 239-247, 1970.

CURLEE, J. Sex differences in patient attitude toward alcoholism treatment. *Quarterly Journal of Studies on Alcohol,* 32, 643-650, 1971.

DAVIES, D. L., SHEPHERD, M. & MYERS, E. The two-years' prognosis of 50 alcohol addicts after treatment in hospital. *Quarterly Journal of Studies on Alcohol,* 17, 485-502, 1956.

Differential Drug Use Within the New York State Labor Force, New York Narcotic Addiction Control Commission. Part of Commission research study: An assessment of drug use within the general population, 1971, 41 pp.

EDWARDS, G., HENSMAN, C., & PETO, J. Drinking in a London suburb. III. Comparisons of drinking troubles among men and women. *Quarterly Journal of Studies on Alcohol,* Supplement no. 6, 120-128, 1972.

EDWARDS, P., HARVEY, C., & WHITEHEAD, P. C. Wives of alcoholics: A critical review and analysis. *Quarterly Journal of Studies on Alcohol,* 34, 112-132, 1973.

ELLINWOOD, E. H., JR., SMITH, W. G., & VAILLANT, G. E. Narcotic addiction in males and females: A comparison. *The International Journal of the Addictions,* 1, 33-45, 1966.

FORT, T. W. A preliminary study of social factors in the alcoholism of women. Masters thesis, Texas Christian University, 1949.

FOX, V. & SMITH, M. A. Evaluation of a chemopsychotherapeutic program for the rehabilitation of alcoholics: Observations over a two-year period. *Quarterly Journal of Studies on Alcohol,* 20, 767-780, 1959.

GLATT, M. M. Treatment results in an English mental hospital alcoholic unit. *Acta Psychiatrica Scandinavica,* 37, 143-168, 1961.

GOMBERG, E. S. Alcoholism in women. In B. Kissin and H. Begleiter (Eds.), *The Biology of Alcoholism.* Volume 4. *Social Biology.* New York: Plenum Press, in press.

GOVE, W. R. & TUDOR, J. F. Adult sex roles and mental illness. In J. Huber (Ed.), *Changing Women in a Changing Society.* University of Chicago Press, pp. 50-73, 1973.

HOLZBERG, J. D. Sex differences in schizophrenia. In H. Beigel (Ed.), *Advances in Sex Research.* New York: Harper and Row, 1963.

HORN, J. L. & WANBERG, K. W. Females are different: Some difficulties in diagnosing problems of alcohol use in women. Paper presented at the First Annual Conference of the National Institute on Alcohol Abuse and Alcoholism, Washington, D. C., June 1971.

HOWELLS, J. G. (Ed.). *Modern Perspectives in Psycho-Obstetrics.* New York: Brunner/Mazel, 1972.

JACOB, A. G. & LAVOIE, C. A study of some characteristics of a group of women alcoholics. Paper presented at the Conference of the North American Association of Alcoholism Programs, Hartford, Connecticut, June, 1971.

JOHNSON, M. W. Physicians' views on alcoholism with special reference to alcoholism in women. *Nebraska State Medical Journal*, 50, 378-384, 1965.

JOHNSON, M. W., DEVRIES, J. C., & HOUGHTON, M. I. The female alcoholic. *Nursing Research*, 15, 1966.

JONES, M. C. Personality correlates and antecedents of drinking patterns in adult males. *Journal of Consulting and Clinical Psychology*, 32, 2-12, 1968.

JONES, M. C. Personality antecedents and correlates of drinking patterns in women. *Journal of Consulting and Clinical Psychology*, 36, 61-69, 1971.

KARPMAN, B. *The Alcoholic Woman*. Washington, D. C.: Linacre Press, 1948.

KENT, P. *An American Woman and Alcohol*. New York: Holt, Rinehart and Winston, 1967.

KINSEY, B. A. *The Female Alcoholic: A Social Psychological Study*. Springfield, Ill.: Charles C Thomas, 1966.

KNIGHT, R. P. The psychodynamics of chronic alcoholism. *The Journal of Nervous and Mental Disease*, 86, 538-548, 1937.

KNUPFER, G. Female drinking patterns. Paper presented at the Fifteenth Annual Meeting of the North American Association of Alcoholism Programs, Washington, D. C., September, 1964.

LAWRENCE, J. J. & MAXWELL, M. A. Drinking and socio-economic status. In D. J. Pittman and C. R. Snyder (Eds.), *Society, Culture and Drinking Patterns*. New York: Wiley, 1962.

LINDBECK, V. The woman alcoholic: A review of the literature. *The International Journal of Addictions*, 7, 567-580, 1972.

LISANSKY, E. S. Alcoholism in women: Social and psychological concomitants. I. Social history data. *Quarterly Journal of Studies on Alcohol*, 18, 588-623, 1957.

MAYER, J. & GREEN, M. Group therapy of alcoholic women ex-prisoners. *Quarterly Journal of Studies on Alcohol*, 28, 493-504, 1967.

MCKINLAY, A. P. The Roman attitude toward women's drinking. In R. G. McCarthy (Ed.), *Drinking and Intoxication*. Glencoe, Illinois: The Free Press, 1959.

MYERSON, D. J. Clinical observations on a group of alcoholic prisoners, with special reference to women. *Quarterly Journal of Studies on Alcohol*, 20, 555-572, 1959.

O'DONNELL, J. A., BESTEMAN, K. J., & JONES, J. P. Marital history of narcotics addicts. *The International Journal of Addictions*, 2, 21-38, 1966.

PARKER, F. B. Sex-role adjustment in women alcoholics. *Quarterly Journal of Studies on Alcohol*, 33, 647-657, 1972.

PEMBERTON, D. A. A comparison of the outcome of treatment in male and female alcoholics. *British Journal of Psychiatry*, 113, 367-373, 1967.

PFAUTZ, H. W. The image of alcohol in popular fiction: 1900-1904 and 1946-1950. *Quarterly Journal of Studies on Alcohol*, 23, 131-146, 1962.

RATHOD, N. H. & THOMSON, I. G. Women alcoholics, a clinical study. *Quarterly Journal of Studies on Alcohol*, 32, 45-52, 1971.

RILEY, J. W., JR. & MARDEN, C. F. The social pattern of alcoholic drinking. *Quarterly Journal of Studies on Alcohol*, 8, 265-273, 1947.

ROBINS, L. N. *Deviant Children Grown Up*. Baltimore: Williams and Wilkins, 1966.

ROSENBAUM, B. Married women alcoholics at the Washingtonian Hospital. *Quarterly Journal of Studies on Alcohol*, 19, 79-89, 1958.

SCLARE, A. B. The female alcoholic. *British Journal of Addiction*, 65, 99-107, 1970.

SCHUCKIT, M. The woman alcoholic: A literature review. *Psychiatry in Medicine*, 3, 37-42, 1972.

SCHUCKIT, M., PITTS, F. N., REICH, T., KING, L. J., & WINOKUR, G. Alcoholism. I. Two types of alcoholism in women. *Archives of Environmental Health*, 18, 301-306, 1969.

WANBERG, K. W. & KNAPP, J. Differences in drinking symptoms and behavior of men and women alcoholics. *British Journal of Addictions*, 64, 347-355, 1970.
WETZEL, R. D. & McCLURE, J. N. Suicide and the menstrual cycle: A review. *Comprehensive Psychiatry*, 13, 369-374, 1972.
WIDSETH, J. C. Dependent behavior and alcohol use in delinquent girls. Paper presented at the meeting of the Eastern Psychological Association, New York, April, 1971.
WIDSETH, J. C. & MAYER, J. Drinking behavior and attitude toward alcohol in delinquent girls. *The International Journal of Addictions*, 6, 453-461, 1971.
WILSNACK, S. C. The needs of the female drinker: Dependency, power, or what? Paper presented at the Second Annual Alcoholism Conference of the National Institute on Alcohol Abuse and Alcoholism, Washington, D. C., June, 1972.
WILSNACK, S. C. Sex-role identity in female alcoholism. *Journal of Abnormal Psychology*, 82, 253-261, 1973.
WOOD, H. P. & DUFFY, E. L. Psychological factors in alcoholic women. *American Journal of Psychiatry*, 123, 341-345, 1964.

8

NEW VIEWPOINTS ON THE FEMALE HOMOSEXUAL

BERNARD F. RIESS

As with so much of psychological and clinical terminology, the word "homosexuality" has been misused and misapplied in numerous ways. For the clinician, the term is generally accepted as a diagnostic label describing a complex sex of personality factors and connoting or implying psychopathology. Also, for the behavioral scientist, the word generally does not differentiate between the male and female whose behavior is thus described. Nor does the average behavioral scientist see the phenomenon as part of a sexual continuum—people are either-or. In most psychological and psychoanalytic writing, the lack of differentiation is endemic. A good illustration of this is the book by Bieber *et al.* (1962) whose major title is *Homosexuality* despite the fact that it includes a study of only males and only male patients. Finally, homosexuality and homosexual have become generalized qualifiers which both describe certain behaviors and simultaneously imply pathology for all those who fit the action. The confusion is increased by the use of the term "latent" homosexuality, often serving to reinforce a diagnosis in the absence of any behavioral act or acts to support the diagnosis.

From the above, it should be obvious that this chapter has a bias, a prejudice in favor of looking at and evaluating what objective evidence there is before coming to any conclusions about the implications of behaviors. This chapter will, accordingly, be organized around a fairly rigorous scheme. This involves, first, a clean, i.e., implicit, assumption-free description and definition of the phenomena under scrutiny. There will

---

Since the manuscript for this chapter was completed, the American Psychiatric Association has removed homosexuality from its official list of psychopathologies and retitled it as a "sexual orientation disorder" which becomes pathology only when it interferes with the emotional or personality functioning of the individual.

then follow a survey of the variables which have been researched as somehow related to homosexuality *in women*. Conclusions from this survey will be compared and contrasted with data obtained from studies of women heterosexuals and male homosexuals. The data will also be looked at in the light of varying theories concerning homosexuality and the so-called homosexual personality. Finally, an attempt wil be made to relate the whole area to the development of self-identity in woman.

WHAT IS HOMOSEXUALITY?

One of the pioneers in the scientific study of sexuality, Kinsey, has this to say about the definition of homosexuality (1948, p. 617): "It would encourage clearer thinking on these matters if persons were not characterized as heterosexual or homosexual, but as individuals who have had certain amounts of heterosexual experience and certain amounts of homosexual experience. Instead of using these terms as substantives which stand for persons or adjectives to describe persons, they may better be used to describe the nature of the overt sexual reactions, or the stimuli to which an individual erotically responds." Thus, overt female-female sexual acts define one kind of homosexuality. The last clause of the Kinsey quotation opens a wider field, for stimuli to erotic responses may be imaginal, affective or unconscious. Sydney Abbott and Barbara Love in *Sappho Was a Right-On Woman* (1972, pp. 26-27) put the question this way: "At what moment does a woman step outside the boundary of acceptable relations with women? When she feels emotion for another woman? If she becomes bisexual? Only if she sleeps for a time exclusively with one woman?" Even if she has had a single sexual experience with a woman, she will be labeled a Lesbian if the experience becomes known. A psychiatrist with many homosexual patients, when asked to define a Lesbian, replied, "A Lesbian is a woman who says she is." Thus, the range of reactions which lead to the name-tag of homosexual is wide indeed.

Another factor needs also to be discussed here. There are some sociological and environmental conditions which facilitate homosexual acting by their enforced restriction of heterosexual experience. Prisoners, isolated from others of the opposite sex, express their sexuality with people of their own sex. This is not meant to imply that heterosexuality is the "normal" form of relationship, but only that sexual appetites and drives seek satiation in whatever form is available. In a California study of female prisoners convicted of felonies, 75-80% of the confined women engaged in homosexual activity, but of these, only 7-10% exhibited or had shown similar behavior outside of jail. Similarly, girls' camps and segregated schools may encourage a given form of sexual behavior. These cultural pressures may prevent the free choice of a love-partner or sex partner and so complicate any clear-cut delineation of homosexuality. In this chapter we shall not deal with women whose choices are determined by their enforced segregation. So too, in this chapter we will not deal specifically with the transient and casual homoerotic encounters of adolescence. This developmental period is one of exploration and testing in which the individual has not made a considered choice of a sexual way of life. Indeed, it resembles more what Stoller has to say about infrahuman homosexuality. "What we call homosexuality in animals is not at all what we see in man. Animals other than man do not choose another of the same sex for intercourse although they occasionally mount one haphazardly for a moment or languidly lick each other's genitalia" (1973, p. 348).

FEMALE HOMOSEXUALITY

One of the significant findings in any survey of homosexuality is that much more is written about and researched on men than on women. Until very recently, female homosexuality was mentioned mainly in case material and not thought worthy of research. Only the outstanding publications and articles will be cited here.

West's (1967) book on homosexuality is very general but does contain some pages on women. Cory's (1963) book on women homosexuals, although endorsed by Albert Ellis, is basically a male homosexual's description of his female counterpart. Magee (1966) has a short, good, layman's approach. The emergence of the women's liberation movement brought with it a more militant approach by Lesbians and several recent publications have added much to the literature but little to research on the topic. Such sociopolitical pressures bear not so mute testimony to the effects of a male dominated world.

More subtle, perhaps, are the points made by Szasz (1961, 1965). This author shows conclusively that naming homosexuality as an illness does not release it from a bias arising from value judgments and inconsistencies. Nowhere are the pseudoscientific rationalizations so apparent as in the distinction between legal penalties for male homosexuality and the legal indifference to similar female behavior. Szasz contends that male homosexuality is a problem for society because the homosexual undermines that most moral and economic value, namely heterosexuality.

It is somewhat in line with this male chauvinist viewpoint to look at the data on frequency of female homosexuality. Most authorities claim it to be much less often found than male homosexuality. Among infra-human primates no exclusive female-female pattern has been reported nor have orgasms resulting from the casual contacts been observed. Even in primitive peoples, Ford and Beach (1951) find few instances. The Mohave Indian culture was the only one in which female homosexuality was tabooed. Of the 76 groups studied by Ford and Beach, in 27 only was there mention of the occurrence of female homosexuality.

Within Western culture there have been two major contributions to frequency data. Kinsey (1953) in his volume on female homosexuality reports 13% of his sample to have had some homosexual experience, but this figure may be high since his total study population was heavily loaded with unmarried women (58.2% of the total). Kenyon (1968) believes, on the basis of "guesstimate," that Lesbianism occurs in the order of one to 45 of adult women in England. No data exist on a time-related frequency distribution.

PSYCHOLOGICAL TESTS AND FEMALE HOMOSEXUALITY

Riess, Safer and Yotive (1974) surveyed all that has been so far published on the personality assessment of women homosexuals, mainly studies which use projective methods but also including some paper-and-pencil tests.

The survey found that most studies suffered from the same methodological errors and difficulties which plague all test research. First among these errors is the use of criteria for women based on signs discovered for males. Whether or not the male signs identify women homosexuals can only be valid when independent study of women has been done. A sign that predicts male sexual behavior may be merely a vocational or so-called masculine attitude on the part of the woman. Second, the signs, particularly on the Rorschach, have a history of inconsistency in selecting even male homosexuals. Finally, the research is contaminated by assumptions derived from Freud's concepts of the "psyche" of the woman. Much of the testing has originated with hypotheses developed from Freudian theory. What is seen by the researcher in the Rorschach protocols is often inferentially related to sexual and homosexual factors. So, if one believes with Freud that homosexuality represents arrested or regressed development, the raw data may be interpreted to bolster or counter the hypotheses. The natural field methodology and the ethological approaches have not as yet been applied to the assessment of female personality whether hetero- or homosexual.

The balance of this section will deal with selected samples of the research data in order both to point to the problems involved in assessment and to show the major consistencies and divergences among the researchers. Since much of the data involves technical features of projective techniques such as the Rorschach, the reader is referred to the original contribution for details. Several of the researchers have given their names to a series of Rorschach scores which have been called "signs" for male homosexuality. These combinations of Rorschach indices will be described only by the names of their contributors and not explicated in the text of this chapter.

Armon (1960) tested two groups of subjects, one of 30 self-identified women homosexuals and the other of 30 heterosexual persons. All were non-patients and had had no therapy. Tests included the Rorschach, Draw-a-Person and the Terman-Miles Masculinity-Femininity Scale. The results of the Rorschach showed no difference in regressive or primitive responses, no difference in fear of masculine hostile-aggressive attitudes, no difference in sexual identity and no difference in pathological thinking. The only differentiating scores showed heterosexual women to have freer emotional reactivity to others than the homosexuals. The DAP drawings were evaluated blindly by clinicians who were unable to separate protocols from the two groups. Armon's conclusion is that "the failure to find clear-cut differences which are consistent for the majority of the group would suggest that homosexuality is not a clinical entity. On the basis of present indications it would seem unwise to make generalizations about female homosexuals as a group or to assume that homosexuality is associated with gross personality disorders. The absence of a dramatic difference between homosexuals and heterosexuals on projective tests should influence the conception that homosexuality is necessarily associated with deep regression and concordant limitations in personality functioning."

Hopkins (1970) specifically studied male Rorschach signs in the protocols of 24 women homosexuals, 24 heterosexual women and five heterosexuals with sexual pathology. Certain signs set off the Lesbian from the heterosexual group: Lesbians gave fewer responses (interpreted by Hopkins as indicating greater reserve), and showed indications of more disturbed relationships with the mother. This latter conclusion was based on responses to Card VII. Only 2% of Lesbians selected this card as one of the most liked compared to 15% of the heterosexuals and 26% of the sexually disturbed.

These studies are characteristic of the projective researches. One other study deserves mention. Freedman (1967) selected two comparable groups, 62 self-identified homosexuals, members of a homophilic association, and 67 organizationally-active heterosexual women. Personal data sheets and two paper-and-pencil personality inventories were used. He found that there was no difference a) in ratings of psychological adjustment, b) in measurements of neuroticism, c) in variability of results, d) in self-acceptance. Where differences appeared at a significant level, heterosexual women were less inner-directed and accepted aggression more easily.

Other studies using questionnaires and personality inventories have been reported by Wilson and Greene (1971) and Siegelman (1972). In both, on a series of instruments, no evidence was found of pathological differences or neuroticism. In Wilson and Greene, surprisingly, the heterosexuals scored somewhat higher on neurotic traits than the homosexuals. However, in both researches, homosexuals tended to be more dominant, a finding also suggested in Hopkins' work. Thus, these studies all agree on the relative lack of differences among homosexual and heterosexual test responses.

The major research finding indicative of differences between the two groups come from England. Kenyon (1968a and b) tested 123 homosexual women and 123 heterosexuals, although the homosexuals were predominantly bisexual with lots of heterosexual experiences. Results from two personality inventories showed greater neuroticism in the homosexual group.

In conclusion, it should be emphasized that all these studies dealt only with middle- or upper-class women and did not differentiate between "exclusive" homosexuals, bi-sexuals or heterosexually married homosexuals.

At this point, it may be of interest to question how the findings about psychological test differences between hetero- and homosexual women compare with similar research on males. Van Aardweg (1969) surveyed the field for male homosexuals. In a thorough analysis of the literature, he comes to these conclusions.

> The Rorschach is useless for the individual diagnosis of personality. . . . There is no specific "homosexual Rorschach" . . . The T.A.T. (Thematic Apperception Test) is probably useful for individual diagnosis of homosexuality as a so-called "broad band" test. Sometimes one may come up with something—perhaps more often not. . . .

There are no indications that a T.A.T. protocol specific for homosexuality can be found, except when the story tells of an overtly homosexual relationship. . . . The T.A.T. lends itself better than the Rorschach to the examination of the phantasy and the inner life of homosexuals. . . .

Among the relationships which did show up, particularly on questionnaire-type material, was a greater tendency toward femininity among homosexuals. This was used by the researchers as an indicator of neuroticism. The definition of neuroticism therefore seems to be influenced by the somewhat archaic stereotypes of the investigator. In other studies, a finding of greater passivity in male homosexuals as exhibited in receptive fellatio was interpreted as neurotic because for a male to be passive is a maladaptive feature and hence neurotic. All in all, it is apparent that the data on male homosexuals are no more conclusive than those derived from testing female homosexuals.

CHARACTERISTICS OF THE FEMALE HOMOSEXUAL

Whether or not one accepts homosexuality as a clinical entity or even as a clinical symptom, there is a need for a systematic description of the people who are so labeled, their origins, early family and sexual history, events during adolescence and early adult life, relationships with people and attitudes toward self.

Such a study needs correlative research, first on a comparison group of heterosexuals and then on a cross-sex study of both homo- and heterosexuals. This is a tremendous task and one that has not been nearly approximated. There are, however, two studies of the female homosexual which are now available and which accomplish in part the description of the "natural history" of their subjects. One of these studies is that of Gundlach and Riess (1968). The other is by Saghir and Robins (1973).

The purpose of the Gundlach-Riess study was to develop some parameters of self-identification as a female. The significance of female homosexuality for this purpose is stated as follows:

It is our belief that training in skills and values, in the preparation for life goals acceptable within our society is different for men and women. Their perceptions of "their" world are different from each other although they live in the same homes, utilize the same equipment, and frequent the same stores and institutions. Hopes, expectations, appraisals of situations, especially those involving human relationships, are markedly different for males and females. Men are indoctrinated to want to be masculine and women to be feminine.

> Insofar as this view is correct, the homosexual is then the result at
> some point of a failure of indoctrination in the socialization of the
> child and its acceptance of a conventionally-expected social role.

Since, therefore, homosexuality represents, in unequivocal behavioral
fashion, a rejection of conventional sex-role activity, a study of its practitioners will reveal some of the ways in which self-identification and social
factors interplay.

In the Gundlach-Riess study, a group of 226 self-identified homosexual,
adult women was obtained through the cooperation of the Daughters
of Bilitis, a female, homophile, national organization. The 234 heterosexual adult women in the comparison group came from friends of the
investigators. Comparability of the two groups was attempted by matching the homosexual respondent with the heterosexual woman of the
same age, educational level, geographical area and size of place of residence over the U.S.A. Again, as in the psychological test studies, the
population was predominantly middle-class white. The subjects in both
groups were non-patients although 41% of the Lesbians and 43% of the
non-Lesbians had had some psychotherapeutic experience. In addition to
these two groups, the research included 24 homosexual and 28 non-homo-
sexual patients, all of whom were in treatment with professional colleagues of the investigators.

For the two large groups, each participant was sent a questionnaire on
early life experiences and sexual behavior. This consisted of 450 items
covering the areas of socioeconomic status, family structure, relations with
father, mother, siblings, recollections of attitudes of their parents to them
and their attitudes to their parents, adolescent and post-adolescent social
life, sexual life and feelings about self as female. Data about the patient
groups were also obtained both from the patients on the same questionnaire and from their therapists on a different questionnaire.

At a later stage, a semantic differential check list for the concepts man,
woman, father, mother, lover, friend was sent to all participants. Similarly,
a booklet in which human figure drawings with thematic stories were to be
completed was distributed to both groups. Because the methodology protected the anonymity of the respondents while still insuring, where necessary, continued mail contact, it was possible to get information not fore-
seen but called for by a study of the questionnaire results.

The data thus generated are much too bulky to be adequately dealt
with in this chapter. Three aspects of the material will be selected for
attention: significant differences between and similarities among (1) the

TABLE 1

Social Relations Before Puberty of Female Homosexual and Comparison Groups

Items	Homo. (N=226)	Comp. (N=234)
1. Before C.A. 12, played mostly with girls	25	42
2. Before C.A. 12, played mostly with boys	31	9
3. Who were your *real* friends?—Girls	57	75
4. Who were your *real* friends?—Neither boys nor girls	18	7
5. a. Subject was found in sex play before C.A. 12	36	27*
b. A big fuss was made over the discovery	19	12*
c. Subject's sex partner was male	27	19*
6. Subject was known as a tomboy	78	48
7. Before menstruation, subject wanted to be a boy	48	15
8. Subject excelled in athletics	54	29
9. Subject idealized or wanted to be like a female teacher	35	16
10. Subject did not want to be like father	26	15
11. Don't remember or didn't have sexual attraction to a male before menstruation	69	45
12. Don't remember or didn't have sexual attraction to a female before menstruation	38	84

* All differences except those marked with a * are significant at least at the .01 level.

homosexual (H) and comparison group (C); (2) the H who had or were in therapy with the H who were not; and (3) comparisons between the male and female H and C groups using the Bieber *et al.* (1962) study for males.

Basing the discussion first on the questionnaire results, there were surprisingly few statistically significant differences between H and C in responses about family and parent-child relationships.

Demological items showing statistically significant differences included: 1) education, where more H than C had less than high school education (36% H, 22% C) and more technical or professional degrees (25% H, 19% C); 2) religion, with more H than C among Catholics (18% H, 7% C) and fewer among Jews (11% H, 25% C). The Protestants divided almost equally (57% H, 50% C); 3) Previous therapy: more H than C had therapy before the age of 20, fewer H had 100 sessions or more and fewer H than C reported treatment as successful (8% H, 18% C). On the remaining items differences were not significant.

An attempt to get at the problems arising from different subsets of each population led to the study of self-concept as more or less feminine in singles, married or lesbian relationships, divorced or separated. In

TABLE 2

Attitudes About Menstruation of Female
Homosexual and Comparison Groups

Items	Homo. (N=226)	Comp. (N=234)
1. Subject felt resigned about first menstruation	29	13
2. Subject felt grown up about first menstruation	23	42
3. Subject felt more attractive in body after first menstruation	10	30
4. Subject felt resentful or ashamed about body after first menstruation	23	7

All differences are significant at least at the .01 level.

TABLE 3

Teen-age Social Behavior of Female Homosexual
and Comparison Groups

Items	Homo. (N=226)	Comp. (N=234)
1. How did you spend your time during your teens? —Socializing in mixed groups	18	41
2. —With boys	10	22
3. There was no or hardly any dating	56	25
4. Did you hug and kiss during high school dating with many boys or with a steady boyfriend?	37	54
5. Subject went beyond hugging and kissing in high school dating	36	47
6. Subject had intercourse during high school dating	12	14*

* All differences except those marked with * are significant at least at the .01 level.

many of the cross-comparisons, the H subgroup was more like a C subgroup than like other H groups. About 10% of the homosexuals were married heterosexually at the time of the study. Twenty per cent had been divorced or separated and 20% had children. A vast majority (83%) of the homosexual women had had a relationship lasting over one year and 17% had a 10-year or longer relationship. Contrasting startlingly to the picture among males, very few women (less than 2% of both H and C) said they sought partners for just a brief encounter.

Tables 1 through 5 are drawn from the chapter by Gundlach and Riess (1968). In most respects they are self-revealing and require little comment here. Generalizing, it appears that homosexuals were more

Table 4

Adult Sexual Attitudes and Relationships of Female
Homosexual and Comparison Groups

Items	Homo. (N=226)	Comp. (N=234)
1. What are your feelings about your femininity as an adult?		
a. decidedly feminine	12	43
b. more feminine than masculine	25	41
c. a little of both	40	16
d. more masculine than feminine	27	1
e. decidedly masculine	2	0*
2. Capacity to have orgasms:		
—easily	58	42
—sometimes or rarely	33	45
3. a. You can have sex without love	27	27*
b. You can have sex only with person you love	64	64*
c. You can have love without much sex	31	19
4. Defloration is a promotion into womanhood	6	25
5. How did you feel when the lover relationship ended?		
a. as if a piece of me were torn off	44	17
b. suicidal	16	4

* All differences except those marked with * are significant at least at the .01 level.

Table 5

You Can't Say the Girls Don't Try

Items	Homo. (N=226)	Comp. (N=234)
1. a. Subject had intercourse with a male	75	94
b. But without climax	42	9
2. Subject was		
a. object of rape or attempted rape	31	21
b. at age 11 or under	13	3
3. Subject had sexual contact or caresses with a female	98	51
4. Subject was married at one time	29	79
5. Time with male partner		
—1 to 9 years	21	48
—10 or more years	12	40
6. Time with female partner		
—1 to 9 years	66	2
—10 or more years	17	0
7. Subject had children of her own	20	64

All differences are significant at least at the .01 level.

involved non-sexually with boys during their early years. They also had less favorable attitudes to their initial menses and socialized less than the comparisons.

As adults, the homosexuals felt less feminine, less a need for purely sexual gratification and were more easily aroused to orgasm than their heterosexual comparisons. Finally, there are data about intercourse with males and caresses or contact with females. Penetration before the age of 17 was experienced by 17% H and 12% C. At ages 17-20, the figures are 28% H and 37% C. Female-female contact occurred with a frequency of 21% for each group before C.A. 10, 24% H and 13% C at ages 11-15, 31% H and 5% C at 16-20 and 22% H and 3% C from 21 to 30. Thus, over half the homosexuals did not initiate their sexual behavior until they were in their late teens or early twenties.

A few other comparisons not found in these tables prove of interest in the quest for differentiating features of the homosexual female. Although more H than C have orgasms easily and frequently, their answers differed to the question, "If you have a fairly permanent sexual partner, who decides when to have sex?" Here 8% of the H group followed their partner's lead as contrasted to 32% of the C women. Also *sexual* activity was less frequent in H than C females ("rarely engage in sex," 42% H, 3% C). Factors other than sex are of importance to homosexual women although sex itself is very satisfying. Less compliance in sex is also true of the H group. Going further into the meaning of the interpersonal relationship, the importance of marriage for the heterosexual was most often stated thus: "to find great happiness and shared love" or "to live with a man who loves ME." The homosexual women's first choices were "her *interest* in ME" and "her kindness and warmth." The meaning of the female-female relationship seems to be different; it depends less on sex than on love and more on warmth, contact, a sense of oneness.

The straightforward tallies of questionnaire data illustrated above were felt to reflect, perhaps, a selective type of recall by the two sets of participants. A new statistical stratagem was then devised to attempt a variant of cross-validational technique. The semantic differential responses were used for these purposes. Each of the concepts—man, woman, father, mother—was described by choices between opposites in 32 sets of adjectives. These choices were obviously independent of and unrelated to the questionnaires answered some months earlier than the semantic differential. The S.D. reactions from all respondents, whether H or C, were thrown into a single data population and a factorial analysis of the four concepts, taken as a single test, was computed. This resulted in the emergence of 14 relatively independent factors. The next step was then to see which women, H or C, constituted the individuals represented by factor 1, 2, etc. The last phase was to look at the adjective choices determining the various factors and to infer some generalizations from the choices. Thus, from the 14 factors and the total population of women, six subgroups of subjects were generated, ranging in size from one containing 25% of the entire group to one of 5% of the population. Each group was defined in terms of extreme scores of factor loadings on one or more of the 14 factors, differing on each factor from the answers of the remainder of the total group. A surprising result was that the four concepts, mother, father, man, woman, each subsumed three factors but the combined factors, woman-mother and father-man, were represented by one factor each.

Turning to the people who constituted each of the six subgroups, the distribution of H and C women was as follows: Group I had 13 H and 37 C; Group 2, 12 H and 22 C; Group 3, 22 H, 10 C; Group 4, 34 H, 1 C; Group 5, 10 H and 24 C; and Group 6, 2 H and 8 C. Thus only in one group (G 4) did the answers significantly discriminate between hetero- and homosexuals. It is clear that expressed choice of descriptive words for father, mother, man and woman did not primarily depend on whether the respondents were homosexual or heterosexual or whether they had therapy or not.

The next question pertains to the factors which describe each group. In G 1, (13 H and 37 C) the women have positive feelings toward man, woman, mother and father, and good family relations. G 2 (12 H, 22 C) is basically anti-mother; G 3 (22 H, 10 C) shows anti-father, anti-mother, anti-man choices; G 4 (34 H, 1 C) is pro-father, pro-mother and anti-man; G 5 (10 H, 24 C) is pro-father and anti-woman and mother. Finally Group 6 (2 H and 8C) is pro-mother, anti-father and anti-woman. Family relationships and attitudes toward men and women do not seem clearly to set off homosexual women from heterosexuals. Even the one wholly H group is pro-father and pro-mother and negative only to man. This certainly casts doubt on the projection of feelings about father to feelings about men in general. It also, by inference, enlarges factors from familial influence to more social and societal pressures. Another finding (Gundlach and Riess, 1967) further suggests the same need to seek explanations along broader lines. These investigators found that more homosexual than heterosexual women were only children or firstborn into families with one other child. Where family size included five or more sizes, the last born tended, if a female, to be more frequently a homosexual. These birth order data are the reverse of findings with males (Bieber, 1962). A recent survey (Riess and Safer, 1973) of birth order among patients at the Postgraduate Center for Mental Health, covering a population of 2474 terminated cases, shows that, regardless of sex, the oldest in small families and the youngest in large families are much more apt to turn up as patients than expected from a normal population. Thus, the situation as regards birth order of homosexual women is the same as that of the population of an out-patient treatment facility and not an isolated phenomenon.

The other important study of homosexuality in a non-patient population was done by Saghir and Robins (1973). They selected two groups of women, 57 homosexual and 43 heterosexual, the former from the Daughters of Bilitis. Each subject went through an intensive, structured interview to "evaluate the homosexual propensity with its antecedents and behavioral manifestations. Specifically, the interview was concerned with data about demographic variables, psychopathological occurrences, the evolution and development of homosexual and heterosexual orientation, the behavioral and sexual practices of each individual, her family relationships and roles and involvements with others and in her particular environment." Thus, the goals of the Gundlach-Riess and the Saghir-Robins study are much the same but arrived at by different means.

Although the two groups of homosexual women came from almost the same sources there were some differences in demographic data. For the Saghir-Robins groups, both homo- and heterosexual, marriage was less frequent than in the Gundlach-Riess material. Single homosexual women constituted 75% of the Saghir-Robins study and only 30% of the Gundlach-Riess. Divorce and separation had a frequency of 23% in Saghir-Robins and 14% in Gundlach-Riess and marriage was 2% in the former and 13% in the latter study. The origin of the study samples may explain some of the observed demologic differences. The Saghir-Robins women were all urban people living in Chicago or San Francisco, while the Gundlach-Riess subjects came from all sections of the United States and from rural and suburban as well as metropolitan centers.

Within the scope of this chapter it is impossible to do justice to the data from the Saghir-Robins book. There are many points of difference between it and the Gundlach-Riess report. To what extent these arise from the smaller number or urban location of the former research remains to be investigated.

Skimming the conclusions from the first study, here is the picture that emerges. In childhood some homosexuals (⅔ of the Saghir-Robins study) were tomboys, but this finding has ambivalent interpretations since it seems to be affected by parental expectations and modeling after teachers and parents. Conscious, overt sexualization occurs later in adolescence among homosexual women and is frequently tied to crushes on women teachers. Homosexual women have had many heterosexual experiences but their homosexual relations are long-lasting and homosexuality is reportedly "rewarding and total in its expression." Voyeurism, sadomasochism and mass sexual activity are rarely found among the homosexual female.

The findings on pathology among the two groups of women show a greater degree of maladjustment among the homosexuals but this is accounted for by a single item—alcoholism. Other homo- and heterosexual adjustment dissimilarities include a greater trend to drop out of college and to have less concern for so-called feminine behavior and dress. "The homosexual woman is not more neurotic or psychotic, although she tends to seek psychotherapy more often." The depression which brings a homosexual woman to therapy is usually a "bereavement" state because of the break-up of a relationship. However, despite these emotional differences, Saghir and Robins found no significant increase in impairment of functioning.

The general conclusions fit into the pattern of other findings. "Homosexuals are not *a priori* sick. Many of them present little or no psychopathology and those who do are rarely disabled by their disorder. . . . We believe that treating homosexuality as a disease and homosexuals as patients is neither scientifically tenable nor actually feasible and practical."

The next comparison goes more deeply into the area of treatment of homosexuals. It seeks to determine what items on the Gundlach-Riess questionnaire separated the women who had therapy from those who did not within both the H and C groups. The data are shown in Table 6. Of the 229 heterosexuals, 98 had experienced therapy in comparison with 90 of the 226 homosexual women. The items in the left hand column are the only ones which statistically and significantly differentiated both H from C and therapy from non-therapy. The first two columns include the percentages on each item from the comparison, therapy and non-therapy subgroups. In the next two columns are shown similar percentages for the homosexuals with and without therapy. The last set of columns gives the significances of differences for the total subsets of therapy—non-therapy and homosexual—comparison groups. Thus, Jewish as a parental religion was significantly more prevalent in the therapy

TABLE 6

Items Significantly Differentiating Percentages of H, C, Therapy and Non-Therapy Women

	C.		H.		Significance of Diffs.	
	No Ther. (131) col. 1	Ther. (98) col. 2	No Ther. (136) col. 3	Ther. (90) col.4	Cols. 1,3 vs. 2,4	Cols. 1,2 vs. 3,4
1. Parents' religion? Jewish	20	**38	8	**26	**	**
2. Did either parent undermine you with the other? No	82	*68	77	**59	**	**
3. Parents' attitude toward you as a girl?						
a) Both accepted me	89	**68	75	**50	**	**
b) Other	2	* 9	8	*19	**	**
4. Was mother sexually seductive?						
a) No	95	**81	84	76	**	**
b) Seductive but unaware	1	6	5	12	*	*
5. Mother usually let me do what I wanted if reasonable	75	**50	63	*48	**	*
6. Response to mother's requests or pressures? Usually comply	51	39	42	**23	**	**
7. How did mother usually punish? Withdrawal	13	**34	10	**21	**	**
8. Did father have a favorite child? No	52	*37	33	27	*	**
9. Did father have a least favored child? No	66	*51	57	*40	**	*
10. Did father encourage or discourage feminine attitudes in you? Neither	53	46	66	53	*	*
11. Father was warm, loving, affectionate	56	**33	41	30	**	*
12. Attitude toward father?						
a) Respect	63	50	50	*32	**	**
b) Love	78	**53	56	46	**	**
13. Father a good parent? Yes, better than average	49	**22	35	**18	**	*
14. Brother or sister seductive before first menstruation? No	78	66	65	56	*	**
15. Recall attraction to male before menstruation? No	31	*15	54	42	**	**

*=.05 level of significance.
**=.01 level of significance.

than non-therapy groups, and also more frequent among heterosexuals than among homosexuals. In general, the progression of disturbance seems to be from the comparisons with no therapy to the homosexuals who had therapy. There are some exceptions to this but the table sufficiently demonstrates that no simple picture of the relationships of women in or not in therapy and homosexuality can be drawn. And, again, the hypothesis that lesbianism is pathological is unsupported.

If one looks to family pathology mainly as productive of homosexuality, many of the items on Table 6 raise some questions about the assumption. For instance, majorities of non-patient homosexuals as well as heterosexuals report acceptance by both mother and father, non-seductiveness by the mother, no partiality on the part of the father, no pressuring attitude toward femininity or masculinity by the father, love for the father, no seductiveness by sibs. It is true that fewer homosexuals than heterosexuals answer in these ways but, despite the statistical significance, the direction of both groups in respect to parents is similar.

So too for the comparisons between the two patient groups. Only a quantitative element separates the two groups of patients, with the homosexual somewhat more extreme than her heterosexual control.

In comparison with the Gundlach-Riess groups, fewer women studied by Saghir and Robins had experienced psychotherapy. Unlike the women in the larger study, therapy was of shorter duration for the California population. Basically the reasons for seeking help in both groups had to do either with depression, the search for insight, relief of guilt or emotional growth. Again only alcoholism clearly differentiated symptomatology in the homosexual from that in the heterosexual woman. Very few of the homosexual group wanted to change their patterns of love-partner choice.

Concluding this section, then, one is forced to agree with the above-cited summary from Saghir and Robins, namely that there is no research evidence for including homosexuality in the list of pathological syndromes. So, one must ask why the "healing" professions feel so strongly that like-sexed love-partner choice is "sick" and should be corrected. To a large extent, this attitude is based on theoretical assumptions about the nature of men and women and their psycho-physiological development as well as the stages of psycho-sexual growth. The following sections will give a capsule view of some of these theories and positions.

The Biological Approach

This is the oldest and most pseudoscientific explanation. It holds that homosexuality, whether male or female, is determined by biological or biochemical factors within the individual. Over the centuries, the identity of these factors has changed from external genital abnormalities such as overt hermaphroditism through chromosomal aberrations, gene determinants, gonadal tissue secretions to hormonal and blood-chemistry deviations.

Against such biologic-organic beliefs, the evidence is overwhelming. In particular, there are the studies by Money (1965) and Stoller (1968), among others. These researchers have documented that parental expectations and rearing within a gender role are far more important as behavioral determinants than are the organic factors. Often the abnormal development of primary and secondary characteristics is not seen until adolescence. Meanwhile, the person is brought up to behave in the gender role of what seemed to be the biologic sex at time of birth. The child developed attitudes and behavior consonant with parental expectations, beliefs and rearing practices. To such an extent was this self and sexual identity built in that surgical reversal of biological sex characteristics had little or no effect on gender behavior. Today, there are few researchers who adhere to a biological cause-and-effect theory of homosexuality, whether of the male or female variety.

The Psychoanalytic Approaches

The major theoretical structures for the development of sexual identity have been based on Freud's psychoanalytic writings or their extensions among his followers. However, here the basic essays have to do with men rather than women, a bias which has held for all analytic writing. To a large extent, homosexuality in women when dealt with by dynamic psychotherapists has been seen as an analog or sometimes a mirror-image of what has been said about men.

Several overt and implicit assumptions pervade the field. These will be listed rather than documented. In the first place, heterosexuality is axiomatically the normal way of making love. Parenthetically, one should reflect on the difference between "making" love and loving. Unless interfered with, all individuals are heterosexual. A second, historical, assumption has been that there is an innate bisexuality in the human organism.

This concept has been resoundingly demolished by Rado (1940) in a classic paper.

A third assumption is that the possession of the penis by the male and its absence in the female is a problem for women whose resolution will determine, to a large extent, the development of a "healthy" adult personality. Freud (1962) held that the three-year-old girl who discovers the difference between her body and that of a boy reacts to the absence of the penis with a lasting feeling of inferiority. This low self-esteem is lifelong, interferes with the development of a secure superego and makes the girl open to more masochistic and narcissistic behaviors. Penis-envy does exist in some women at some time in their development but there have been few research studies or even clinical case histories which have separated penis-envy from jealousy of the preferred status of the boy, his greater freedom and the greater reinforcement by his parents of "masculine" attitudes and behavior.

A final axiom must be mentioned. This is the overriding importance ascribed to the development during the third to sixth year of life, the "oedipal" period. Since all beings are heterosexual, the son's reaction to his mother becomes more and more explicitly expressed in hugging, kissing, and snuggling, with a response from the mother which sets him off as a man. The mother's incest anxiety will lead to some rejection of the son's advances and forces an identification with the father. Here arise fears of castration which have to be resolved during adolescence by sexual experiences. Homosexuality is then seen either as a regression or fixation to or at a pre-oedipal stage.

What then of the girl? She has discovered and been traumatized by the absence of a penis. During the oedipal phase she does not fear castration since she has nothing to castrate. Blaming her mother for the organ-deprivation, the girl seeks a penis from her father which is rapidly converted to a symbolic penis in the form of a wish to bear her father's child. Thus maternity is a result of penis-envy. However, the woman's role in intercourse was seen by Freud as passive-receptive and hence the development of the female is in the direction of passivity and compliance. The early, pre-oedipal activity components are suppressed and the passive-compliant rewarded. One result of the repression of aggression is its internalizing and redirection against the self—hence female masochism.

Bieber (1962) sees homosexuality as always pathological and always a defense against fear of heterosexuality. Since any accommodation which exists to an unrealistic fear is necessarily pathological, homosexuality is therefore pathology. Where both parents are psychologically disturbed, where the father is detached and hostile and the mother close-binding and seductive, the son is likely to be homosexual. The mirror-image of this constellation accounts for female homosexual development to some authors who extrapolate from the Bieber conclusions. Thus one expects for the woman a seductive father and rejecting mother.

A different orientation occurs in writings by Ovesey (1963). This authority sees homosexuality as arising from three different adaptational adjustment styles. One has to do with pleasure and gratification from like-sexed genital contact, a second adaptation represents an attempt to solve serious dependency problems and the third arises from attempts to assert power. The latter two are certainly not sexual but come from feelings of inadequacy, defectiveness and inability to survive as an adult. Such conflicts may be resolved by seeking maternal-like dependency status or by compensation through denying the weakness and acting out in a power-seeking manner. Ovesey calls such types of behavior "pseudo homosexual."

Fenichel (1945) is one of the few orthodox psychoanalysts who deal specifically with female homosexuality. He saw two etiologic factors: repulsion from heterosexuality as a result of the castration complex and the carrying out in an adult life of early fixation to the mother.

A good summary of factors theoretically associated with homosexuality in women is to be found in two chapters by Romm and Wilbur in Marmor's (1965) volume on sexual inversion.

In summarizing the explicit theories of female homosexuality, the emphasis almost throughout has been on the early identification of the daughters with the mother and on the trauma of the discovery of the lack of penis. To date, there has been very little evidence other than case-histories contaminated by the *a priori* biases of the clinician for the hypotheses generated by the theories. It should also be clear by this time that one does not do psychotherapy with a woman because she is homosexual but, and only sometimes, because her homosexuality is just one of the many factors causing her to seek help. The old maxim that "it is more important to know what kind of person the disease has than the kind of disease the person has" can be restated for the homosexual woman. It is indeed more important to know what kind of person the homosexual is than what causes the homosexuality.

IF AND WHEN FEMALE HOMOSEXUALS NEED HELP

We come finally to the treatment of those women who seek help and who present homosexual relationships as the problems. Rather than give a series of protocols, an attempt will be made to outline paradigms for investigating and assessing the problem. Once the nature of the individual and its relationship to the choice of a sexual or love partner has been established, therapy does not differ from that involved in any other type of case.

A good starting point for dealing with any person who comes in for help with homosexuality is to question the nature, extent and behavioral aspects of the sexual choice. In practice, this implies that the therapist recognize the wide range both of behaviors and origins and avoid regarding homosexuality as a clinical entity. A second essential is not to generalize from what is known about homosexuality in males to women. Such occurrences as cruising, one-night stands, aversion to genitalia of the opposite sex, identification with the cross-sexed parent may be true of many male homosexuals but are rare among females. It is important, also, and particularly in initially establishing a working relationship, that the therapist clearly indicate that, in and of itself, the choice of a like-sexed love partner is not necessarily pathological. If the therapist cannot in good faith and belief make this assertion, treatment becomes difficult if not impossible.

With these precautions in mind, the usual therapeutic practices take over. Among the specific questions which must be answered in dealing with female homosexuality, the most difficult is "why do you feel homosexuality is your problem?" The working through of guilt, shame and/or isolation is designed to make possible a rational choice of partner. In developing a healthy attitude toward the partner, be it woman or man, the homosexual patient faces many of the situations etiological to all emotional disturbance. Identification with parents, childhood experiences with parents, sibs, teachers and friends, sexual explorations and behavior are all equally determinative of neuroses whether the presenting symptom is or is not homosexuality. Concepts such as penis-envy, pre-oedipal fixation and other analytic terms may be explored but must not be considered as pathognomic for female homosexuality. Sometimes such behavior will be a manifestation of "acting-out," at others of an ego-syntonic mode of combating second-class citizenship or male chauvinism. Tomboyishness, when found, is to be analyzed, but not labeled as specific for homosexuality.

One of the major diagnostic issues in the treatment of women who are homosexual is why they prefer a woman to a man companion. Is this an answer to exploitation, mistreatment or abuse by a male in childhood, adolescence or adult life? Is the choice based on sensory-affective preferences, for instance, the desire for loving, not necessarily genital, contact? These needs, i.e., skin contact, closeness and warmth, were reported by the Gundlach-Riess respondents as more important and meaningful than genital contacts. As a by-product of this need-satisfaction relationship, one might list the much longer duration of lesbian love-pairings than those found among males. From all the data of research studies of women, a predominant influence to be investigated in treatment is the kind, level and force of parental expectations of and attitudes to girl children.

For many years, the male homosexual in his adult partnership choices was held to be almost untreatable, if and when he was motivated to change his life patterns. Today, there is much more optimism about the outcome of therapy. Most authorities agree that women homosexuals who come for help about their selection of life and love style are more amenable to help than their male counterparts. It has been hypothesized that this is true because of the greater frequency of experienced heterosexual behavior and the absence of male genital aversion in the woman.

Two recent treatments of female homosexuality are instructive in terms of an attempt to see the behavior in the light of new data about the psychological structure of the female. Eisenbud (1969) deals with the fantasy and the reality strivings of women in a male world, although she still has recourse to such concepts as penis-envy and castration fears. McDougall (1970) in a most stimulating volume by Chasseguet-Smirgel (1970) sees homosexuality as "characterized by a continual *acting-out* of an internal drama in the outside world in an attempt to maintain ego identity. There are many neurotic mechanisms at work but they fail to protect the ego with regard to its sexual identity. . . . The risk of losing the identity-emblems thus acquired makes the homosexual liable to severe depressive episodes. . . ." It is encouraging to see these contributions to a study of the female emanating from female authorities.

In concluding this chapter, it must be emphasized again that there are no evidential bases for the belief that female homosexuality *qua* homosexuality is pathological in a psycho-dynamic sense. It may be an expression of rejection of the male-dominated world and hence anti-establishment. Second, one must be extremely cautious in applying the same rules-of-thumb or of-head to men and women. We have had as yet no attempt to write the psychology of woman from the point of view of all the new data accumulated by researchers and growth experiencers. Finally, there is the matter of the woman who wants to change her style of love relationship. Like any other decision, this desire must be challenged, analyzed and the existence of both options opened for examination. Only when choice is freely made can there be a real change in the patient. So too for these patients, it must be made clear that the homosexuality, like heterosexuality, can serve to perpetuate a neurotic or psychotic life-style. If the neurosis is dealt with, the choice of a love-partner can be made independently of the sex of the partner.

REFERENCES

ABBOTT, S. & LOVE, B. *Sappho Was a Right-On Woman*. New York: Stein and Day, 1972.

ARMON, V. Some personality variables in overt female homosexuality. *Journal of Projective Techniques*, 24, 292-309, 1960.

BIEBER, I. ET AL. *Homosexuality: A Psychoanalytic Study of Male Homosexuals*. New York: Basic Books, 1962.

CHASSEGUET-SMIRGEL, J. (Ed.). *Female Sexuality: New Psychoanalytic Views*. Ann Arbor: University of Michigan Press, 1970.

CORY, D. W. & LEROY, J. D. *The Homosexual and His Society: A View from Within*. New York: Citadel, 1963.

EISENBUD, RUTH-JEAN, Female homosexuality: A sweet enfranchisement. In G. D. Goldman and D. S. Milman (Eds.), *Modern Woman*. Springfield, Ill.: Charles C Thomas, 1969.

FENICHEL, O. *The Psychoanalytic Theory of Neuroses*. New York: Norton, 1945.

FORD, C. S. & BEACH, F. A. *Patterns of Sexual Behavior*. New York: Harper Bros. and Hoeber, 1951.

FREEDMAN, M. Homosexuality among women and psychological adjustment. *Dissertation Abstracts*, 28, 4294B, 1967.

FREUD, S. *Three Essays on the Theory of Sexuality*. J. Strachey (trans.). New York: Basic Books, 1962.

GUNDLACH, R. H. Childhood parental relationships and the establishment of gender roles of homosexuals. *Journal of Consulting and Clinical Psychology*, 33, 136-151, 1969.

GUNDLACH, R. H. & RIESS, B. F. Birth order and sex of siblings in a sample of lesbians and non-lesbians. *Psychological Reports*, 20, 61-62, 1967.

GUNDLACH, R. & RIESS, B. F. Self and sexual identity in the female: A study of female homosexuals. In B. F. Riess (Ed.), *New Directions in Mental Health*. New York: Grune and Stratton, 1968.

HOPKINS, J. The lesbian personality. *British Journal of Psychiatry*, 115, 1433-1436, 1969.

HOPKINS, J. Lesbian signs on the Rorschach. *British Journal of Projective Psychology and Personality Study*, 15, 7-14, 1970.

KENYON, F. E. Studies in female homosexuality, psychological test results. *Journal of Consulting and Clinical Psychology*, 32, 510, 1968a.

KENYON, F. E. Studies in female homosexuality. IV. Social and psychiatric aspects. *British Journal of Psychiatry*, 14, 337-350, 1968b.

KINSEY, A. C. ET AL. *Sexual Behavior in the Human Male*. Phila.: Saunders, 1948.

KINSEY, A. C. ET AL. *Sexual Behavior in the Human Female*. Phila.: Saunders, 1953.

MAGEE, B. *One in Twenty: A Study of Homosexuality in Men and Women*. London: Secker and Warburg, 1966.

MARMOR, J. (Ed.). *Sexual Inversion*. New York: Basic Books, 1965.

MCDOUGALL, J. Homosexuality in women. In J. Casseguet-Smirgel (Ed.). *Female Sexuality: New Psychoanalytic Views*. Ann Arbor: U. Mich. Press, 1970.

MONEY, J. (Ed.). *Sex Research: New Developments*. New York: Holt, Rinehart and Winston, 1965.

OVESEY, L. The homosexual conflict: An adaptational analysis. In H. Ruitenbeck (Ed.), *The Problem of Homosexuality in Modern Society*. New York: E. P. Dutton, 1963.

RADO, S. A critical examination of the concept of bisexuality. *Psychosomatic Medicine*, 2, 459-467, 1940.

RIESS, B. F. & SAFER, J. Birth order and related variables in a large out-patient population. *Journal of Psychology*, 85, 61-68, 1973.

RIESS, B. F., SAFER, J., & YOTIVE, W. *Projective Tests of Homosexual Women*, 1974. (In press: mimeo available from senior author.)

ROMM, M. E. Sexuality and homosexuality in women. In J. Marmor (Ed.), *Sexual Inversion*. New York: Basic Books, 1965.

SAGHIR, M. & ROBINS, E. *Male and Female Homosexuality*. Baltimore: Williams and Wilkins, 1973.

SIEGELMAN, M. Adjustment of homosexual and heterosexual women. *British Journal of Psychiatry*, 120, 477-481, 1972.

STOLLER, R. *Sex and Gender*. New York: Science House, 1968.

STOLLER, R. J. Psychoanalysis and physical intervention in the brain. In J. Zubin and J. Money (Eds.), *Contemporary Sexual Behavior*. Baltimore: Johns Hopkins Univ. Press, 1973.

SZASZ, T. S. *The Myth of Mental Illness*. New York: Hoeber, 1961.

SZASZ, T. S. Legal and moral aspects of homosexuality. In J. Marmor (Ed.), *Sexual Inversion*. New York: Basic Books, 1965.

VAN AARDWEG, G. J. M. Male homosexuality and psychological tests. *International Mental Health Research Newsletter*, 11, 7-11, 1969.

WEINBERG, M. S. & BELL, A. P. *Homosexuality: An Annotated Bibliography*. New York: Harper and Row, 1972.

WEST, D. J. *Homosexuality*. Chicago: Aldine, 1967.

WILBUR, C. Clinical aspects of female homosexuality. In J. Marmor (Ed.), *Sexual Inversion*. New York: Basic Books, 1965.

WILSON, M. & GREENE, R. Personality characteristics of female homosexuals. *Psychological Reports*, 28, 407-412, 1971.

Part IV

CONTEMPORARY PSYCHOTHERAPIES

9

WOMEN IN BEHAVIOR THERAPY

ARNOLD A. LAZARUS

Long before the advent of Women's Liberation, behavior therapists were training women to be self-sufficient, socially assertive, and to stand up for their rights. Unlike psychoanalytic theory, significant sex differences are by no means an integral part of social learning theory or behavior theory. On the contrary, research by behavior theorists has indicated that gender role differences are greater within each sex than between men and women (Mischel, 1966). Thus, there is nothing whatsoever in behavior theory that can lead to any sexist attitudes—no concepts like "penis envy" or "castration anxiety," no insistence upon so-called "vaginal orgasms," and no credence is given to any other prejudicial sex-typed response patterns. Yet we live in a culture where sex stereotypes still predominate. We also live in a culture where millions have been conditioned to accept ill-defined concepts of "masculinity" and "femininity."

No matter how desirable one may regard egalitarian divisions and interactions between the sexes, the everyday realities present a different picture. I see women who feel cheated and deprived because their husbands fail to live up to stereotyped notions of red-blooded American masculinity. I see downtrodden women who suffer unbeknownst because their husbands do live up to a certain stereotype of the All American Man. I am consulted by women who feel trapped, confined, exploited and abused. I am also consulted by women who ardently desire to be overwhelmed, ensnared, bound and restricted. The heterogeneity of complaints and afflictions nevertheless demands viable treatment goals and objectives. A personalistic outlook (Lazarus, 1971) calls for specificity and respect for individual differences in selecting appropriate therapeutic goals.

It should perhaps be mentioned that a personalistic approach empha-

217

sizes individual freedom but upholds the moral precept that people are best discouraged from harming themselves or others. However, since social roles are learned (and therapy is often a matter of unlearning self-limiting roles and acquiring new and personally fulfilling roles in life), the competent therapist does not avoid the responsibility of challenging negative roles, no matter how vigorously promoted by society at large, that impinge upon the psychological growth of individuals or specific groups. Long before it was fashionable to do so, behavior therapists questioned why so many women believe that "femininity" necessarily implies a range of indirect, docile, subservient, emotionally labile, and deliberately inept behaviors. It is unfortunate that we live in a culture that promotes various types of hypocrisy, that discourages personal openness, that favors numerous social inhibitions, and that upholds a tradition of personal dishonesty in the name of tact, or considerateness. Within these corruptive confines, women have the doubly demanding task of skillfully playing these nefarious societal games while pretending to be stupid at the same time.

Therapists (unlike theorists) inevitably place positive or negative value upon various categories of behavior—e.g., adaptive, deviant, asocial, etc. The value judgments of behavior therapy are such that "assertive behavior" is generally preferred over unassertive or submissive behavior—for men and women. There are no double standards. Hypersensitivities are regarded as impediments to successful functioning. Inhibited patterns of social or sexual interaction are considered unfortunate. Timidity and reticence are usually replaced by frank and forthright expressions of basic needs and feelings. The stereotype of the defenseless little woman has never been upheld in the behavior therapy literature. Thus nearly two decades ago, Lazarus and Rachman (1957) reported the case of a 34-year-old woman who suffered extreme anxiety coupled with feelings of inadequacy and inferiority and who, in addition to receiving desensitization therapy, "was instructed in the use of *assertive responses*," so that she became an individual in her own right and rapidly gained generalized self-confidence.

Lazarus (1968) reported the following case:

> The wife of a wealthy lawyer was rendered miserable by the fact that her husband refused to allow her to pursue part-time work. She desired to escape from "domestic drudgery" for a few hours each day, but her husband stubbornly insisted that her place was in the home and glibly argued down her objections and protestations. He refused an invitation to discuss matters with the therapist on the

grounds that he was too busy. A program of behavior rehearsal remedied the situation after three sessions. The therapist role-played the husband and easily argued down the wife's pleadings and protests. The dialogue was tape-recorded, and the playback was described by the client as "typical of our arguments at home." The therapist played the tape again, stopped it at judicious points, and suggested appropriate rejoinders that the client might have inserted. The scene was rehearsed several times. Occasionally the therapist modeled appropriate responses by playing the client's role. After the third session, the therapist, role-playing the husband, was unable to win the argument by means of rhetoric or verbal abuse. The client was then pronounced capable of confronting her husband. At the next session she reported having won his consent and duly obtained part-time employment. The husband, in turn, reduced dissonance by outspokenly supporting the virtues of "working wives."

But as we proceed beyond the techniques of behavior therapy and examine the relationship within which these techniques are administered, a dimension seldom explored in the behavior therapy literature comes to the fore. When a male behavior therapist conducts relaxation training with a female client, factors other than the autonomic effects of tension release probably have a bearing on the outcome. The latter was clearly illustrated in a letter from a woman who had never met me but whose husband had purchased my relaxation cassettes (Lazarus, 1971a). She reported her initial reaction as follows:

My husband brings the tapes home from work in his briefcase. He brings a little tape recorder too. After the children are asleep, he sets the recorder up on the desk in our bedroom. I lie on the bed, nervous and expectant. This is too intimate. It makes me uncomfortable. We are going to let a strange voice into our bedroom. It is voyeuristic, eerie, a disembodied voice in our bedroom. I lie still, controlling my nervousness. My husband turns the switch, and the most relaxed, well-modulated voice I have ever heard fills the room. It is soothing, hypnotic. The voice is giving directions to bodies— any body, my body. It is talking about and to my feet, legs, trunk, shoulders, head. It is giving my body directions to let go. The voice is under my clothes, clinging to my feet, climbing up my legs. What will the voice do when it comes to the trunk? Will it say pubic area, breasts? No, it is too intimate. Turn it off. I love the sound of that voice. It gets from the legs to the head without uttering forbidden words. How did it do that? Does the voice know what my body looks like? Does it know that I take a bath every day? My legs and armpits are shaved? That I have skin soft as velvet? . . . I sit up and rub the back of my neck. The voice echoes in my head. I can't imagine talking face to face with the person who belongs to that voice. We are too different.

If the foregoing is indicative of the fact that even an impersonal cassette recording has an impact that transcends peripheral stimulus-response analysis, it is obvious that a myriad of personal influencing factors enters into all behavior therapy techniques. The question to ask is if there is any way of determining in advance which factors can deliberately be invoked to enhance therapeutic outcomes. In this chapter we will be concerned mainly with when and how certain women are definitely helped rather than hindered when treated by male behavior therapists. Conversely it is worth inquiring on what grounds the decision is reached to refer a woman to a female rather than a male behavior therapist.

The first consideration, as I have shown elsewhere (Lazarus, 1971; 1973), deals with *expectancy fulfillment*—people enter therapy with certain expectations, and the effectiveness of therapy is often closely linked with the fulfillment of these expectations. Thus, people who enter therapy believing, for instance, that hypnosis will facilitate their progress may possess a self-fulfilling prophecy that should be incorporated into their treatment. Similarly, my clinical findings indicate that if someone believes, for example, that an older man will be more helpful in treatment than a younger person, appropriate matching of client and therapist (where feasible) is advisable. And for present purposes, if a woman believes that another woman is likely to be more helpful to her than a man, referral to a female therapist would be indicated. Conversely, when a woman prefers a male therapist to a female therapist, it is better for her to enter therapy with whomsoever she feels more optimistic. Of course, it would be naive to assume that one simply follows the client's prescriptions without examining the motives behind a given preference. However, it is usually poor therapeutic practice to argue with clients, and it is well worth remembering that the patient often knows best.

Apart from clear-cut preferences or prejudices, the decision as to whether a male or female behavior therapist is preferable in a given case depends on many factors. Some individuals maintain that women should always be treated by women, that men cannot possibly empathize with women, and that help given by a man to a woman only subjugates her further. This blanket statement lacks any substantiating data. Fortunately, a lengthy rebuttal of such a position is not necessary for only a few extremists seem to embrace that point of view. Indeed, it is clear that for many women there may be distinct advantages in working with a male therapist who is capable of providing a very different male model than the ones to which she is accustomed. She is thus provided with the wherewithal to relate in a different (more constructive) way. Let us say that she is accustomed to living with a domineering father, an authoritarian husband, and has had numerous contacts with professional men (e.g., doctors and lawyers) who have always cast her in the helpless little girl role. Such a woman can gain enormous personal freedom from relating to a male therapist who enables her to test out different roles. If she succeeds in breaking free from her frustrating role stereotype, she gains not only new degrees of freedom and new ways of relating to men, but also a greater sense of autonomy and self-worth. Nonetheless, it is self-evident that when a male therapist treats a female client, a number of distinctive features may inhibit or retard therapeutic progress. The most obvious element concerns the degree of sexual attraction on either or both parts. Does this have a significant bearing on determining treatment outcomes?

When carefully scrutinizing my case notes in order to assess the role played by sexual attraction on therapeutic outcomes and follow-ups, it was easy to divide this factor into four parts: (1) women who found me sexually attractive but to whom I was not attracted; (2) women whom I found sexually attractive but who were not attracted to me; (3) women who found me sexually attractive and vice versa; and (4) women who were not attracted to me and vice versa. The foregoing was measured in two ways. The application of Orlinsky and Howard's (1966) therapy session report (see Appendix B of my book *Behavior Therapy and Beyond*) elicits information on a 3-point scale as to whether the client felt sexually attracted. The use of this instrument following the Desert Island Fantasy Test (Lazarus, 1971) is particularly useful as the fantasy test has seductive overtones. Sexual attraction was also assessed by perusing case notes. (I routinely jot down significant affective responses that emerge during each session.)

Before commenting on these results, one special point must be emphasized. Behavior therapy is primarily a goal-oriented, problem solving enterprise in which the therapist's didactic role as a trainer or teacher-clinician deflects attention from "transference" or the patient-therapist relationship onto significant issues in the client's life outside of the treatment dyad. The only time I explore the patient-therapist relationship is when therapy is not proceeding apace and negative aspects within the treatment dyad appear to be impeding progress. At the same time, most behavior therapists do not seek to remain detached, ethereal or enigmatic but enter the treatment arena as real people and thereby enable their clients to react to them more realistically. In essence, behavior therapists endeavor to be "positive reinforcers" without responding to their clients as sexual objects and without enticing their clients to regard them as anything more than significant change agents. Nevertheless, people will be people, and men and women closeted together week after week, engaging in relaxing, instructing, and various retraining activities, will find that extraneous feelings of affection, antipathy, gratitude, irritation, adoration and disgust may facilitate or impede the attainment of their main therapeutic objectives.

Returning to the role played by sexual attraction on treatment outcomes, after carefully reviewing over 100 case notes, I could detect absolutely no significant trend or pattern. Therapeutic duration and outcome seem unaffected by my subjective feelings—women to whom I was attracted responded no better and no worse to my ministrations than those whom I did not find attractive. Similarly, women who were attracted to me showed no advantages or disadvantages over those women who were not attracted to me. The only exceptions were a few instances where women expressed very strong positive feelings for me which seemed to interfere with therapy.

Unlike psychoanalysts, behavior therapists cannot interpret positive or negative statements directed at them in terms of "transference projections." Unrealistic feelings and expectations probably enter into nearly all interpersonal relationships, but, as previously stated, the behavior therapist is sufficiently "real" for his clients to respond to him as a person, or at least to significant aspects of his behavior. When therapy seems to be sidetracked by various distortions and false perceptions, one may often remedy the situation by simply emphasizing certain realities. Thus, when a 26-year-old woman who sought help for her marital problems was making no headway, I asked her if something between us was hindering her progress. She was evasive during the session but then sent me the following note. "I am enormously attracted to you and cannot separate you as a person and as a therapist. When I am with you I have marvelous sexual fantasies and fail to follow our conversation in a coherent fashion." I responded by writing her a letter stressing the fact that she probably envisaged me as someone who was always therapeutic, understanding, tolerant and undemanding. I underscored the fact that outside of a therapeutic relationship I would make certain demands, be unprepared to accede to certain wishes, and would undoubtedly display various behaviors that would tarnish her one-sided picture of me. When I broached the subject during the next session she preferred to ignore it, but thereafter her attention was no longer riveted on me but was directed at the treatment objectives at hand. Therapeutic progress was clearly facilitated by my reality oriented response.

An exception worth reporting concerns a young woman who confessed that she had "enormous feelings of love" for me and said, "I am walking around in a body suffused with love." I responded by saying, "Thank you, I'm pleased." I then asked, "Can you make this love work for you?" She laughed and said, "I already have. I see myself now as a loving person; that is my core, my jewel . . . I also feel ready now to take the psychological risks you spoke about, to do the things that will change my life." Instead of analyzing and interpreting her feelings of love for me, I further emphasized the fact that she was now capable of experiencing strong positive feelings in general. Subsequent sessions capitalized upon this newfound capacity so that she was able to consolidate love bonds with significant others.

I cannot recall any cases where women with feelings of strong antipathy towards me remained in therapy. They probably terminated treatment and sought out someone more congenial for them. But those cases —men and women—who arouse negative feelings in me are given frank feedback directed at their specific negative or annoying behaviors, not at them as people. A typical excerpt from a session with a 32-year-old woman follows below:

Her: I hate all men. I hated my father, I hated my brothers, I hate my husband, and, and I even think I hate my son.

Me: I guess you would add me to that collection.

Her: I don't think of you as a man.

Me: (Laughing) Oh, wow! I guess that was the ultimate put-down.

Her: You can take it anyway you please. I didn't realize you're so sensitive. I'm just saying you're my doctor, period.

Me: Well, as I've mentioned many times, you do come across in a very angry and combative manner.

Her: That's your opinion.

Me: There's nothing to gain from arguing about it. I'm simply sharing a feeling with you. And I think this style of yours has a lot to do with your general problems.

Her: Don't lecture me! Please don't give me lectures.

Me: Okay. No lecture. Just a feeling. I feel under attack.

Her: Poor defenseless little you!

Me: You're not being at all constructive.

Her: Okay, if I were a man I wonder if you would still hand me that crap about being hostile and combative, or perhaps your male chauvinism is showing.

Me: I don't think there has to be war between the sexes. I think people can respond to one another as people, and I don't have one standard of assertiveness for men and another for women. . . . You're being aggressive, you're not being assertive for a man or for a woman.

Her: That's all baloney. You can't help taking sides with your own sex.

Me: Does that mean you'd do better with a woman therapist?

Her: I hate men but I don't trust women. You can't get rid of me that easy.

Me: I'm not trying to get rid of you. I would like to find a way of cutting through your aggression so that you can express your feelings assertively. You can't hide from yourself and from others the fact that you are basically a warm and caring person.

Her: Stop being cute with me. I see through your motives. With me that sort of soft soaping will get us nowhere.

Me: You remind me of the stereotyped man with a taboo on tenderness.

Her: Tenderness! That's a good word. You bet I don't want to be tender and stomped into the ground or something.

Me: You know something funny? I see your tough facade, your combative veneer, as the very thing that gets you stomped on by others. As the one time popular song put it, you could "Try a Little Tenderness."

As the foregoing case progressed, the heart of the matter amounted to certain issues that are almost a societal cliché by now. Raised by a domineering father who valued his two elder sons and relegated his only daughter to second class citizenship, she grew up feeling angry but inadequate, resenting her subservient mother and craving but never receiving the full acceptance of her father. Now at age 32, following her programmed script, she was a housewife and mother, professionally untrained, understandably resentful, ambivalent, confused and essentially unfulfilled. She obviously rejected the notion of receiving treatment from a woman because she was "brainwashed" into perceiving her own sex as inferior. In a sense, she seemed to need permission from a man (a father figure?) to engage in useful activities that would take her away from husband and family for a few hours each day. A benevolent therapeutic outcome followed her newfound willingness to study journalism, take up pottery, and obtain part-time work selling real estate.* I had encouraged her to attend a woman's consciousness raising group, but after a few meetings she dropped out protesting that the members were "too far into the Women's Movement," that they were telling her how to feel and what to think, that she disapproved of them, and believed that "in the long run they will be cutting off their own noses." It seemed that her early conditioning prevented her from attaching sufficient value to women *per se,* but she was nevertheless able to acquire a certain sense of autonomy, freedom, self-worth, and independence from working with a male behavior therapist.

A limiting aspect of all therapy is that it depends so largely upon the skills, values and specific limitations of the person administering the procedures. A middle class housewife consulted me for the treatment of panic attacks, generalized anxiety, depression and feelings of gross inadequacy. Her husband was callous, domineering, insensitive, demanding, and enjoyed suppressing every vestige of her potential self-worth, independence and initiative. I embarked on a course of conjoint therapy and I also saw the woman individually. She was rife with clichés about female inferiority and male dominance, but her self-derogatory statements seemed to belie various strengths and many potentially positive attributes. We were making some headway in therapy—she was finally beginning to realize that her individuality could blossom and she would yet remain a good wife, an honorable daughter, and a loving parent. I moved to a new work locale, and she consulted a woman behavior therapist in preference to a male therapist whom I had recommended. The woman behavior therapist, who views herself as liberated and fully emancipated, nevertheless reversed the therapeutic ground that I had covered. She reinforced the client's dependency upon her husband, undermined the notion that she would ultimately be far better off being less dutiful, and actively discouraged her from becoming more of an individual. In short, while the woman's anxieties were somewhat ameliorated, she is even less of a person now than she had been before consulting me. The spark is gone, and she lives out the downtrodden role of a suburban housewife who has relinquished all of her individual rights. Thus, she was encour-

---

* As Nathaniel Branden (1971) points out, "incalculable damage has been wrought by the conventional view that the pursuit of a productive career is an exclusively masculine prerogative, and that women should not aspire to any role or function other than that of wife and mother. A woman's psychological well-being requires that she be engaged in a long-range career; she is not some sort of second-class citizen, metaphysically, for whom mental passivity and dependence are a natural condition" (p. 131).

aged *by a woman* to adopt a male dominated role, thus avoiding conflict and anxiety, but at the expense of her individuality.

Those who make the error of assuming that a militant feminist is synonymous with a liberated woman seem to forget that warfare exists only where conflicts remain unresolved. In behavior therapy we aim to teach women how to be assertive and truly emancipated from an oppressive regime of domestic drudgery;* how to be successful while never hiding their intellectual prowess and never denigrating their own achievements; how to be genuinely uninhibited, fully recognizing their rights and gently but persuasively showing many of their exploited sisters how to modify a wide range of unfortunate proscribed roles. Such a woman is at peace with *men,* with *women,* with *people,* and with *herself.* For an excellent account of various assertive training procedures for facilitating the growth of women, the reader is referred to the paper by Patricia Jakubowski-Spector (1973).

In the course of therapy I have encountered many women who needed to learn from a man that all males are not insensitive, unemotional, unperceptive, tough-minded creatures preoccupied with things rather than with people. I have spent an inordinate amount of time trying to teach men and women—husbands and wives, brothers and sisters, lovers or casual acquaintances—how to relate to one another as people. Often this worthy goal could not have been achieved were it not for able female co-therapists. The impact of a significant remark in therapy would frequently owe its power to a sex-linked variable. "That remark had to come from a *man.*" "She had to hear it from a *woman.*" "That was helpful because we (a male and a female therapist) both agreed so strongly with each other."

One of the most iniquitous situations one so frequently encounters in therapy is the plight of the middle-aged woman. One sees highly intelligent, well-educated women who have been out of the employment market for 20 years or more. In our success-oriented society, these women have

---

* Lest the reader conjure up a T.V. commercial that equates "freedom from domestic drudgery" with a new oven cleaner, or perhaps a musical mop that permits the "little woman" to hum a tune while shining her floors, let it be emphasized that behavior therapists provide an entirely different antidote. Women can overcome domestic drudgery by instituting two basic changes: (1) An equitable load of daily chores needs to be delegated to all household members. (Some women may require considerable assertive training in order to accomplish this end.) (2) Positive reinforcements outside of the home—preferably work experiences that prove emotionally and financially rewarding—are necessary to provide an identity that transcends the role of dutiful wife and/or mother.

often forfeited their own careers and professional growth for the sake of husbands who then define themselves as "successes" and regard themselves as worthy of more interesting and stimulating companions. Similarly, we frequently encounter relatively uneducated middle class women who, after serving husband and family for more than two decades, are rejected for a young, usually professionally trained woman, who offers "intellectual compatibility." In an upwardly mobile society, women who depend on men for their own status and self-esteem are in a precarious position. A great deal of ingenuity is demanded from the therapist in combating these unfortunate trends. It is not an easy task to convince women that extrinsic virtues are a poor basis for the development of enduring self-worth. Yet, successful therapy is predicated on the assumption that people can be taught to appreciate intrinsic values and that they can learn to cultivate a repertoire of behaviors that reflect genuine warmth, empathy, integrity, dignity, etc., and to place personal value upon these basic qualities. The point is that neither men nor women who place exclusive value on extrinsic beauty, achievements, power, financial wealth, and public acclaim can ever develop an enduring sense of self-esteem.

In therapy, one often sees women who suffer dreadfully while passively enduring brutal, tyrannical behavior from despotic men. Some women have sought therapy after literally having teeth rammed down their throats by uxoricidal mates. At this juncture in history, it usually requires a male to intercede meaningfully when combating the sexist attitudes and utterly chauvinistic reactions of the men who perpetuate the foregoing relationships. These men would only scoff and jeer at the efforts of a female therapist who would dare to intervene on behalf of a suffering sister. Even when a male therapist interacts with these men on behalf of a female client, considerable care must be exercised to avoid any tenderhearted or sentimental appeals.

Throughout this chapter I have touched on various situations where a male therapist seemed preferable to a female therapist, or where co-therapy with a male and female therapist had distinct advantages. Apart from the instances already cited, under what circumstances do I usually refer a female client to a female therapist? The most succinct answer to this question is: where a crucial element of change seems to require a female rather than a male role model. When might this occur? Perhaps the most typical situation is when a timid, inhibited, unassertive woman remains unresponsive or refractory to my attempts at assertive training. Many women regard self-assertion as incompatible with "femininity" and tend to regard assertive behavior in men as a cultural expectation. Women in our culture learn to be indirect and to rely on "feminine wiles." Even in my *groups* certain women remain unresponsive to the fact that the more assertive female group members may readily serve as role models. They tend to perceive these assertive women as having been beguiled by male authoritarianism into acting in a forthright and outspoken manner which runs counter to their "basic femininity." However, suspicions of this kind may readily be dispelled when a female therapist—without a male "guru"—spells out the virtues of assertive behavior and then models the basic differences between assertive and aggressive responses. Similar effects may be observed in all-women groups (cf. Jakubowski-Spector, 1973).

In keeping with the above, I have treated numerous women whose generalized anxiety and subjective misery were allayed by my therapy, but who nevertheless retained heavily indoctrinated attitudes of basic inferiority concerning their own sex. Referral to a female therapist capable of demonstrating that a woman does not have to accept a subservient role can prove invaluable. A case in point concerns a divorced woman whom I managed to convince that remarriage was not a *sine qua non* for her future happiness. Although the profound depression which initially led her to consult me had lifted, I nevertheless remained vaguely uneasy about her progress. I encouraged her to join a woman's consciousness-raising group. After she had been in the group for several months, she effected some subtle but significant changes which led me to realize that my uneasiness was due to the fact that, despite her therapeutic gains, she had become emotionally dependent upon me and was more concerned about pleasing me than in becoming her own person. The consciousness-raising group disabused her of the notion that unless a woman is pleasing some man at least some of the time, she is not a proper woman.

In a paper on consciousness-raising groups, Brodsky (1973) stresses the fact that "the C-R group starts with the assumption that the environment, rather than intrapsychic dynamics, plays a major role in the difficulties of the individuals." The same may be said of behavior therapy. It soon becomes obvious that when emphasis is placed upon environmental factors that maintain deviant behaviors instead of looking for putative dynamics or speculative genetics, a very different picture emerges. And behavior therapy is predicated on the assumption that even if a factor is due to organic processes, learning principles may nonetheless be employed to remedy the situation. Thus, when certain writers justifiably attack the psychiatric establishment (e.g., Chesler, 1972) it is too bad that they fail to recognize the fact that behavior therapy has something unique to offer all victims of environmental oppression. Behavior therapy aims to equip people (regardless of sex) with coping devices and numerous interpersonal skills, so that they become more capable of dealing with many environmental pressures and thereby attain a genuine sense of mastery and personal fulfillment.

REFERENCES

BRANDEN, N. *The Psychology of Self-Esteem.* New York: Bantam Books, 1971.

BRODSKY, A. M. The consciousness-raising group as a model for therapy with women. *Psychotherapy: Theory, Research and Practice,* 10, 24-29, 1973.

CHESLER, P. *Women and Madness.* New York: Doubleday, 1972.

JAKUBOWSKI-SPECTOR, P. Facilitating the growth of women through assertive training. *The Counseling Psychologist,* 4, 75-86, 1973.

LAZARUS, A. A. & RACHMAN, S. The use of systematic desensitization in psychotherapy. *South African Medical Journal,* 31, 934-937, 1957.

LAZARUS, A. A. Behavior therapy and marriage counseling. *Journal of the American Society of Psychosomatic Dentistry and Medicine,* 15, 49-56, 1968.

LAZARUS, A. A. *Behavior Therapy and Beyond.* New York: McGraw-Hill, 1971.

LAZARUS, A. A. *Daily Living: Coping with Tensions and Anxieties.* Chicago: Instructional Dynamics Inc., 1971a.

LAZARUS, A. A. "Hypnosis" as a facilitator in behavior therapy. *The International Journal of Clinical and Experimental Hypnosis,* 21, 25-31, 1973.

MISCHEL, W. A social learning view of sex differences in behavior. In E. Maccoby, *The Development of Sex Differences.* Stanford: Stanford University Press, 1966, pp. 56-81.

ORLINSKY, D. E. & HOWARD, K. I. *Therapy Session Report.* Chicago: Institute for Juvenile Research, 1966.

10

THE THERAPY OF WOMEN IN THE LIGHT OF PSYCHOANALYTIC THEORY AND THE EMERGENCE OF A NEW VIEW

ESTHER MENAKER

The psychology of woman, as indeed all of psychology, belongs clearly to the realm of behavioral science, which differs markedly and in important ways from the hard sciences. In dealing with human behavior, despite great advances in the field of neurophysiology, only the simplest and most primitive aspects of behavior are amenable to the experimental method which would make their significance directly verifiable in the way we are accustomed to expect from the application of scientific method. Not only are the individual variables enormously complex, but in assaying behavior the social framework in which it takes place presents us with a constantly changing variable which must be taken into account. The result of these complexities is that more truth is observable than provable. I make this point at the outset because generalizations and theoretical formulations about women have been made either from a biased viewpoint without regard for the social framework—and this has been one of the great shortcomings of psychoanalysis—or "studies" with attempts at quantification have been undertaken based largely on subjective reports of women themselves concerning their reactions and experiences, often within the context of an ideological bias. This does not discredit the observations in their entirety, but it places them definitely outside the field of exact science. This fact should alert us to the *relative* truth of such theories and observations.

The truism that we live in a time of rapid social change has special significance for psychology and therefore for the psychology of women which is the particular concern of this paper. A veritable psychological "laboratory" has been created by the opportunity to make comparative psychological observations within changing sociological frameworks, and this within remarkably short time spans. Theoretical formulations about women, like all psychological formulations, are conditioned among other things by the social background in which they are made. Early psychoanalytic theories were limited by a lack of awareness of the role of the social background. Conclusions based on observations of pathologic behavior, reaction or symptom were not only transferred *in toto* to theories of normal development, but were made into generalizations that were to be applicable for all time. Since psychoanalysis was the first psychology to be concerned in depth with all those areas of human thought and emotion that had previously been neglected by psychologists, and since many of its findings have significantly enlarged and deepened our understanding of human behavior, it is understandable that it could not have considered all the dimensions involved. Embedded in a general theory of human personality, Freudian thinking developed its own theory of the development of the feminine personality, especially of feminine sexuality.

Let us examine the problems for which women sought help at the time of Freud, how Freud dealt with them and what theories he derived from his observations. Despite the fact that Freud's first patients, and perhaps those throughout the period in which his major theories of personality were taking shape, were women, his theory of feminine psychology derived from his conclusions regarding the psychological development of men.

It is important therefore to review briefly and in broad outlines Freud's major concepts regarding the growth and development of the male personality, bearing in mind that Freud's theory of personality is a predominantly psycho-sexual one, since it stemmed from his theory of neurosis in which he saw sexual conflict as a primary cause. The conception of conflict, in turn, rests on certain basic discoveries: the existence of a dynamic unconscious in which the impulse life of man resides; the importance of early childhood sexuality and its destiny within the familial experience; and the fact of childhood amnesia and the repression of unacceptable and anxiety-producing wishes and drives. Thus the male child, by virtue of his developing childhood sexuality, is caught in a conflict between his sexual wishes, which are directed toward his mother, and the fear of his father toward whom these wishes have placed him in a position of rivalry. The fear is a fear of the loss of that very organ, namely his penis, which is the focus of his erotic wish. This is the classic conception of the oedipus complex and of castration anxiety which has become so familiar to Western culture as to be widely accepted as an inevitable part of normal human experience. This syndrome of oedipal wishes and castration anxiety was also, for Freud, the core of the neuroses.

But now, Freud asks, what becomes of these wishes, what is their fate, how is the conflict resolved and how does its resolution influence the development of personality? Obviously the oedipal wishes are destined to frustration, first because the actual physical equipment of the child lacks the capacity for their realization, and secondly because the fear of castration results in the boy's giving up of his erotic wishes in favor of keeping his penis. In this process he identifies with those aspects of his father's personality which he experienced as prohibiting the fulfillment of his erotic desires *vis-à-vis* his mother. It is in this process of introjection that the core of the boy's superego—of his conscience—is laid down.

For the little girl's psycho-sexual development Freud advanced a different course of events, but one in which the issue of the penis—in this case its absence—was crucial. The sight of the boy's penis and the concomitant awareness of her own lack result in profound feelings of inferiority and in penis envy. To compensate for her lack the little girl turns toward her father in terms of an oedipal attachment and in the unconscious fantasies of childhood hopes for a child from him. This wish is of course destined to disappointment and gradually the little girl turns away from her father. But the downfall of the oedipus complex is much more diffuse and gradual, and is not based on an overriding fear, namely fear of castration, as it is for the boy. According to Freud this fact results in a much weaker superego in the female than in the male.

The phallocentric nature of these theories of psycho-sexual development is clear. Everything is focused on the penis—on its presence or absence—and the little girl is seen as an *homme manqué* who must ultimately make the best of things and be resigned to accepting a child instead of a penis. A major task of therapy, from the orthodox viewpoint, is to help the woman patient achieve this resignation—to accept her femininity as compensatory, as second best! When we consider that Freud has so often been criticized for an extreme biologic orientation, it seems strange that his psycho-biologic thinking, i.e., the connection which he makes between biology and psychology, is so distorted and convoluted. It would be an anachronism indeed if, in the history of life on our earth and with the evolution of sexual differentiation, a creature ultimately emerged whose evolved conscious awareness should on a biologic basis also include a dissatisfaction with the plan of nature.

Horney (1964) in 1922 was fully aware of the fallacy of such a premise on biological grounds. The "assertion that one half the human race is discontented with the sex assigned to it and can overcome this discontent only in favorable circumstances is decidedly unsatisfying, not only to feminine narcissism but also to biological science." Such dissatisfaction can only be the result of social attitudes and pressures, not of biological givens. Because Freud's theory of personality and his concept of motivation are based largely on the fate of instinctual drives, he considered these as constants, overlooking the fact that in human psychology the forms of their expression and the effect which these forms have on the development and nature of personality are dictated largely by social and cultural factors.

Undoubtedly Freud observed penis envy in his female patients, and little wonder in a culture in which men were preferred. Freud's own familial situation in which he was so clearly favored by his mother as against his sisters is stereotypic for the culture and period in which he grew up (Jones, 1953) and had much more freedom, many more rights, privileges, and opportunities for self-fulfillment. The women who consulted Freud were indeed thwarted—thwarted by the values and sexual mores of their society and by the denigrated image of them which the male dominated culture projected onto them. For many of them their frustrations (and Freud was concerned principally with sexual frustration) were expressed in neurotic symptoms, often of a hysterical nature, and it was for these that they sought help. Thus Freud's theories of feminine sexuality arose out of his therapeutic work with a specific population in a specific time and place.

We owe much to the results of Freud's observations: the nature of psychic conflict, the struggle between wish and anxiety, the emergence of unconscious motivation and its subsequent repression, the nature of symptom formation, its defensive function and its isolation from the total personality. But because Freud, caught in the masculine values of his time, generalized from a limited, socially-conditioned group of cases to a universal psychology of women, and failed to perceive that his conclusions were *relative* to his field of observation, we are burdened with a one-sided theory of the psychosexual development of women. The one-sidedness of his theory is further reinforced by the fact that his concern with ego psychology came late in the history of psychoanalytic theory, with the result that the emphasis on sexual development in the formation of personality, for men as well as women, far outweighs the inclusion of ego factors. A concern with these, since they seem more directly influenced by cultural factors than the life of the instincts, would have called for greater awareness of the social framework.

A number of Freud's followers modified, added to, or disagreed with Freud's view of the personality of woman. Ruth Mark Brunswick (1970), for example, pointed out the importance of the pre-oedipal phase, i.e., the attachment of the little girl to her mother, which in many cases persists throughout life either in positive or negative form and interferes with the woman's capacity for establishing normal relationships with men. Both Josine Müller (1970) and Karen Horney (1964) do not regard penis envy as a primary determinant in the psycho-sexual development of women, but report the awareness of vaginal sensations at an early age in little girls. Horney takes the very important view which is biologically sound that a female child is a woman from the start and not only from puberty, as Freud thought, and that departures from the normal development of femininity are influenced by social factors. This is the first important inclusion of the social framework as a determinant in the development of the feminine personality.

A number of analysts who observed penis envy in their clinical experience have placed a different interpretation upon it than Freud's. Thus Chasseguet-Smirgel (1970) describes Melanie Klein's belief that the little girl—under the sway of her oedipal impulses and in response to her dominant feminine instinctual components—"orally desires the paternal penis; this wish then becomes the prototype of the genital, vaginal desire for the penis." "The introjection of this penis forms the nucleus of the paternal superego (in both sexes); the sadism linked with this phase makes this earlier superego a terrifying one." Ernest Jones (1953) thinks that penis envy in the little girl "is merely a regressive defense in the face of the wish for the penis during intercourse with the oedipal father."

It is striking that the psychoanalysts, whether in agreement or disagreement with Freud, looked for an explanation of the development of female personality (and for that matter of the male as well) in exclusively sexual terms, disregarding the larger perspectives which a concern with historical and social factors would have contributed. Nowhere is the pansexualism of Freudian theory more clearly illustrated.

In the early history of psychoanalysis there is an exception to this in the work of Otto Rank (1958), whose departure from the Freudian movement has regrettably resulted in a general neglect of his prolific writings. However, in the current climate of the women's liberation movement, although expressed some forty years ago, his views which take a wide historical dimension into account are most timely today. In *Beyond Psychology* there is a chapter entitled "Feminine Psychology and Masculine Ideology." Rank begins by saying that "It has become a truism that man from time immemorial has imposed his masculine way of life upon woman, both individually and collectively." The profoundest root cause for this fact as seen in its earliest expression in mythology and primitive religion lies in man's need for immortality, a need which "woman satisfies through her reproductive function in and with the child." In this need of man to deny his mortal nature, his having been born of mortal woman—that is, to blot out his mother-origin—is to be found the dynamic drive for man's religious, social and artistic creativity through which he not only proves his supernatural origin (religion) and capacity (art) but also tries to translate it into practical terms of social organization (state, government)." Human civilization has experienced a gradual masculinization and a movement away from the veneration of female creativity which characterized certain ancient religions and civilizations.

In modern times this masculinization is reflected, among other things, in man's denigration, through his rational psychology, of the so-called "feminine" traits of emotionalism and irrationality—traits which Rank sees as representing certain human qualities of a positive nature. He takes issue with Freud's "masculinity complex," that is, the woman's desire to be or become a man, seeing it as Freud's need to explain human behavior from a patriarchal point of view. The world in which Freud functioned was sexualized by man's interpretation of it and woman was sexualized in terms of man. But, Rank emphasizes, woman "has always wanted and still wants first and foremost to be a woman, because this and this alone is her fundamental self and expresses her personality, *no matter what else she may do or achieve.*"

The human need to actualize to the fullest one's psycho-biologic destiny is, to my mind, basic, for men as well as women. However, this need is always fulfilled within a social context which defines and delimits it in terms of roles. Human adaptive flexibility and the capacity to learn, however, make possible a wide range of role definition—a definition which is determined largely by historical time and social structure. In the inner life of individuals the carrying out of a role is mirrored in imagery —the self image and the image of others that are created as a person observes and experiences others in interaction with them. Thus, for example, we acquire ideas of what is feminine, what is womanly or manly.

In a time of social change like our own, if we return to the issues of the psychology of women, the changes in role and in imagery make it eminently clear that we cannot define femininity by outer behavior, i.e., by the carrying out of a role. The role may change—a woman may become an engineer or have an administrative post in government, roles previously and more generally taken over by men—but her self-image, her inner feeling about herself, may be quite feminine. This will depend on the presence or absence of a social stereotype which is projected upon her, and on her own inner strength in resisting the imposition of the stereotype, and on the security of her self-definition.

What is important here is that self-definition is not achieved primarily by the carrying out of a role, be it social or sexual. Ideally woman is not defined in her own eyes, and hopefully in those of society, by what kind of orgasm she has, or by whether she prefers to be a wife and mother, or have a career or profession. Just as motherliness cannot be measured solely by the amount of time that a mother spends with her child, so femininity cannot be defined by an assigned role.

Unfortunately, there have been many attempts on the part of women to resolve their inner conflicts by what Ruth Moulton (1973) has called a "frantic flight into domesticity." This is only one aspect of the more general human attempt to achieve a secure inner core of self by living out what society, or psychoanalysis, or scientific findings, or an ideology regards as a norm. The process is more apparent in the psychology of women because woman as an individual, woman as "personality," is more in the making; the history of her individuation is younger and is currently more in flux than that of man.

For many individuals a specious sense of security is achieved if the self-image and the social stereotype correspond. However, when the social stereotype ceases to be unified, when there are numerous sub-cultures each with its own norm and when in turn the norms for role definition are in a state of flux, the individual who seeks security largely through compliance with the social stereotype is at a loss. While to some extent a period of rapid social change will precipitate minor and transitory identity crises in almost all individuals, the neurotic and the socially disadvantaged individual—and I regard women as in many ways socially discriminated against—will be more vulnerable in terms of self-definition. It is precisely for the resolution of conflicts of this nature that the modern woman seeks psychotherapeutic help.

In this connection, I should like to describe the case of a young married woman who came to me because of depression and obsessive doubting to illustrate the typical dilemma of many contemporary women whose mature lives are taking place at a time of social change, of changing goals and values. There are many cases which I might have chosen, especially those of young, unmarried women, which would perhaps point up more dramatically the problems, conflicts and anxieties which the new sexual morality has created, and the therapeutic problems which are thereby brought about. I have chosen Marie because the respective roles of individual intrapsychic conflict and of the influence of the social framework, and their interaction, are so clearly brought out in her case. Thus one can see, in treating her psychotherapeutically, the specific contributions of psychoanalytic knowledge and understanding, and the need to enlarge this understanding to include the social dimension.

When Marie first consulted me she was in her early thirties, had been married for about ten years and had three children ranging in age from approximately nine to four years. She was married early in her college years to a graduate student who later became a successful and respected economist. Marie was a person of unusually high intelligence with a brilliantly logical mind. She herself had professional interests in the field of social work, and some years later, with the help of therapy, was able to combine her career with her functions as wife and mother. However, this result was only achieved after a long struggle, for it was precisely the conflict between her maternal role and her need for intellectual gratification through work that seemed unresolvable to her. She felt this conflict and its symptomatic expression in obsessive doubting to be the cause of her depression.

While there were undoubtedly times during her marriage, which was by and large a good one, when she was alienated from her husband and her sexual life was consequently ungratifying during such periods, the sexual issue was in no sense central to her feelings of dissatisfaction and unhappiness. Her complaints and resentments in relation to her husband revolved around his failure to participate sufficiently and more actively in the life of the family. Since she was involved in study and work, and in her domestic tasks as well, she was often overwhelmed by a feeling of injustice in regard to the unequal distribution of responsibility. Furthermore, her emotional need for companionship and for the sharing of the parental role and the familial experience, as well as her wish to make good some of the deprivations of her own childhood by vicariously enjoying her children's interaction with a father, was thwarted by her husband's withdrawal. This is a frequently heard complaint in modern marriage, and I think it is the result of a new conscious awareness and overt expression on the part of women of expectations for participation and companionship from men, which they had long felt but which social change has permitted them to voice. It is a clear example of how a changing psychology of women automatically calls for a modification in the psychology of men.

Marie had an extremely unhappy and lonely childhood, the details of which I will describe presently. In itself, apart from the social factors which gave it its specific expression, it could have accounted for her depression. And, indeed, some years before coming to me, when she lived in another city, Marie had consulted a psychoanalyst, hoping for help with her doubts and conflicts. Instead an attempt was made to indoctrinate her with a fixed set of norms and a definition of her role which only served to confuse her further, and to fill her with guilt for not measuring up to the standard. She was told that her normal feminine role was to be a wife and mother and that the expression of needs other than these was neurotic—probably an expression of masculine strivings. She was even advised on the upbringing of her children—when it was appropriate to be firm; when she was being too self-effacing in her permissiveness and self-sacrifice. While it is not only quite conceivable but inevitable that her neurotic conflicts as they reflected her own childhood experiences would result in neurotic attitudes toward and interactions with her children, the fact that these were expressed to her by the therapist in the form of norms only filled her with more uncertainty, increased her doubt and guilt, and consequently lowered her self-esteem. I make this point to bring out the dangers implicit for a patient, especially in a formative phase of life and in a time of social change, in the imposition of the therapist's values—more especially if they derive their authority from what he regards as "scientific findings." This has been one of the unfortunate misapplications of psychoanalysis.

Marie's parents ran a small business in which both father and mother participated. The little girl was turned over to maids—most frequently very incompetent maids who knew little about the proper rearing of children. She remembers the loneliness that she felt in the face of their disinterest and lack of participation. Her relationship with her mother was no better. Her mother was tyrannical and unendingly critical. There was little about her daughter that pleased her: she criticized her appearance, her dress, her friends, her bookish and intellectual interests. Nor was the criticality balanced by positive feelings. Marie was a sort of Cinderella in the house, for as she got older she was given household chores which took most of her free time; one of these involved the care of her younger brother. Often she missed going out with friends or playmates on a Saturday afternoon because she had not finished the housecleaning, and if she began her work especially early in the morning in order to fin-ish in time to enjoy the afternoon her mother would find additional things for her to do. There was a mean exploitativeness in her mother's attitude and behavior to Marie, so that the growing girl had little happy recreation in her childhood.

She felt her father to be a weak man, who loved her, but was never able to stand up to the mother, and never protected his daughter against her. When she and the father were alone together there was a pleasant companionship between them which vanished with the appearance of the mother. This benign and if somewhat tepid love of her father, how-ever, was of extreme importance, for it gave her the basis for the capacity to love a man and later her sons. It has been my observation that girls whose relationship to the father is either lacking or primarily hostile have great difficulty in forming successful and stable attachments to men. Either their needs are so urgent that they become unduly demanding, or their hostility to the father is transferred overtly or covertly to the men with whom they seek a relationship.

The need for a father in the development of normal femininity, with special emphasis on sexuality, is ably described in a review of Seymour Fisher's, *The Female Orgasm,* by Alex Comfort (1973):

> the greater a woman's conviction that love objects are not depend-able, and must be held onto, the poorer her capacity for full response. This may come about through loss of a father, or childhood depriva-tion of the father's role. . . . Deprived of a stable father-figure, the non-orgasmic in this study seemed to be unable to face the blurring of personal boundaries which goes with full physiological orgasm.— Fathers are there to imprint girls for sexual adequacy.—It ought to be a salutary check on the idea of fatherless upbringing as a contri-bution to Women's Lib, an idea which no primatologist would regard with favor.

Throughout her developmental years Marie was conscious of hating her mother. There was in this case no therapeutic task of uncovering hidden or unconscious resentments and hostilities, nor even of unearthing unacceptable love feelings, although there were certainly bonds and at-tachments on the level of identifications which later in life manifested themselves in the patient's behavior with her own children—much to her distress. It was to the ego level of conflicting identifications and of uncertainty of self-definition that her obsessive doubting and her depres-sion could be traced—not primarily to an unconscious conflict between love and hate as is more usual for the obsessional neurosis. She had an overwhelming fear of being like her mother and sought female models throughout her life, in the form of the mothers of her friends, teachers, women of accomplishment whom she admired, to counteract identification with her mother. In her relationships to her children, her efforts were bent on being all that her mother was not—a loving, accepting and affirming mother.

It is not hard to see that her personality was built too exclusively on a defensive reaction against incorporation of her mother and insufficiently on healthy processes of autonomous ego development. The result was an uncertainty about who she was, which frequently spilled over into the area of values, especially regarding the upbringing of children. This rejection of the mother as a model for the building of the core of the ego is a common problem for women, and to my mind its roots do not lie in the fact, as the classic psychoanalysts would have it, that the mother failed to give them a penis, but in the lack of sufficient, affirmative love on the part of the mother for the female child. This has both social and individual historic causality and the two are inextricably intertwined. By "affirmative love" I mean that quality of love from the mother which accepts, respects and has affection for her child as a separate and individual human being, and which regards her femininity positively as an intrinsic and valuable aspect of her being. The capacity for such love on the part of the mother resides in her personal history and in the influences of society as well.

The lack of value placed on woman and the assignment to her of inferior roles throughout the ages in Western as well as Eastern civilizations have resulted in a denigrated self-image which is passed on from mother to daughter throughout history. A mother who does not sufficiently love herself in the sense of affirming her womanliness cannot fully love her little girl. Thus for the little girl the limitations and frustrations of her individual history are reinforced further by the attitudes of society. The rebellion in many female children and in the lives of many young women against the identification with the mother is healthy testimony to the power and strength of the ego in its drive to achieve self-actualization and autonomy. Most frequently this rebellion is expressed consciously as a wish to assume a role different from that of the mother—not to be a household drudge, not to have one's life limited by the duties of wife and mother, not to be economically dependent upon a man, to have an independent career. These goals have a validity of their own even if they are formulated in the name of rebellion; but the deeper and more unconscious rebellion is one which struggles against the incorporation of the mother's devalued self-image, against the mother's self-hate which would, if taken into herself, become part of the daughter's conception of herself. Such self-hate is, of course, also the basis for depression.

For Marie, as well as for many young women of our time, the conflict between the maternal role and career is not to be understood solely on the more superficial level of not being able to do justice to both roles, with a concomitant fear and guilt reaction because of the possibility of not being an adequate mother (although this conflict exists), but on a deeper level, it is a struggle for self-esteem, a struggle to break the chain of socially inherited feelings of inferiority.

To my mind, the conflict for many individual women cannot be resolved exclusively through the assumption of roles more valued by society than the domestic one, although such breaking of the bonds of socially assigned role is of the utmost importance. The struggle for self-esteem and ego autonomy involves a fundamental psychological separation from a mother whose unconscious attitudes include a denigration of her female child. The use of psychoanalysis, not in its orthodox form, nor in its traditional attitudes toward femininity, but with special emphasis on the subtler and more unconscious processes of ego growth and development, can be helpful.

Marie's obsessional neurosis, therefore, took place largely in ego terms, most specifically in the area of values and in terms of her self-conception. Her doubts centered around whether a specific action, usually regarding her children—for example, whether a particular school was appropriate for her youngest child, was optimally expressive of her maternal concerns. She compulsively wished to be the mother which her own mother was not. She had defensively to negate the identification with her mother. Her superego constantly reiterated to her "Do not do what your mother did." But she was never certain, for inevitably a part of her mother did in fact reside in her. She had insufficient surety in her own autonomy for the separation to take place easily. And that part of her ego which did separate left a vacuum within her personality from which a large part of her depression stemmed. She wanted, in fact, to be loved by a mother.

The unfulfilled longing left its melancholy imprint on her character. This was further reinforced by the critical aspect of her superego which represented her mother's critical attitude toward her. To give this up would have meant a further separation from her mother. There were times in her treatment when she masochistically preferred to maintain her bad self-image, thereby keeping her critical mother image within her

(Menaker, 1953); at other times her independent ego asserted itself and fought off the demons within. In this struggle she was aided, not only by the understanding of the psychological processes in depth which her analysis provided, but by my encouraging, at every possible point, her active participation in the work that interested her and my affirmation of her as a woman, a mother and wife, but above all, as a human being. I thereby helped her to exorcise the bad mother image within and to substitute for it a more benign introject—one whose social values were more consistent with her interests and abilities and with the opportunities that a changing society offered to women. I was the antidote to her mother, raising her self-esteem and helping her to fulfill her capacities.

It is my conviction that, in doing this, I did not approach her with preconceived psychoanalytic norms of feminine psychology nor did I impose my values upon her, but freed her to consolidate her own wishes —wishes to be a good mother—wishes to have a career. These had previously been unfree and guilt-ridden because they were held down by the inner spectre of her mother's values as they reflected individual personal and social attitudes. This introjection was, of course, associated with guilt for my patient because of profound hostility which her mother's denigrated estimation of her had engendered. The hostility in turn added to depression already present because of profound feelings of inferiority.

It seems to me that this case illustrates the personal origins and destructive effects of a psychic conflict centering around the female role, in the intricacies of familial interactions, most especially in the relationship to the mother. But it also points up the continuum between social and psychological causative factors, for the mother's attitudes toward the role of woman are as much the product of the long history of social attitudes as they are of individual personal development. It also becomes clear that a resolution of such conflicts cannot be achieved *solely* through the assumption of social roles or activities—notably those previously most frequently assigned to men. Such participation in new roles must follow upon a personal resolution of intrapsychic conflicts which have created a bondage to the past. The exercise of new roles, however, *once an inner freedom from destructive introjects has been achieved*, can support the growth and formation of an autonomous ego, and raise the level of self-esteem.

The struggle of women today to achieve selfhood, self-esteem and equality with men solely through the exercise of roles other than the domestic one, while eminently understandable and I think transitional, has led to a confusion between role and ego—ego to be understood principally in this context as self-definition. As I have previously stated, no human being can be adequately defined by his or her assumed role. To attempt to do so is to create the characterless and purely symbolic figures of a play in which individuals are designated, not by name, but by role: the prince, his friend, the mother, the doctor, etc. But who are they as people and how do they think of themselves? It is true that the self-image is powerfully conditioned by the surrounding social attitudes. In fact the self-image of a little girl begins to be formed in a social situation—namely in the family, as I have already described it in the case of Marie. But not only is the familial attitude the product of a long history of human development, but current social attitudes are strongly reinforcing. Therefore a change in the traditional role of women through changing social attitudes and values creates an opportunity for the acting out of new and socially more valued roles. The competent carrying out of these redounds to the increased self-esteem of woman, which in turn strengthens her ego.

However, the task of achieving self-definition in depth—for men as well as women—cannot be accomplished exclusively through the assumption of roles. The inner growth of an independent ego depends first upon the relationship of the individual to his introjects, i.e., to what extent they will become acceptable models for identification processes upon which the growth of the ego depends; secondly, upon the successful resolution of conflicting identifications; and thirdly upon the individual's openness to new experiences and the capacity to internalize them as aspects of evolving ego processes. The more such inner growth approximates the ego-ideal of the individual—and the ego-ideal is strongly influenced by social values—the greater will be his sense of self-esteem and therefore of ego-autonomy.

In this realm, women have characteristically special problems, both psychologically and sociologically. Being of the same sex as their mothers makes them more dependent upon them than men would be for the growth and development of ego through the processes of incorporation and identification. They must identify with a woman in order to become a woman psychologically, and a child's first experience of woman is the mother. Thus for the little girl the inevitable internalization of the mother as a part of normal ego development is more critical than it is for the boy, for whom the identification with the father is the more critical factor in the achievement of identity as a male. In the process of such internalization the incorporation of aspects of the mother's femininity will include those socially inherited attitudes toward women—or the reaction against them—to which the mother herself has been subject.

It is precisely at this point that psychological and social factors meet, for social attitudes and values are transmitted through the psychological processes of internalization from generation to generation. The chain is broken through the emergence of strong and exceptional individuals who strive for ego identity beyond and outside the conventionally accepted norms. Such individuals become the foci of social change (Menaker, 1965), and their creative role consists in delineating new values, goals and norms, i.e., in creating the opportunity, through the emergence of new ego-ideals, for others who are themselves motivated in similar directions to internalize their values and thus to achieve greater self-actualization. I see a major task of psychoanalytic therapy in its contemporary garb to be the freeing of the individual from conflict-producing identifications in order to make room for the incorporation of new values. This is especially true for the treatment of women, the formation of whose personality is currently more undetermined because of social change.

While I have intentionally failed to place major emphasis on the issue of sex in relation to feminine psychology since so much has already been written on this subject, and much has been said about the general psychology of women based too exclusively on her sexual role, it would be negligent to omit the influence of changing sexual mores and a changing sexual morality upon the conduct of the psychotherapeutic process. Despite the disclaimer of psychoanalysis (Hartmann, 1960) that it operates almost entirely free of value systems, it becomes clearer in the light of changing norms that psychoanalysis does indeed have norms and that its therapeutic function is delimited by them. For example, what was previously defined by psychoanalysis as sexual varietism and considered a pathologic condition is increasingly difficult to distinguish from the usual sexual behavior of many young people today. If one is to avoid the judgmental use of norms, the issue in therapy becomes one of addressing oneself to the inner conflict surrounding behavior—and since the individual has come to treatment, there is conflict—rather than to the behavior itself.

The classic analyst may counter that psychoanalysis has always focused on the inner conflict through its emphasis on intrapsychic dynamics, and has eschewed direct comment upon behavior. But this is only a partial truth, and the therapeutic interaction is subtler and more complex than to exclude the influence of the analyst's norms and values, whether they are derived from subjective attitudes or objective theoretical convictions, upon his evaluation of the analytic material. This is especially true in the differentiation of defensive from *bona fide* action. If, for example, he holds strongly to the penis-envy theory of feminine psycho-sexual development, he is likely to interpret aggressive behavior or resentful attitude toward men or toward a particular man in an appropriate situation exclusively in terms of such envy. He may be blind to the fact that these reactions may be legitimate manifestations of self assertion whose proper expression is permissible within a changing social framework. Or if he is committed to the "clitoral-vaginal transfer theory" as propounded by Freud and many of his followers, he will be unaware of recent biological motivation: Is it "acting out" in the name of some unconscious gratifi- as a manifestation of masculine strivings. He may also be inclined to evaluate a wish for a career or a vocation outside the home (see case of Marie, described above) as a flight from the role of wife and mother, instead of as a wish for the optimal fulfillment of ego potential.

Greater freedom in sexual behavior in the light of greater social permissiveness is not always easy to evaluate in terms of deeper psychological motivation: Is it "acting out" in the name of some unconscious gratification? Is it a defensive use of sex to overcome unrelatedness and loneliness? Or is it a legitimate expression of need that takes a specific and differentiated form in the case of different individuals? The answer to these questions cannot come through the dogmatic application of a theory to the therapeutic situation, but only through an unbiased investigation of the total personality in each individual case, which must include an openness to the factors of social change which form the background for his functioning and influence his conception of norms, goals and ideals against which he measures himself.

Thus is the Freudian concept of normality, i.e., the ability to work and love with a minimum of conflict, challenged not as a formal generalization, but in its specific content—a content which changes and takes shape in an historic social context. This is especially true at the present time for the psychology of woman, for woman is evolving to new levels of ego autonomy and integration, and as woman evolves, so must man change. The task of therapy, as I see it, is to bring all that is valid in psychoanalytic understanding and all that is added to that knowledge through further open-minded investigation of personality, especially in the area of ego psychology, to bear on facilitating that evolutionary process.

REFERENCES

Brunswick, R. The pre-oedipal phase of libido development. In J. Chasseguet-Smirgel (Ed.), *Female Sexuality*. Ann Arbor: University of Michigan Press, 1970, pp. 24-28.

Comfort, A. A girl needs a father. *The BBC Listener*, 89, 549-550, April 26, 1973.

HARTMANN, H. *Psychoanalysis and Moral Values.* New York: International Universities Press, 1960.

HORNEY, K. *Feminine Psychology.* New York: Norton, 1964.

HORNEY, K. The dread of woman. In J. Chasseguet-Smirgel (Ed.), *Female Sexuality.* Ann Arbor: University of Michigan Press, 1970, pp. 31-32.

JONES, E. *The Life and Work of Sigmund Freud.* Vol. I. New York: Basic Books, 1953.

JONES, E. The early development of female sexuality. In J. Chasseguet-Smirgel (Ed.), *Female Sexuality.* Ann Arbor: University of Michigan Press, 1970, pp. 36-38.

KLEIN, M. Psychoanalysis of children. In J. Chasseguet-Smirgel (Ed.), *Female Sexuality.* Ann Arbor: University of Michigan Press, 1970, pp. 33-34.

MENAKER, E. Masochism: A defense reaction of the ego. *Psychoanalytic Quarterly,* 22, 205-220, 1953.

MOULTON, R. Sexual conflicts of contemporary women. In E. G. Wittenberg (Ed.), *Interpersonal Explorations in Psychoanalysis.* New York: Basic Books, 1973.

MÜLLER, J. The problem of the libidinal development of the genital phase in girls. In J. Chasseguet-Smirgel (Ed.), *Female Sexuality.* Ann Arbor: University of Michigan Press, 1970, pp. 30-31.

RANK, O. *Beyond Psychology.* New York: Dover Press, 1958.

SHERFEY, M. J. The evolution and nature of female sexuality in relation to psychoanalytic theory. *Journal of the American Psychoanalytic Association,* 14, 28-128, 1966.

11

WOMEN IN THERAPY — A GESTALT THERAPIST'S VIEW

MIRIAM POLSTER

Not long ago, in a weekend workshop for couples, we had divided into two groups, husbands and wives. Off by themselves, the women were asked to close their eyes and fantasize what one of their days might be like if they were men instead of women. Afterwards, as we shared our fantasies with each other, one of the women reported how in her fantasy she had started walking through her house from one of the back bedrooms, all the way through the house, and how, as she walked through each of the rooms, she hadn't picked up a single toy or piece of clothing or newspaper, she hadn't closed a single drawer or closet door, she hadn't turned out a single light or mopped up a single spill, and finally she had just walked straight through the house and out the front door, closing the door behind her. After she finished telling us her fantasy, there was a soft crackle of laughter, smiles of recognition and kinship and a chuckle of admiration at her fantasied resolution.

Now I had met the husbands of these women. They were not brutes, bullies or martinets who insisted that household duties be performed with militaristic timeliness and dispatch. But these women didn't seem to need that, anyhow. They had arrived at the point where they felt compelled to do things they didn't really want to do and which they could get out of doing only by special effort, like fantasizing, or under special conditions, like illness. Somehow, they had constructed for themselves standards of behavior that they felt obliged to live up to and which often bore only slight resemblance to the actual pattern of their own personal needs.

A double thread runs through the stories of many of the women I see, married or unmarried. On the one hand, they feel trapped in a round

247

of commitment and activities which keeps them busy but leaves them feeling unsatisfied, frantic and unfulfilled. On the other hand, adding insult to injury, they do not even experience themselves as having a hand in making many of the decisions about how they are to live. They feel locked into a situation—a career decision, a relationship or a life-style—which they didn't elect or which has turned out to have hidden consequences they didn't foresee, but which they feel powerless to change or to abandon. They bottle up the feelings and desires which they believe they can't express, either because expressing them will cause more trouble than they already have or because it won't make any difference anyway and they will only wind up feeling more frustrated and impotent. So they become skillful at learning how to dance when somebody else leads.

The difficulties any person experiences in life will reflect his or her own particular limitations and these, in turn, will relate to the prohibitions and limitations which society imposes on each of us. If a woman is married, societal patterns will have a lot to say about how her husband views the marriage and what expectations he has brought to the relationship. Her own personal bent will, correspondingly, determine how hemmed in she may feel by these expectations and how committed she is to living up to them, whether she finds them compatible or not with her own needs. Single or married, at work she will encounter the expectations her colleagues carry in with their lunch pails or briefcases and her response to built-in expectations also pervades her experiences as a woman at school, within her family and among her friends.

It is a major hunk of work for a woman to integrate all of these inclinations and influences and to come up with a harmonious personal sense of herself where no experience need be discriminated against as inadmissible or unworthy.

As a child, all of her experience was viewed freshly and uncritically. She made her own standards for what she wanted to do and what she didn't want to do, spinning them out of the shining thread of her own sensations and values. She could play as happily with shit as she could with mud. Only gradually did she begin to learn that some things that made her happy weren't supposed to and some things which weren't so pleasing to her were, nevertheless, better regarded and were to be more highly valued. She began to distrust knowledge based primarily on her own experience and to introject, to swallow whole with the same lack of criticism, the precepts of other stronger and wiser people around her. She began to exchange pure joy for secondhand wisdom. In doing this she had her first exercise in learning how to deny or disapprove of some of the most beautiful parts of her own experience.

But these denied or disowned parts of herself did not just meekly disappear. The imprint of firsthand living is not so easily erased. The taste of honey lingers somewhere in one's insides and sends up vague traces of something better than the present watered-down experience which is only an inadequate substitute. Somewhere underground, her original knowledge of joy sits uneasy and only too ready to contradict or sabotage the surface confluence agreed upon by her shrewder and more politic socialized self which denies the primal zest and richness that she knows can underlie her actions.

Eventually, these antithetical characteristics freeze into postures of mutual alienation and stand-off; this is the genesis of her own personal polarities, those internal contradictions which nourish ambivalence and fatigue. Perls (1969) formulated the concept of polarities into the basic characters of topdog versus underdog, but there is more diversity than this in the cast of polarities making up the composite which is any particular woman. Topdog and underdog imply merely that in these polar struggles one of the opponents appears to be winning or to have the upper hand. However, any characteristic aspect of a woman can spawn its own polar counterpart. So, contests can rage on internally between a woman's ruthlessness and her tenderness, between her conventional self and her rebel, between her meekness and her arrogance. Any woman is a composite of many Dr. Jekylls and Ms. Hydes.

To the extent that a woman keeps herself out of touch with one of the polarities engaged in her personal conflicts, she is ensuring her own immobility and impotence. Rooted in her submerged and disowned underdog are the seeds of change and movement. Like all the disenfranchised, her underdog has little to lose and everything to gain from change. When she remains out of touch with this unacknowledged part of herself, she is, in effect, silencing her own protest against the *status quo*. The parts of herself which she refuses to give ear or voice to remain isolated and unavailable as a support for informed action. They are relegated to underground activities, dissension and sabotage. This is what underlies her sense of being trapped or crammed with unexpressed and inexpressible feelings.

In gestalt therapy, a central focus of our work is the individual's responsibility for shaping his or her own existence. In spite of how her environment leans on her, a woman, nevertheless, has to know how to engage with it in ways which will be nourishing and zestful, not just successive acts of self-betrayal. She is creating her own life, bit by bit. She needs all her energy and ingenuity to come up with hours, days and years that she feels she has had a hand in shaping. To do this, she has to be able to integrate her awareness of sensations, actions, wants, values, relationships and all the raw material of her life with her own personal willingness and skill in using this awareness as her basis for action.

When her awareness is unprejudiced and unimpeded, when she has no stake in keeping parts of her experience alien and unknown, her actions can spring expressively from native mobilization. Her sense of her life is that it has flexibility, surprise, enthusiasm and movement. She experiences herself as a free agent, acting from her own needs, making choices from a range of possible alternatives and being free to change whatever she becomes aware of as unsatisfying or toxic.

An example of this is the experience of one woman who came to realize, in her awareness of the tyranny that her family and their rigid upbringing had imposed on her, that she had even furnished her entire house according to their dictates and not at all to her own taste! In addition to standards of interior design, she had also swallowed much of what the family had to say about such virtues as thrift, frugality and conservative behavior. One day we were working with her distaste for her furniture and how angry she was with herself for feeling so stuck with it. She was far from poor and could probably have afforded to chuck it all and simply refurnish. I instructed her to use her anger and give herself a lecture on what she might do with her herd of white elephants. She was a woman of rich imagination and exuberant sense of drama, and she swung into the assignment with energy. Her ideas ranged from burning it and collecting the insurance to giving it all to a charitable organization and claiming it as a tax deduction. But her eventual solution illustrated an important and basic principle in gestalt work with polarities, in this case her esthetic self and her practical self. Resolution of a conflict, in its most effective and enduring form, usually involves respecting both parts of the polarity and merging them into a course of action which represents a synthesis or an alliance of these previously disparate parts. Her solution turned out to be a house sale, leaving her house bare, cannily getting top dollar for her unwanted furniture (even selling some of it to her relatives!), and winding up with a healthy bankroll to finance her refurnishing.

Now all of a woman's actions may not be this exciting or have such a sense of turnaround. Life is not so unstintingly generous. But even when a woman performs humdrum tasks, if she experiences herself as not locked into doing them she is free to recognize that she regards these tasks as necessary and *chooses* to do them rather than delegating them to someone else or letting them go undone. She is also free to stop doing them when she senses that the psychological cost to herself has become more than she is willing to pay.

The experience of being stuck, on the contrary, consists of finding one's present status malnourishing, distasteful or even downright poisonous but feeling unable to do anything but hang on to it. A woman may know exactly what it might take to turn her life around, but such changes may frighten or repel her. On the other hand, she may only vaguely want something more or something different than she has right now, and this amorphous discontent scares her, or results in her feeling guilty, despondent or overly demanding.

What a woman finds unwelcome about making changes in her own life is, at least partly, a projection. That is, what scares her or repels her or makes her feel guilty is the unknown or the unacceptable or the reprehensible *in herself*. What she fears about making changes is primarily the re-awakening of aspects of herself, unpredictable, untried, alien, demanding and leading to consequences she is not sure she is willing to permit. Her self-doubt also has an introjective core. It is the accumulation of the judgments and values of other people which she has taken in and adopted as her own and which she feels uneasy about questioning. Unchallenged, these foreign doctrines govern her actions from a position analogous to that of a distant ruler sending out edicts, which are not to be questioned, to the inhabitants of a territory he has conquered. Instead of viewing herself as a population of potential and unrealized capacities which she might explore, she fears rebellion and the overthrow of her established routine and is immobilized by this fear. She keeps herself in check like an uneasy dictator who fears change. This is how she has arrived at her current impasse—unhappy with her present life, but afraid or unwilling to try new behaviors or adopt new values which might lead to resolution. As a way of relieving herself of the responsibility for this situation, she projects outside of herself her own unwillingness to change and decides that she has no effect on an immutable and intransigent world. She is stuck.

One young married woman deplored the boredom of her life with a husband whom she considered dull, unadventuresome, overweight and her social inferior. Some of these things were true about him, but he was also generous with her, listened to her periodic tirades without getting too angry, and had enough emotional resilience to come out of these combats still loving her and not bearing any grudges. He worked at an unskilled job where he was his own boss and dealt with machinery which he loved. He was not a milktoast; he was an easygoing guy with a good sense of humor and a no-nonsense attitude towards himself and the world around him. He was pretty well informed, had some interest in politics, but mostly he liked his job, his family and his friends.

She was filled with the idea that she was really better than all this, too good for such a husband, and wanted to split. Where she wanted to go and what she planned on doing when she arrived were inconsequential details that she couldn't be bothered with. She admitted that she very much liked the financial and material comfort she had with him, and he came in very handy when there were practical issues that demanded attention. She had very little tolerance for handling frustration in a creative way, she would get bogged down in emotional upheavals, and his good-humored patience was indispensable at these times. This was not a very good omen for her independent function without him.

During our work together, interestingly enough, she changed very little. He lost weight, became more active in volunteer political organizations, began to read more and talk to her about what he was reading—but she was still not satisfied. She had a great stake in not recognizing change, since she wanted to retain her picture of herself as a woman burdened with an inferior husband. This freed her of the necessity to do anything about making changes in herself that might move her out of her own boredom. Of her own shortcomings she remained steadfastly unaware, and when her husband confronted her about them on those occasions when he was moved beyond endurance, her response was tears and hysteria.

This elevated picture of herself had been handed to her by her mother, along with the family recipes. But all she had was a vague sense that she was cut out for better things, and there was very little substance behind these feelings. Her first chore was to learn how to make her own life interesting without blaming her boredom on her husband and expecting him to do something about it. We worked at making her more aware of the specific things she wanted from her husband, and she began to give up expecting him to be a mind-reader and divine what she wanted. She began to take a couple of courses at the local university extension program. Not grand actions, surely, but initial steps in shaping her own movement out of boredom.

The need to keep from making changes imposes certain conditions on a woman. She has to keep herself from becoming aware of attractive possibilities for action either within herself or in her environment. She has to keep new directions from becoming fascinating or compelling enough to disturb and arouse her. She has to construct and maintain an equilibrium for herself where she can exercise just enough sensitivity to know that she is unhappy, but not enough to discover or invent what she might do about her own unhappiness.

There are several ways she can keep herself in this condition. For the most part, they consist of not allowing her own experience to become sharp enough, figural enough, to articulate clearly what is bothering her. Whenever an individual has a stake in things-as-they-are, she has to do something to obscure the native flux that all living things display. To keep phenomena which *are* changing appearing as if they are not changing at all, she has to prevent herself from seeing them clearly, in rich detail, as well-defined and active figures against the background of her general orientation to her life. In the above example, the young wife had to learn to see change in her husband, as well as work towards changes in herself.

One way of not perceiving clearly is to play dumb or vague by remaining unaware of specifically what she may not like about her present situation. She can't identify what displeases her. Nothing is actually wrong. She has a lovely home, or a good job, or a fine husband, or great kids, or good people to work with, and she can't conceive of how to change anything when nothing is wrong. She blurs her own experience and keeps herself in the dark as a way of short-circuiting the excitement and the arousal to action that awareness brings. Awareness calls for responsive and expressive behavior; it tips the balance against inaction.

Take the example of another married woman, beautiful and intelligent, doing well at a job which she found interesting, loving and being loved by her husband, but still feeling that there was something missing. One day she was recounting her experience with one of the administrators in the agency where she worked. It had been an unsatisfactory interview where she had failed to get her point across to the older woman who had brushed aside her questions, giving her only perfunctory answers and hurrying her out of the office. My patient made excuses for her supervisor, saying she was busy, that she probably had many other things on her mind, and that she had to take other people into consideration and wasn't free to devote herself to just one person's needs. Then she fell silent. I asked her what she was aware of, and she replied that she was holding her breath and she was clenching her teeth. I instructed her to breathe more deeply and regularly and to attend to what happened when she did this. She observed that her teeth remained clenched, but that now she also noticed some tension at the back of her throat. I asked her to make some sound when she exhaled, incorporating the tension in her throat and the clenching of her teeth. What emerged was a somewhat throttled but unmistakable growl. She looked startled at making such a sound. I asked her whom she felt like growling at, and after a pause she said, "You know, I don't really mean what I said about my supervisor. I think she's giving me lousy supervision and I'm angry at her for not giving me the kind of supervision I need." Another moment's pause, "And I'm mad because *I* made it easy for her! *I* let her get away with it!" This led to a chain of memories of instances when she had made it easy for people to ignore her, or not take her seriously, or not give her the information she wanted from them. I told her I would play her supervisor and we would start the interview over again and this time to make sure that she got what she needed and didn't let me squirm off the hook. To do this she had to mobilize more of her own aggressive energy, to the point where, when I began to rise out of my chair as if indicating that the interview was over, she put one forefinger against my chest and pushed me back into the chair saying, "I'm not done with you yet!" When we finished she looked lively and vigorous. Subsequently she became more active in getting what she wanted, not only from her supervisor, but also from doctors and salespeople whom she had previously allowed to intimidate her.

Another way for a woman to avoid moving directly against her predicament is to retroflect, to direct her disapproval of something back against herself in the form of a blanket condemnation. She condemns herself totally as inadequate or unworthy. Other people are stronger, more capable, more knowledgeable or just plain nicer than she is. Other women manage a home and kids and a job and go to school, and *they* aren't worn to a frazzle and shrewish like she is. Or they have special talents or ideas and even though they live under some of the same conditions she does, *they* manage to come up with creative and sparkling answers. *They* are more virtuous, less self-centered, less selfish and they never complain about their troubles. Everyone else seems so happy and competent, why is she the only malcontent? All of her troubles exist because she is so incompetent, and she engages in a constant round of self-accusation and blame.

As an example of this, I remember a young woman who was creative, hardworking, generous and loving to her family with these talents. When she was able to do something that made her happy, she was as radiant as a sunrise, and often the things that made her happy were things that made life better for her husband and kids, too. Often—but not always. There were some things she wanted to do for herself; she wanted to paint, and teach practical nursing, in which she was trained, part-time, and more generally to establish an island of personal competence and achievement not rooted in her own home. Her husband gave superficial approval to these ambitions. As long as they didn't interfere with her care of the kids or her maintenance of the house, or her serving as hostess to his family and business associates, and as long as it didn't involve his having to take up the slack in the family living arrangements, it was okay with him.

Her husband was a reliable, conscientious and hard-working young man. He took his responsibilities seriously. He took everything and everyone else seriously, too. But what he didn't know about was joy, grace, luminosity and free-flowing love, and he was choking these very qualities right out of his wife. She was ripe for such a bargain, it turned out, because her mother, a conventionally practical woman, had dismissed as trivial her daughter's very real artistic talent and had left her a set-up for anyone who continued the routine. Her husband differed from her mother superficially in that he was indulgent and condescending instead of harsh, but he, too, put her down in his own way. She was so snowed by his good qualities that she believed she was too demanding and he was a saint even to put up with her. He agreed with her and treated her with a tolerant benevolence that bordered on the ludicrous, except that it had such tragic repercussions. I worked with them as a couple on those few occasions when he was willing to come in. Mostly, he thought it was his wife's problem, an effective defense, and he was generously willing to pay for her treatment. So we worked alone, she and I.

Our sessions focused on her becoming aware of what she wanted and how she might get it without needing anything from her husband. If this sounds like a mixture of subversion and autonomy, for many women it boils down to just such a method. She became an expert, using the proceeds from the sale of several of her paintings to hire someone to do some of the work at home that didn't need her personally. She also got into touch with her own attractiveness, began dressing with more dash and began to hear some of the admiring things that people other than her husband had to say about her. She even considered taking a lover, but decided against it because she really loved her husband, pompous as he was, and reasoned that it would cost her more anguish than she wanted. Her sense of her own worth began to equal her estimate of her husband's worth, and she started to teach him some of the things she needed him to know, like how to make love better. She even realized that in some ways he was more fragile than she, and her loving could more realistically cope with his needs, as well as her own. What she accomplished in therapy was to stop believing exclusively in outside authorities and to look to herself as a person whose experience and authority were at least as valid as theirs. When we terminated, she had a more accurate appraisal of both herself and her husband. She was past the idolatrous worship of him that was the obverse of her own self-condemnation.

Another way that some women paralyze themselves is to make their goals so grandiose or drastic that they can't get started on such vast plans. What they conceive it would take for their own personal improvement is a grand societal reformation or family upheaval or graduate degree or administrative position that would give them prestige and clout. Even if this is true, which in some sense it always is, this is not where she can get started. The trouble with these ambitious plans is that they sound so elegant and far-reaching that they become a substitute for action. A woman asserts that she could run her own advertising agency, but she just can't get someone to stay with the kids while she would be away. Another wants a graduate degree, but hates to do required reading. This settling for eternal and obsessive planning with no consummatory action is what Perls called "mind-fucking."

One young woman, lethargic and indolent in her sessions with me, would engage in repetitious denunciations of a society where people didn't care about one another and where women were relegated to subservient roles. But she sat for hours in my office expecting all of the action to come from me, and putting nothing into the pot. I was supposed to lay some kind of therapy on her which would change everything while demanding very little action from her. My aim, whenever she tried to engage me in this way, was to do something which would compel her to take over an active role. So, every time she complained about the evils of the society, I would get her to move out of her usual listless protest by engaging the offenders in an imaginary dialogue or by playing the part of the transgressors defending themselves or by any other means I could come up with to energize her.

One day she began to complain, logically enough, about my not being more active in our session. I asked her to scold me and to tell me what she wanted from me. As she berated me, I directed her to listen to what she was saying. Before long, she became aware that she was assuming a subservient role in our work together, perpetuating right in my office what she had ascribed to society's ill will. Our sessions changed after that, with her assumption of more responsibility for the conduct of her own therapy. Her energy was not so devoted any more to pointless harangues and focused instead on the specifics she wanted to change in her own life; she switched her major at school, selected a new advisor whom she found she could really talk to and joined a couple of activist groups where she began to act on her social grievances in the company of kindred spirits.

In working with a woman who feels stuck, it becomes important to ascertain whether she expends more energy in emphasizing the objections to movement than in supporting her own positive momentum. Many women specialize in throwing roadblocks in their own paths, cluttering up their experience with side issues that obscure and distract from the central concerns, leaving them worn out and with little energy left for the main event. There is usually much for her to be discontented about, but she prevents herself from doing anything about it because she is so hedged in with conditions, precepts, moralisms, projections, contingencies, qualifications, corollaries—ad infinitum—all of which must be considered. And considered they are, endlessly, until she begins to sound like a broken record. I recall the fantasy of one woman who was reciting all the contingencies she had to consider before she could do something she wanted to do. I asked her to fantasize that each one of these considerations was a bar in a cage that she was making for herself. As she named each one of the objections she was putting up, she was to picture it as one of the bars. She built a marvelous cage for herself; she had enough objections to ring herself in completely.

Growing up a woman in our society leaves a psychological residue that cripples and deforms all but the most exceptional women. It is no comfort to know that the same distortions also pervade growing up a man and with some of the same unhappy consequences. There is also no comfort to be found in the fact that some of the best teachers of these principles are themselves women, who ought to know better from their own experience. Our society reinforces in women dependent, exploitative and defensive behaviors aimed at procuring conventional and stereotyped rewards. For the woman who is disdainful of either the method or the rewards, there is frequently much trouble and meager compensation. No wonder many women give up the fight. For those who persevere in trying to establish an independent sense of their own identity, it is still not without cost in the form of nagging self-doubt, criticism from others and displacement of energy into dealing with side issues and irrelevancies.

For example, one woman was doggedly independent and resented the marginal status of a single woman who couldn't call a man for a date with the same freedom that he could call her. The artifice of sitting at the phone and waiting for him to take the initiative was galling. Many times she just wouldn't wait, but even when she called, knowing it was as much her right as his, she felt precarious and unsure of her welcome. In addition to the universal doubt about whether or not someone wants to hear from you when you are the one making the overture, she was worried about the onus of the aggressive female. This kind of defensiveness pervaded many of her actions so that even the simple act of having to put air in her bicycle tires and needing the gas-station attendant to show her how to use the air hose for the first time aroused in her the disgust at looking like another dumb female who didn't understand mechanical contraptions. Our work together was devoted to getting her off the ground and making her strong, assertive energy work for her, rather than against her. She had to learn how to keep her own motor running, how to be as much as she could be and how not to water herself down in order to minimize trouble. She was strong enough to tolerate trouble better than weakness any day. But the fact that she had to work so hard to establish and maintain her own independent function is a black mark against a society that insists on caricatures of women instead of fully dimensional self-portraits.

Even for women who appear to accept the traditional roles and outwardly function well, there is still a hidden personal toll. Physical complaints, boredom, feelings of fatigue, problems about their own sexuality are evidence that all is not well with them, either.

One woman came to see me complaining of feeling tired and with head throbbing even when she woke up first thing in the morning. Her doctor had found nothing wrong with her physically and she was desperate. One day, as we worked with her chronic headache, I asked her to attend to her pain and to observe what it felt like. She answered that it felt like a heavy sandbag on top of her, bearing down and oppressing her. I told her to take ownership of the sandbag, to fantasy that *she* was the sandbag and was pressing down on her own throbbing head. She began to speak as the sandbag, "Here I am, right when you wake up and I'm going to stay with you all day, too. I'm going to press down on you and tell you all the things you have to do and I'm going to remind you about all the things you left undone from yesterday. . . ." Tears came to her eyes and she spoke about how she never seemed to let up on herself, even when she was exhausted, always goading herself with lists of chores to be done, always feeling she never did enough. "I do this to my husband, too. I ask him to do something and I don't let up on him, I nag at him until he gets it done and I make him miserable and mad, and then I feel like such a bitch!" I remarked that she didn't have to go on sandbagging herself and her husband if she didn't want to, and asked if she had any ideas about how she might quit this. She continued to talk about how unrealistically high her expectations were from herself and others. As she went on, she evolved a system for herself whereby she would decide which chores she felt were really essential and wanted done right away, and which were less important and could be done whenever someone had the time. She also worked out a motto which she put at the top of her list: "Remember, the sun will rise tomorrow even if I don't pull it up." She was able to stay with this scheme, too, and her headaches went away, along with the discarded sandbag.

Another woman complained that she was overly concerned about her bowel habits, worrying about constipation and drinking prune juice whenever she hadn't had a daily bowel movement. She was constipated, but not seriously, and where she had got the idea that she had to have a daily bowel movement she didn't know. She described how attentive she was to both the quantity and quality of her stool—and was usually not very pleased with what she had produced. I asked her to try some homework—not to look at her bowel movements at all, just to shit and then flush the toilet. The very next week she reported that her constipation was gone! Once she stopped evaluating herself and allowed herself just to produce freely, she could just produce shit freely, too. No more prune juice either, nor did the constipation come back for the next year and a half that we saw each other.

I believe that a mode frequently resorted to by women is retroflection, turning back against themselves something they would like to do to someone else or have someone else do to them. It is the recourse of people who have only a minimal expectation of having enough impact on their environment to make it produce what might satisfy them. So they give up their expectation and settle instead for a self-contained action; they do for themselves or to themselves what they would like done for or to them, or what they might like to do to someone else. Often they turn back against themselves their unexpressed feelings of resentment, disappointment, criticism, deprecation and hostility. I remember one woman who, unwilling to criticize her husband who was away a good deal on business trips, made the back of her scalp raw with scabs as she picked at herself instead.

Sexual difficulties in women frequently revolve around a retroflective nucleus of resentment and self-punishment. A fringe benefit, of course, is that in some cases this also permits some punishment of another person as well as herself.

One woman, married for about 12 years with three children, began suddenly to find intercourse with her husband excruciatingly painful. A gynecological examination revealed no physiological explanation for her discomfort. She was a bright, spunky woman with definite opinions of her own and good insight into the problems of other people, but unable to soften up long enough to see when or how she was defeating herself. We did some work focused on getting her to relax the sphincters of her vagina, moving her pelvis more freely and coordinating her breathing with a feeling of openness throughout her body, not just in her nose and mouth. These exercises were successful in freeing her own feelings of sexual want, but when she got close to her husband she was dismayed to find that she stiffened up and couldn't move softly and loosely into the contact that both he and she wanted. One day she was talking about her father, an overbearing, dictatorial and deeply disrespectful man. Most of her early life had been spent in resisting his insistence that she meekly knuckle under to his orders and opinions. I asked her to fantasy that her father was sitting in the empty chair in my office and to express her feelings directly towards him. She told him of her resentment at his steamroller style, how he just ran over people who opposed him and how the only way she had escaped was by just not taking any crap from him. I asked her what she felt as she said this. She replied that she felt tight and tense all over, just short of trembling. I asked if this was how she felt in her vagina, too. She replied that it was. I directed her to intensify her tightness until she felt she was as tense as she could be, to hold it for a moment longer, and then abruptly let go. There was a moment when she let her breath go after holding it while she had tensed up, and her face softened from its grim expression. She began to yield to crying. She shook her head and said through tears that she remembered how she had hated her father and that she thought she was all through with that, had settled it long ago. I said that it seemed to me that she had stored up all her resentment and centered it in her vagina, where she was still acting as if she wasn't going to take anything from a man, even if she loved him. She closed her eyes for a minute at the sudden rush of self-recognition and wordlessly nodded her head.

A woman in trouble is frequently a woman whose sense of her own boundaries is both rigid and fragile. Her I-boundary (Polster and Polster, 1973), her personal tolerance for permitting awareness to grow and

ripen into contactful interaction with her environment, is severely restricted by her inability or reluctance to risk takeover. Her selectivity
for contact—which is determined by the I-boundaries she has chosen to
maintain for herself—will govern the style of her life, dictating the
choice of friends, lovers, husbands, work, geography, fantasy, lovemaking,
childrearing and all the other experiences which are psychologically relevant to her life. If she allows herself to become figurally aware of aspects
of herself or her life which displease or frustrate her, she risks allowing
this growing tide of awareness to surge into a direction which might lead
to action. If she is unwilling to risk this, she becomes committed to a
policy of unawareness and inaction.

Awareness is a way of keeping up to date with herself and her current
experience. It is a preamble to lively engagement and expressive interaction in the present moment. It is an antidote to remaining fixed in past
commitments or outgrown values. The woman who is aware of her wants
and can express them experiences herself as being on target and moving
towards a sense of completion and release. With the completion of a
cycle of awareness-wanting-action, she is free to continue her contemporary interaction with her own experience rather than becoming mired in
incomplete and unfulfilled wanting.

Awareness is no guarantee against pain or unhappiness. It means that
she may indeed perceive clearly the dead-end quality of a lifeless relationship, she may recognize that a work scene is sterile, she may acknowledge that something she once wanted is, in actuality, no longer what
she wants now. It also means that she must take the responsibility for
creating and/or perpetuating this unhappy state of affairs.

But until her sense of responsibility and ownership is acknowledged—
and eventually welcomed—there is no therapeutic leverage for movement.
She has to learn to cherish her awareness because of the information she
can glean from it to guide and orient her in making her own decisions
and taking subsequent action. She has to want to know herself well so
that she can move with grace and spontaneity, confident enough of her
own flexibility so that error or second thought needn't scare her. She
has to be able to commit herself to a course of action, *not* in perpetuity
but in existential enthusiasm. Awareness is a necessary ingredient in
this kind of living.

I have found that my own womanhood is a very important factor in
my work as a therapist. With some women it adds an expectation of
being understood in a way no man could understand them. This
leads to a willingness to be open, to discuss things with me that they

might "confess" to a man but that they can "tell" me. It leads also, I believe, to their becoming more confronting, less docile, less cowed by their therapist. Taking me on in an argument makes the odds seem a little more in their favor; I swing enough weight as a therapist, at least I am also a woman. It gives me an advantage in working with women because there is a diminished likelihood that they can brush aside my disagreeable comments or observations as less relevant to them because I "don't really know how it is." I *do* know how it is, I have been there and I am still there. This gives a resonance to our relationship that can amplify what I do and say.

My being a woman also enhances my value as a personification of other possibilities of being-a-woman. It is not unusual for a woman to ask me if I juggled the same set of problems she is trying to keep in the air. How did I deal with the conflict between marriage, children, personal and professional needs? Do I ever have trouble with my kids? Do I ever feel rejected or unsure of myself? Have I ever lost a baby? Do I feel the responsibility dumped on me for aging parents? These questions demonstrate an incontrovertible parallel that she is drawing between herself and me. My answers, when I give them, are surely not intended to provide instructions for imitation. When I can, I answer more about *how* I arrived at an answer, about what my contingencies were, than about the actual solution of a particular problem. That way she and I can work towards inventing new answers, personally and uniquely applicable to her.

This is not to be taken as a statement that I believe women should be in therapy with other women and men should seek help only from other men. There are important therapeutic rewards, as I know from personal experience, when women work with a male therapist and men work with a female therapist. The basic human dimension of *personhood* is at stake in therapy—moving beyond stereotypes of man or woman into the full articulation and integration of everything any individual can be when all aspects of one's experience are available.

A good woman has pungency, flexibility, suppleness, energy, responsiveness, tenderness, toughness, grace, depth . . . so does a good man. She doesn't play favorites with these qualities. She needs them all to go about the serious business of creating her own life.

REFERENCES

PERLS, F. S. *Gestalt Therapy Verbatim*. Moab, Utah: Real People Press, 1969.
POLSTER, E. & POLSTER, M. *Gestalt Therapy Integrated*. New York: Brunner/Mazel, 1973.

12

ANNA O. – PATIENT OR THERAPIST?
AN EIDETIC VIEW

AKHTER AHSEN

The case of Anna O.—in real life, Bertha Pappenheim—was first mentioned in 1893 in a paper jointly authored by Sigmund Freud and Joseph Breuer. Her case history was subsequently reported in full in their book *Studies on Hysteria* (1895).

According to this account, Anna, whose hysterical symptoms were first manifested in 1880, showed great sensitivity for poetry and fantasy, and, at the same time, a very strong and critical intellect. This is one of the many paradoxes which characterize the case of Anna O. and which were not given full recognition during treatment. These paradoxes, however, proved to be critical factors in a strange history of self-therapy. It will be the purpose of the present paper to examine the ways in which this innovative form of therapy, devised by a patient for her own cure, restored her to the vigor of full health, and to a level of functioning far higher than she had previously enjoyed. In examining this question, I propose first to describe the case of Anna O. as reported in the literature; then to describe the patient's participation in social work and in literary creativity in the post-treatment period; to give a brief account of the public acclaim that was given to her, notably at the time of her death; and, finally, to discuss in some detail the procedures by which she came to formulate a new branch of therapy.

Anna O. was a young woman who was deeply devoted to her father. In July 1880, when Anna O. was twenty-one years old, her father fell ill of tuberculosis. Such was the physical and emotional energy she contributed to his nursing care that by degrees her own health came to be grossly deteriorated, with accompanying weakness, anemia, and distaste for food. By December of that year, she had developed a severe cough, which Breuer was called in to treat.

263

Due to this deterioration of her health, Anna was forced to give up her nursing duties. Thereupon, she developed a number of symptoms, including a convergent squint, severe disturbances of vision, and

> paresis of the muscles of the front of the neck, so that finally the patient could only move her head by pressing it backwards between her raised shoulders and moving her whole back; contracture and anaesthesia of the right upper, and, after a time, of the right lower extremity. The latter was fully extended, adducted and rotated inwards. Later the same symptom appeared in the left lower extremity and finally in the left arm, of which, however, the fingers to some extent retained the power of movement. So, too, there was no complete rigidity in the shoulder-joints. The contracture reached its maximum in the muscles of the upper arms. In the same way, the region of the elbows turned out to be the most affected by anaesthesia when, at a later stage, it became possible to make a more careful test of this. At the beginning of the illness the anaesthesia could not be efficiently tested, owing to the patient's resistance arising from feelings of anxiety (Breuer and Freud, 1895).

This description indicates a typical nursing posture which Anna was still reliving in fantasy; but Breuer seems not to have grasped its meaning.

During this time, Anna had a routine of falling into a somnolent state in the afternoons, which lasted until about an hour after sunset. After this, she would wake up saying, "tormenting, tormenting." At other times, she would find it difficult to speak, and gradually she became completely deprived of speech. For two weeks she was completely dumb and, in spite of making continuous efforts to speak, she was unable to utter a syllable.

Gradually, under Breuer's care, the symptoms left Anna, and she left her bed at last on the first of April, 1881. Four days after this improvement, her father died and Anna O. succumbed to her illness again. A violent outburst of excitement was followed by a profound stupor. She emerged from this state with a highly restricted field of vision, so that when a bunch of flowers was presented to her, she could see only one flower at a time. She complained of being unable to recognize people, and, as she said, had to do laborious "recognizing work," which involved guessing a person by recognizing a small feature and remembering him from this small clue. As her mourning symptoms isolated her, people seemed to her to become wax figures without any connection with her. Finally, she recognized only Breuer. As long as Breuer was talking to her, she was always in contact with reality, and lively, except for interruptions caused by "absences," her customary way of dealing with her internal states. Now she only spoke English, and the nurse learned to communicate with her somewhat in this language. She was able to read French and Italian, and if someone asked her to read aloud passages in these languages, she would produce with extraordinary fluency and promptness an admirable extempore English translation.

Anna O.'s illness was aggravated by an incident involving a consultant who was brought in ten days after her father's death. Although she conversed with Breuer, she persisted in completely ignoring the consultant. Breuer interpreted this neglect as a "negative hallucination." The consultant physician then forced Anna to notice him by blowing smoke into her face, whereupon Anna got up, rushed to the door and fell unconscious, and, on regaining consciousness, experienced a short fit of anger and a severe attack of anxiety. Breuer had great difficulty in calming her down. That evening Breuer left Vienna, and when he came back after several days, he found Anna much worse. She had gone without food the entire time, and was consequently in a state of physical deterioration, and her mind was filled with anxiety which revealed itself in visions of terrifying figures, death's heads and skeletons. As she experienced these images, she acted them through and in part put them into words, so that the people around her were aware to a great extent of the content of her consciousness. Within two months after her father's death, her condition had worsened. As strong suicidal impulses appeared, she was transferred to a country house. The move was followed by three days and nights completely without sleep or nourishment, by numerous attempts at suicide, by smashing of windows, and other aberrant actions. After this, she became quieter, allowed the nurse to feed her, and took chloral at night.

The pattern of waking at night and sleeping in the afternoons, connected with nursing her father, had been carried over into her own illness. As mentioned earlier, after a deep sleep in the afternoon, she would grow restless, tossing to and fro, repeating "tormenting, tormenting," with her eyes shut all the time. While preoccupied with her internal imagery, she would give a clue in the form of a few muttered words, and if someone picked it up, she would start telling some story, first hesitatingly and then, later on, more fluently. The starting point or the central motif of these stories was, as a rule, a girl anxiously sitting by a sick-bed. A few minutes after finishing the narrative, Anna would wake up, calm and comfortable. She called this state "gehäglich," an invented word she substituted for the regular German "behäglich," meaning comfortable. After her father's death, the content of these poetical compositions centered on events that had annoyed her during the day, but now this facility diminished, and she seemed to show no further progress. To overcome this, Breuer arranged for Anna to be brought back to Vienna, where her inventive and narrative gifts returned immediately, and she was once more amiable and cheerful.

Breuer, however, became concerned that Anna was not showing steady and increased improvement in Vienna; in fact, there was even marked deterioration of her psychical condition in December. She then became excited, gloomy, and irritable, and Breuer's attempts at having her give regular expression to her internal imagery were unsuccessful.

Then came Anna's spectacular performance in self-therapy. Toward the end of December 1881, she began to tell Breuer, "nothing new but only the imaginative products which she had elaborated under the stress of great anxiety and emotion during the Christmas of 1880" (Breuer and Freud, 1895), that is, the Christmas following her forced removal from her father's bedside. After she had re-experienced these scenes, she felt greatly relieved. Many things were confused in her mind, but one thing was clear—that her father had died—and this knowledge remained in her consciousness most of the time. Now her pictorial experiences, which we will call eidetic experiences, burst forth powerfully, and, as Breuer puts it, "She was carried back to the previous year with such intensity that in the new house she hallucinated her old room so that when she wanted to go to the door she knocked up against the stove which stood in the same relation to the window as the door did in the old room." Anna was now reliving the previous year, not in a general or indefinite manner, but day by day, in calendar sequence. Breuer did not suspect what was happening until, during her eidetic state, she talked through whatever had excited her during the same day, in the December of 1880 and of 1881. This reliving of the previous year day by day continued until the illness came to a final end in June, 1882. Breuer became aware of this day-by-day reliving through an accidental happening, when one morning Anna told him laughingly that, although she had no idea why, she was angry with him. The same evening she relived the experience imagistically; and from a reading of Anna's mother's diary, Breuer came to the realization that he had annoyed Anna very much on that very date a year ago. The day-to-day reliving of 1881 came to a critical stage when Anna began to re-experience even earlier events which took place during the incubation period of her illness between July and December

1880. It soon became evident that most of her symptoms and imagery disturbances were related to this period.

Anna O. was now firmly resolved that the whole treatment should be finished by the anniversary of the day on which she had been moved to the country. Accordingly, in June, she entered her "talking cure" with the greatest energy and accomplished the cure, as predicted by her. On the last day she re-arranged the furniture in the room so that it resembled her father's sick room, and then reproduced the terrifying hallucination which, according to Breuer, constituted the root of her whole illness.

One night her father had a high fever, and she sat at his bedside, awaiting arrival of a surgeon from Vienna who was to operate on him. At that time they were living in a country house where snakes in the field behind the house had given Anna a fright on earlier occasions. While sitting at her father's bedside, with her right arm over the back of a chair, Anna fell into a waking dream in which she saw a black snake emerging from the wall to attack her helpless father. She tried to ward off the snake, but found herself paralyzed, as her right arm had "gone to sleep." The anesthetized arm's fingers then seemed to her to turn into little snakes with death's heads (the nails), and, in her terror, she tried to pray but language failed her. The whistle of the train which was bringing the doctor broke the spell. As this core experience, and others, were relived by her, she overcame her hysterical symptoms one by one, and recovered from her illness, as she had determined.

At this point, the clinical picture shows some confusion. While Breuer reports that Anna went traveling, conflicting statements are made by Freud. Jones (1953) states:

> Freud has related to me a fuller account than he described in his writings of the peculiar circumstances surrounding the end of this novel treatment. It would seem that Breuer had developed what we should nowadays call a strong countertransference to his interesting patient. At all events he was so engrossed that his wife became bored at listening to no other topic, and before long jealous. She did not display this openly, but became unhappy and morose. It was a long time before Breuer, with his thoughts elsewhere, divined the meaning of her state of mind. It provoked a violent reaction in him, perhaps compounded of love and guilt, and he decided to bring the treatment to an end. He announced this to Anna O., who was by now much better, and bade her good-by. But that evening he was fetched back to find her in a greatly excited state, apparently as ill as ever. The patient, who according to him had appeared to be an asexual being and had never made any allusion to such a for-

bidden topic throughout the treatment, was now in the throes of an hysterical childbirth (pseudocyesis), the logical termination of a phantom pregnancy that had been invisibly developing in response to Breuer's ministrations. Though profoundly shocked, he managed to calm her down by hypnotizing her, and then fled the house in a cold sweat. . . .

The poor patient did not fare so well as one might gather from Breuer's published account. Relapses took place, and she was removed to an institution in Gross Enzersdorf. A year after discontinuing the treatment, Breuer confided to Freud that she was quite unhinged and that he wished she would die and so be released from her suffering. She improved, however, and gave up morphia.

In 1932, Freud wrote a letter to Stefan Zweig regarding Anna O.'s case (1960). He said:

> What really happened with Breuer's patient I was able to guess later on, long after the break in our relations, when I suddenly remembered something Breuer had once told me in another context before we had begun to collaborate and which he never repeated. On the evening of the day when all her symptoms had been disposed of, he was summoned to the patient again, found her confused and writhing in abdominal cramps. Asked what was wrong with her, she replied: "Now Dr. B's child is coming!"
>
> At this moment he held in his hand the key that would have opened the "doors to the Mothers," but he let it drop. With all his great intellectual gifts there was nothing Faustian in his nature. Seized by conventional horror he took flight and abandoned the patient to a colleague. For months afterwards she struggled to regain her health in a sanitorium. . . .

Some further speculations may be added to Freud's reporting of the phantom pregnancy from his *On the History of the Psycho-analytic Movement* (1914). Freud wrote:

> In his treatment of her case, Breuer was able to make use of a very intense suggestive *rapport* with the patient, which may serve us as a complete prototype of what we call "transference" today. Now I have strong reasons for suspecting that after all her symptoms had been relieved Breuer must have discovered from further indications the sexual motivation of this transference, but that the universal nature of this unexpected phenomenon escaped him, with the result that, as though confronted by an "untoward event," he broke off all further investigation. He never said this to me in so many words, but he told me enough at different times to justify this reconstruction of what happened. When I later began more and more

resolutely to put forward the significance of sexuality in the aetiology of neuroses, he was the first to show the reaction of distaste and repudiation which was later to become so familiar to me, but which at that time I had not yet learnt to recognize as my inevitable fate.

There seems to be nothing in existing records to substantiate Freud's comments. It is, indeed, possible that Freud doubted the efficacy of Anna O.'s healing through images, since it would be a complete contradiction of his own technique of treatment through the study of resistances. In the present writer's opinion, Freud may thus have tried to make a case that Anna O. was not actually cured of her hysterical condition.

Whatever the actual sequence of events, there is a good deal of evidence to support Breuer's statement that Anna O. embarked on a long series of travels after her treatment. She blossomed with fulfillment in her true identity as Bertha Pappenheim. Some called her "saintlike," others, "overwhelming and powerful." It has been said that she "spoke like a prophet," and "sounded like a visionary." Her travels were motivated by a firm purpose—after the turn of the century, Bertha Pappenheim made repeated on-the-spot studies of social conditions in the Balkans, Russia, Galicia, and Palestine. During her many travels—which brought her to Salonica, Lemberg, Lodz, Warsaw, St. Petersburg, Moscow, Smyrna, Jaffa, and in 1909 to London and Washington—women's problems, social work, and problems of education were uppermost in her mind (Jensen, 1970). Bertha Pappenheim's work spread, in large measure, through the institutions and societies she organized, founded, and inspired. As she developed expertise in these areas, she organized women volunteers for service and donations. She evolved careful and comprehensive social work procedures which allowed for thorough investigation of background and appropriate recommendations. Nurseries, foster home and adoption placement, vocational guidance agencies, clubs, homes for working girls were all projects she began. Of major concern were health and child care and providing a healthy social atmosphere in the institutions.

Two questions occupied Bertha Pappenheim's mind most of all—prostitution and illegitimacy. Both those social evils appeared to be connected with the legal status of women under the Jewish civil law. Unmarried women could not share in the community and if an abandoned wife (*agunah*) could not obtain a legally valid Jewish divorce or prove her husband's death, she could not remarry; if her husband, on the other hand, had become father to another woman's child and she was unmarried, he could then become that woman's husband and abandon his wife. Yet, a wife was not allowed to divorce the husband. A wife who had a child after being abandoned could not compel support from the father since she was still legally married to the first husband. The existence of unmarried mothers was denied; illegitimate children were not supported (Edinger, 1958, 1968, Freeman, 1972).

Another problem of young Jewish girls being delivered by Jewish merchants for white slave traffic was an unpopular matter in which the rabbis and others silently acquiesced by passivity or turning their heads aside while accepting tainted money for support of the synagogue. For Bertha Pappenheim, religion was "to bear humbly what is law; to feel actively responsible for law" (Edinger, 1968). Further to this, she said: ". . . everybody who is not against the meanness of our community is for it" (Edinger, 1968). In 1907 she reported:

> In the "traffic in girls" merchants as well as merchandise are mostly Jewish. We know that family life today is not what it used to be, that the men, both fathers and sons, do not protect themselves and their homes from being soiled and that the dirt cannot be washed away by the tears of deceived and damaged women. Many of the girls who indulge in prostitution know that they have only one value, that of the sex object (Karpe, 1961).

Bertha Pappenheim met the challenge of her time head on, "to study the miserable condition of the Jewish people and to improve the protection of women, girls, and children" (Edinger, 1968) for as she said, "Neither sex nor age nor religion nor party can be an excuse to remain quiet. To know of wrong and to remain quiet makes one partly guilty" (Edinger, 1968. In 1902, Bertha Pappenheim formed the *Weibliche Fürsorge* (Care by Women), the basic institution for Jewish welfare work at Frankfurt, composed of volunteer women who learned through it the latest in social work techniques. In 1903 she founded the *Girls' Club*, a social society intended for the "daughters" of the orphanage who had gone out into the working world and wanted a place for recreation and continuing education. In 1904 Bertha Pappenheim formed the *Jüdischer Frauenbund* (Federation of Jewish Women), and was elected its president. This national federation became part of the German Federation of Women's Organizations and was counterpart to Protestant and Catholic social work organizations. Its work included central support for orphanages and hospitals, and the financing of training facilities for Jewish social workers and nurses. The *Jüdischer Frauenbund* also put out a paper, which Bertha Pappenheim edited (*Encyclopaedia Judaica*).

In 1907, she left the *Jüdisches Mädchenhaus*, or Jewish Orphanage for Girls, as director, and established, with money from a relative, a shelter called *Heim des Jüdischen Frauenbundes*, at Neu-Isenburg, which provided care for Jewish unmarried mothers, and unstable and delinquent girls. In 1909 she visited Lillian D. Wald's Henry Street Settlement in New York. She traveled to Rumania and in 1910 she gave a speech in London at the International Congress to Fight White Slave Traffic. In 1911 she traveled to the Middle East and Russia. She visited brothels, slums, and social welfare institutions in Greece, Turkey, Jerusalem and Egypt. In 1911 she also presented a report to the German National Committee Against White Slavery. She sent educators and nurses from the Frankfurt orphanage to Galicia.

In 1912 she visited the part of Poland incorporated into Russia, Russia, and then Galicia. As Russian-Jewish girls were brought to Germany to work in the munition factories, she set up local welfare work facilities for them. Hit hard by inflation, she traveled to maintain and gather support for her work and led study groups at the "Lehrhaus," under the direction of Martin Buber and Franz Rosenzweig, on the ethics of social work. She also organized seminars on social action for the prevention of physical want, lack of food, and fuel. In 1914, Bertha Pappenheim was elected to the board of the German Federation of Women's Organizations. She also inspired the founding of the World Congress of Jewish Women (Rabin, 1934).

Bertha Pappenheim's literary efforts were no less notable. In 1899, she translated into German Mary Wollstonecraft's *A Vindication of the Rights of Woman,* and financed its publication. In the same year, she wrote a satirical play entitled *Women's Rights,* which centered on the problems of destitute and abandoned women, and the injustices suffered by women workers. In 1890, Bertha published *In der Trödelbude* (In the Rummage Store), a collection of stories, each one narrated by an old item in an antique shop. Other literary media which she used included shadow-plays, songs, and prayers.

In 1900, Bertha Pappenheim authored a pamphlet entitled "Zur Judenfrage in Galizien" (The Jewish Problem in Galicia), describing the miserable conditions and poverty which prevailed in that area. She hoped to arouse Jewish social conscience to action, and emphasized the importance of education for young Galician women. She became familiar with the dire circumstances of these people through the Galician immigrants. She later visited Galicia and in 1904 discussed in "Zur Lage der Jüdischen Bevölkerung in Galizien" the damage done should a woman's personality be left to remain undeveloped and uneducated.

Since she was drawn to studying the past, she enjoyed translating documents of women's life in the ghetto, and old family charts. During her researches, in 1910 she "excavated" the *Memoirs* of Glückel von Hameln. Bertha also translated into German the *Maaseh Buch*, a book of Yiddish folklore with ethical content and the *Tze'enah Ure'enah*, a homilectical commentary and exposition of the Pentateuch very popular among women and written by Jacob ben Isaac Ashkenazi especially for them.

In 1913, Bertha Pappenheim published the dramatic trilogy *Tragische Momente* and in 1916 she published a collection of stories entitled *Kämpfe*. In 1924, her first collection of travel letters was published under the title *Sisyphus-Arbeit*, with Part II appearing five years later.

A paper written shortly before her death shows clearly Bertha Pappenheim's abiding concern for the fate of Jewish women in particular and for the fate of all women in general. In the *Jewish Woman* (1934) she stated:

> . . . no adult education, can repair today the sin against the Jewish woman's soul and thus against all Judaism by excluding the unknown woman from the Jewish sense of being and by cultivating only her physical strength for the service of man. . . . I see the logical and tragic consequence in that women and mothers of the recent past were not able to raise their children with respect for the spirit of tradition (Edinger, 1968).

On May 28, 1936, this great, spiritual, passionate and sensitive woman died. She was a courageous and deeply religious person who, in Dora Edinger's words, devoted her life to "social justice and had educated women toward this goal" (Edinger, 1958). She was, in brief, "a German feminist fully convinced that only by achievements in the field of education and social work could women prove their right to full citizenship" (Edinger, 1958). In a special July-August memorial issue, a "Gedenknumner," of the monthly paper of the *Jüdischer Frauenbund*, tributes were published from her "daughters," co-workers, board members, and many others who knew of her and of her work. It described her achievements in local, national and international social work and her artistic and literary interests. Bertha Pappenheim was later commemorated with a postal stamp in the "helpers of humanity" series issued by the West German government, and was written up in the Holy Land Philatelist, Israel's Stamps in 1955.

In the final analysis, however, the words of Martin Buber on the occasion of her death will stand for all time as testimony to her worth as a rare human being (Edinger, 1968):

> There are people of spirit and there are people of passion, both less common than one might think. Much rarer are the people of spirit and passion. But the rarest is passion of the spirit. Bertha Pappenheim was a woman of passion of the spirit.
> She had to become severe, not hard but severe, lovingly severe, demanding much, full of passion—because all was what it was, and remained what it was. She lived in days which could not bear the white fire; they did not see it, did not even believe that it still existed.
> But it did exist. This white flame burned in our days. Now it is extinguished. Only her image survives in the hearts of those who knew her.
> Hand on this image. Hand on her memory. Be witnesses that it still exists. We have a pledge.

Anna O's technique of self-therapy seems to rely heavily on eidetics, a phenomenon later experimentally studied by the Marburg school of Germany and clinically systematized by myself (Ahsen). Apart from her achievements in feminism and social work, she was the first in psychological history to use eidetic images for exploring what troubled her, and anticipated by forty years a significant remark made by O. Kroh in 1922 that a truly objective, internally oriented psychotherapy system would be developed through eidetics. Assuming Breuer's descriptions of Anna O.'s talent for image-formation to be correct, Anna would be known in present-day terminology as an eidetiker, i.e., an individual who has a natural talent for vivid imagery experience. However it is now common knowledge that eidetic images are not specific to artists and other creative persons only, but they also appear in all other people, as part of the developmental process, and their vivid traces are preserved in the areas of distress and conflict. It is precisely in the latter sense that Anna's achievement turned out to be epoch making, in the true sense.

Eidetic images are characterized by their vividness. They represent a cross section of the image phenomena. They relate to fantasies, being akin to images which appear in a variety of mental phenomena, have a hallucinatory vividness, and resemble dreams, daydreams, and literary metaphor. In traumatic memories, eidetics reproduce actual historical data with detailed exactness. They are spontaneous, interior, demonstrable, repeatable, affect-laden images which appear over the developmental line and influence the mind of the adult in a powerful way. Capable of releasing a real somatic response, following certain laws of symbolic and mechanical operation, a simple eidetic image automatically sets off a complex mental reaction and elaborates the mind's dynamics through its own experiential exposition. The individual, when experiencing an eidetic image, "sees" it in the literal sense of the word, and while "seeing" it he is always in possession of his usual, normal consciousness in the sense that he knows that what he is seeing is internal.

Penfield's experiments (1952) in which he touched the temporal cortex of his patients with a weak electrical current transmitted through a galvanic probe show neurological evidence of the same phenomenon. He concluded that everything which was once in the conscious awareness of the person is recorded in detail, stored in the brain, and capable of being played back. Each electrode evoked a single precise recollection and not a generalized memory, as in a high fidelity tape-recorder.

Breuer's descriptions of the way in which Anna O. experienced her problems bear a remarkable similarity to eidetic descriptions, although at the time of his reporting, eidetics were not known. We will take each of these aspects under consideration.

Regarding Anna's natural ability toward imagery, Breuer said:

> There were two psychical characteristics present in the girl . . . which acted as predisposing causes. . . .
> (1) . . . an unemployed surplus of mental liveliness and energy, and this found an outlet in the constant activity of her imagination.
> (2) This led to a habit of day-dreaming (her "private theater") . . . this habit prepared the ground upon which the affect of anxiety and dread was able to establish itself . . . when once that affect had transformed the patient's habitual day-dreaming into a hallucinatory *absence* (Breuer and Freud, 1895).

What specifically does Breuer mean by *absence?* He describes Anna's states of consciousness as follows:

> Throughout the entire illness her two states of consciousness persisted side by side: the primary one in which she was quite normal psychically, and the secondary one which may well be likened to a dream in view of its wealth of imaginative products and hallucinations, its large gaps of memory and the lack of inhibition and control in its associations . . . the patient's mental condition was entirely dependent on the intrusion of this secondary state into the normal one . . . not only did the secondary state intrude into the first one, but—and this was at all events frequently true, and even when she was in a very bad condition—a clear-sighted and calm observer

sat, as she put it, in a corner of her brain and looked on at all the mad business. This persistence of clear thinking while the psychosis was actually going on found expression in a very curious way. At a time when, after the hysterical phenomena had ceased, the patient was passing through a temporary depression, she brought up a number of childish fears and self-reproaches . . . (Breuer and Freud, 1895).

Could Anna have fabricated or deliberately attempted to guide things? Of this, Breuer says:

. . . I always found the patient entirely truthful and trustworthy. The things she told me were intimately bound up with what was most sacred to her. Whatever could be checked by other people was fully confirmed. Even the most highly gifted girl would be incapable of concocting a tissue of data with such a degree of internal consistency as was exhibited in the history of this case. It cannot be disputed, however, that precisely her consistency may have led her (in perfectly good faith) to assign to some of her symptoms a precipitating cause which they did not in fact possess. But this suspicion, too, I consider unjustified. The very insignificance of so many of those causes, the irrational character of so many of the connections involved, argue in favor of their reality (Breuer and Freud, 1895).

In her reporting, the factual consistency was surprising.

. . . in the patient's memory they [episodes regarding deafness] were so clearly differentiated, that if she happened to make a mistake in their sequence she would be obliged to correct herself and put them in the right order; if this was not done her report came to a standstill. The events she described were so lacking in interest and significance and were told in such detail that there could be no suspicion of their having been invented. Many of these incidents consisted of purely internal experiences and so could not be verified; others of them (or circumstances attending them) were within the recollection of people in her environment (Breuer and Freud, 1895).

As is commonly known regarding eidetic experiences, unless the sequence of the experiences is maintained, progression will not properly take place (see Penfield, 1952). Anna defined them clearly in her mind stepwise and would not be deterred from the healing experience by glossing over them in a haphazard manner.

Even as a brief sketch, Anna's steps for self-therapy appear to have a definite significance as a treatment procedure for various emotional problems. Her steps appear to touch the potency of the individual's own internal resources, the capacity of the mind to direct its own course in the appropriate direction, until the cause of the problem is imagistically surfaced and overcome by confrontation. This central motif of Bertha Pappenheim's self-therapy is amazingly profound and potent, and when methodically applied, it ensures results better than most systems. The elements of this procedure are essentially the same as appear in the present writer's approach to psychotherapy based on a more systematic use of the eidetic phenomena (cf. *Eidetic Parents Test and Analysis*, 1972, and *Basic Concepts in Eidetic Psychotherapy*, 1968).

THE PRIVATE THEATER OF THE MIND

Emotional problems can be treated without intervention by another individual, and without labels, in what Anna O. called "the private theater of the mind," in which internal emotional life is experienced by the individual in intimate detail through the imagizing process. Seclusion is essential to this process, so that the individual can grow without facing oppression and control from outside. This private theater of the mind acts as an oasis of imagery and serves as an agent of discovery, expression and growth.

ATMOSPHERE

Eidetic analysis, undertaken in the true spirit of self-analysis, involves imagistic self-experience in specific problem areas, so that life situations are clarified through lifelike visual images. It represents a whole new way of looking at mental life, not through another person's ideas and views, but through one's own mind's eye. Such an approach becomes a key to solving the perpetual mental war between various interpretations of mental states which leave one angry, confused, and helpless. It presents a direct, fresh, and easily understood method of arriving at an intimate, personal understanding of one's own problems.

"What is an eidetic?" Someone said, "It is like a yesterday's memory, though it may come from the distant past. If you experience a recent memory visually, this re-activation of past experience resembles the eidetic experience."

TWO ROLES

While using eidetics for self-analysis and therapy, one takes up the challenge of playing two roles: therapist and patient. As a patient, you proceed by making a list of your problems or symptoms, and, as a therapist, you faithfully write down everything concerning the images in the form of a daily journal.

EXPERIENCING THE SYMPTOM

After making a list of the problems or symptoms, the procedure requires one to retire to a room, relax and experience the problem situations or symptoms in detail, allowing them to permeate the mind fully. Stay in this state until you are deeply involved in that experience. If, for instance, your symptom is a sharp pain in the knee, re-create that pain in the mind, and concentrate fully on it.

EMERGENCE OF AN EIDETIC

During or immediately after a concentrated experience of problems and symptoms, you should see an image emerging on the mental horizon. This visual image is called an eidetic. Look at this image over and over again. Do not try to intellectualize or reason. As you repeat the eidetic many times over, you should become aware of its meaning spontaneously. This meaning will precede, accompany, or follow a physical feeling associated with the image. Find out if this feeling is painful or pleasurable or causes relaxation or tension inside you.

SELF-TEST*

After having experienced the eidetic fully, you are ready to test the eidetic in order to feel out the possibilities contained in it.

In order to test the eidetic systematically, first actively evoke and tantalize the image to make its visual detail and contents clear. Next, handle the image in all possible ways by projecting it over and over again, dealing with the persons who appear in the eidetic, experiencing them and talking to them. React to the various aspects of your image with openness; do not control or inhibit any emotions, memories, or associations. Try to experience all details, and write them down. By the time you have created all this mind data, you will have come to know a lot of new material, and you are ready to handle the experience in a manner which will resolve what was revealed in it.

---

* A complete list of eidetic test situations is provided in *Eidetic Parents Test and Analysis* (Ahsen, 1972).

SOLUTION

After having tested the eidetic image in the ways described above, you should arrive at a spontaneous understanding of the situation represented in it. At this point, a specific aspect of your problems or symptoms will fall in line with what is revealed in the eidetic. Repeated projection and experiential reliving of the eidetic will enable you to handle the experience and allow the eidetic to evolve in its normal patterned course. The basic stages of solution are set out below, with brief examples from my own clinical work.

1. *Progression*

The repeated attention or concentration paid to an eidetic will cause the original eidetic to evolve into a series of new eidetics. The new visual pictures will gradually progress until they arrive at a final solution image. For example, a female patient suffering from a chronic excruciating pain at the back of her head for three years overcame her symptom completely when she experienced an image progression. The initiating eidetic involved an actual traumatic memory of cold rain falling on her head, for many hours. The original eidetic multiplied into a series of eidetics elaborating various stages of the trauma, which spread from the head to various parts of the body. After the eidetic progression was experienced completely, the trauma was overcome, and she was healed of the symptom.

2. *Emanation*

While concentrating on an eidetic, your own image appearing in it may gradually change into an active self-image containing positive overt expression and feelings of release. The new, active self-image reactively develops out of the previous passive self-image showing some form of weakness such as fear or fixation. Many times the active self-image emerges spontaneously, while at other times you can actively see it leaping out of the previous self-image. For instance, a female patient who was tormented by feelings of jealousy concerning a sibling who had received too many gifts on a certain occasion in the past saw herself in the image as depressed and uncared for. Then she suddenly saw another image of herself leaping out of the previous self-image, and the new self-image appeared to be very angry and aggressive. For the first time she found that she could overcome her tormenting feelings by seeing the new self-image acting the way she had felt at that time.

3. *Catharsis*

When an eidetic is repeated, it creates a powerful impact in the mind so that the individual deeply experiences associated emotions, such as grief, anger, and a variety of body feelings, such as trembling. While concentrating on an eidetic, a strong catharsis of the original situation contained in the eidetic develops, leading to reliving and overcoming of the emotion involved. For example, a patient suffering from frequent, severe asthmatic attacks for several years had received psychotherapy and had been tested for possible allergies, without cure. However, the eidetic images evoked in the very first hour revealed the problem to be rooted at an age when the patient had been treated cruelly by her nanny. The actual eidetic involving persecution by the nanny brought to the surface the underlying anger which the patient had experienced at that time. Concentration on the eidetic resulted in a powerful catharsis of her anger at the nanny and cured her of the symptom of asthma completely.

4. *Interaction*

While projecting an eidetic, you may merely view the picture or instead interact with the persons appearing in the picture. This interaction involves behaving toward a person in the eidetic in a manner which provokes a reaction from him or her in the image. In this manner, you can express anger, love, and so on; or introduce a new situation element into the projection which forces the person to respond or react in a certain manner. For instance, a patient who suffered from lack of feelings believed that his father could not respond positively to his mother because she was domineering. He saw an eidetic of the parents in which they were running in a vast, open countryside and the mother was running faster than the father. He said, "I see clearly that she is dominating. The only alternative my father has is to sit down and not cooperate. This is how I have always felt as a man." The patient was asked to interact with the parental images by asking the mother to slow down and cooperate with the father, and asking the father to brace up and run faster. The mother appeared cooperative in the image, but the father was still very resistant. This spontaneously created an awareness in the patient that his father was really a resistant person, and that his own resistance was similar to his father's. This changed the character of his self-centered thinking.

5. *Insight*

By repeating the eidetic, concentrating on it, allowing it to evolve, or becoming aware of the emotions present in it, you can look at an old problem from a new experiential angle. Thus, instead of merely reacting in the old manner or pacifying yourself with erroneous and limiting notions, you can develop a completely new experiential outlook, through eidetics.

Penfield's experiments involving evoked recollections through application of a stimulating electrode threw light on the character of the new meaning or insight present in the eidetic. Lawrence S. Kubie, a renowned psychoanalyst and one of the discussants on Penfield's paper on "Memory Mechanisms," described this evidence as important to the future of psychotherapy. According to him Penfield's evidence "shed light on one of the critical limiting factors in psychoanalytic therapy: or, to put it in more general terms, it may explain a limiting factor in the psychotherapeutic leverage of any form of psychotherapy which depends upon the use of words to recapture 'memories' in the pursuit of 'insight.' "

Penfield's evidence, which described meaning or insight as experiential rather than rational, also provided a definition of meaning which bypasses the psychoanalytic verbal meaning, as well as Pavlov's conditioned reflex theory on which much of behaviorism rests. The insight experienced through eidetics flows directly from the eidetic as something deeper than a psychoanalytic insight or behavioristic learning. Such an insight evolves spontaneously, hits deeper and lives longer.

Eidetic exploration and experience have been relevant to a variety of emotional problems ranging from psychosomatic ailments, hysterias and phobias, to schizophrenia. This has been copiously brought out in the published case histories of the present author. Eidetic methodology works in a highly specific manner, dealing with the root cause of the emotional problems, demonstrating the link as well as the healing process. It is astonishing to note how an attack of the common cold can be stopped through an eidetic in the duration of a single session, how an anorexia unsuccessfully treated by a psychotherapy approach and medication can be cured within a few sessions. As a rule, specific images have been found to have a curative effect on symptoms such as ulcerative colitis, resulting in the healing of the symptoms within a few weeks; menstrual pain has been linked with specific image situations of trauma or anger in the patient, with treatment through the specific image resulting in a definite cure. The indirect relationship of images with the symptoms of hysteria and phobia was long known but now eidetics help us to understand the symptoms and achieve results rapidly and definitively.

The cure of severely resistant cases is an especially interesting feature of treatment through eidetics. Eidetics offer a dependable methodology for handling of ailments that have remained perplexing to present-day medical and psychotherapy procedures. These cases appear to respond to eidetics with speedy results. The case of Mrs. Jay reported by Akhter Ahsen and Arnold A. Lazarus (Lazarus, 1972) demonstrates how such a severely resistant case can respond to the eidetic procedures. In this case, the use of behavior therapy had completely failed to achieve results and the patient had in fact regressed; but she responded to eidetics with a fast recovery from severe irrational anxiety, chest pains, palpitations, nausea, pins and needles, dizziness, and extreme feelings of personal unworthiness.

The treatment of schizophrenia through eidetics is the most fascinating correlate of Penfield's findings. It involves the repairing of the general splitting process by presenting meaning-carrying eidetic images and allowing connections to emerge through the visualization process. Penfield emphasized that the presence of meaning was an integral function of the evoked images, and that the interpretive and meaning-building process was inherent to the evoked response. In my own eidetic work on schizophrenia, I found the principle extremely useful, since avoidance patterns, flat or inappropriate affect, and inability to relate to the environment could be cured when these processes were experientially dealt with through eidetics. Because eidetics produce meaning and affect of their own accord, they gradually help to integrate the schizophrenic's emotional life. The eidetic procedure relates to and elucidates emotional details, gradually helping to stem deterioration and to evolve feeling and thought consistency. In the schizophrenic, eidetic images create an atmosphere of relevance spontaneously and on this is established the basis of reconstruction. In the treatment of schizophrenia, eidetics may well represent the most purposeful, appropriate and emotive vehicle of cure known to date.

However, the main attraction of eidetics does not lie merely in the possibility of cures over a wide spectrum of ailments, but in what the eidetics signify for mankind in general. As Pavlov (1936) said so clearly and so feelingly, there are "two categories of people—artists and thinkers. Between them there is a marked difference. The artists . . . comprehend reality as a whole, as a continuity, a complete living reality, without any divisions, without any separations. The other group, the thinkers, pull it apart, kill it. . . . This difference is especially prominent in the so-called eidetic imagery of children. . . . Such a whole creation of reality cannot be completely attained by a thinker." Then Pavlov goes on to say that in the average person the two are found together rather than apart. This is precisely where the importance of the eidetic imagery lies.

What Pavlov said about the individual also holds true about society. There comes a period in human history when thinking assumes a negative posture and needs to be redeemed by the artistic process. It is possible that a whole era of Man can think itself into a trap, and spin without resolving anything, instead creating new problems. When an age decays and uses words as a manipulative weapon to perpetuate what has already lost relevance, the eidetic becomes the symbol of much-needed fresh experience. In this sense eidetics not only serve an important function in the psyche of the individual, they also represent a sociological mode for the progress of civilization.

Because the man tends to control the conception of his Age with almost complete obsession, it is the woman who appears to carry the first corrective thrust in the form of a natural imagery release. Against the containing and belligerent verbal man, woman becomes the symbol of a new world, containing a dream of condensed eidetic imagery. The new life made of this condensed imagery tends to superimpose itself over the mistakes of the Age, and in this superimposition the dead habit coalesces with intense, outward moving imagery. Vocalization of this condensed imagery is the beginning of woman's identity, role, and her true creative power. A verbal psychology developed by man revolves around man, and it is bound to become a man against woman psychology. A psychology based on eidetic processes saves man and woman from this emotional exclusion by creating a way toward awareness of true human needs. Such a psychology which bypasses labyrinths of rational manipulations is an elixir for both woman and man.

REFERENCES

AHSEN, A. *Basic Concepts in Eidetic Psychotherapy.* New York: Brandon House, 1968.

AHSEN, A. *Eidetic Parents Test and Analysis.* New York: Brandon House, 1972.

BRAM, F. M. The Gift of Anna O. *British Journal of Medical Psychology,* 38, 53-58, 1965.

BREUER, J. & FREUD, S. *Studies on Hysteria.* New York: Avon Books, 1966.

EDINGER, D. *Bertha Pappenheim* (1859-1936). A German-Jewish Feminist. *Jewish Social Studies,* 20, 180, 1958.

EDINGER, D. *Bertha Pappenheim: Leben und Schriften.* Frankfurt-am-Main: Ner Tamid-Verlag, 1963.

EDINGER, D. *Bertha Pappenheim: Freud's Anna O.* Highland Park, Illinois: Congregation Solel, 1968.

ELLENBERGER, H. F. Book Review: *Bertha Pappenheim: Leben und Schriften* by D. Edinger. *Journal of the History of the Behavioral Sciences*, 2, 94, 1966.

Encyclopaedia Judaica (Cecil Roth and Geoffrey Wigoder, Eds.), Jerusalem Encyclopaedia Judaica. New York: Macmillan, 1971-1972, 13.

FREEMAN, L. *The Story of Anna O.* New York: Walker, 1972.

FREUD, E. L. (Ed.), *Letters of Sigmund Freud.* New York: Basic Books, 1960.

FREUD, S. On the history of the psycho-analytic movement. *Standard Edition*, XIV.

Holy Land Philatelist, Israel's Stamps, June, 1955.

HOMBURGER, PAUL. Re: Bertha Pappenheim. New York: *Der Aufbau*, May 7, 1954, 19.

JAENSCH, E. R. *Eidetic Imagery.* (Trans. by Oscar Oeser). New York: Harcourt Brace, 1930.

JENSEN, E. M. Anna O.—A study of her later life. *The Psychoanalytic Quarterly*, 39, 269-293, 1970.

JONES, E. *The Life and Work of Sigmund Freud.* Vol. I. New York: Basic Books, 1953.

KARPE, R. The rescue complex in Anna O.'s final identity. *The Psychoanalytic Quarterly*, 30, 1-27, 1961.

KROH, O. *Subjektive Anschauungsbilder bei Jugendlichen.* Eine psychologische-pädagogische Untersuchung. Göttingen: Vandenhoeck & Ruprecht, 1922.

LAZARUS, A. A. (Ed.). *Clinical Behavior Therapy.* New York: Brunner/Mazel, 1972.

PANAGIOTOU, N. & SHEIKH, A. A. *Eidetic Psychotherapy: Introduction and Evaluation.* *International Journal of Social Psychiatry*, London, in press.

PAVLOV, I. P. (1936). *Conditioned Reflexes and Psychiatry.* New York: International Publishers, 1941.

PENFIELD, W. Memory mechanisms. *A.M.A. Archives of Neurology and Psychiatry*, 67, 178-198, 1952.

RABIN, E. The Jewish woman in social service in Germany. In: *The Jewish Library.* Third Series (Rabbi Leo Jung, Ed.). New York: The Jewish Library Publishing Co., 1934, 299.

The Universal Jewish Encyclopedia (Isaac Landman, Ed.). New York: The Universal Jewish Encyclopedia, Inc., 1942, 8.

WERBLOWSKY, R. J. ZWI & WIGODER, G. (Eds.). *The Encyclopedia of the Jewish Religion.* New York: Holt, Rinehart and Winston, 1965.

13

THE TREATMENT OF SEX AND LOVE PROBLEMS IN WOMEN

ALBERT ELLIS

Whether women, just because they are female, have any different or greater sex and love problems than men is a highly debatable question. On the one hand, we have outstanding female writers and researchers, such as Mead (1955) and Thompson (1973), insisting that women are distinctly different from (though hardly inferior to) men and that therefore they have special kinds of sex-love difficulties. On the other hand, we have equally prominent and authoritative feminists, such as Chesler (1972), de Beauvoir (1953), and Millet (1971), claiming that practically all the "unique" psychological and sexual "disturbances" of women are culturally incited and that if male chauvinism stopped rearing its ugly head these "unique" problems would become practically nonexistent.

No one presently seems to know the indubitable answer to this important question, since all the published evidence is, to say the very least, inconclusive. What does seem reasonably clear is that whatever are women's "intrinsic" or "natural" sex and love problems, these difficulties tend to become enormously exacerbated in any male dominated culture. If women are easily prone, as they may possibly be, to viewing themselves as inadequate and undeserving, to being overly dependent and in dire need of others' love and approval, to letting themselves be sexually exploitable, and to unconsciously repressing or consciously suppressing their sexual arousability and orgasmic capacities, their "proneness" in these respects is certainly abetted by the tendency of a vast majority of human cultures—which generally tend to be male supremacist—to espouse a double standard of morality, to exploit women's weaknesses, and in one way or another (and usually quite significantly) to give females only second-class citizenship.

284

The sex-love problems to which women are so frequently heir are therefore in large part social and are inextricably meshed with the existing social order (Seward, 1973). If full, or even notable, solutions to some of these problems are ever to be achieved, this order will probably have to be significantly modified. For example, if females are to stop putting themselves down for having "unfeminine" bodies, the extremely unrealistic views of Hollywood, the TV industry, and the bathing beauty concepts of what the ideal female form absolutely *should* be would better undergo drastic revision (Ellis, 1961, Frumkin, 1973). For even the teachings of an efficient system of psychotherapy—like rational-emotive therapy—are going to be impeded if a woman's therapist shows her that she doesn't *have to* conform to societal standards of physical beauty while practically every movie and TV presentation that she sees tells her that she *does*.

Granting that women's sex-love difficulties are importantly intertwined with the social fabric in which they are reared and reside and that the elegant solution to these problems includes significant social change, the question still arises: What are some of the most common problems in this area with which, for one reason or another, women are afflicted and how, even within the existing social context, can these problems be therapeutically ameliorated? It is to this question that the present chapter will largely be devoted.

The vast majority of women today seem to suffer from one or more fairly serious love and sex difficulties. This may be seen as an exaggerated and alarmist statement, but let me hasten to add that I would make exactly the same assertion about the vast majority of men. Even if I forget about the literally thousands of clients whom I have worked with over the last 30 years, and even if I stick to the evidence I have gained from detailed conversations with hundreds of non-clients whom I have met during the same period in many different parts of the United States and Canada (and more occasionally in various other parts of the world), I would still stand by this declaration. From eighty to ninety per cent of the males I have talked to are afflicted with some significant degree of inability to love, and of insensate jealousy, engaging in sex more for ego-raising games than for intrinsic enjoyment, varying degrees of impotence, compulsive homosexuality or virulent antihomosexuality, sexual anxieties and phobias, or other kinds of love-sex hangups. Come to think of it, I think I could easily (and safely) say ninety to ninety-five per cent!

So women, even in our male dominating culture, are hardly unique in their sexual and amative problems. But since this chapter, by arbitrary delimitation, is designed to be about women and sex, let me stick to that aspect of human affairs. And let me now list some of the main sex-love disturbances to which, on the basis of my many clinical and nonclinical intimate contacts with females, I think women in our culture (that is, Western civilization) are prone. I shall also try to show how each of these difficulties can be effectively treated by applying some of the principles of rational-emotive therapy (RET), which I have developed and practiced during the last 20 years (Ellis, 1962, 1972a, 1972b, 1973, 1974, Ellis and Budd, 1974, Ellis and Harper, 1971, 1972).

Love Slobbism

Women, as Lord Byron poetically and perspicaciously noted over a century ago, tend to make love not merely *an* important part of their lives but their whole existence. Although the women's liberation movement may eventually change this, it has not yet done so to any considerable extent. The average female, married or unmarried, believes that she *has* to be part of an intimate twosome; that she *must* be securely companioned by someone who dearly cares for her until the very end of her days; and that, if she has children, they've *got to* be interested in and want to regularly relate to her. When there is any good possibility—as there assuredly is, in the course of her everyday existence—that her dire need to love and be loved may not be successfully fulfilled, she often turns herself into a love slob and literally or figuratively licks the ass (or penis) of any man, woman, or child whose approval she thinks she absolutely must, must, must have. When her attempts to nail down love guarantees appear to be failing, she commonly makes herself feel desperately lonely, alienated, depressed, worthless, hopeless, or suicidal.

Love slobbism is a severe symptom of disturbance—or what I call point C (emotional Consequence) in the A-B-C's of rational-emotive psychology. It usually follows after, at point A (an Activating Event), a woman has been unable to find a suitable love partner or has found a potential mate and been rejected by him. Since most women (like most men) do not fully understand how emotional Consequences really occur, they falsely believe that Activating Events (A) cause these Consequences (C), and tell themselves (and others): "My lover rejected me and that made me depressed. His leaving me hurt me very much."

Hogwash! Activating Events (A) virtually never cause emotional Consequences (C). The real issue is B—the individual's Belief System, which *interprets* and *evaluates* the events at A. What happens, therefore, when a woman gets rejected, at A, and feels and acts like a love slob (that is, utterly dependent, depressed, and self-downing) at C, is that she believes, at B, a set of sane and insane, rational and irrational ideas. And it is almost entirely these ideas (or attitudes, values, philosophies, or Beliefs) which determine whether or not she will take on the self-defeating behavior of love slobbism.

First, almost every woman who feels seriously hurt and depressed when her lover (or would-be lover) rejects her, tells herself and firmly holds a set of rational Beliefs (rB's). These usually are: (1) "I don't like being rejected by someone for whom I care." (2) "I wish he had accepted instead of rejected me." (3) "Because I got rejected, that is quite unfortunate, sad, and disadvantageous." (4) "If I keep getting rejected and never succeed in establishing the kind of ongoing, fairly permanent relationship that I want with another person, that will be even more unfortunate and inconvenient." (5) "Therefore, I'd better try to win this partner back—or else find someone else I care for who will truly care for me."

If the woman who was rejected rigorously stayed with these sensible, rational Beliefs (rB's), she would only tend to feel sorry, regretful, sad, frustrated, irritated, annoyed, and determined to change her life for the better—that is, to find, in one way or another, a suitable love partner. But she would *not* feel hurt, depressed, or worthless. To feel these latter Consequences (C), she would almost invariably go on to a highly magical, empirically unconfirmable set of irrational Beliefs (iB's).

Such as? Such as: (1) "It's *awful* that my mate (or potential mate) rejected me!" (2) "I *can't stand* being rejected!" (3) "I *should have* been more beautiful, intelligent, and loving so that he then would not have rejected me." (4) "Because I didn't do what I *should have* done with him, I am a rotten person, a worm!" (5) "Since I'm so worthless, every partner I go with will recognize this, and I will *never* maintain a successful, ongoing relationship with a desirable person." (6) "If so, life won't be worth living at all, and I might as well kill myself than face such a horrible, hopeless existence!"

It is these, irrational Beliefs (iB's), rather than the woman's being rejected (at point A), that cause her anguish, despair, and acute love slobbism (at point C). Even if she *continually* got rejected at A, and thereby failed to get what she wanted in the way of a deep, satisfying love relationship, this kind of steady rejection would merely be frustrating, depriving, and thwarting. Only by her irrational *evaluations* would she make it demeaning and depressing.

The solution? Pretty obvious, if I, as a therapist, can help this woman use rational-emotive psychology. For I then merely try to induce her to go on to D—to Dispute her irrational Beliefs. Thus, I persuade her, by teaching her the logico-empirical method of challenging and questioning her irrational hypotheses about herself and the universe, to Dispute as follows:

1. "Why is it *awful* if your mate (or potential mate) rejects you?" Answer: "It isn't! For *awful* means, first, *more than* obnoxious and unpleasant; and how could anything be *more than* very frustrating and unpleasant—even rejection by a person whom I deeply love? Secondly, if I say a thing is *awful* I really mean that because it is highly undesirable, it shouldn't, mustn't exist. But *why* shouldn't things I don't desire, like rejection, exist? No reason whatsoever! Whatever exists exists! Only God can mandate away unpleasantness; and, obviously, I'm no God!"

2. "Where is the evidence that *I can't stand* being rejected?" Answer: "Clearly, there isn't any. Of course, I'll never *like* rejection; but I can damned well stand what I don't like! No matter how many times I am rejected by someone for whom I care, I'll still survive. What's more, I can even—at least, if I stop my whining—be happy surviving without him: though not, perhaps, *as* happy as I would be if I survived with his love."

3. "Why *should* I have been more beautiful, intelligent, and loving so that he then would not have rejected me?" Answer: "Only because I stupidly *think* I should! It would have been fine had I possessed exactly the kind of traits that he adores and if he consequently loved me. But just because *it would be desirable* if I had x or y or z hardly means that I *should* or *must* have it. There is no reason, in fact, why I must be *anything;* and I'd better accept that reality!"

4. "Even if I didn't do what I could have done to get him to accept me, how does it make me a rotten person or a worm for my acting so badly?" Answer: "It doesn't. Although my *traits* and *performances* can legitimately be rated, there is no accurate way of rating *me*, my totality, my essence, or my being. *I* consist of thousands of traits, some good, some bad; some of them one way today, much different tomorrow. I may, for example, be good at writing, but that hardly makes me a *good person*. And I may be bad at sex, but that doesn't make me a *bad individual*. All people, including me, are much too complex to be given a global, total rating. There are no human worms and there are no human angels. All humans are simply human—never subhuman or superhuman. I'd

better, therefore, acknowledge the bad or inefficient *things* I did that may have kept me from winning him, but I'd better not say that the rating of those things (which I can helpfully use to change them) is the same thing as the rating of me. I, as a person, am not really ratable, even though most of my individual acts and performances may be."

5. "Is it likely, if the person who rejected me finds me (or, more accurately, my traits) of so little worth to him, that all other men whom I find attractive will recognize my total worthlessness and that I will therefore never be able to maintain a successful, ongoing relationship?" Answer: "Hardly! Individual tastes widely differ, and some males will accept me for the very reasons why he rejected me. If he and many others reject me, that will tend to prove that *it will be difficult* for me to find the kind of partner I want. But difficult only means difficult—and not impossible. If I really am handicapped in finding the kind of person I want because some of my traits are not too attractive, then maybe I'd better look harder and work more energetically to discover and win this kind of partner."

6. "Is it true that if I never find the kind of sex-love partner I desire, life won't be worth living at all and that I might as well kill myself than face such a horrible, hopeless existence?" Answer: "Of course not! My life will, of course, be *less* enjoyable without a good sex-love relationship than it would be with one. But there are many other things I can enjoy besides sex, love, and mating, and if these things are entirely unavailable to me for the rest of my days (which is highly unlikely, if I get off my butt and keep seeking them!), that's really going to be sad. But not awful or terrible—for I can still find *something* to make my life meaningful and happy!"

If, therapeutically, this rejected and despairing woman will Dispute, at D, her irrational Beliefs (iB's), and if she will continue to vigorously Dispute them until she no longer devoutly holds them, or until she at most subscribes to them lightly and occasionally, she will almost invariably be able to change her disturbed feelings, at C, from hurt, depression, horror, and withdrawal to sorrow, regret, frustration, and annoyance—or from highly inappropriate and self-defeating to distinctly appropriate and self-motivating feelings. She won't feel deliriously happy or even indifferent about being rejected—for those emotions, too, would be inappropriate and self-sabotaging—but she will feel suitably sad and concerned; and will be able to use these feelings to help herself in her future quest for sex-love acceptance.

Love slobbism, in other words, doesn't stem from a woman's strong *desire* or *preference* for relating intimately to others but from her grandiose *demand, command,* or *need* that she so relate. She makes herself into a love slob by sanely wanting intimacy and then by insanely escalating her wanting into a whining dictate. When she logically and empirically—that is, rationally—Disputes (at D) her own puerile demandingness and de-escalates it into a strong (though not necessitous) desiringness, she solves her emotional problem, learns to live with (though not necessarily like) harsh reality, and increases her chances of getting what she wants in the future. Her love slobbism then tends to evaporate.

SEX-LOVE HOSTILITY

While most women (like most men) put themselves down when they act inadequately or get rejected by someone for whom they care, some heavily create feelings of hostility and rage rather than (or in addition to) feelings of shame and worthlessness when they are sexually or amatively thwarted. A typical example, in this connection, is the woman who is in an emotional relationship where the man, her lover or husband, says that he cares for her but keeps acting in a manner that she thinks is not too loving and seems to be interested in other women, too. At point A (the Activating Event) she observes his seeming lack of interest and at Point C (the emotional Consequence), she becomes intensely jealous and hostile. Because of her jealousy and hostility, she frequently becomes so obnoxious in her behavior toward her partner that she appreciably helps to ruin their relationship.

In this kind of sex-love problem, B, her Belief System, is again the key issue. For no matter how much she tends to think that A causes C—"He lied to me about that other woman he is interested in, and he thus upset me and made me angry!"—she really causes it by her own rational and irrational Beliefs. Her rational Beliefs (rB's) probably are: "He is neglecting me and I don't like that! I wish he were only enamored of me and it is most unfortunate that he isn't!" As in the illustration used under love slobbism, if she stayed with these Beliefs, and these alone, she would feel appropriately sorry, disappointed, and annoyed—but hardly insanely jealous and angry.

Her hostility comes from her concomitant irrational Beliefs (iB's); namely: "How horrible it is that he is treating me like this! How can he act so unfairly! He shouldn't be acting that way at all; and what a louse he is for behaving the way he shouldn't!" These Beliefs are almost completely magical, unrealistic, and unprovable because: (1) It isn't *horrible* (that is, more than 100% unpleasant) that he is treating her this way—only highly inconvenient. (2) Even if he is acting unfairly (which, of course, he may not be), he can easily act in that manner, and has every right, as a fallible human, to make mistakes and commit injustices. (3) It would be lovely for her, no doubt, if he acted more lovingly. But that is hardly a reason why he *should, ought,* or *must* act that way. (4) He may indeed be behaving lousily but that hardly makes him, as a total human, a louse. In many other respects, toward her and others, he probably behaves quite unlousily, even remarkably well. She is therefore foolishly damning *him,* instead of some of his *behavior.*

The solution to this woman's problem of jealousy and hatred, therefore, is to work hard at changing her B's—her Beliefs—instead of inappropriately overfocusing on A (someone else's attitudes, emotions, and behavior) and C (her own feelings which stem from her irrational Beliefs). In looking at her irrational Beliefs—her demandingness about her husband or lover—she might also well look at some of her own irrational B's about herself—her underlying assumptions that she *must* have some man's complete and utterly guaranteed love if she is to accept herself and live a reasonably happy existence. It might, indeed, be *preferable* if her chosen partner deeply cared for her forever. But why *must* she depend on the attainment of a *preferable* state of affairs. Clearly—if she thinks about it and gives up her grandiose demands—she mustn't.

SEXUAL INADEQUACY

If we go by ideal standards of sexual arousal and orgasmic achievement, most civilized females are frequently or usually inadequate. For it is only the rare woman who easily becomes aroused, who doesn't require some special condition (such as an intense romantic attachment to her partner) to let herself go sexually, who never is guilty about masturbation, who quickly comes to orgasm, who can almost always climax during intercourse, and who can achieve a minimum of several orgasms a week. Every study of female sexuality that has ever been done tends to show that even among selected women who are partly picked for their "normal" sexuality, high incidences of various kinds of sexual disability tend to exist (de Martino, 1969, 1973, Fisher, 1973, Kinsey, Pomeroy, Martin, and Gebhard, 1969, Masters and Johnson, 1966, 1971, Singer, 1973, Sorenson, 1973).

Even if we go by much less ideal standards and consider as sexually inadequate only those women who have great difficulty in becoming sexually aroused and who never or rarely achieve any kind of orgasm, we still are left with a quite sizable number, and a great many of these females tend to have some kind of psychological problem, particularly that of anxiety (Ellis, 1961, 1965a, 1965b, Masters and Johnson, 1971). Their irrational Beliefs (iB's), in these instances, overlap with the same kind of Beliefs that they are telling themselves about love and rejection, except that they are more specifically about sex failure.

By way of illustration, let us consider Sally G., who came to see me because she only occasionally came to a climax even when her lovers massaged her clitoral region for fifteen or twenty minutes and who recently had been becoming completely turned off to sex, so that virtually nothing aroused her. "The man I am going with now," she said, "is great. There's not a thing he wouldn't do to satisfy me. He really cares and *wants* me to be satisfied. And I love him for that—as well as for many other things. But nothing seems to work any more, and if it continues like this, I'm sure I'll ruin the best relationship I've ever had."

"And how do you feel about all this?" I asked.

"Feel? How would anyone feel in my position? Depressed, of course. Depressed like I've never been depressed before!"

Already, after knowing Sally for only a few minutes, I thought I knew the basic answer—and the solution—to her problem. For that is the advantage of an efficient theory of psychotherapy, such as RET. Give me A and C—which most clients are fully aware of and can exposit in from five to fifteen minutes—and I almost always know what B and D are. And also what can be done with and about them, to help solve the client's emotional difficulties.

Just to make no mistake about this, however, (since even the best psychotherapists are hardly infallible!), I asked, "While you're having sex with your lover, what exactly are you saying to yourself? What are you thinking, at what I call B (your Belief system), about yourself, your partner, and the sex act itself?"

"Oh, that's easy. I'm saying many things to myself—all bad. I'm saying, first, that it's taking too long for me to get aroused. That I'll probably never come to orgasm. That he must be getting bored. That this will ruin our relationship. That there's something really wrong with me. That I might as well kill myself, if this keeps up!"

"Very sexy thoughts, I must say!"

"You're right. They're as sexy as the kitchen sink. But I *know* what's going to happen—or *not* happen. I really *know*, after all the experience I've had, the very dreadful experience I've had, recently. So what do you expect me to be saying to myself—that everything is glorious and I'm going to get sixteen orgasms before he can say Ms. Robinson?"

"No, I don't expect anything. But the point is: *you* do."

"I do?"

"Yes, you expect—or demand—that it *shouldn't* take so long for you to get aroused. That you've *got to* come to orgasm. That he *must not* get bored. That you *have to* maintain a good relationship with him. That there *ought not* be something wrong with you. That you *need* a good sex life to be a happy human being."

"Well, what's wrong with *those* expectations? *Shouldn't* I get aroused more easily, have orgasms, and maintain a good relationship with my lover? Why *shouldn't* I?"

"Because—if you stop to think about it (which few humans, alas, do)— there pretty obviously aren't any absolutistic shoulds, oughts, musts, necessities, got to's, or have to's in the universe. Not, at least, as far as anyone has ever scientifically proven."

"Nonsense! Don't I *have to* respond better sexually if I am to keep him or any other reasonably sexy man satisfied?"

"No, of course not. It would, in all probability, *be better* if you were sexually more arousable and orgasmic; but ten thousand *it would be betters* never equal a single *should*. For "it would be better if I were sexier" means that *the chances are* that if you were you would please your lover and *probably* have a more satisfying relationship with him. But some lovers, actually, might find your sexiness *dis*pleasing; and some would love you more without it."

"Damned few!" retorted Sally.

"Yes, probably. But the mere fact that most of your lovers most of the time would love you more if you were more arousable and orgasmic still doesn't equal (1) I *must* be loved and am a thoroughly worthless skunk if I am not, nor (2) There is an inalterable law of the universe which states that I *have to* be sexy to be loved.

"Are you trying to tell me that I must think in terms of "it would be betters" rather than of "musts" if I am to overcome my feelings of sexual anesthesia?"

"No—not you *must think that way*, but *it would be better if you did!*"

Whereupon I proceeded to show Sally that she had at least two serious emotional problems—or inordinate demands on herself—which seriously interfered with her functioning. First, she demanded and commanded that she be easily and fully sexually arousable, and because she was focusing so intently during the sex act, on "I must succeed at sex; it's terrible to fail!" she was not focusing on sexually exciting stimuli (such as her lover's body or his feelings for her) and was foredooming herself to failure.

Once Sally had sex (at A), told herself that she absolutely *had to* succeed (at B), and thereby brought on anxiety and frigidity (at C), she then perceived what was happening at C and turned this into another A and B. Thus, at the new A (Activating Experience), she experienced panic and sexlessnes. At the new B (Belief System), she told herself, "It's horrible to be sexually inadequate! What a thorough, unlovable slob I am for being so inadequate!" At the new C (emotional Consequence), she then felt even more inadequate and hopelessly depressed.

Sally, in other words, had *two* intense fears of failure: first, her fear of failing sexually, which deflected her from thinking of arousing stimuli and which caused her to be frigid; and second, her fear of being worthless for *being* sexually inadequate. This same kind of doubleheaded fear is common in nonsexual disturbances as well. An individual is extremely anxious *lest* he or she fail at school, work, or social affairs; then, when anxiety actually brings on failure, he or she is exceptionally anxious *about* this anxiety and about the actual failure. Consequently, people circularly put themselves down, become panicked about being panicked, depressed about being depressed, and feel worthless about feeling worthless.

The therapeutic solution I employed with Sally was similar to that I have used in many other cases of sexual inadequacy. It consisted of several cognitive-behavioral methods which are often employed in RET.

Antiawfulizing

Sally was shown that *nothing* is awful, horrible, or terible in the entire universe. Her unarousability and lack of orgasm were to be seen as decidedly unpleasant and handicapping, but never as *more* than that. Although she was left with the feeling that it is highly *desirable* to succeed (that is, enjoy herself) sexually, she was induced to give up the irrational idea that she *should, ought,* and *must* succeed.

Sensate Focus

Sally was given the activity homework assignment of having steady sex relations with her lover (which she had been recently avoiding) and of focusing, during these relations, mainly on pleasing each other rather than on desperately trying to achieve orgasm. This is the method first reported by Semans (1956) and later highly publicized by Masters and Johnson (1971), which encourages sex partners to divert themselves from anxiety by concentrating on "This sensation is enjoyable!" rather than upon "Suppose I fail! Suppose I fail!"

Unconditional Self-Acceptance

Sally was shown how she could completely accept herself as a human being *whether or not* she succeeded sexually and *whether or not* she was anxious. She was shown that humans are only human—not superhuman or subhuman—and that as she accepted herself fully with all her inevitable fallibilities, she could stop trying to *prove* and simply *be* herself.

Desensitizing

Whereas many behavior therapists, such as Wolpe (1958) and Lazarus (1971), might have used imaginative desensitizing or reciprocal inhibition by helping Sally to think of increasingly dangerous sexual situations and relax her body (and temporarily allay her anxiety with this diversion method) every time she felt anxious, I instead used *in vivo* desensitization, as I have been doing in RET ever since I first formulated the method in 1955. I induced her gradually to do more risk-taking sexual things, both with her lover and with several other attractive men with whom she wanted to experiment. At first, she would merely hold hands with these partners; then she would kiss and pet lightly with them; then she would try heavy petting (the sensate focus); and finally she would try intercourse. As she went through this hierarchy of "riskier" procedures, she would consciously antiawfulize and convince herself that any kinds of failures were unfortunate but not catastrophic.

Sexual Imaging

Masters and Johnson tend to be wary of sexual imagery because they are afraid that if inadequate individuals are encouraged to think highly sexual thoughts they will tend to set up worrisome images or thoughts as well, and will thereby become more anxious. I have found for many years, however, that actively directed imaging techniques often work very well to induce sexual arousal and orgasm (Ellis, 1965a, 1972c). With Sally, I therefore helped her to imagine the same kind of highly eroticizing fantasies when she was having sex with male partners that she spontaneously employed during masturbation, and she soon found that this kind of imagery frequently worked beautifully to create and enhance her arousal. At first, she tended to resist this procedure, since her masturbatory fantasies were rarely of her lover but often of two or more powerful thugs who totally overpowered her and forced her to have sex with them against her will. But when she was able to allow herself to have this kind of fantasy when she was with her lover (or with other men) she found that it was usually quite effective in getting her aroused, and that it could later be switched, just before the point of orgasm, to fantasies involving her actual partner and of having loving contact with him.

Rational-Emotive Imagery

Rational-emotive imagery (REI) is a special kind of cognitive-emotive-behavioral technique originally developed by Dr. Maxie C. Maultsby, Jr. (1971), who built upon the work of Brande (1936), Coué (1923), Maltz (1960), and Peale (1952). However, in the particular form that I generally use it, it becomes a technique that is almost diametrically opposed to rather than consonant with Peale's "power of positive thinking." As I explained it to Sally, in the course of her second session:

"Close your eyes, right now, and fantasize, just as vividly as you can, that you are having sex relations with your lover. Can you do that?"

"Yes."

"All right. Continue, in your imagination, having sex with him. But picture, quite vividly, that little or nothing is happening. You are not getting in the least aroused; the whole thing is a complete bust; and he is becoming quite irritable and disappointed in you, because you are failing. In fact, he's wondering and making overt remarks about your continually failing and he's indicating that he's beginning to suspect that you're just a dud, sexually, and that you're not likely to ever satisfy any man in that respect. Picture these scenes just as dramatically as you can. See that it really is happening!"

"I can see it. I can clearly see it now."

"Fine. How do you feel? How do you honestly feel, right in your gut, as you envision this kind of sexual failure?"

"Awful! Depressed!"

"Right. That's the way you normally feel when you think of this kind of thing happening. Now, change the feeling in your gut to a feeling of *only* disappointment and frustration. Keep the same fantasy in your head, exactly the same picture, but *only* feel sorry, disappointed, and frustrated. *Not* awful, *not* depressed. *Only* disappointed. Can you do that?"

"I'm having great trouble feeling that way. It's hard!"

"I know. But I'm sure that you can do it. You do have the power to change your feelings—if only for a short time. So try some more. Feel *only* disappointed and frustrated. See if you can do that."

(After a pause): "All right. I guess I can do it."

"Do what?" I asked.

"Feel *just* disappointed. It keeps running back into depression. But I can feel it, at least for awhile."

"Good. I knew you could. Now, what were you thinking about to make yourself feel that way?"

"Let's see. I guess I'm thinking, 'It isn't the end of the world. I really would *like* to be much more aroused and please Henry. But I don't *have to.*'"

"Yes? Anything else?"

"Yes, I guess: 'I'm not a rotten person, even if I *never* get very sexy again. It's only *one* of my traits, sexiness, and it isn't *me.* If I lose that, I still very much have the *rest* of me.'"

"Fine. That's exactly what you could continue to think, if you want to feel disappointed but *not* depressed. For you *aren't* a rotten person, if you're not sexy. There *is* much more to you than that. And you *can* enjoy yourself, and even have a good love relationship going, if you never get very sexy again."

"Yes, I see right now that I can."

"Right! Now, if you will practice this rational-emotive imagery technique every day, for a minimum of ten minutes a day, for the next few weeks, if you really keep practicing it, it will become more and more a part of you. You'll see, more clearly than you ever did, that you have a *choice* of what you think when you envision sex failure, that you can *choose* to feel sorry and disappointed—or awful and depressed. And you will *get used to* feeling the former and not the latter, until it becomes almost an automatic part of your thinking and feeling. Up to now, you have really been vigorously practicing the opposite—that is, *making yourself* feel depressed whenever you think, as you often do, of not becoming aroused or orgasmic. Now you can *make yourself* feel differently, until you 'naturally' keep feeling that way. So every day, for the next few weeks, practice this kind of rational-emotive imagery that we have just done, until it becomes 'second nature.' Will you do that?"

"Yes, I will," said Sally. And she did practice it steadily for the next few weeks, and reported that when she did have sex with her lover, and she began to feel depressed at the thought of failing, she quickly and almost automatically was able to make herself feel sorry and disappointed instead. After a few weeks, she even had trouble feeling depressed! And she was then able, much easier and better than before, to practice intense sexual imaging of an exciting nature and to sometimes arouse herself considerably and to come to orgasm.

Operant Conditioning

When Sally failed to carry out her homework assignments—particularly that of going to bed with her lover or with other men when she was afraid of failing and wanted to escape from facing her problem—she was put on a self-contracting basis, according to the techniques developed by Goldfried and Merbaum (1973), Homme (1969), Premack (1965), Meichenbaum (1971), and Skinner (1953, 1971). She agreed that she would only reinforce or reward herself (by reading and listening to music, which she greatly enjoyed doing daily) *after* she had carried out her homework assignments and that she would penalize herself (by doing at least an hour's onerous housecleaning each day) when she shirked any assignments. Although she was at first reluctant to enforce this self-contracting procedure, when she finally got around to doing so she found that it distinctly enhanced the likelihood of her carrying out the RET *in vivo* desensitizing assignments.

These were some of the main cognitive-emotive-behavioral procedures that I used with Sally. After seven once-a-week therapy sessions, she began to be moderately aroused with her lover (but not with other men), and by the twelfth session, she was regularly experiencing orgasm again, usually after from five to ten minutes of clitoral region massage by her partner. She also reported that although we had never specifically discussed her problems at work—she was a junior high school teacher in a very rough school and was afraid that she would lose her job if she didn't keep better order in her classes—she had realized that she had the same kind of enormous fear of failure in this area as she had in the sex-love area, and had worked on this fear and significantly ameliorated it by using procedures similar to those we had been employing to help her sexually. So, although we almost exclusively discussed her relationship problems, she had been able to use the RET principles and practices to help her in other important areas of life.

SEXUAL AND GENERAL UNASSERTIVENESS

Up to recently, perhaps the great majority of women, particularly in Western "civilization," have been much less assertive than it would have been preferable for them to be. Although women's lack of assertiveness tends to be something of a general trait, prevalent in many aspects of their lives, its sex-love aspects are notably pernicious. Thus, in our society, females tend to avoid actively pursuing relationships with males they care for. They often avoid taking the sex initiative, even when they are highly desirous, both before and after marriage. They go along with hypocritical double standards of sexual morality, even when actively discriminated against by these standards. They pretend that they are sexually satisfied when they really are not. They go along with male demands, even when they feel sexually indifferent or revolted. They refrain from instituting separation or divorce proceedings, in spite of the unsatisfactory state of their marriages. They easily go along with conventional child-rearing traditions that make them virtually slaves to their children. They meekly accept work and household duties without asking sufficient support or cooperation from their husbands. Etcetera!

RET has always been in the forefront of those therapies that promulgate assertion training. It especially does so by activity homework assignments. Thus, females in individual or group rational-emotive therapy are frequently given graduated series of assignments that finally enable them to pick up attractive males in public places (such as dances, singles gatherings, or bars); to phone their men friends instead of passively waiting for the men to call; to make sexual overtures when they wish to do so; to ask their partners to engage in sex-love practices that they particularly enjoy; to stop taking too much responsibility for their children; and to do many other "unfeminine" things that they truly would like to do (Wolfe, 1973).

If they have great difficulty in asserting themselves in these ways, they are frequently put through role-playing forms of behavior rehearsal, in the course of their individual or group therapy sessions. Thus, a shy and meek woman may be rehearsed, in the course of a group session, to ask a man to dinner, to go to a party alone and break in on the conversation of three people who are talking together, or to ask her lover to bring her to orgasm through oral-genital relations.

As usual, these behavior therapy aspects of RET are invariably accomplished by teaching women clients the philosophic A-B-C's of assertiveness and nonassertiveness. Susan G., for example, had the problem of never going after the male she really wanted when she and her woman-friend, Josephine, went to a social affair together and were approached by a couple of men. She almost always stood quietly by while Josephine picked the man she clearly wanted—who normally was easily the more attractive of the two—and maneuvered him into taking her home while Susan was left with the less desirable male.

Although Susan benefitted, during her RET sessions with activity homework assignments, assertion training, and operant conditioning in connection with forcing herself to be almost as determined as Josephine was in getting the man she wanted, a real breakthrough in this connection was not achieved until she finally, during her fifth session, saw what the A-B-C's of her unassertiveness were all about. Part of our dialogue during this session went as follows:

Susan: I'm afraid I blew it again! In spite of the great rehearsal we did last week, I went to a dance with Josephine last Saturday and let her do exactly what she's done twenty times before with me. And this time the guy I wanted obviously was much more interested in me than in her, and he and his friend, in fact, got talking to me first when Josephine was off in the ladies' room. Nonetheless, she just maneuvered herself into the front seat of the car with him, when they were taking us home, pushed me into the back seat with the other guy, and then got the good one to drive me and the other guy to my place first and to drive off with her to her place. And I just let her do it! I could have killed myself for not speaking up and insisting that the good guy was really with me. But I didn't speak up!

Therapist: Because?

Susan: Oh, I don't know. I just didn't.

Therapist: Just? You mean, don't you, that you told yourself something very specific, and *then* you "just" didn't speak up to her. Or, in other words, at point C, the Consequence, you unassertively kept your mouth shut after, at point A, the Activating Experience, she arranged to let the "good guy" sit in the front seat with her and drive her home. Now the point is—what is point B, your Belief System, that led you to act so unassertively at C?

Susan: Well, I certainly know what my rational Belief was at B!

Therapist: What? What was it?

Susan: "There she goes again, that bitch! Going after what she wants, no matter what I want—and no matter what the guy wants. What a vile way to act!"

Therapist: You mean, that was your *almost* rational Belief. The first part, "There she goes again!" is an observation, and probably correct. The last part, "What a vile way to act!" is your rational evaluation or Belief. For, according to your wishes and the way you would like things to turn out, it would have been better had she acted otherwise.

Consequently, your evaluative conclusion, "In view of what I would want to have happened, and in view of the fact that I've told her about how displeased I am about the way she's behaved in the past and agreed with her that she was not to do this again, her action or behavior is indeed vile," is a reasonable or rational conclusion. But you are making an irrational judgment, too. What is that?

Susan: Oh, you mean about my designating her as a bitch?

Therapist: Yes, why is that an irrational—rather than a rational—Belief?

Susan: Because she *acts* bitchily but is not necessarily *always* going to do so.

Therapist: Yes. Accurately stated, she is a woman with highly bitchy behavior, and she might well behave that way again. But she *could,* at least theoretically, act better in the future, while *a* bitch, or someone who is a bitch to the core, could not. What, moreover, about your *condemning her* for acting bitchily?

Susan: Oh, yes. We've been through that before, too. And I guess you're right. I didn't get what you were saying about this, at first, because I really believed that people who act consistently bitchily *should be* condemned. Now I'm beginning to see that maybe it is better to avoid them, but that to condemn them means putting them down as being *totally* lousy. I'm beginning to agree with you about this, although I couldn't see it at first.

Therapist: All right: so it's irrational for you to call her *a* bitch, however bitchy her behavior may be (and even continue to be). What else are you saying, at point B, to make yourself give in to her when she goes after the fellow you want, and who you think wants you?

Susan: I guess, "If I interrupt and contradict her nerviness, she'll hate me and maybe never go out with me again."

Therapist: Right. But that, too, is merely an observation—and perhaps a true one. If you hold your ground and deflect her from waltzing off with the fellow you want, she may well hate you and refuse to go out with you again. But what's your evaluation, your irrational evaluation, of that possibility?

Susan: Mmm. I'm not sure. I don't know.

Therapist: You *do* know. Look for it!

Susan: No. My mind's blank.

Therapist: Well, unblank it! What would virtually any woman tell herself if her friend agreed not to go off with a male who was interested in her and then actually did so?

Susan: That that's a dirty deed!

Therapist: Yes, but that's a rational Belief again. For it probably *is,* empirically speaking, a dirty deed. Now, what's the irrational Belief?

Susan: (Looks puzzled. Silence)

Therapist: And that dirty deed is—? What?

Susan: —Awful!

Therapist: Right! "It's *awful* that Josephine did that to me again! How *could* she do it? She *shouldn't* have done that dirty deed."

Susan: Right! she *shouldn't* have done it.

Therapist: Why the hell *shouldn't* she?

Susan: Well, I wouldn't do it to her, for one thing.

Therapist: And *therefore* she shouldn't do it to me? Does that really follow?

Susan: No. I see what you mean. No matter how I would behave, she has a perfect right to behave as she does.

Therapist: Even though you don't *like* her behavior?

Susan: Yes, even though I don't like it.

Therapist: And how about your statement, which you probably keep making to yourself, "How *could* she do it?"

Susan: She damned well could! In fact, she did!

Therapist: Yes, she easily can do whatever she does. The answer to the question, "How can she do this to me?" is almost invariably, "Easily!" In fact, it would be very hard for her *not* to do it—wouldn't it?

Susan: Yes, in Josephine's case, it certainly would be!

Therapist: And how about your irrational Belief, "She shouldn't have done that dirty deed!" Well?

Susan: Well, of course, that's nonsense. I can't command that she not do what she does.

Therapist: You can—but it won't get you very far! You don't control her behavior; and your command says that you should control it—that "Because I don't like it, she shouldn't do it!" Drivel!

Susan: Yes, I see now. I am not God. I can only control myself—and *hope* or *wish,* not *command,* that people like Josephine will control themselves.

Therapist: Right. Now, let's review. Spell out the A-B-C's that you are making up about Josephine; and how you could Dispute, at D, your irrational Beliefs, at B.

Susan: All right. At A, she agrees not to be too pushy about walking off with all the attractive men we meet together, especially when one seems to be interested in me. And she then actually does me in and maneuvers the better of two guys to take her, instead of me, home. At C, I feel angry at her, but do nothing to stop her.

Therapist: Right. Because at B—what?

Susan: At B, I'm first telling myself, rationally, that she's doing a dirty deed to me, and I don't like it. Then I'm telling myself, irrationally, that she *shouldn't* be doing that bitchy deed and is *a* bitch for doing it.

Therapist: Correct. Now, what can you do, at D, to Dispute your irrational Belief?

Susan: Ask myself, *"Why* shouldn't she be doing that deed?" and "How does it make her *a* total bitch for doing it?"

Therapist: Exactly. And your answer, or the new philosophic Effect, at E?

Susan: That people behave the way they behave, including Josephine. That *it would be nice* if she didn't behave that way, but that's no reason why she *shouldn't.* And that she isn't *a* bitch, but merely a fucked up human who often acts bitchily.

Therapist: Good! I think you hit it right on the head. Except that we both made a mistake, you and I, and got so hung up on your anger at Josephine that we forgot the other very important C or Consequence: Your not assertively speaking up for yourself and trying to stop her from waltzing off with this "good guy." How about that A-B-C's of your inertia and unassertiveness?

Susan: Yes, we forgot that. But I can see that even without our discussing it, I have been getting myself all set to change it.

Therapist: How?

Susan: By—uh—. Well, let me do it A-B-C-wise again, just to get it utterly clear in my head and to aid my dealing with it next time.

Therapist: Fine.

Susan: Let me start with C, the way it tells you to do on your Homework Report. At C, I act unassertively and feel anxious. At A, Josephine is, as usual, trying to get her way and make off with the more attractive guy. Because at B, I am first telling myself, rationally, "I don't like her behavior, and I'd better stop her before she gets away with it!" But at B, I am also telling myself, irrationally, and much more strongly, "If I stop her, she won't like me—and that would be terrible! I *must* have Josephine's approval, even if I keep losing the guys I want because I let her go after them first." And my irrational idea, at B, is the real thing that makes me act so unassertively and weakly at C.

Therapist: Exactly! And what could D and E be?

Susan: Uh, let me see. D—"Why would it be terrible if Josephine doesn't like me?" And: "Where is the evidence that I *must* have her approval?" E—"It's not terrible if Josephine doesn't like me—only inconvenient. And it even has it's conveniences! And there is no reason why I *must* have her approval, though it would be nice if I did have it."

Therapist: Right. And what behavioral Effect do you think you'd get, at E again, if you kept Disputing your irrational Beliefs persistently and strongly?

Susan: I think I'd begin to speak up, to assert myself in going off with the good guy, and probably much more often get what I really wanted.

Therapist: I think so, too. Why not try it and see? Force yourself to see the bullshit you are telling yourself, at B, and to Dispute it vigorously, at D. Also: let's give you the actual homework assignments of (1) speaking to Josephine again about this general problem that you have with her and (2) definitely speaking up and challenging her the very next time she attempts to walk off with a male in whom you are interested.

Susan: I'll definitely work on that.

And Susan did work on it and over the next few months became so assertive that she usually ended up with the "good guy" whenever she and Josephine went to a social affair and met two males. Moreover, she began to be more assertive, at the same time, on her teaching job, with her family members, and with the males she dated. So her general as well as her sex-love assertiveness significantly increased.

SUMMARY

Rational-emotive therapy deals with various sex-love problems of women (and, of course, of men) in a comprehensive, cognitive-emotive-behavioral way. It often employs a wide variety of therapeutic methods. But it does not do so merely in an eclectic, pragmatic way because one or more of these methods may work. It is primarily interested in helping women make a profound philosophic change, so that they will not only be able to overcome their existing emotional problems but also tackle any other difficulties that are likely to arise in the future. It is preventive as well as therapeutic, and it follows the educational rather than the medical, psychodynamic, or encounter model (Ellis, 1972d). It essentially teaches troubled individuals to understand and employ the logico-empirical method in regard to their own thinking, feeling, and behavior rather than merely in regard to external problems (Ellis, 1971, 1972c).

RET accepts women in their own right and not merely as part of a man-woman relationship. It assumes that they are all individuals, with significant differences from all other individuals. It assumes that simply because they exist and are human they have a right (though not a necessity) to survive, to be as happy as they can teach themselves to be, to live in and get along satisfactorily with members of their social group, and to relate intimately (and sometimes sexually) to personally selected members of this group. It teaches women, in the pursuit of these individual and social goals, to accept themselves fully and unconditionally— that is, to rate their traits, deeds, acts, and performances (in order to know what they like and help themselves to get what they like) but *not* to rate their selves, beings, essences, or images (in order to become holier-than-thou and get into some kind of mythical heaven). While attempting to be ruthlessly scientific and empirical, RET is at the same time humanistic, egalitarian, and devoted to maximum utilization of self-choosing. Patricia Jakubowski-Spector (1973) and many other counselors who especially try to help women with problems of assertiveness frequently note that RET is the main cognitive-behavior therapy of choice. It is hardly surprising that I enthusiastically agree.

REFERENCES

BRANDE, DOROTHEA. *Wake Up and Live!* New York: Simon and Schuster, 1936.

CHESLER, PHYLLIS. *Women and Madness.* New York: Doubleday, 1972.

COUE, E. *My Method.* New York: Doubleday, Page, 1923.

DE BEAUVOIR, SIMONE. *The Second Sex.* New York: Knopf, 1953.

DE MARTINO, M. *The New Female Sexuality.* New York: Julian Press, 1969.

DE MARTINO, M. *Sex and the Intelligent Woman.* New York: Springer, 1973.

ELLIS, A. *The American Sexual Tragedy.* New York: Lyle Stuart and Grove Press, 1961.

ELLIS, A. *Reason and Emotion in Psychotherapy.* New York: Lyle Stuart, 1962.

ELLIS, A. *The Intelligent Woman's Guide to Manhunting.* New York: Lyle Stuart and Dell Books, 1965a.

ELLIS, A. *The Art and Science of Love.* New York: Lyle Stuart and Dell Books, 1960, 1965b.

ELLIS, A. *Growth through Reason.* Palo Alto: Science and Behavior Books, 1971.

ELLIS, A. *Executive Leadership: A Rational Approach.* New York: Citadel Press, 1972a.

ELLIS, A. *How to Master Your Fear of Flying.* New York: Curtis Books, 1972b.

ELLIS, A. *The Sensuous Person: Critique and Corrections.* New York: Lyle Stuart, 1972c.

ELLIS, A. Emotional education in the classroom: The Living School. *Journal of Clinical Child Psychology,* 1 (13), 19-22, 1972d.

ELLIS, A. *Humanistic Psychotherapy: The Rational-Emotive Approach.* New York: Julian Press, 1973.

ELLIS, A. Empirical confirmation of rational-emotive therapy. *Counseling Psychologist,* 1974 (in press).

ELLIS, A. & BUDD, KATHIE. *Bibliography of Articles and Books on Rational-Emotive and Cognitive-Behavior Therapy.* New York: Institute for Rational Living, 1974.

ELLIS, A. & HARPER, R. A. *A Guide to Successful Marriage.* Hollywood: Wilshire Books, 1971.

ELLIS, A. & HARPER, R. A. *A Guide to Rational Living.* Hollywood: Wilshire Books, 1972.

FISHER, S. *The Female Orgasm.* New York: Basic Books, 1973.

FRUMKIN, R. M. Beauty. In A. Ellis and A. Abarbanel (Eds.), *Encyclopedia of Sexual Behavior.* New York: Jason Aronson, 1973, 216-227.

GOLDFRIED, M. & MERBAUM, M. *Behavior Change through Self-Control.* New York: Holt, Rinehart and Winston, 1973.

HOMME, L. *How to Use Contingency Contracting in the Classroom.* Champaign, Illinois: Research Press, 1969.

JAKUBOWSKI-SPECTOR, PATRICIA. Facilitating the growth of women through assertive training. *Counseling Psychologist,* 4, 75-86, 1973.

KINSEY, A. C., POMEROY, W. B., MARTIN, C. E., & GEBHARD, P. H. *Sexual Behavior in the Human Female.* New York: Pocket Books, 1969.

LAZARUS, A. A. *Behavior Therapy and Beyond.* New York: McGraw-Hill, 1971.

MALTZ, M. *Psychocybernetics.* Englewood Cliffs, N. J.: Prentice-Hall, 1960.

MASTERS, W. H. & JOHNSON, VIRGINIA E. *Human Sexual Response.* Boston: Little, Brown, 1966.

MASTERS, W. H. & JOHNON, VIRGINIA E. *Human Sexual Inadequacy.* Boston: Little, Brown, 1971.

MAULTSBY, M. C., JR. Rational-emotive imagery. *Rational Living,* 6 (1), 24-27, 1971.

MEAD, MARGARET. *Male and Female.* New York: New American Library, 1955.

MEICHENBAUM, D. *Cognitive Factors in Behavior Modification.* Waterloo: University of Waterloo, 1971.

MILLET, KATE. *Sexual Politics.* New York: Doubleday, 1971.

PEALE, N. V. *The Power of Positive Thinking.* Englewood Cliffs, N. J.: Prentice-Hall, 1952.

PREMACK, D. Reinforcement theory. In D. Levine (Ed.), *Nebraska Symposium on Motivation.* Lincoln, Nebraska: University of Nebraska Press, 1965.

SEMANS, J. Premature ejaculation: A new approach. *Southern Medical Journal,* 49, 353-358, 1956.

SEWARD, GEORGENE. Sex and the Social Order. In A. Ellis and A. Abarbanel (Eds.), *Encyclopedia of Sexual Behavior.* New York: Jason Aronson, 1973, 979-986.

SINGER, I. *The Goals of Human Sexuality.* New York: Norton, 1973.

SKINNER, B. F. *Science and Human Behavior.* New York: Macmillan, 1953.

SKINNER, B. F. *Beyond Freedom and Dignity.* New York: Macmillan, 1971.

SORENSON, R. C. *Adolescent Sexuality in Contemporary America.* New York: World Publishing, 1973.

THOMPSON, CLARA. Femininity. In A. Ellis and A. Abarbanel (Eds.), *Encyclopedia of Sexual Behavior.* New York: Jason Aronson, 1973, 422-427.

WOLFE, J. L. What to do until the revolution comes: An argument for women's rational therapy groups. Talk presented at the University of Wisconsin, November, 1973.

WOLPE, J. *Psychotherapy by Reciprocal Inhibition.* Stanford: Stanford University Press, 1958.

14

CREATIVE EXITS: FIGHT-THERAPY FOR DIVORCEES

GEORGE R. BACH

Even though I myself initiated the term "creative divorce" in the book *The Intimate Enemy* (Bach and Wyden, 1968) several years ago, I now feel that I must have had my tongue in cheek when I wrote it. For the divorce process is inherently traumatic, and to call it "creative" may be taken as an inappropriately glib cavalier gesture, or too slick to show respect for the complexity of the paradox that term displays. It is more responsible to ask: under what conditions can any given divorce be experienced as "creative," or at least as therapeutic? One may want to ask, still more specifically, what kind of interventions by a psychotherapist, who is being consulted by a woman about to enter into a divorce situation, would aid in turning an intrinsically traumatic, stressful, destructive, and painful process into a growth-stimulating one? And further, one ought to be clear, as a psychotherapist, what kind of intervention would tend to reinforce a sense of failure, guilt, disappointment, outrage and retaliation? In keeping with the theme of this book, I shall try to answer these questions from my clinical experience gained in years of consultation with women clients in the throes of divorce.

Thirty years ago, when I saw my first divorce-stressed female patient, Benjamin Franklin's classic reference to the unmarried person as "the odd half of a pair of scissors" still was the prevailing social attitude. Then (in the forties) any attempts on my part to turn the failure of a marriage into a therapeutic, let alone a "creative," experience, were vigorously resisted by my respectably middle-class clients (then in Cleveland Heights). Then all I could do was stand by while they vented their fury, bemoaned their

The author gratefully acknowledges valuable assistance received from Joan Hotchkis, Luree Nicholson, Stephanie Bach, and Keith McCoy.

extreme disappointment, cursed their miserable fate, licked their ego-wounds and swallowed their pride. They asked for help in their search for a new mate, or for aid in regressive returns to their original family refuges. Then psychotherapy with a divorce-traumatized woman was a "healing" tactic to facilitate a self-recovery process and to provide support and understanding in a judgmental, anti-divorce milieu. Today, this is still true, but only for those now "old-fashioned" ladies who are failing to participate fully in the main current of American feminine thought—the thrust toward's woman's self-assertion.

But for those of my present female clients who fully participate in the spirit of the times that supports a significant psychological metamorphosis of female selfhood from a secondary-dependent towards a primary independent role, I am not nearly as much limited to the supporting function of a recovery agent. Rather, in both group and individual consultations, many times a divorce can become a *discovery* process. The divorce process can indeed be therapeutically restructured to provide the first stepping-stone to freedom, not only from a stressful marriage but freedom for wholesome self-development through independent singlehood.

In growing segments of society all over the world, the female destiny —which many now call her "curse"—to live in tandem rather than solo style is now repelling rather than compelling. The economic and sexual liberation of woman has radically diminished her need for the "sacred halo of marriage." This evolution of gender status shows that the "need" to be married and to raise a family was society-bound and role-determined rather than rooted in a primary psycho-biological, let alone instinctive, nesting urge. In addition to movements for economic and sexual freedom, a humanistic revolution has occurred which places the search for self-identity above the quest for a mate. What used to be considered an unquestionable requirement for female life-fulfillment has become a voluntary choice. An increasing number of intelligent women are opting for singledom. And they demand that the single condition be respected as an acceptable life-style for everyone, male and female, never married or divorced, with or without children! And they resent being type-cast anew by an equally restrictive stereotype which views singledom somewhat derogatively (or enviously?) as "swingledom," thereby inferring that the main interest in the single life-style is to gain easy access to the mechanized sex-games the "swing-fringe" ploys in *Playboy,* and now also *Playgirl,* magazine style.

The marital condition has now been widely unmasked as a security trap which exploits in both male and female certain regressive propensities, such as possessiveness, jealousy, and dependency. The emotional harm of having a tag-along identity by living vicariously for or through another person or as "a team" has been exposed by millions of unhappily married women seeking psychotherapy. Other millions of divorcées are willing to share their hindsight about how little their marriages added to their emotional development, self-confidence and self-actualization. And the old argument "stay together for the children's sake" has lost its credibility completely due to the discovery that children are much less— if at all—traumatized by a reasonably managed divorce than their parting parents. On the contrary, the divorce may bring the child closer to its mother and father, each as persons rather than in their parental roles. Furthermore, a new level of intimacy can be attained by dating singles which more often than not is more authentic than any marriage-romance ever was. This I fully explain in my book *Pairing* (Bach and Deutsch, 1970).

In this new single-oriented society, the psychotherapist can aid in making clear any discoveries of growth and gains to be made, rather than merely losses to be recovered. These gains can be experienced while undergoing the change from a married to a divorced state, not waiting until "the wounds are healed." This can be done by full awareness and experimentation with the many opportunities for *aggressive self-assertion* that are inherent in the divorce crisis.

Erich Fromm speculates that humans when threatened would rather flee that fight (Fromm, 1973). Exiting spouses tend to do just that: get out without a fight—often sneak out, run away, disappear without a trace. Culturally the female has been more counseled to flee than the male, who is more encouraged to fight. Therefore, it is at times necessary for the therapist to define and point out what these opportunities for aggressive self-assertion are. For, even with her back to the wall, the typical lady in marital distress will postpone as long as possible displaying out into the open her tiger-rage.

Among the most common of these occasions for legitimate expressions of aggression in terms of righteous wrath are:

1. Flushing out the cover-up of illicit lovers.

2. Confronting third parties in person with their attempts to snatch away the husband.

3. In cases where the husband wants a divorce but seeks to throw the blame on her by making *her* so disgusted and upset that *she* will feel like leaving: confronting the husband with his manipulative tactics and

insisting that the responsibility for the breakup fall where it properly belongs.

4. Demanding a radical stop to the mistreatment and/or total neglect of the children by their father.

5. Cutting short the husband who is biding his time to "drop the axe."

6. Uncovering attempts by the husband to elicit loyalty from friends and relatives on his side with totally fabricated stories of the lady's misdeeds, etc.

7. Calling the police when hubby becomes physically violent or threatens to do so.

8. Bringing in a close friend to assist as counsel in an altercation about breaking up when the husband is overwhelming, either physically or intellectually or by the sheer quantity and speed of verbiage.

9. Insisting that an emotionally noncommunicative husband at least respond to her feelings.

10. Where the husband says he wants to leave but is vacillating about doing so, aggressively insisting that he "either proposes specific and realistic improvements, or gets out!"

The therapist can reinforce positive learning that potentially can be experienced by helping the person participate fully, to become totally involved in the crisis of parting, rather than passively allowing others— the ex-husband, the family lawyer, friends, neighbors, children, or a new lover—to "manage" the conflictful proceedings. The intelligent woman appreciates, even welcomes, the new assertive attitudes, roles, and behaviors required during the divorce crisis. It not only invites but requires innovative thinking, new responsibilities, courage, new contacts, new procedures, and frequently new social and physical environs. The challenge here for the therapist is to come up with the most creative ways of dealing with this existential newness—for which, traditionally, no familiar models can be drawn on to imitate.

In this light the female can experience her divorce as the major initiatory act towards a new self-assertive life-style. However, this novelty can be very scary and resistance to its full utilization—even enjoyment—may show itself in various impatient flight reactions, such as moving quickly into a new marriage and/or letting the lawyers fight it all out with a passive attitude of resignation: "Let him have anything he wants—all I want is my freedom."

One of the major reasons for resistance against full experimentation with new behavior patterns is the culturally conditioned *aggression-phobia* which handicaps the female in her fight for the freedom to be herself. Nothing illustrates this better than several unique experiences I had during World War II. In 1941 I spent part of my graduate student field work at an aircraft (bomber) factory trying to train male (chauvinist) foremen to learn how to accept and cooperate with female welders and other women factory workers. Then I succeeded more often only when I trained the women—at the same time as I trained the foremen to more than just "tolerate" them as a necessary evil—to assert themselves, to display that their learning capacity and, later, their manual skills most assuredly equalled those of the fighting men they replaced.

A year later, at the University of Iowa, as an assistant to the late Kurt Lewin, the founding father of the group-dynamics movement in psychology, I was part of a team of psychologists charged with the task of helping female officers of the WACS stationed in their national training headquarters in Des Moines to accept their officer status and learn how to assert their authority over men lower in rank, without either feeling uncomfortable, incongruous and/or becoming excessively "ball-cutting." How to maintain the identity of "femininity," while performing productive services skillfully and effectively in a traditionally male-dominated environment, was a tough challenge for these women. Having had the opportunity to assist some to take and enjoy this challenge to transcend traditional sex-role limitations then (1941-1943) helped me later in individual and group psychotherapy with women who consulted with me about their divorce crisis.

When I ask myself what interventions and consultations on my part seemed the most helpful to women in situations which demand of them new attitudes and new behavior styles, I would choose again the training in using aggression constructively.

To counteract the tendency to avoid active partaking of the new behavior possibilities that present themselves in the "change-of-state" situation, and to aid the female in learning how to overcome aggression-phobia and in adopting new constructively aggressive modes of acting and communicating, I—with the help of my associates—have designed aggression-games, rituals, and "love-fight" techniques. These are learning aids which encourage the female in therapy to explore and experiment with aggressive styles of being-in-this-world, which she never before associated with being feminine. She can be aggressive in her own behalf, but loses her élan in the tandem. Over one hundred heuristic "exercises" which help individuals to develop more fully their potential for creative and constructive aggressive have been clinically tested for their effectiveness in aiding in the development of self-assertion, which is of specific relevance to the female in the divorce crisis. Many of these have been previously published in a training manual (Bach and Bernhard, 1971).

The full utilization of aggression in the service of a creative and therapeutic divorce is one of the objectives of our "exit-fighting" procedures, which include "The Un-wedding," a ritual counterpart of the wedding ceremony. To illustrate these procedures, as well as the process of utilizing the divorce as a springboard for aggressive self-assertion on the part of the female—both as the leaving or as the left partner—I am including unedited protocols written by women in therapy with me at the time of parting from a centrally significant loved-one.

In consulting with hundreds of couples in the throes of divorce, it was possible to identify among the infinite variety of pair-specific marital problems *one* common incompetence: *They do not know how to have a good, fair fight. They do not know what to do with anger, their own or their partner's. They do not even know how to confront and bring into the open their differences, which they tend to assume to be "irreconcilable." When they feel forced by intolerable stress into an argument, they escalate irrationally, fight dirty, hit below the belt, hit and run, take sneaky potshots, entrap and ambush one another. They will "Watergate" their hostilities through concealed underground aggression. They will form unholy alliances, typically secret ones, whereby some temporary relief and comfort are fleetingly enjoyed at a heavy expense of later expanding and intensifying the original conflicts. And—perhaps worst of all—they do not know how to get out without provoking dangerous hostilities!*

We have found that when partners learn how to fight their way out—fair and square—the divorce process becomes a "growth stimulus." Managing the exit creatively involves constructive behavior changes. Constructive aggression training prevents alienation caused by below-the-belt blows to bodies and souls, which characterizes wild exits. As they learn how to fight, and sometimes because of it, many a partner feels that—even though they dread the emotional stresses and the social stigma of divorce—marriage is not for them, at least not the one they are in, and they are glad to get out. Here again—on the way out—aggression properly managed can play a therapeutic role.

Doing therapy with divorcées highlights the special problems the female in our culture faces, compared to those of the male. Two sorts of chauvinistic role-typing tend to make it especially difficult for the female to turn a "marriage-failure" into a growth-stimulating scene. First, because the creative style of divorcing requires self-assertive aggression, the female is handicapped by the sweet, nice stereotype of friendly, cooperative, *non-aggressive* characterizations of "femininity." Also, she usually has little or no successful pre-divorce experience with living within an aggressive life-style, which is traditionally associated with masculinity. Secondly, the female divorcée (and/or widow) tends to be regarded by formerly friendly married female friends as a predatory threat—"better keep her away from my husband." This threat is reinforced by a male chauvinistic tendency to "chivalrously" offer sexually oriented consolation services to ex-married women now without husbands. It follows that the female divorcée is in a special quandary and requires specialized guidance.

Furthermore, the divorce problems are not made any easier for the female by her sexual disposition. The female sexual functioning, in general, and the consistency of her orgasmic capacity are significantly disturbed by separation, especially the experience of being the one who is left rather than leaving. In spouse-separated males no analogous increase in impotence can be clinically detected. In fact, typically, the abandoned male tends to seek and and often finds consolation in new relationships that are sexually more fulfilling than the old home bedroom fare. And this may be in the nature of a visit to the massage parlor after seeing a porno movie. In contrast, most left females become, especially during the readjustment phase, even more suspicious and cautious of entering into new intimacies. Being divorced reinforces further their separation anxiety. The following research findings by Dr. Seymour Fisher are relevant here:

> The prime difference between women who are high and low in orgasmic consistency concerns their anxiety about *losing* what they love. The low-orgasmic woman, as contrasted to the high-orgasmic, feels that persons she values and loves are not dependable, that they may unpredictably leave her. She seems to be chronically preoccupied with the possibility of being separated from those with whom she has intimate relationships (Fisher, 1973).

MARITAL EXITS: THE ART OF UNCOUPLING

Separation anxiety and other stress-producing behaviors associated with the breaking of an intimate bond are growth-hindering habits. They are learned behavior patterns that can be unlearned and replaced by new, more productive ways of uncoupling. Marital exits are more often than not marred by intense, negative emotions, punitive retribution, harsh blamesmanship, bitter disappointments, and physical violence. The latter relatively easily escalates into the extreme of spouse-killing. Mate-killing is often associated with one partner wanting to leave and having to shoot or knife or poison his or her way out because the other blocks the exit in some violence-provoking way. Or the leaving partner may get killed later as the death-penalty for breaking the lifelong vows (Bach and Goldberg, 1973).*

To render marital exits less traumatic with less destructive consequences, an *exit-fight-training* program suggested itself as an adjunct to our fair fight training methods originally designed to aid in the preservation of marriage and family life (Bach and Wyden, 1970). Exit fight training—EXT for short—is a method of training divorcing partners to do so not in a phony, so-called "civilized" manner, but in an authentic style which yields a maximum of learning, stimulates new orientations and minimizes the trauma that is inherent in the breakup of any intimate bond for which deep commitment once genuinely existed.

*Reducing the Divorce Trauma by Practicing
Constructive Exit Fighting*

Shakespeare said that lovers' partings are "sweet sorrow." The paradoxical nature of parting is experienced by all *significant others,* and is not necessarily limited to lovers. The exit exercises are designed to fully experience the paradox, and thus not be rattled or embarrassed by it.

The following pages give two eyewitness reports of a therapy group ritual called the *unwedding,* the purpose of which is to ease the pangs of separation and to attempt to draw some last lessons from the history of the marital rift. Retrospective learning can compensate for the destructive painful aspects and transform the situation into a *creative divorce,* that helps wounds to heal.

Unwedding rituals may also serve to reduce the chance that bitter disappointment and hate, too often fanned by selfish divorce shysters and destructive ally-friends, will escalate into retributive strategies and very expensive battles, some of which have cost lives.

The setting of the unwedding is usually towards the end of either a thirteen-week constructive-aggression lab course or an extended marathon weekend session. All lab-group members, before sanctioning the unwed-

---

* For a more detailed report of the author's spouse-murder research, see G. R. Bach and H. Goldberg: *Stop Being So Nice—You're Killing Me,* New York: Doubleday, in print, 1973.

ding, will have had the opportunity to have all the information they need for deciding for or against the wisdom of having an unwedding at all.

Blessing of Unbound Ties: A Report of My Unwedding
by Jane X

Twelve hours into the marathon we broke for some sleep and we drove to a motel nearby where Jim insisted on sleeping in separate beds; a pretty strong declaration because we had been sleeping in the same bed at home. I felt banished. I did not want him to make love to me, but I thought we had both enjoyed cuddling. I was hurt, and then remembered grimly that I "nauseated" him.

Early the next morning, Jim and I had a confrontation and our conflict revealed the vast distance which separated us. I realized that the distance was deepened to an abyss by the fact that he truly did not love me; he could not have loved me and still have done the hurtful things he had done to me. Dr. Bach asked me, "Are you ready now for an unwedding?"

And suddenly the truth blazed before me—continuing to hold onto Jim could only mean further hurt for me as he tried to get away from my desperate grasp. I then convinced everyone present that I earnestly wanted an unwedding to stop subjecting myself to pain—for I saw clearly that Jim would continue to hurt me as long as I permitted him to. I cared for myself—which I couldn't do before, knowing that I was too weak to tear myself away from him.

After Jim convinced the group that he, too, wanted a release from our marriage, we chose our "unbridal party"—with unbest man, minister, and unbridesmaids. I had lunch with my four maids and Debbie somehow managed to obtain a plastic glass filled with sour-sweet daiquiri for the five of us to sip at lunch as we talked about the fulfilling life ahead for me, now that I had decided to relinquish the dreams and hopes which had tortured me with their lack of fulfillment for so long.

"There are lots of nice men around," Rose said.

"I'll say," Pat added. "And you have an advantage over women who haven't been married—you can take your time in choosing another husband, you know there isn't any rush."

"And you're so fortunate not to have any children—you can really be free all the ways," Marcia pointed out.

"What career plans do you have?" inquired Gretta, bringing me sharply into confronting reality. Suddenly came rushing upon me the tremendous complexity of remaking my life—I would have to find a place to live, and either start back to work teaching English in junior high school, or go back to the University for further training in counseling and guidance, an interest I had begun to develop last spring.

I had many grave decisions to make, but the idea that they would be my decisions, that they would not be dependent upon where Jim could live because of his advanced training, brought these choices into a more exhilarating perspective. I was my own person again. I could do what I wanted and I savored that thought throughout lunch as we talked of other things—where good apartment areas were in Los Angeles, what the format of the unwedding ceremony would be. . . .

After lunch, Jim, tense and anxious, came to me and asked to speak with me alone. We went downstairs to the "waterfall room," paneled in dark wood, carpeted in deep red wool shag, with a dry waterfall of artificial rocks in the corner. We sat on the floor and he said, "I am very worried and need assurance from you. I'm agreed that you will reproach me after our unwedding and make me feel guilty for rejecting you and not carrying through our mariage vows. I couldn't stand that. I know I've hurt you so much in the past—and your pain has made me very unhappy."

For the second time since I've known him, I saw Jim cry. His tears were anguished sobs and they came from very deep within him where they had been constrained for so long. In a hoarse wail he begged me to reassure him that I really did want to go through with the unwedding ceremony, that I would not go back on my vows to set him free, that I would not torture him with my unhappiness.

I looked into his tear-filled eyes and told him, meaning every word with all my heart: "We have made our decision. I have made my decision based on what I realize is best for my happiness. I know now that you cannot fulfill the hopes and dreams I had for our marriage. And I know that I must give them up—we have a way to relinquish them forever in our promise to set each other free, to realize the death of our marriage and the birth of our new, separate lives. I fully believe that we can be happier apart. I really *know* that, and I will not deny this knowledge later!"

A relieved and grateful look eased the anguished lines of his flushed and tear-streaked face and he smiled and said in a choked whisper, "Thank you!" I felt very strong then. I was no longer a weepy clinging girl. I was a woman and I was responsible for myself, and this responsibility meant not vacillating after making such an important and difficult decision.

Our unwedding party met with Dr. Bach under the eucalyptus trees in the warm afternoon sunlight to plan our ceremony. We could hear the St. Bernard puppy snuffling about, the gardener trimming the hedges, and the swallows chirping as we sat in our aluminum lawn chairs and joined hands in meditation.

"What God hath joined together, let no man cast asunder lightly, without due thought and consideration. But when it becomes apparent that a marriage is a mistake, that the individuals are tied to one another to each other's harm, then the bond must be broken in order that the individuals can be released to live happier, more fulfilling lives than they can realize together."

We planned a candlelight ceremony with an India Raga as our music. Pat offered me her silk hostess gown to wear, so much more fitting than my black pants and orange blouse! I felt very regal in her long, lustrous, striped robe, and fully dressed down to slippers which matched and gold bracelets for my arms. While our guests were arranging themselves, Marcia said, "Flowers, you must have some flowers to carry—all brides are late, so an unbride can be late too—I'll find some flowers outside!"

Nervously I walked back and forth waiting for her return, peeking into the next room where our ceremony would soon take place, our new lives commence. Finally Marcia came back with flowers gathered from the garden and we entered the room together as Jim and his unbest man came in from the other room. We met in the middle of the darkened room and gazed into each other's eyes, shining in the candlelight.

We joined hands and our minister tied a blue wool paisley scarf around our clasp. We sat down and each gave our pledge to liberate each other. Our minister asked: "Do you, after careful and sincere consideration, choose to set this man free? To live his own life, independent of your expectations? And do you vow to give up your hopes and dreams for your marriage, understanding fully that you have promised to relinquish them forever? Do you pledge to always remain friends? To free yourself from bitterness and not to harbor anger and contaminate other relationships with enmity against your former mate? Do you promise to take the lessons of your unhappiness to enrich your future life, your vision widened by suffering which you will not regret, knowing that you are a fuller person for it?"

"I do."

"In the presence of your understanding and compassionate friends, seeing that you are indeed earnest in your intention to liberate one another, I pronounce you unmarried." The minister untied the scarf and Jim took off my ring, giving it to his unbest man to keep in trust—forever, I knew. I took my flowers from Marcia and gave them to our minister saying, "I present these flowers in token of the death of our marriage. Good-bye, Jim."

"Good-bye, Jane."

I knew the men were going to take me into the next room for a welcome back party—but I was quite surprised to find myself raised above their heads and carried there! What an exhilarating joy I felt at each man presenting himself to me—giving me his congratulations, his welcome, his hopes for my happiness.

And what beautiful presents these dear men gave me! Some read me poems—thoughtfully chosen, sincerely read. Others gave me the picture of themselves they had drawn our first night. One friend presented me with a drawing of a beautiful golden tree soaring to the sky in exuberant foliage, full of life and promise! I received a turquoise piece of paper with the carefully lettered words, "Bless You." And truly I did feel blessed, enraptured with my new freedom to respond to the warmth of these beautiful, giving men. I felt so filled with their love, I felt shining and lovely. My last gift was a little five-cent pack of Kleenex—which seemed to me a little funny—I felt so happy then that I could not imagine ever crying again. But it was a most practical gift and I now realize that although I have buried the hopes and dreams I had for our marriage, I am still yearning and mourning what I gave up. And I expect to feel intermittent pangs for some time. I truly loved Jim and it would be false to my deep feelings to try to suppress my grief. But my sadness now is not remorse; I do not regret our years together and I do not feel bitterness that it is now over."

The next protocol of another unwedding was written by a participant-observer rather than the principal character.

The Unwedding (by Joan Hotchkis, Actress, Writer and Participant in Several Marathon Groups)

In Rick and Shirley's unwedding, which occurred four years ago, I took part as a spectator and a participant.

My therapist uses group rituals to define and support a behavior change. He feels that our present-day culture is barren of them, because the old rituals no longer apply to modern life and therefore people no longer use them. New ones need to be invented, such as the unwedding, which is the celebration of a *creative divorce,* just as the wedding joyfully ritualizes the beginning of a creative partnership. I only wish I'd known about it at the time of my own divorce and could have been unwed from my husband with dignity and social support instead of the post-mortem shame we both suffered.

I was an unbridesmaid in Rick and Shirley's unwedding, which took place after a thirty-six hour marathon. Married couples attended the marathon, as well as some singles and divorcées like myself. My struggle —or "growth edge," as we call it—was to clarify and strengthen my identity, a fuzzy thing that lived beneath my phony behavior, which consisted mainly of seductive ploys towards men. For years I'd been leaning heavily on the image of the Femme Fatale and now as middle age washed over me—I was forty-one, with my beauty fading—the image had become obsolete. It had never served me well anyway, restricting me to a role instead of nourishing me with a true sense of womanhood, But at this particular marathon, which came early in my therapy, I was still clinging to it.

The couple to be unwed had gone through many hours of fair fighting and I'd listened, horrified, to the dreadful things they'd done to each other in the name of domestic peace, I didn't much care for either of them. Compassion had never been my strong suit. He was a bitter young psychiatrist, silent and vengeful, and she was the PTA prototype I'd been avoiding all my life through my femme fatale pursuits. I couldn't connect with their real suffering—until the ritual of the unwedding.

The unbridesmaids prepared Shirley for the ceremony, brushing her hair and decorating her with flowers from the garden, while the unushers kept Rick company in a separate room. When it was time, we all gathered together in the same room. The ungroom and the unbride sat on chairs facing each other, close enough to touch. The women clustered behind Shirley, giving her support and all the men stood behind Rick. Our thera-pist stood in the middle like a kind of High Guru. He asked them to hold hands and then he wrapped their marital clasp in a scarf and held it tight while saying some words about the importance of this occasion and the commitments they'd made during their fair fights to treat each other and their children with respect during the divorce proceedings. Then the unbride's "minister," someone she'd chosen from the group, spoke to her, defining her unwedding as a beginning as well as an end, reminding her of her worth as an independent woman and her opportunity now to expand all her potentials. The ungroom's minister made a parallel address to him.

Then with a sweeping, ceremonial gesture the High Guru unwrapped the scarf. He asked the couple to disengage their hands, rise and kiss each other goodbye. They did so, tears streaming down their faces as well as everyone else's. I too was deeply touched though my tears were trapped in my throat. He instructed them to turn away from each other and walk to opposite sides of the room and asked all the men to follow the unbride, to crowd around her lovingly, touching her cheeks and lips with kisses and filling her ears with affirmation of her attractiveness as a single woman, thereby signifying her reentry into the Love Market. All the women followed the ungroom and did likewise.

Follow-Up on Unweddings

Of the 52 individuals from twenty-six "unwedded" couples, 33 remain convinced one to four years later that the ritual helped them on to new levels of growth. Four ex-partners remarried each other and report a different, better marriage was the result. They're reunited after taking a long holiday from each other. One lady liked the ritual at the time, but later began to hate it in retrospect, especially when she found out that her ex-hubbie seems to have a better post-divorce time than she has. The rest of the initial group of the unwedded moved away and we were unable to follow them up at all. These preliminary follow-up results seem to us sufficiently encouraging to continue the therapeutic ritual of the unwedding in carefully prepared and selected cases who come to us for the purpose of aiding their exit.

PREVENTION OF VIOLENT EXITS: SHOOTING YOUR WAY OUT

Tragic instances of lethal punishment were triggered by exits, when one of the partners wanted to leave while the other wanted no breakup. This could be either the agent or the victim. The person blocking the exit may get shot to remove the barriers to freedom. Another pattern is to administer the death penalty to the leaving partner some time after he or she has left, when the fact of permanent separation has sunk in. These violent exits give us pause to reflect upon how such mayhem could be prevented by the use of more constructive ways of living through the pain of separation and the pangs of shattered hopes and spoiled dreams.

Because many intimates tend to become irrationally hostile when faced with a stressful exit situation, the probability of violent destructive behavior exists more commonly than is known. We have developed some further "exit-exercises" as means to familiarize people—married or not— with constructive ways of exiting, so that they need not push any panic buttons when and if a parting situation confronts them.

Good Riddance: Aggressive Exit-Training

The painful task of undoing meaningful bonds is obviously not limited to broken marriages. In fact, unmarried pairs have mini unweddings all the time, at the average time lapse of five months and nine days. According to our research on pairing, this is the standard duration of adult love relationships in an active, deeply involved state. After that a gradual alienation, a fading out without a sharp exit occurs, *provided the dénouement is mutual.* However, in the frequent case where only one partner is disenchanted while the other's interest is maintained, sometimes on an intensified level, the parting is again much sorrow and little sweat! For such a situation our trainees are encouraged through practicing an exercise called *Release Me!*

Purpose: The *Release Me* exercise is designed to help the partner who wants out but feels hindered by the unwillingness of the clinging vine to let go. This exercise is similar to *A Thousand Times No!!!* The strategy here is based on the assumption that one of the reasons the clinger clings is that the "want-out" person has up to now behaved ambivalently. This "off again—on again" manner always rekindles the hopes of the clinger. The purpose of this exercise is to make it crystal clear *that there is no way other than out.* When the clinger really believes that he has no chance at all to succeed in keeping the want-out partner, he will be more accessible to a creative exit ritual. Also, he is less likely to resort to retributive hostility later on.

Procedure:

1. The want-out partner engages the clinger in a fair persistence-resistance confrontation. At least one witness from each side is invited and must be present. In the invitation to the exercise the clinger is reassured that he has a chance—to test whether his previously vacillating partner *really wants out.*

2. As a warm-up the witnesses and principals engage in a series of persistence-exercises to arrive at a *No-Yes* score for the two protagonists. The issue of leaving is totally *taboo* in this round.

3. After an intermission designed to relax everyone, witnesses invite and engage each other in *A Thousand Times No* shouting match. The "yes-no" routine is modified to "Stay!" versus "Out!" ("No, *you can't leave!*" versus "Yes, *I want to go!*")

4. It is important that the want-out partner keep at it until actual, real collapse. Anything less is unconvincing. Only a truly unambivalent "want-outer" can do this.

5. The witnesses offer their observations, including their perceptions of the urgency and genuineness of the need to exit on the part of the one who wants out. The witnesses can help the clinger to acknowledge the reality of the partner's commitment to exit.

6. The clinger now asks for help to get over the fixation on the want-out partner and for assistance in the digestion of a sense of loss.

7. In the spirit of good will and fellowship, arrangements are made to plan a creative exit ritual in the near future. The want-out person is invited, and hopefully accepts under the condition that the issue of parting is a *fait accompli* and not to be reopened again.

Exit Options

Another exercise, *Exit Options,* has the purpose of helping partners who definitely *want out,* but feel hostilely hindered by a clinger who won't give up.

Procedure:

1. If you feel you are in a caged situation (at home, at work, or ?), and definitely want out, but are afraid or don't know how to do it, engage your core lab partners in a *Huddle Session* devoted to figuring out all the options for an effective exit.

2. Listen to your lab group exit suggestions for information only. Take notes and enter them on a piece of paper.

3. Homework: When alone take time to reflect. Write a list of every exit possibility you—with the help of the log notes—can conjure up. Take plenty of time and fight off a numb fearful dumbness by inner dialogue.

4. After you list all options, mark them plus or minus to indicate those you might choose and those you might discard as ineffective. Use the "exit options" listed by trainee Suzie Q. as a sample for format—not content.

The background is that the clinger (the "he") in the report below has made her physically afraid, because he has beaten her once when she first told him that she wanted out. She enjoyed masochistically getting beaten and sported her black eye with the pride that comes from being wanted that much!

My Exit Options, by Susie Q.

I could toss A out the door. This is unrealistic. I'm not big enough or strong enough or even oriented along this line of physical activity. It would be like a fly trying to move a mountain and A would be angry. The fly would be squashed.

I could ask him to get out of my life and leave me alone. This might not be bad, but his reaction would be defensive and hostile if I worded it as stated. Besides I do want to maintain a business contact with him and a friendship if possible.

I could wish him away. This is not realistic—it is dreaming only. This is a waste of time, no action here.

I could start reading Women's Lib materials and become enthralled with their philosophy. I see him as wanting a woman who follows his every lead, stays home, and does what he says. He doesn't like Women's Lib because they take away from other more pressing problems and they are a front for people's weaknesses. He would be disgusted with me if I started agreeing with their philosophy. It would also create a phony argument that would cover the real problem.

I could start being a WASP with a great deal of prejudice. I have enough problems without assuming more. I hate this approach. It is ugly and very "unpeople." It is a "hate" approach.

I could just be here, stop my 8:30 P.M. phone curfew, and go out with other men. This would be disastrous because his wrath would be aroused. I would be the creator of a problem and the victim. He wants me to assume the above responsibilities and to not do them without saying so first is lying to him and myself.

I could act uninterested, unconcerned and uncaring—bored in other words. This would be a lie too. I do care about him. I just feel like we can't work because of what I want. I'm not often bored so I'd be acting.

I could ask for the ring back that I gave him. This would cut it off successfully. I don't like this because I would feel childish. I made it for him and gave it to him, and now he can do what he pleases with it.

I could tell him what is happening with me. I want to tell him that I do want to be in a married state again some day. This means that I want a man to share in the financial responsibility, to live with me, sleep with me every night (almost anyway) and be accessible to help raise any forthcoming children, plus grow as people out of our association. As I read this, I see that he has indicated that he would do some of this so I'm really hung-up in the "legal" way. I want less distance between us. Therefore, because these things won't be, I want to be free to go my own way (and find someone else). The part in parenthesis could be threatening. He's married so he definitely doesn't fit that criteria.

This is honest, however, it could be dangerous and threatening. I've talked about this before and I'm changing now or he will see it that way. I don't want to make him angry. In reality I'm more certain of what I want. I don't really believe we can work or that we belong together as a "semimarried" couple. Friends who visit, work together, share time, and maybe even have a sexual relationship are O.K. but no strings or restrictions. He'll say "huh" probably and leave and I won't know if it's over or what. Then if I go about my business he'll get angry. I might have to change what I want in terms of what can be.

I could send him a letter. This could be an alternative, but I feel uncomfortable about it because I'm not doing it myself. I would also worry about his anger.

Back to Exercise: Exit Options

5. Present the listing of your exit options to the lab at the next meeting. Listen to further suggestions. Then choose one and carry out your plan—if it's constructive. Consider using the format of one of the Exit Rituals, such as *Release Me!* followed by a softening *Exit Ritual;* perhaps you may want to try your mind on designing a version of the *Unwedding,* even if you are not married to a clinger.

It might be of interest to note that Susie Q.'s lab group rejected all of her exit-options and, sharing her fear of violence and feeling protective towards her, suggested another, rather unoriginal exit-option: *Call Your Lawyer* and have him write the clinger a kindly desist letter. Susie Q. opted for that. The clinger received the warning letter. Susie Q. moved, address unknown, and the clinger kept away ever after.

SUMMARY AND CONCLUSIONS

The current thrust towards feminine self-assertion has created a new climate that favors a growth-stimulating, rather than a wound-licking, approach in psychotherapy with women in the throes of divorce. However, to take full advantage of this challenge for the fulfillment of feminine growth potentials, women need therapeutic "coaching" to overcome their cast sex-role, which has rendered their conflict-coping styles effective. To wit: Fleeing rather than fighting; undercover male manipulation; passively depending on "allies" (lawyers and friends) to fight their divorce battles for them; masochistic victimology; unimpressive anti-male furies— etc. These and many other counterproductive styles of divorce crisis-coping are viewed in this chapter as symptoms of a more fundamental, culturally conditioned feminine handicap: *incompetence in the constructive and effective use of anger and aggression.* The various ways a psychotherapist can help women to overcome their aggression-phobia and their hostility-distortions, and train and coach them in constructive *love-fight techniques* are explained. Specific attention is focused on the creativeness of the actual exit, because wild and rough exits reinforce the traumatic side of divorce, often tragically. Training methods to prepare partners for "creative exits" are described, and several case histories are presented to illustrate some of the processes involved, such as the *unwedding.*

The selected case histories also show some clinical results which lend support to the following central notion: learning to utilize anger and aggression constructively can help intelligently self-assertive women to turn their divorce-crises into a significant improvement of their existential lot in life. Divorcing creatively, rather than destructively, is seen as a new capability which adds to the emergence of a mature feminine identity. This emergence of a self-assertive femininity, hopefully, will give mankind a new model of how to utilize human frustration and aggression in growth-furthering rather than growth-hindering ways.

REFERENCES

BACH, G. R. & BERNHARD, Y. *Aggression Lab: The Fair Fight Training Manual.* Dubuque: Kendall/Hunt, 1971.
BACH, G. R. & DEUTSCH, R. *Pairing.* New York: Wyden, 1970.
BACH, G. R. & GOLDBERG, H. *Creative Aggression.* New York: Doubleday (in press).
BACH, G. R. & WYDEN, P. *The Intimate Enemy.* New York: Morrow, 1968.
FISHER, S. *The Female Orgasm.* New York: Basic Books, 1973.
FROMM, E. *The Anatomy of Human Destructiveness.* New York: Holt, Rinehart and Winston, 1973.

15

CONSCIOUSNESS-RAISING GROUPS AS THERAPY FOR WOMEN

BARBARA KIRSH

The thesis of this paper is that consciousness-raising groups in the women's movement are an alternative solution to traditional psychotherapy for solving women's problems. The growth of the women's movement is an indication of widespread dissatisfaction among American women. Sociological concepts of minority group status and role conflict will be used to explain the structural, cultural and individual sources of dissatisfaction among women. The factors conducive to the rise of the women's movement will be examined and consciousness-raising groups will be discussed as a possible solution to the defined problems.

Both traditional psychotherapy and consciousness-raising groups function as personal change mechanisms; however, a sociological analysis reveals significant differences in their structure, ideology and outcome. The individual is the unit of change in psychotherapy. In contrast, the goal of the consciousness-raising groups is to change the social structure and culture through the individual. A psychotherapeutic point of view explains problems in terms of personal inner dynamics, while a feminist perspective looks to the socio-cultural context as explanation for what appears to be individual conflict, tension or discomfort. The consciousness-raising groups advocate working upon both the individual and society as a means of solving women's problems.

Central to the analysis in this paper is the assumption that social structure, culture and the individual are integrally related. We can consider "role" to be the mediating link between the social structure and the individual. Sources of women's role conflict and dissatisfaction can be identified and understood in terms of the social structure: economy, government, laws, marriage, religion, education. Other sources of role conflict are in cultural patterns: contradictory role expectations, unattainable goals, or outdated values, for example. In this discussion, "role" can be understood as "units of conduct which by their reoccurrence stand out as regularities and . . . which are oriented to the conduct of other actors" (Gerth and Mills, 1953, p. 10). The power of roles is so great that it has been asserted that a person's perception, sense of time and space, motivation, self concept and psychological functioning are "shaped and steered by the specific configuration of roles" incorporated from society (Gerth and Mills, 1953, p. 11).

The social structure is made up of organizations of roles. This blueprint is colored in with the shared symbols of culture, including values, beliefs, attitudes, norms, and expectations. An important aspect of roles is how they are evaluated and arranged in society. The concept "status" refers to the position of the roletaker in the social hierarchy.

Women, as a group, are currently experiencing changes in their roles. It has been said that role expectations confronting women are vague and undefined, and also contradictory (Gove and Tudor, 1973, Angrist, 1969, Steinmann and Fox, 1966, Friedan, 1963, Goode, 1960, Komarovsky, 1946, Parsons, 1942). It is thus not surprising that "most clients of psychotherapists are women" (Hurvitz, 1973, p. 235). Having posited role theory as a method of analyzing women's "problems," it is necessary to examine the female role complex and its sources of conflict in order to formulate ways of resolving the conflict.

Sex role, or gender role, is the first and most pervasive role an individual acquires in the socialization process (Polk and Stein, 1972, Holter, 1970, Angrist, 1969, Banton, 1965, Parsons, 1942). Beginning at birth, a person's behavior is shaped and reinforced to conform to what his or her society considers appropriate sex role behavior. Most segments of our society consider "masculine" behavior to include the basic attributes of dominance, assertiveness, rationality, achievement-orientation, ego strength, intelligence, creativity and bravery. "Femininity" is thought to include the basic traits of passivity, emotionality, kindness, nurturance, dependence and selflessness (Block et al., 1973, Broverman et al., 1970).

These normative sex role-related traits are being challenged by the social movement for women's liberation. The ideological impetus behind this movement for change is the analysis that not only are individuals differentially socialized on the basis of ascription (supposedly inborn characteristics), but that society values the male role more than the female role (Holter, 1970, Rosenkrantz et al., 1968, Lynn, 1959, McKee and Sherriffs, 1957). The dominant culture values the male role and associated traits as the social structure inducts males into positions of power. These related trends have a vast effect on individuals of both sexes. According to Holter, "Inherent in the acquisition of these personality characteristics by males and females is a certain structuring of society. Males are defined as power-holders, women as the opposite. This disposes men to try to maintain sex differentiation. The acquisition of submissiveness of women disposes them to accept their own position as well as men's. The definitions of masculinity and femininity thus contribute directly to the maintenance of these traits" (p. 196). The legitimized power or control over half the population by the other half on the basis of ascription is termed sexism.

Hole and Levine (1971), in their discussion of the women's movement, state: "It is crucial to an understanding of feminist analysis to recognize that the stated goal of feminism is freedom; and feminists argue that freedom can be achieved only by the elimination of sexist sex-role stereotyping. For, role-typing is built on a power structure of male dominance, and the exercise of power by definition destroys freedom. . . . It is upon their perception of sexism as the underlying ideology of society, molding social institutions, social relationships, and individual psyches, that feminists base their analysis, define their goals, and undertake activities to effectuate these goals" (p. 196).

Having proposed that sex role is a source of conflict for women, we turn to an analysis of how sex role is used to determine position in society, how sex roles are culturally evaluated and the psychological effects of this evaluation, and how individuals are taught to conform to sex role expectations. The three sociological levels that will be examined regarding sex role are the social structure, culture and the individual.

SEX ROLE IN RELATION TO THE SOCIAL STRUCTURE, THE CULTURE, AND INDIVIDUAL SOCIALIZATION

Many "personal" problems women experience arise from the cultural attitude of prejudice (a stereotyped negative set of attitudes) and structural discrimination (a stereotyped negative set of behaviors). Examination of the population designated as "women" reveals minority group status and role characteristics (Freeman, 1971, Hacker, 1951, Myrdal, 1944). Louis Wirth (1945) defines a minority group as "a group of people who, because of their physical or cultural characteristics, are singled out from the others in the society in which they live for differential and unequal treatment. . . . Minority status carries with it the exclusion from full participation in the life of the society" (p. 347). Note that access to power, not statistical frequency in the population, is the key defining concept of a minority group. As an example, blacks in South Africa are a minority group because they have no direct power, although they are a vast majority of the population.

An examination of the power structure in the United States indicates the extent to which women are excluded. According to Amundsen (1971), the corporate economy is in effect controlled by the boards of directors of a small number of large corporations, banks, and insurance companies. All 884 people comprising the boards of the top 20 industrials, the top 15 banks and the top 15 insurance companies are men.

At the present time, 40% to 50% of all American women of working age are employed. In 1966, the average salary for full-time workers was $7396 for white males, $4777 for black males, $4279 for white females, and $3194 for black females (Amundsen, 1971). Only 3% of working women earned more than $10,000 in 1968, as compared with 28% of male workers. Women who worked full-time in 1968 earned about 58% as much as men working full-time (Women's Bureau, U.S. Department of Labor, 1971).

The myth that women seldom work out of necessity is proven false by the following statistic. In 1970, two-thirds of the working women in the United States were either single and had to support themselves, were the supporting heads of families, or were married to husbands who made less than $5000 a year (Amundsen, 1971). In 1970, 5.6 million families were headed by women; the median income of all woman-headed families in 1969 was under $4000 (Amundsen, 1971).

Education does not necessarily help a woman obtain economic security: "A woman college graduate can expect to earn $446 less per year than a white male who has only graduated from elementary school" (Amundsen, 1971, p. 35).

About 65% of working women are employed in clerical, sales or service positions. In the higher paying job categories, women make up 22% of university faculty, 9% of scientists, 7% of physicians, 3% of lawyers, 1% of engineers, 1% of federal judges and 4% of state legislators. In 1968 only 65 women had ever served in the House of Representatives and only 10 in the Senate. Only 3 women have ever been elected governor and these 3 succeeded their husbands (Amundsen, 1971).

Men hold almost all positions of power in the mass media, major foundations, universities, the C.I.A., the F.B.I., religious institutions, the stock market, and the military; there have been only 2 women appointed to Presidential Cabinet posts and no woman has ever been a Supreme Court Justice, Vice-President or President (Amundsen, 1971).

Women are almost nonexistent in positions of direct power in the American social structure. The cultural attitudes of prejudice and the structural behavior of discrimination function to instill minority group character traits in little girls. As girls grow up, they receive two strong messages from their surroundings: they live in an egalitarian society where individual initiative enables anyone to achieve success (Amundsen, 1971, Hole and Levine, 1971), and females hold no power in society and can only be wives and mothers. The logical conclusion is that women are second-class citizens because they deserve nothing better (Freeman, 1971). Little girls are prone to develop traits typical of minority groups (Allport, 1954, Myrdal, 1944): dislike for their own sex, negative self-image, insecurity, self blame, a submissive or "shuffling" attitude, identification with males and low aspirations (Hacker, 1951).

There have been some studies dealing with cultural attitudes that result from and perpetuate female minority status. In one such study exploring female prejudice against other females, Goldberg (1972) presented college women with literature from six professional fields (2 "masculine," 2 "feminine," and 2 neutral). The subjects were divided into two experimental groups; all read the same six articles, but half saw a female name on the article, the others saw a masculine name. The booklets containing the articles were balanced so that three women authors and three men authors appeared in each set. The students evaluated the articles and judged those with male names to be of higher quality than those (identical) articles with female names. This was true even for more acceptably "feminine" fields such as education and dietetics. Goldberg feels this documents the cultural tendency for women to perceive other women as inferior to men and for women to allow this expectation to bias evaluations of male and female achievement.

Broverman, Vogel, Broverman, Clarkson and Rosenkrantz (1972) summed up a series of studies they had done on sex role stereotypes. They had administered questionnaires to a range of individuals, including college students and mental health professionals to determine the subjects' current sex role standards. They found that among the populations they sampled, "the positively valued masculine traits form a cluster of related behaviors which entail competence, rationality, and assertion; the positively-valued feminine traits form a cluster which reflect warmth and expressiveness" (p. 61). Included in what was called the male competency cluster are "being independent, objective, active, competitive, logical, skilled in business, worldly, adventurous, able to make decisions easily, self-confident, always acting as a leader, ambitious" (p. 66). The stereotypic perception of women embodied a general lack of these traits.

The traits seen as male are considered more socially desirable by the public and more functional in terms of achieving the more prestigious rewards in our society. Both sexes incorporate the better and worse aspects of the stereotypical sex role in their image of themselves and thus, according to Broverman et al., "women tend to have more negative self-concepts than do men" (p. 75).

American culture negatively evaluates the female role and its associated traits; women perceive this evaluation. Various forms of psychological conflict and discomfort result from this perception of the culture and of the often subliminal realization that few women attain success or power. Being in a negatively evaluated, unprestigious role may impair a person's self-concept.

Findings have suggested that accepting the traditional female role complex of wife and mother is negatively related to ego strength (Gump, 1972). College women who planned careers in addition to marriage and motherhood had higher ego strength scores than women who intended to limit their roles to the wife-mother combination. Gump concluded that the "more purposive, resourceful women are less traditional in their sex-role orientation" (p. 91).

Interviews and projective tests show that women who strongly commit themselves to the role of mother are more likely to experience depression in middle-age, when the children leave home, than women with other sources of self esteem (Bart, 1971). Bart also examined cross-cultural data on middle-age and found that loss of being needed as a mother is related to depression in societies where women's status goes down in middle-age. This is explained by the prestige and reward system in many cultures that values beauty and ability to bear children as the measure of a woman's worth. The cultures in which women's status increases tend to value the knowledge and competencies of old people; in these cultures with an institutionalized "sage" role for old women, little stress occurs in middle-age.

Bogart and Muhr (1972) conducted an experiment in which male and female students received altruistic or aggressive responses from a male or female "stooge." General attitudes toward men and women were measured before the experiment, and attitudes toward self and supposed partner were obtained after the experiment. When ratings for self esteem were analyzed, it was found that females had worse attitudes toward themselves than males, and were more affected by hostile response from a male. Women saw themselves as "good" if the partner responded in a positive manner, and as "bad" if the response was hostile. The women in general had lower self-esteem when their partner was male. Bogart and Muhr summarize, "Women as a group do appear to possess some of the psychological attributes of other minority groups, particularly negative self-attitude, negative attitude toward other members of one's group and positive attitude toward members of the majority group, in this case, males" (p. 9).

Conflict over achievement in women motivates an "avoidance of success," according to Horner (1968). A fear of being considered unfeminine, or deviant, inhibits self-confident competition and achievement. An interpretation of this finding is that women see almost no successful women who could function as role models; the examples of successful achievement in daily life and in the public imagination are male, not female. A woman who desires to succeed in a field not traditionally considered "feminine" opens herself up to social ostracism; if she succeeds in her goal, she will likely experience interpersonal rejection, she will have to prove and reprove her competence, and in general, she will suffer the stigma of being deviant. Thus, we surmise that the scarcity of women in important structural positions inhibits younger women from feeling such success is possible for themselves. The cultural attitude that women are only fit to become mothers and wives is perpetuated by structural discrimination that discourages other roles. It is the socialization process, to a large extent, that works to channel males into so-called "masculine" roles and females into "feminine" roles.

Commenting on how children learn sex roles, Mischel (1970) says, "Sex-typed behaviors, like all other social behaviors, depend to a large extent on observational learning and cognitive processes. Such learning can occur without any direct reinforcement to the learner. . . . People learn sex roles through their eyes and ears by observing other persons and events and not merely from the consequences they get directly from their own overt behavior" (p. 29).

Sex role learning begins during the first year of life. In our society, it is traditionally the mother who interacts with the infant most of the time. Hoffman (1972) suggests that the mother's "early behaviors toward the infant are not deliberate efforts to teach the child his proper sex role, but she has internalized society's view and acts accordingly. She acts toward her son as though he were sturdy and active and she is more likely to show pleasure when his behavior fits this image. Her daughter is her doll—sweet and delicate and pink. The mother's behavior reflects this perception, and if the child exhibits behavior consistent with the female stereotype, such as dependency, she is not as likely to discourage it as she would with the son" (p. 141).

There have been several studies that have found specific differences in parental attitudes toward sons and daughters. For example, Goldberg and Lewis (1969) found that mothers encouraged more dependency in girls than in boys; also, mothers talked to and touched their six-month-old daughters more than sons. Sears, Maccoby and Levin (1957) found that parents allowed boys to express more physical aggression than they allowed in girls.

After reviewing the research on sex differences in early socialization experiences, Hoffman (1972) concludes: "Since the little girl has (a) less encouragement for independence, (b) more parental protectiveness, (c) less cognitive and social pressure for establishing an identity separate from the mother, and (d) less mother-child conflict which highlights this separation, she engages in less independent exploration of her environment. As a result she does not develop skills in coping with her environment nor confidence in her ability to do so" (p. 147).

Other socializing agents besides parents that teach cultural sex role stereotypes are media (television, books, newspapers) and school. In a study on picture books for preschool children, Weitzman (1972) found that the portrayal of the characters reinforces traditional sex stereotypes. Females are underrepresented in the stories; Weitzman says that even when girls and women appear in the books, they "play insignificant roles, remaining both inconspicuous and nameless" (p. 1128). Boys have adventures and lead diverse, independent lives; girls in the picture books are usually passive, indoors and serve men and boys. Boys work and play together but girls are isolated from each other and are defined in terms of their relation to men and boys. Almost all of the women are identified only as wife or mother, while a wide range of occupations is open for the men. Little girls are rewarded for being pretty, boys are rewarded for being clever and achieving.

Joffe (1971) studied a progressive nursery school that carefully tried to avoid teaching sex stereotyped behavior to boys and girls. Even here, though, subtle influences from some of the teachers motivated sex-typed behavior. For example, girls were complimented on how nice they looked in dresses, boys were more rewarded for aggression than were the girls. The songs, storybooks and games were stereotyped. All the teachers were female, encouraging the belief that only women should or do take care of children.

We see that socialization from such institutions as the family, school, and media attempts to induct an individual into the culture and the mainstream social structure. The process of social learning transmits values, knowledge, traditions and language; channels biological drives; and attempts to prepare the individual to function in society (Gerth and Mills, 1953). The most intense and overt socialization occurs in infancy and childhood; however, social learning continues at more moderate rates throughout life (Inkeles, 1969, Neugarten, 1968, Brim, 1966, Becker, 1964). In a complex and industrialized society such as ours that experiences rapid change, early childhood socialization tends to be inadequate for all the contingencies of adult life (Emmerich, 1973, Inkeles, 1969). Brim suggests that socializing agents, such as parents and schools, should move away from teaching specific attitudes and habits and, instead, should provide the individual with general traits conducive to flexibility, creativity, initiative, insight, self-determination and intelligent responses to new situations (Brim, 1966).

Neugarten (1972) talks about the outdatedness of the traditional wife-mother role. She says that in 1966, "the average woman left school at age 18 . . . married at age 20 . . . her first child was born within one year, her last child was born by the time she was 26, and her last child was in school full-time when she was only 32. Her last child married when she was 48, her husband died when she was 64, and she herself could expect to live to 78, or almost 80. Thus, our average woman could look forward to some forty-five years of life after her last-born child was in school" (p. 211). With these social facts in mind, it seems obvious that socializing little girls to become only wives and mothers and excluding additional roles for women is highly dysfunctional and a source of conflict.

Socializing children to be prepared for social change and encouraging flexibility are part of the solution for role conflict; the other part of the solution is establishing agents to resocialize adults, and to alleviate personal conflict and stress that occur in times of bewildering variety of role expectations (Inkeles, 1969, Brim, 1966).

PSYCHOTHERAPY AND CONSCIOUSNESS-RAISING GROUPS
AS RESOCIALIZATION

Psychotherapy and consciousness-raising groups may both function as resocialization. The search for personal and social change may be seen as a conscious desire to alleviate role ambiguity and conflict, to redefine one's status or position and to clarify and improve one's self concept.

There are commonalities in the social contexts that foster a flourishing of social movements and psychotherapies. Modern, industrialized societies tend to experience a high degree of cultural confusion, with social change battering down established behavior patterns and values (Inkeles, 1969, King, 1956). Conflicting values and norms encourage decreased social integration and the diversity of role expectations may generate interpersonal tensions (Frank, 1972, Szasz, 1970, Cottrell, 1969, Inkeles, 1969, King, 1956).

It must be remembered that individuals create social movements, although social movements arise in a specific socio-cultural context and have the manifest purpose of effecting social change. When established patterns and relationships no longer satisfy an individual's needs, susceptibility to new or different patterns emerges. Feelings of frustration and alienation may combine to activate a search for new meanings, goals, relationships, values and life-style (Toch, 1965, King, 1956).

In a changing heterogeneous society, it is likely that many people will perceive similar dissatisfactions with their roles and statuses; communication among these people may develop further consciousness of their discontent, and with continued interaction, they may formulate plans for concerted activity in the form of a social movement (Killian, 1964, King, 1956). Hope that an improved future is possible by means of a social movement encourages sharing of problems and group exploration of solutions (Toch, 1965, Killian, 1964, King, 1956).

Therapy is a more individualistic source of personal change, or resocialization, in such a socio-cultural milieu. Frank (1972) believes that psychotherapies abound ". . . when more traditional ways of maintaining morale are weakened by rapid shifts in social mores and cultural values . . . the forms of psychotherapy most in demand at any given time embody the value systems of that era. Obviously, the more congruent the world-view of the therapist is with that of his patient the more easily he can combat the latter's sense of alienation and meaninglessness" (p. 35).

Frank's enumeration of common "symptoms" of psychotherapy patients seems to correspond to role conflict. He says, "Candidates for psychotherapy, despite the diversity of their presenting complaints . . . have at least one feature in common: they are unhappy and this unhappiness usually is related to stressful interactions with others. They experience anxiety, depression, resentment, or other dysphoric emotions, and all forms of therapy, when successful, ameliorate these feelings. Improvement in therapy also seems to be accompanied by heightened self-esteem and feelings of mastery or control over oneself and the environment" (p. 31).

Thomas Szasz agrees with Frank's relativistic view of therapy and formulates his definition of what has been labeled "mental illness": Szasz believes that "mental illness" is merely the manifestation of conflicting values, a struggle with the problem of how to interact in a satisfactory way with other people (Szasz, 1970).

Szasz's definition of the problems of many psychotherapy patients seems close to role conflict. We can find a common frame of reference to compare and contrast psychotherapy and consciousness-raising groups. Consciousness-raising groups have the same attributes that Jerome Frank (1972) observes in all psychotherapies: a supportive and confidential relationship; a specific setting; a world view or rationale that makes comprehensible a person's perceived dissatisfactions; and a set of activities suggested by the rationale involving the individual and the other perception-sharers (p. 36).

There has been some controversy within the women's movement as to the labeling of consciousness-raising groups as therapy (Brown, 1971, Hanisch, 1971, Zweig, 1971, Morgan, 1970). The negative connotations of the word "therapy"—a cure for the demon "mental illness"—and the underlying assumption that women's problems are individualistic, not social—probably discourage some feminists from use of the term. However, some notion of "therapeutic" or beneficial change is necessary to formulate sociological and clinical comparisons of individual change in the psychotherapeutic situation and the consciousness-raising group. The concept of beneficial individual change used here has the flavor of Alan Watts' (1961) model of therapy as personal liberation: the process includes "transformation of consciousness, of the inner feeling of one's own existence" and "release of the individual from forms of conditioning imposed . . . by social institutions" (p. 25).

In contrasting traditional psychotherapy and consciousness-raising groups, we find differences in the structure and ideology of these two personal resocialization mechanisms. The basic difference in the structures is that the patient-therapist relationship is unequal and hierarchical, contrasted with the peer equality among women in consciousness-raising groups. The basic difference in the ideologies is that traditional psychotherapy stresses adjusting the inner workings of individuals to fit society; consciousness-raising groups emphasize the need to change society by showing individuals that their "personal" problems are rooted in socio-cultural phenomena.

Some stress-producing elements that impinge on women's full function-ing are present in the structure and ideology of the patient-therapist re-lationship; in contrast, consciousness-raising groups are set up so that both structure and ideology encourage fuller attainment of human po-tential and social change.

A critique of the patient-therapist relationship, using a traditional medical model, by Chesler (1971), characterizes the interaction as un-equal in that the therapist (usually a man) is in the position of authority over the woman patient. The woman expresses her dissatisfactions or unhappiness to the male authority and asks for his help. Her frustrations are kept under control by the interpretation that they are symptoms of a personal "mental illness"; no comparison with other women's problems is made and organization to change objective social conditions is not considered. The therapist traditionally reinforces talking rather than motivation for social action as a cure. (Of course, in contrast to this model, some forms of behavioral therapy encourage activity to change the patient's life situation.) Chesler mentions that therapists generally don't accept social sources of discomfort and deny the woman's reality by inter-preting her view of herself and her problems in terms of psychological rhetoric to which only the therapists have access. The nature of the pa-tient role denies the legitimacy of the woman challenging the profession-al's perspective. Laing (1967) also discusses denial of the patient's reality as a drawback in therapy.

Hurvitz (1973) discusses psychotherapy as a form of social control. He states firmly, "Psychodynamic psychology, with concepts such as 'Electra complex,' 'penis envy,' 'vaginal orgasm,' etc., has fostered a view of women as appendages to men, as less developed human beings, and as 'natural' or 'instinctive' mothers and homemakers, fostering conditions and attitudes that create problems for many women. Psychotherapy thus presumes to help these women overcome their problems by inducing them to accept the very conditions that give rise to their complaints" (p. 235).

Broverman et al. (1970) explored what behavior is considered "healthy" in men, women and adults (sex unspecified). Mental health clinicians answered a questionnaire and the authors conclude that the results indi-cated "a powerful negative assessment of women. In effect, clinicians are suggesting that healthy women differ from healthy men by being more submissive, less independent, less adventurous, less objective, more easily influenced, less aggressive, less competitive, more excitable in crises, more emotional, more conceited about their appearance, and having their feelings more easily hurt" (p. 4). The standard of a healthy adult was the same as for a healthy male. A double bind therefore exists for women because different standards apply to women and to adults. Women cannot easily at the same time manifest traits considered healthy for both women and adults. This corresponds to Simone de Beauvoir's statement (1970) that, especially among psychoanalysts, "man is defined as a human being and woman as a female—whenever she behaves as a human being she is said to imitate the male" (p. 47).

In their discussion of this double standard of mental health, Broverman *et al.* state that this is a problem stemming from "the clinicians' acceptance of an 'adjustment' notion of health, for example, health consists of a good adjustment to one's environment. . . . An adjustment notion of health, plus the existence of differential norms of male and female behavior in our society, automatically leads to a double standard of health. Thus, for a woman to be healthy, from an adjustment viewpoint, she must adjust to and accept the behavioral norms of her sex, even though these behaviors are generally less socially desirable and considered to be less healthy for the generalized competent, mature adult" (p. 6). The authors emphasize that clinicians seem to accept the traditionally circumscribed role of women and in doing so, "help to perpetuate the stereotypes. Therapists should be concerned about whether the influence of the sex-role stereotypes on their professional activities acts to reinforce social and intrapsychic conflict" (p. 6).

As mentioned previously, some of the discomforts women experience result from their minority status. Helping a minority individual better accept her social definition and play the "feminine role" does not change the source of her discomfort, but forces the person to deny her perceptions of dissatisfaction and discomfort. She is urged to continue using male standards of herself as the criteria of her behavior rather than attempting to display whatever urges she feels, regardless of the social sex-typing of those urges. Assertiveness, intellectuality, overt sexuality and independence are some of the characteristics which might be defined as overly masculine and unsuitable for a woman. According to studies such as Broverman *et al.* (1970), the analyst's standards or prejudices may influence whether the manifestation of such behavior indicates "mental illness" in a woman.

As a sociological phenomenon, women's consciousness-raising groups function to take the power of standard maker out of the out-group's possession; feminists attempt to define themselves and determine what behaviors women may exhibit. An effect of taking the power of definition away from male therapists is to change the source of approval. A group that determines how it should act and in what manner it should be treated considers itself the final judge of its goals; approval-seeking is turned in on the group and it does not feel emotionally-dependent on an out-group for approval. This is a common step in developing a sense of unity in a social movement (Killian, 1964).

Until recently, when people had problems in living and went to therapists for help, both members of the contract assumed that adjusting the patient to better fit society's demands was an integral part of therapy. However, a feeling now exists that when those demands include outmoded or constricting sex role standards, more conflict can be resolved if the standards or role expectations and the individual's self-image are changed, rather than forced into an old mold. Some women have discarded the idea of therapy as a form of personal change and structured alternative mechanisms of resocialization: the consciousness-raising groups in the women's movement.

THE WOMEN'S MOVEMENT

To understand the consciousness-raising groups, we must first examine the women's movement. Basic questions include: what is the women's movement; why did the social movement occur when it did; and what do the movement's different structures and ideologies offer women?

According to Holter (1970), certain conditions are generally necessary for sex role frustration to be organized into concerted activity for change. Contact among dissatisfied women who identify with each other's situations, an ideology, and organizational abilities are among Holter's prerequisites for a women's movement.

Acker and Howard (1972) concur with Holter that contact and identification are essential. They comment that, unlike other minority groups, women live with the majority group (men) and have few legitimate activities with other women that could challenge the male monopoly of interpersonal and structural power. "Where there is interaction, it tends to center on the women's relationships to husbands and children. . . . Women do not feel a sisterhood with other women, but see other women through a fine gradient of status distinctions constructed on the basis of their male affiliations. These distinctions inhibit communication among women as autonomous individuals and make it difficult for women to see the similarities in their basic situation as women" (p. 5).

A communication network emerged in the 1960's (Freeman, 1973) as women who were already committed to effecting social change participated in various social movements. Some of the earliest and strongest support for the women's movement originated on university campuses where large concentrations of young, left-leaning women interacted (Acker and Howard, 1972).

An ideology evolved, based on the premise that institutions and culture in the United States (and, indeed, in most of the world) are prejudiced in favor of men and discriminate against women; and that sex role socialization and stereotyping must be changed. Of course, feminism is not new; the basis of these ideas, as well as activist believers, existed a century ago. The movement had been almost nonexistent for nearly 50 years, though, and these core beliefs are the most prominent ones to surface in the late 1960's. At present, a diversity of ideological positions exists throughout the movement, but these ideas are fairly constant—the various branches of the women's movement reinterpret "individual conflicts as the consequence of social-structural factors" (Acker and Howard, 1972, p. 21) and analyze women's position as that of a minority group.

The organizational skills which Holter posits as necessary prerequisites for a movement (1970) developed in different forms, depending on which branch of the movement demanded the skill. The two main divisions of the women's movement are the reform or women's rights organizations (e.g., National Organization for Women, Women's Equity Action League) and the radical small groups, known as rap or consciousness-raising groups (Hole and Levine, 1971). The former branch works within the social structure for such changes as establishment of day care centers, repeal of abortion laws, legal suits against job discrimination and election of women to public office. The more radical segment works on a grass-roots level, hoping to change individual and cultural images, norms, attitudes and behaviors. The source of organizational training for the reform groups was largely established institutions such as government agencies, political parties and media and business. The members of the small groups preferred more anti-hierarchical, amorphous structures and came out of left-wing social political institutions (student groups, civil rights agencies, peace movement groups). There is much overlap and cooperation between these branches; N.O.W. may organize rap groups and the small group members may work on specific projects. Generally, the extent of radical or reformist activity and beliefs within the two branches is decided on the local level.

Observers in the social sciences have pondered why the women's movement emerged in the late 1960's (Ferriss, 1971). The theories of height-ened expectations followed by disappointment (Davies, 1969) and relative deprivation (Merton, 1957) give insights to this problem.

Many women participated in, or at least sympathized with, the civil rights movement, the peace movement, the student movement, and the Black Power movement. It was expected that the American ideals of equality, freedom and opportunity for all would finally be enlarged to include the underprivileged, including women. Also, in the 1960's, the counterculture or hippie movement emphasized respect for each person, regardless of status; dress modes became more androgynous and alternate living styles became popular (communes, group marriages).

If any general theme emerges from the 1960's, it is a desire for self-determination, an urge to re-establish personal control over a puzzling array of new, frequently changing social stimuli. A widespread feeling existed that urged people to work for self-actualization, to attain self pride and to expand the choice of legitimate beliefs and life styles. Mani-festations of this feeling were the push for Vietnamese self-determination, draft resistance, and the slogans, "We shall overcome," and "Black is beautiful."

Women's expectations were raised, but even within the social move-ments that called for radical change, women were delegated the un-prestigious positions and tasks the men did not want. Students for a Democratic Society (SDS) was as traditionally sexist as the Pentagon (Freeman, 1973, Piercy, 1970).

Economic indicators, such as wage differentials between males and females and the sex of people in powerful positions, had not significantly changed between 1950 and 1970 (Freeman, 1973). However, during these years, the cultural context had evolved from a Cold War quietism and conservatism to radical confrontation politics.

As social awareness of poverty, inequality and injustice grew, some women were sensitized to their own second-class citizenship. Using the dominant or powerful majority group (white males) as a yardstick, some women felt relatively deprived. Several other factors which contributed to a latent dissatisfaction with the female role were the near-perfection of birth control which freed women from unwanted pregnancy; changing social norms encouraging small families because of overpopulation; more women entering higher education in an affluent era; more women work-ing at underpaid jobs; and longevity, creating a need for enlarging the wife-mother role into an occupational role during the long, "empty nest" period of life.

This is a brief sketch of the socio-cultural context in which the women's movement emerged. For a more complete analysis, see Hole and Levine, 1971 and Freeman, 1973.

Consciousness-raising groups are structured to promote personal and cultural change. The small groups usually have from four to twelve members. The groups are established either through informal channels, such as word-of-mouth, or more formal channels, such as local women's centers or women's organizations. The members live close enough to each other to meet at least once a week. The meetings are usually held at members' homes; they may be at one specified place, such as an area women's center or university building, or may rotate from home to home. The length of time spent at each meeting varies, but is usually from two to five hours.

A "successful" group may meet from three months to as long as two years, or more. To stress the underlying unity of all women, some diversity of members is a goal of most groups. Age, race, class, education, work experience, marital and parental status, heterosexuality-homosexuality are criteria that can be varied for more or less heterogeneity. Some groups are established for predetermined reasons, such as to discuss the problems of divorced women with children, or problems facing women within a profession; others are set up for less well-defined purposes and evolve broader goals as the group continues. A general purpose is to expand one's awareness of what it means to be a woman in the current social and cultural context. Groups that begin through friendship channels tend to be more homogeneous; those arranged randomly through formalized intermediaries, such as N.O.W., tend to be more diverse in membership.

The ideology of the small groups in the women's movement demands that the groups be leaderless; lack of hierarchy and moving toward equality are strong values. Sometimes a woman who has experienced a previous rap group helps start the group. She gives ideas for discussion topics, facilitates the members in warming up and getting acquainted, and may help the group set some norms and standards. She generally attends only one to three meetings and then leaves the group to itself. After that, the group is leaderless and stresses that each member is equally responsible for achieving the group's purposes.

Political and social realizations arise in interaction with the telling of personal experiences and feelings. Each woman must view herself as an "authority" since she knows her own experience best; the ideology of the group is developed as an outcome of personal experience—thus, the popular slogan that "the personal is political." This process is akin to R. D. Laing's (1967) "politics of experience."

Some norms that commonly evolve in rap groups include allowing a member to speak without interruption and without criticism; not dwelling on personal problems without generalizing the source or manifestation of the problem to the rest of the group and other women; not dominating the discussion or competing for speaking time; feeling that the group is important enough to arrive on time and only miss meetings for valid reasons; being tolerant of other group members' feelings, different life-styles and backgrounds; being supportive of the other women and yet not offering specific advice.

The discussion topics are sometimes decided upon a week in advance, or they can appear spontaneously at a meeting if a woman presents an issue of personal importance that arose during the week. Some guidelines for rap groups that circulate in women's movement publications offer topic suggestions. Examples of discussion starters are the following: what do you like most and least about being a woman; do you interact differently with men than with women; do you compete with women; how did you learn about sex and what were your first sexual experiences; what would you like to be and what would you like to change about yourself; when did you first perceive discrimination and when do you experience it now; what is the division of labor in your family?

One method of examining the literature on consciousness-raising groups is to look first at group change, or the stages the group goes through, and then at individual change. These phenomena interact and are only analyzable in theory; in practice, they may not be readily discernible as separate entities. It is necessary for the group to evolve for individuals to change, and the changes the members experience motivate the group transformations.

The group development has been best described by Allen (1970). The four group processes that frequently appear as stages building upon previous development are what Allen calls opening up, sharing, analyzing, and abstracting. These stages may overlap somewhat; however, the knowledge and experiences gained in each stage are a basis for success in the subsequent processes.

Opening Up

The beginning of the group involves the opening up stage. Each member tells personal experiences and the group gets a feel for its diversity and similarity. Warmth and understanding are offered in exchange for personal confidences and deeply-felt emotions. Allen states: "In its early stages a group usually fosters a feeling of intimacy and trust which frees women to discuss their fears and problems. This is because most women have been isolated and alone and the group experience is the first time they have found others who like themselves are frustrated with their lot as women in this society" (p. 24). Closeness results from this stage. In the supportive atmosphere, all expressions of feelings are accepted. There is no competition or judgmental attitude toward experiences, emotions, beliefs or life-styles.

Sharing

The expression of inner feelings and needs expands, after a certain amount of time, to the teaching of group members by sharing commonalities. This expansion involves changing the focus of attention of each discussion from individuals to the group as a whole. The subtle and overt prejudice and discrimination that group members have experienced are discussed first as individual feelings and perceptions, then as the introduction to social and political phenomena affecting all women. According to Allen, "Through experiencing the common discussion comes the understanding that many of the situations described are not personal at all, and are not based on individual inadequacies, but rather have a root in the social order. What we have found is that painful 'personal' problems can be common to many of the women present. Thus attention can turn to finding the real causes of these problems rather than merely emphasizing one's own inadequacies" (p. 26).

An important function of this stage is overcoming the negative stereotype that women cannot band together for instrumental purposes and that women do not like each other. Deep friendships result; warmth and a general excitement in anticipation of the group meeting prevail. The women in the group feel reinforced by the hopeful mood and a tendency develops that encourages cooperation with other women to solve status and role problems. A final function of this stage is to overcome frustration and self-doubt and to channel energy into personal and social change.

Analyzing

The third stage is that of analyzing; the group reaches beyond personal or group-wide experiences and looks into the position of women in society. Questions are asked regarding why women are a devalued group, how this is maintained and how to change this status. One problem encountered in this phase is combining subjective thinking and feeling with objective analysis. This process of synthesis continues, as new feelings and experiences lead to new theories, and those theories bring to light past feelings and experiences. The ideology grows with personal exploration.

Abstracting

Abstracting is the fourth process and it is a continuation of analyzing. Allen calls this building "a vision of our human potential" (p. 29). In this process, the group examines institutions to determine how they "fulfill or prevent the fulfillment of human needs, how they work together and how they must be changed" (p. 30). The group itself is examined as to its role in forming ideology and serving as an impetus for social change outside itself. Its usefulness as a unit initiating a sense of emotional warmth and support, personal change, or serving as an educating agency or task-oriented group is appraised.

In her summary of the group process, Allen cautions that the four analytically-distinct stages are not discrete time periods. In practice, they mesh together after the preliminary opening up. She states that "one does not graduate through the various processes until one is only abstracting to the exclusion of all else. Analyzing and abstracting are only valid processes if they continue to be rooted in the present feelings and experiences of participants. The order may be fixed but the processes themselves are ongoing" (p. 30).

The structure and ideology of the rap groups combine to facilitate change in those aspects of the feminine role that the group members desire to re-evaluate. The role characteristics associated with minority group status particularly come under scrutiny. A successful group stimulates a member's awareness of herself as a woman and of society's perceptions of her. Changes in sex role characteristics occur chiefly under the two headings of feelings about self, and feelings about other people and society.

A number of studies have been done on personal change in women's consciousness-raising groups. They are all recent; some have not yet been published. The methods that have been used to collect data are intensive interviews, participant observation and questionnaires. It is generally remarked by the authors that feminists refuse to be studied by either men or women who are unsympathetic to their beliefs. Thus, the usual social scientific study, in which there is a clear-cut separation between the subjects and the investigator, examiner neutrality, and concealment of the true purpose of the project from the subjects stands no chance of recruiting feminist groups as subjects. All the studies reported herein have what some may term "bias" in that the authors enlisted the support of the subjects and had to prove the sincerity of their social-political views before any exploration could begin. Either by the selection process by which investigators were interested in feminists, or by the power of personal influence in converting neutral social scientists, all the authors were feminists by the time their project terminated.

The change that is found in attitudes toward the self, in the course of the consciousness-raising group, relates to the fact that "women, like some other low status categories in society, have a tendency to turn aggression or blame inwards, on both the individual and the group level" (Holter, 1970, p. 40)." A central purpose of the group is to make the members aware of the extent to which they were influenced by sex-stereotyped socialization, and the pervasive cultural reinforcements that perpetuate minority group behavior. Many of the perceived inadequacies are the result of being taught not to adopt healthy adult behavior traits, but instead to exhibit so-called feminine characteristics. The tendency to be submissive, dependent and overly-nurturant leaves an individual with low aspirations, a fragile sense of self and a need for approval from others. Problems tend to be attributed to inferiority and personal incompetence. The group helps to focus the causes of these feelings; members recount early experiences illustrating how they were taught to display concern for others, but to stifle achievement-oriented activity. Political, economic and social causes of these feelings are analyzed during the group; the individuals turn the society and culture into the units of analysis and find motivation to work to change both self and environment.

By means of unstructured, nondirective interviews, Cherniss (1972) compared women currently in rap groups with matched controls who did not consider themselves feminists. Cherniss states: "There was considerable variability, but in virtually every case, involvement in the movement was for these women an experience of personal change. After only a few months of participation, the women seemed to undergo a number of profound changes in style and outlook. They began to see themselves and the world around them in a very different light, and this change in attitude and perception seemed to be accompanied by significant changes in behavior" (p. 122).

Cherniss found participation in the women's movement small groups to take the appearance of a "program of development" (p. 119). The women involved attempted to understand their past in terms of cultural norms and expectations for their sex, they tried to redefine themselves in terms of inner sources of identity (rather than as daughter, wife, mother, or girlfriend), and to decide upon future goals and modes of behavior that involved the "real" self rather than the merely "feminine" roles of self. Cherniss found that a basic issue dividing the feminist subjects from the other women was the centrality of the mother-wife role among the control subjects. The feminist women had other or additional roles and interests to augment their identities.

Cherniss noted that the feminist respondents were moving in a direction of independence, autonomy, activity, mobility, self-esteem and self-acceptance as the characterizing styles of relating to the world and themselves.

Another "therapeutic" gain from the group was a redefinition of the mother, which resulted in more sympathetic understanding of the mother's social constraints, and decreased guilt, anger and depression in the mother-daughter relationship. The strengths of the mother were recognized and appreciated, while weaknesses were accepted in line with the pressures, frustration and penalties of the role. The mother was accepted as part of the "sisterhood" of women.

Cherniss remarked upon the sense of trust and intimacy that developed among the women in the group. They established a sense of community with their common cause. As noted widely in the rap group literature, a strong feeling of support seems to unite the groups and helps each member make the desired changes in self and life situation. Frequently, the group is the first situation in which the women work closely with other women in an intimate atmosphere without competition or labels imposed by male-dominated culture (e.g., sexy, pretty, ugly, blonde, dumpy).

Part of the process of the rap group involves what Cherniss calls "finding one's anger" (p. 120). As the women become sensitized to sex prejudice and discrimination, anger at the various manifestations of this attitude and behavior appear more and more frequently. Sensitivity sharpens to situations at work, to division of labor in the home, to lewd remarks in the street, to movie portrayals of women, male-biased language, the exclusion of women from history books, and multitudes of other examples. The anger usually reaches a catharsis, after which strength and determination to change self and society, hopefully, result.

In Micossi's (1970) article on consciousness-raising groups in the women's movement, she discusses an "increase in self awareness" (p. 85). The group, as a conversion mechanism to feminism, provides a new perspective and awareness of oneself as an individual and as a woman. Micossi states: "Once a woman becomes aware of the nature of the traditional role, she cannot act as before. And this is a painful jolt for the converted woman. The extent to which our lives are played out through sex roles is considerable. And when suddenly a woman invalidates these roles for herself she becomes disoriented, and normal interaction is disrupted. Her identity must be reconstituted, new forms of action constructed and people and objects in her environment reassessed" (p. 87).

Micossi mentions a "rise in self-esteem" that occurs in a woman after the self awareness; the "self hatred that comes with failure and disappointment is hurled outward in a liberating catharsis" (p. 87). Personal problems are seen in a cultural context and the individual burden is relinquished. The newly found self takes responsibility for acting upon life situations to establish positive changes.

In a study by Acker and Howard (1972), interviews with feminists revealed striking background similarities. For example, many of the women had close childhood relationships with their fathers which fostered high self-esteem and high expectations; some of the women had been independent early in life and had learned to be responsible for themselves. Acker and Howard say that though "the women in our samples seem to have emerged or grown into feminism . . . participation in consciousness-raising groups contributed importantly to the development of a feminist identity and world-view for many of our respondents" (p. 21). The groups functioned to define each member as more competent; women interacting without reference to male-defined statuses helped establish new self images and identities and to renovate role patterns.

Acker and Howard note that for women who were isolated, especially, the "group discussions were probably more analogous to therapy groups in which individuals can ventilate anger, frustration and fear, safely removed from the situation and relationships which generate these feelings" (p. 23).

Newton and Walton (1971) conducted intensive interviews with women in rap groups. They report five major changes in the individuals involved. First, the women experienced an altered world view in which they perceived "women as a group with definitive characteristics" (p. 33), and society as divided into two major groups, males and females. Identity changes occurred, including different feelings about body image. For example, there were changes in clothing and cosmetics; more significantly, the women felt comfortable and accepting of their bodies, more physically and sexually competent. There were changes in reference groups and interpersonal relationships: feminist women became the primary reference group and relationships with men turned more egalitarian. There were changes in job-career orientation; many women felt ambivalence toward professionalism and male-dominated institutions, and made efforts to work for movement-oriented activities. Finally, the group members felt "an enhanced sense of self-acceptance and worth, and a lessening of guilt and self-doubt (p. 38).

A participant observation and interview study of consciousness-raising groups in Montreal, by Krug (1972) found two main problems that were worked upon: relationships among women, including competition, need for honesty, and explorations of prejudice; and the differences that occur in behavior when women interact with men as compared with behavior among women. These specific groups Krug studied moved from concentration on personal concerns to political activity. Generalizing about the group members, Krug stated: ". . . these women are generally people of heightened personal and social awareness who are strongly concerned with effecting improved relationships with themselves and with others, male and female alike" (p. 7).

White (1971) interviewed feminists after consciousness-raising group membership, and found improved self image. The women reported more self respect, higher ambitions, more independence and more confidence. There was also decreased prejudice toward other women. Relationships with men became more equal, involved less stereotyped "feminine" role-playing, and tended to be more platonic than romantic. Among the reasons the women posited as leading to their feminism were "wanting to become a full person and needing to be free" (p. 33).

A participant observation study by Whiteley (1973) includes statements by the group members that seem to express the profound personal changes that the women perceived in themselves. The most significant changes relate to feelings about self, and feelings about other women.

> I used to think that if I wanted to have a really good discussion with someone about ideas, I had to go to a man. And I now realize I turned that belief back on myself unconsciously and felt insecure about myself intellectually. In the process of coming to respect other women's minds, I came to have more respect for my own.

Before this, I usually avoided doing things with groups of women—I guess I really bought the notion that things done with "just women" were somehow less worthwhile, less important and enjoyable

In the group I learned greater acceptance of myself and trust in my own reactions and wants, whether or not they fit stereotyped feminine behavior. When I learned that many of my feelings were not a "sickness" but shared by other women, I felt stronger and less disappointed in myself.

A common complaint about women's groups is that they make women angry. My own experience is that the group didn't "make" me angry. It just helped me discover that I was. I had told myself I felt depressed. Now I have some sense of being angry and can begin to ask myself what I'm angry about and work on the problems.

CONCLUSION

Clearly, there are conflicts inherent in women's roles and status at the present time. This paper examined role conflicts in terms of cultural prejudice against women, structural discrimination against women, and sex role socialization that attempts to teach personality characteristics which will channel the sexes into their "proper" roles and statuses. The detrimental effects of these practices were also discussed.

Social-historical factors created latent role dissatisfaction in women, and a woman's movement was mobilized when contact occurred among women who perceived this dissatisfaction, and an ideology and organizational skill developed in the population experiencing sex role conflict.

Consciousness-raising groups arose as resocialization agencies and alternative structures to psychotherapy for resolving role conflict. These groups are effective in developing an awareness in women of the culturally accepted feminine role and behaviors. The rap groups encourage a critical evaluation of sex roles and of the attitudes and behaviors that perpetuate stereotyped roles. The groups offer alternative behaviors, attitudes and world view in a supportive atmosphere conducive to change. The conversion process motivates activity to change self, culture and social structure; some rap groups themselves enter into direct action after the initial period of raising the members' consciousness.

It has been proposed by some observers that traditional psychotherapy serves more as a mechanism for social control than for innovative resocialization for women, implying that the childhood socialization process taught the "proper" roles, but failed in individual cases. Charges have been made that traditional psychotherapy attempts to instill the same basic values and behaviors that socialization agencies (parents, schools, media) and indeed, mainstream male-dominated culture, failed to instill.

In contrast, women's movement consciousness-raising groups aspire to round out sex roles to encompass positive human traits. These traits should ideally be acceptable in men and women in a more humanitarian, androgynous society.

Although consciousness-raising groups and psychotherapy are posed as alternatives in this paper, and their major differences are stressed rather than similarities, in reality they often serve as problem-solving mechanisms for the same people, sometimes simultaneously. And therapies differ, of course, in their specific practices and amount of attention given to social and cultural influences; assertive training and behavioral techniques are quite different from Freudian and other medical-model therapies. As any other group of people, therapists differ in their amount of social sensitivity and prejudice. This realization may account for the wide demand for feminist therapists at the present time.

Certainly, some women have problems that are not directly derived from role conflict or low status; however, therapists and clients should be aware of cultural roles and stereotypes that function to bind the feet, or at least the mind, of men and women who might work to renovate outdated, dysfunctional attitudes and behavior.

Women's roles have been posited as important stress-producing elements in women's lives. As a culturally-defined minority group, women are delegated unprestigious roles and are taught devalued personality traits. There is nothing innately inferior with the wife-mother role complex or with such "feminine" traits as dependence, emotionality, nurturance and passivity; rather, the problem is that such roles and traits are constricting when assigned to a group on the basis of ascription when the other half of society is freer to decide its roles on the basis of achievement. It will be a better, happier, more fully-functioning society and culture that guarantee freedom for both men and women, of all races and ethnic groups, to have feelings and exhibit behaviors designated as positive human qualities, not merely positive "feminine" or "masculine" qualities. The structural power would no longer be dominated by one group and cultural attitudes of prejudice toward the less-powerful group would disappear.

Such a society would not expend energy to adjust its members to outdated, rigidified roles, but would encourage all people to develop their own unique abilities. Thus, feminist theory is not merely pushing women into what is currently defined as socially desirable (i.e., masculine) in terms of succeeding in the existing society; instead, feminists of both sexes suggest that the existing culture and social structure be extensively changed to more fully actualize and accommodate everyone.

REFERENCES

ACKER, J. & HOWARD, M. On becoming a feminist. Paper presented at American Sociological Association, New Orleans, 1972.

ALLEN, P. *Free Space: A Perspective on the Small Group in Women's Liberation.* Washington, New Jersey: Times Change Press, 1970.

ALLPORT, G. W. *The Nature of Prejudice.* Cambridge, Mass.: Addison-Wesley, 1954.

AMUNDSEN, K. *The Silenced Majority: Women and American Democracy.* New York: Prentice-Hall, 1971.

ANGRIST, S. S. The study of sex roles. *Journal of Social Issues,* 25, 215-232, 1969.

BANTON, M. P. *Roles: An Introduction to the Study of Social Relations.* New York: Basic Books, 1965.

BART, P. B. Depression in middle-aged women. In V. Gornick and B. K. Moran (Eds.), *Woman in Sexist Society.* New York: Basic Books, 1971, pp. 163-186.

BECKER, H. S. Personal change in adult life. *Sociometry,* 27, 40-53, 1964.

BLOCK, J., VON DER LIPPE, A., & BLOCK, J. H. Sex-role and socialization patterns: Some personality concomitants and environmental antecedents. *Journal of Consulting and Clinical Psychology,* 41, 321-341, 1973.

BOGART, K. & MUHR, M. Sex, self-perception and the perception of others. Paper presented to the Eastern Psychological Association, Boston, 1972.

BRIM, O. G. Socialization through the life cycle. In O. G. Brim and S. Wheeler (Eds.), *Socialization after Childhood: Two Essays.* New York: Wiley, 1966.

BROVERMAN, I. K., BROVERMAN, D. M., CLARKSON, F. E., ROSENKRANTZ, P., & VOGEL, S. R. Sex role stereotypes and clinical judgments of mental health. *Journal of Consulting and Clinical Psychology,* 34, 1-7, 1970.

BROVERMAN, I. K., VOGEL, S. R., BROVERMAN, D. M., CLARKSON, F. E., & ROSENKRANTZ, P. S. Sex-role stereotypes: A current appraisal. *Journal of Social Issues,* 28, 59-78, 1972.

BROWN, J. Editorial. In J. Agel (Ed.), *The Radical Therapist.* New York: Ballantine, 1971.

CHERNISS, C. Personality and ideology: A personological study of women's liberation. *Psychiatry,* 35, 109-125, 1972.

CHESLER, P. Patient and patriarch: Women in the psychotherapeutic relationship. In V. Gornick and B. K. Moran (Eds.), *Woman in Sexist Society.* New York: Basic Books, 1971.

COTTRELL, L. S. Interpersonal interaction and the development of the self. In D. A. Goslin (Ed.), *Handbook of Socialization Theory and Research.* Chicago: Rand McNally, 1969.

DAVIES, J. C. Toward a theory of revolution. In B. McLaughlin (Ed.), *Studies in Social Movements: A Social-Psychological Approach.* New York: Free Press, 1969.

DE BEAUVOIR, S. *The Second Sex.* New York: Bantam Books, 1970.

EMMERICH, W. Socialization and sex-role development. In P. B. Baltes, and K. W. Schaie (Eds.), *Life-Span Developmental Psychology: Personality and Socialization.* New York: Academic Press, 1973.

FERRISS, A. L. *Indicators of Trends in the Status of American Women.* New York: Russell Sage Foundation, 1971.

FRANK, J. The bewildering world of psychotherapy. *Journal of Social Issues,* 28, 27-44, 1972.

FREEMAN, J. The origins of the women's liberation movement. *American Journal of Sociology,* 78, 792-811, 1973.

FREEMAN, J. The building of the gilded cage. In A. Koedt and S. Firestone (Eds.), *Notes from the Third Year.* New York: Notes from the Second Year, 1971.

FRIEDAN, B. *The Feminine Mystique.* New York: Norton, 1963.

GERTH, H. & MILLS, C. W. *Character and Social Structure.* New York: Harcourt, Brace and World, 1953.

GOLDBERG, P. Are women prejudiced against women? In C. Safilios-Rothschild (Ed.), *Toward a Sociology of Women.* Lexington, Mass.: Xerox, 1972.

GOLDBERG, S. & LEWIS, M. Play behavior in the year-old infant: Early sex differences. *Child Development,* 40, 21-31, 1969.

GOODE, W. Norm commitment and conformity to role status obligations. *American Journal of Sociology,* 66, 246-258, 1960.

GOVE, W. R. & TUDOR, J. F. Adult sex roles and mental illness. *American Journal of Sociology,* 78, 812-835, 1973.

GUMP, J. P. Sex-role attitudes and psychological well-being. *Journal of Social Issues,* 28, 79-92. 1972.

HACKER, H. M. Women as a minority group. *Social Forces,* 30, 60-69, 1951.

HANISCH, C. The personal is political. In J. Agel (Ed.), *The Radical Therapist.* New York: Ballantine, 1971.

HOFFMAN, L. W. Early childhood experiences and women's achievement motives. *Journal of Social Issues,* 28, 129-156, 1972.

HOLE, J. & LEVINE, E. *Rebirth of Feminism.* New York: Quadrangle Books, 1971.

HOLTER, H. *Sex Roles and Social Structure.* Oslo, Norway: Universitets-forlaget, 1970.

HORNER, M. S. Sex differences in achievement motivation and performance in competitive and non-competitive situations. Unpublished doctoral dissertation, University of Michigan, 1968.

HURVITZ, N. Psychotherapy as a means of social control. *Journal of Consulting and Clinical Psychology,* 40, 232-239, 1973.

INKELES, A. Social structure and socialization. In D. A. Goslin (Ed.), *Handbook of Socialization Theory and Research.* Chicago: Rand McNally, 1969.

JOFFE, C. Sex role socialization and the nursery school: As the twig is bent. *Journal of Marriage and the Family,* 33, 467-475, 1971.

KILLIAN, L. Social movements. In R. E. Faris (Ed.), *Handbook of Modern Sociology.* Chicago: Rand McNally, 1964.

KING, C. W. *Social Movements in the United States.* New York: Random House, 1956.

KOMAROVSKY, M. Cultural contradictions and sex roles. *American Journal of Sociology.* 52, 184-189, 1946.

KRUG, T. Women's lib: Consciousness-raising in Montreal. On file at the Montreal Ethnographic Data Bank, Sir George Williams University, Montreal, Canada, 1972.

LAING, R. D. *The Politics of Experience.* New York: Ballantine, 1967.

LYNN, D. B. A note on sex differences in the development of masculine and feminine identification. *Psychological Review,* 66, 126-135, 1959.

McKEE, J. P. & SHERRIFFS, A. C. The differential evaluation of males and females. *Journal of Personality,* 25, 356-371, 1957.

MERTON, R. K. *Social Theory and Social Structure.* Glencoe, Ill.: Free Press, 1957.

MICOSSI, A. L. Conversion to women's lib. *Trans-Action,* 8, 82-90, 1970.

MISCHEL, W. Sex typing and socialization. In P. H. Mussen (Ed.), *Carmichael's Manual of Child Development.* New York: Wiley, 1970.

MORGAN, R. *Sisterhood Is Powerful.* New York: Random House, 1970.

MYRDAL, G. *An American Dilemma.* New York: Harper, 1944.

NEUGARTEN, B. L. Adult personality: Toward a psychology of the life cycle. In B. L. Neugarten (Ed.), *Middle Age and Aging.* Chicago: Univ. of Chicago Press, 1968.

NEUGARTEN, B. L. Education and the life-cycle. *School Review*, 80, 209-216, 1972.

NEWTON, E. & WALTON, S. The personal is political: Consciousness-raising and personal change in the women's liberation movement. In B. G. Schoepf, (Chw.), Anthropologists Look at the Study of Women. Symposium presented at the American Anthropological Association, 1971.

PARSONS, T. Age and sex in the social structure of the United States. *American Sociological Review*, 7, 604-616, 1942.

PIERCY, M. The grand coolie damn. In R. Morgan (Ed.), *Sisterhood Is Powerful*. New York: Random House, 1970.

POLK, B. B. & STEIN, R. B. Is the grass greener on the other side? In C. Safilios-Rothschild (Ed.), *Toward a Sociology of Women*. Lexington, Mass.: Xerox, 1972.

ROSENKRANTZ, P., VOGEL, S., BEE, H., BROVERMAN, I., & BROVERMAN, D. M. Sex-role stereotypes and self-concepts in college students. *Journal of Consulting and Clinical Psychology*, 3, 287-295, 1968.

SEARS, R. R., MACCOBY, E. E., & LEVIN, H. *Patterns of Childbearing*. Evanston, Ill.: Row, Peterson, 1957.

STEINMANN, A. & FOX, D. Male-female perceptions of the female role in the United States. *Journal of Psychology*, 64, 265-279, 1966.

SZASZ, T. S. *Ideology and Insanity*. New York: Doubleday, 1970.

TOCH, H. *The Social Psychology of Social Movements*. New York: Bobbs-Merrill, 1965.

WATTS, A. W. *Psychotherapy East and West*. New York: Ballantine, 1961.

WEITZMAN, L. J. Sex-role socialization in picture books for preschool children. *American Journal of Sociology*, 77, 1125-1150, 1972.

WHITE, H. R. Becoming a feminist. Unpublished honors paper, Douglass College, 1971.

WIRTH, L. The problem of minority groups. In R. Linton (Ed.), *The Science of Man in the World Crisis*. New York: Columbia University Press, 1945.

WHITELEY, R. M. Women in groups. *The Counseling Psychologist*, 4, 27-43, 1973.

Women's Bureau. *Underutilization of Women Workers*. Washington, D. C.: U.S. Department of Labor, 1971.

ZWEIG, M. Is women's liberation a therapy group? In J. Agel (Ed.), *The Radical Therapist*. New York: Ballantine, 1971.

Part V

THERAPY AND AGENCIES

16

WOMEN IN INSTITUTIONS: TREATMENT IN PRISONS AND MENTAL HOSPITALS

EPHRAIM M. HOWARD and JOYCE L. HOWARD

"Them as got, gits. Them as ain't, gets took."

INTRODUCTION

Few of us recognize this bit of folk wisdom as an up-dated version of the Gospel of Matthew, 13:12, in which it is more eloquently expressed as, "Unto them that have shall be given. And from them that have not, shall be taken away even that which they have not." As we examined the dehumanizing and depersonalizing effects of institutionalization, we were continually reminded of this passage from the gospels. The undesirable aspects of institutions and their equally negative effects on *all* inmates have been well reported by Goffman (1961) and others; here the focus is on female inmates.

Our concern is whether women and men in the United States are treated differently in prisons and mental hospitals, and to what degree this differential treatment may be affected by race or ethnic origin. Furthermore, we questioned whether attitudes in American society at large, where women are the majority but have traditionally been treated as a semi-oppressed minority, would be carried over into our institutions of residential treatment. Our survey also encompasses the manner in which women and men are committed to institutions and the various ways in which they are released. We will consider separately the intake, residential

The authors express their appreciation to Shirley Willner of the Biometry Branch of NIMH for her cooperation in providing information and mental health data, to Amber Jones and Barbara Rabe for their generous assistance in obtaining information, and to Leslie Ota of the Rutgers University Library in New Brunswick, who always knew where to find the needed information.

357

and discharge phases for the existence of differential treatment. Similarities and differences between the two types of institutional processes will be discussed in a summary section. Interestingly enough, some of the differences noted with respect to treatment were not in the directions indicated by other writers. Where our findings differ from those of other investigators we will try to show how our conclusions were reached.

Our general conclusions may be summarized as follows:

1. Correctional institutions and mental hospitals rarely achieve their limited stated goals, let alone the idealized ones usually verbalized in our society.
2. The differential treatment afforded women and men in institutions generally reflects the differential treatment accorded to the different sexes and races in our society; however, the differences in treatment noted are not always in accord with preconceived or popular notions.

BACKGROUND

Treatment is defined here as the entire process by which people enter the institution, all aspects of their lives within the institution and the procedures by which they leave it. Under the category of correctional institutions or prisons we have included federal, state, city and county institutions. Separate data were obtained from the relevant agencies in the states of California, New Jersey and New York as well as from the Bureau of the Census, the National Institutes of Health and other governmental bureaus.

Confidential interviews were conducted with 53 offenders, ex-offenders, patients and ex-patients of mental hospitals, volunteers who have worked with both groups in pre-release planning and post-release adjustment and the staffs of mental hospitals and the prison and post-prison system. These interviews provided information not available from other sources.

Past and current data were reviewed to determine trends.* Inasmuch

---

* The compilation of statistical information is difficult. Terms utilized, as well as their definitions, change with time and, in several instances, specific crimes (in the case of correctional institutions) and diagnoses (in the case of mental institutions) no longer have the same names or meanings that they once had. Also, different states or other reporting agencies choose different definitions, even for reports made at the same time. In addition, there is often little uniformity or consistency in the use of definitions. Furthermore, many states and other agencies collect and report only those statistics which they require for obtaining funds or record keeping. Such data may not be particularly helpful for evaluative or other informational purposes.

Many statistics on mental illness which were carefully kept in the 50's were dropped as our focus is on women, we have evaluated the data according to the total number per 100,000 of the *same sex* in the reporting population rather than the usual term of per 100,000 (with no consideration as to sex distribution). In addition, we reversed the usual procedure by listing women per 100* men rather than the traditional format of men per 100 women.

WOMEN IN PRISONS

Although female criminality has been discussed in varying degrees throughout history and many theories proposed, virtually all the early material on penology relates to men. Some of the first discussions of women's reformatories were contained in reports to the International Prison Congress of 1910, but they did not give very complete descriptions of existing facilities (Lekkerkerker, 1931). It was not until 1926 that a separate chapter on women's reformatories appeared in a general work on penology, and Lekkerkerker's (1931) was perhaps the first comprehensive study in this area. Other studies published as recently as 1971 support Lekkerkerker's assertion that institutions for women should be separate from those for men, and should preferably be headed by women (Eymon, 1971, Monahan, 1941). Yet, in 1964 there were only 29 separate institutions for women, including one in Puerto Rico, one in Washington, D. C. and one federal institution (Eymon, 1971). The most recent Directory of Correctional Institutions and Agencies available to us (1972), listed a total of only 37 such institutions and, of these, 31 were headed by women and 6 by men.

Typical of this lack of attention paid to the problems of female offenders, the first mention before a national forum occurred in 1970 at

---

by the 70's. Interestingly, prison data are becoming increasingly available and the kinds of information published are expanding in such states as California.

Penology, it will be recalled, is that branch of criminology which deals with prison management and the reformatory treatment of criminals; *criminality* relates to the quality of being criminal.

Since our focus is on differential treatment, we made no special examination of data relating to either prostitutes or female drug addicts. Prostitution, the traditional "woman's crime," has been discussed at length elsewhere: some say it was the major way women exhibited their criminality (e.g., Lombroso and Ferrero, 1958; Hollander, 1922).

* The statistic "women per 100 men" was obtained from the raw numbers and is only indirectly related to the rates per 100,000 of same sex in the population. This statistic does *not* indicate the proportion of women in the overall population who are involved in a particular category (the latter comes from the rate per 100,000 of same sex in the population). However, it *does* show the relative proportions of women and men involved in that category.

the One Hundredth Annual Congress of Corrections. Even there, only two papers on this subject were presented (Proceedings, 1971).

At this point it is important to consider certain key issues raised by Pollak (1950). In his summary of many studies of female criminality, Pollak posed the following questions: " (1) Are crimes in which women participate exclusively or to a considerable extent offenses which are known to be greatly under-reported? (2) Are women offenders generally less often detected than are men offenders? (3) Do women if apprehended meet with more leniency than do men? It seems that each of these questions will have to be answered in the affirmative and that the long discussion which has centered around the apparent sex differential in crime may have been based on a statistical deception."

Although ". . . criminal statistics are probably the least reliable of all statistics because they undertake to measure something which is designed to escape measurement" (Pollak, 1950), they provide the only data we have on entry into the system.

Far more crimes are committed than are reported, and only a small fraction of those reported are cleared by arrests and the report does not always include the sex of the offender. Of those arrested, only a fraction are charged and a still smaller number tried and found guilty. For example, using reported crimes as the basis, in 1970 only 19.8% were cleared by arrests; 16.7% of all reported crimes resulted in persons being charged; and 5.6% of crimes reported resulted in the person being found guilty (*Crime in the U.S.*, 1971). Accordingly, there is no way of determining whether differential treatment existed because we have no knowledge of how many women were involved in these reported crimes.

Pollak (1950) claims that specially lenient attitudes prevail in all levels and that "Men hate to accuse women and thus indirectly send them to their punishment, police officers dislike to arrest them, judges and juries to find them guilty, and so on." Our current information, 20 years later, may disagree with the degrees of implied chivalry of that statement, but there continues to be differential treatment from the very beginning of the process, with women appearing to be treated preferentially. For example, some interviewees reported: "Women say they're needed by their children and lots of people buy it. Some who never even see their kids can pull that and get away with it. Just let a man try it—no dice."

The percentage of crimes committed by women has been increasing and, accordingly, the arrest rate of women has risen. Perhaps this increase in crime rate for women reflects the effects of ongoing societal changes or crises on social behavior in general and that of women in particular

Table 1

Total Arrest Rates in the U.S.A. for 1952 and 1970

Year	Raw Number		Number per 100,000 of same sex in the reporting population*		Percent arrested	
	Women	Men	Women	Men	Women	Men
1952	120,005	990,670	1022	8549	11.0%	89.0%
1970	946,897	5,623,576	1217	7622	14.4%	85.6%

* Use of "number per 100,000 of same sex in the reporting population" permits valid comparisons to be made over the 18-year gap even though there are differences in the size of reporting populations and in proportion of women in the general population of the U.S.

(Einsele, 1971). This change may also result from the changes in sex differentiated roles in our society. As women are less closely supervised we can expect a decrease in sex differences in crime (Sutherland and Cressey, 1970).

We encountered many such statements in the literature as "When serious crimes are considered as a group, arrests in males in 1960-1970 were up 73 per cent and female arrests increased 202 per cent (*Crime in the U.S.*, 1971)." Also "Long-term arrest trends, 1960-1970, revealed that arrests for young females under 18 years of age increased 204 per cent, while arrests for young males under 18 rose 98 per cent" (*Crime in the U.S.*, 1971). These statistics notwithstanding, the reluctance to arrest women apparently persists.

By using the arrest rate per 100,000 (Table 1) and the total population in 100,000's, we can obtain a rough measure of the actual numbers of women involved. When the approximately 19% increase in the rate of women arrested per 100,000 in the population is considered together with the increase in number of women in the U.S.A., from 1952 to 1970, the number of women arrested rose from 804,000 in 1952 to over 1,269,000 in 1970, an increase of over 50%. It is this increase in arrests to which much publicity has been given.

The arrest rates for some of the crimes for which women are beginning to be arrested in ever increasing numbers are shown in Table 2. This breakdown shows how the distribution of arrests has changed. While women, the majority in the population, represent a disproportionately small number of those arrested, there is a slight trend toward equality of proportional representation. It is not clear whether these data reflect a trend toward equalizing the social treatment afforded the two sexes, or whether women are assimilating the societal norms of the dominant male group.

TABLE 2

Arrest Rates in the U.S.A. for Some Crimes, by Sex,
for 1952 and 1970

Crime and Year	Number per 100,000 of same sex in the reporting population*		Arrests for this offense as a percent of total arrested		Percent of those arrested for this offense who are	
	Women	Men	Women	Men	Women	Men
Total						
1952	1022	8549	100%	100%	11%	89%
1970	1217	7622	100%	100%	14%	86%
Murder						
1952	2.07	9.02	.20%	.11%	19%	81%
1970	2.54	14.71	.21%	.19%	15%	85%
Aggravated Assault						
1952	17.47	84.82	1.71%	.99%	17%	83%
1970	20.45	149.16	1.68%	1.95%	13%	87%
Larceny-theft						
1952	47.17	296.26	4.62%	3.46%	14%	86%
1970	221.27	601.62	18.18%	7.89%	28%	72%
Drunkenness						
1952	322.73	4039.80	31.60%	47.30%	7%	93%
1970	137.53	1905.02	11.31%	24.90%	7%	93%
Narcotic drug laws						
1952	3.96	22.77	.40%	.27%	15%	85%
1970	69.58	396.11	5.72%	5.19%	16%	84%
Stolen Property; buying, receiving, possessing						
1952	1.26	13.97	.12%	.16%	8%	92%
1970	7.38	75.58	.60%	.99%	9%	91%

* Reporting population: 1952—23,334,035; 1970—151,604,000.

Drunkenness is the only category for which there has been a decrease in the rates of women and men arrested. The rates for all of the other crimes considered rose, ranging from an increase of .47 per 100,000 for women arrested for murder to an increase of 174.1 for women arrested for larceny-theft. Extending these rates to the entire population resulted in an increase of 1019 in the nationwide arrests of women for murder between 1952 and 1970, and an increase of 193,649 in the arrests for larceny-theft over the same period. Larceny-theft was the only category in which the per cent of women arrested changed greatly over the 18 year period, doubling from 14% in 1952 to 28% in 1970.

It is clear that the increased number of people arrested necessitates a change in treatment procedures. Otherwise we are in danger of being

TABLE 3

Persons in Correctional Institutions in the U.S.A., by Sex,
for 1950 and 1970*

Year	Number**		Number per 100,000 of same sex in the population of the U.S.		Percent of those in prison who are	
	Women	Men	Women	Men	Women	Men
1950	12,995	251,562	17.13	336.09	4.9%	95.1%
1970	19,052	293,620	18.27	322.92	6.1%	93.9%

* Excludes Alaska and Hawaii. Data for 1950 are presented rather than for 1952 as in Tables 1 and 2 since available prison data for 1952 did not include the city and county institution information. Data presented include these institutions for 1950 and 1970 and hence may be compared to overall arrest rates which include persons who might be sentenced to all institutions.
** Excludes 20,252 persons in institutions in 1970 where no breakdown by sex was reported.

swamped by numbers and cost. Accepted attitudes toward those considered as needing institutionalization must be changed and new techniques developed for dealing with the problems of those who violate social norms. With limited exception, notably in California, our society has not been willing to make the necessary socio-cultural adjustment to the increase in numbers. California's approaches, although not approved by some professionals in correction, have resulted in lowered costs, reduced recidivism and crime rates no worse than elsewhere (Ryan, Beer and Bales, 1970). The need for such changes is particularly important in the case of women whose treatment has been patterned on that of men rather than meeting female needs.

Our interviews showed that women are often propositioned during the arresting process, the implication sometimes explicitly stated, being that the arrest will not occur if the woman is "cooperative." However, the arrest process is usually completed regardless of the degree of "cooperation" displayed and the woman feels, and is, doubly betrayed. While women are less likely to be sexually molested by fellow prisoners than are men, the dangers of such molestation by institutional staff remain (Davis, 1968). In addition, our interviews showed that either male physicians or female personnel made the body searches of women and that men were searched by male physicians or male personnel.

Differential treatment is equally apparent at the next stage of the criminal justice system, incarceration. Women were only 4.9% of the resident population in correctional institutions in 1950 and 6.1% in 1970, although they constituted 11% of the arrests in 1952 and 14% in 1970.

The percentage of those in state and federal institutions who were women dropped from 3.5% in 1950 to 2.9% in 1970. Inasmuch as these state and federal institutions generally receive offenders with more serious offenses, it might be said that the proportion of severe crimes committed by women has decreased slightly over the 20-year period 1950-1970. This evaluation, however, is in contradiction with popular beliefs which reflect the absolute numerical increase rather than the change in proportion.

Due to the limited availability of data from states, the only direct comparisons we can make with the 1970 overall data are for California and New York. In 1970, the percentage of women in the institutions of the New York State Department of Correctional Services was 2.9% and the corresponding figure for California was 3.0%, both figures being in close agreement with the national averages. Also, 4.8% of those in all correctional institutions in New York State in 1970, including city and county jails, were women (*Directory*, 1972), as compared with the nation-wide figure of 6.1% (Table 3).

Comparison of arrest rates with commitment rates for the State of New York for 1970 again supports the idea of preferential treatment being accorded to women. In 1970, women constituted 15.25% of those ar-rested (*Reported Offenses*, 1972) but only 4.8% of those in the correc-tional institutions.

Thus, both statistics and interviews support the notion that preferen-tial treatment is accorded to women during the entry phase into the prison system. As we shall see, such differentials exist throughout the system and take the form of worse rather than preferential treatment during the remainder of the correctional process.

Intake

One of the first steps in the intake process is classification. All of the authors cited thus far are in agreement with Davenport's (1972) state-ment that "We must treat the person not the offense. . . ." In attempting to do this, classification systems for men were developed. These systems serve two purposes: First, to provide the type of security arrangements deemed necessary to protect society—this is generally a function of the severity of the crime. Second, to consider the personal characteristics of the individual insofar as these reflect a possibility for skills training and rehabilitation. We found no evidence of the development of a separate classification system for women. If any system was used, it was an adaptation of that used for men.

Since most states have, at best, only one institution for women, all con-victed women, hardened felons as well as fledging misdemeanants sen-tenced for over one year, are sent to the same facility. Exceptions exist only when the city or county jails are suitable for some of these offenders. By contrast, in most states an effort is made to separate experienced male felons from misdemeanants or less dangerous criminals.

Skills Training

In evaluating the California programs before 1968, Spencer and Bere-cochea (1971) stated that, "It is obvious that the selection of the courses in the vocational training programs at C.I.W. (California Institution for Women) was based on their practical contribution to the ongoing opera-tion of the institution rather than an assessment of either the labor market or the potential employee." In our interviews we found similar limitations existing today in institutions in other states. This has re-sulted in a ". . . limiting effect upon the development of skills which are relevant to the labor market."

We did not encounter any location, except California, where poten-tially useful training such as paramedical, practical or vocational nursing, or training as nurse's aides was available, yet such skills can be learned and are in demand. In 1968, California started a program in vocational training in cooperation with a nearby college. All paroled program par-ticipants obtained stable full-time employment in the medical field and none had returned to prison (Spencer and Berecochea, 1971). This 100% success was four times greater than the usual results of training programs based on institutional needs. Also, these figures confirm that programs oriented towards upgrading previous skills and which offer "professional training in marketable skills with follow-up job placement may hold substantial rehabilitative potential."

While interviewees agreed that most of the programs for men were limited or irrelevant in the same sense as those for women, it was also agreed that there was a wider variety of choices available and that male offenders could obtain training which might be helpful in finding employment.

Work Release

In most states work release programs are available to offenders nearing the end of their sentences. These programs permit the offender to leave the prison each day, work in a nearby community, and return to prison at night. Again, there is a difference in the treatment accorded women and men. Work release programs for women have only recently been started, in most instances not until after they were proven successful in men's institutions. Because of the poor skills training programs for women, a disproportionately small number of women offenders are able to participate, and—to compound the difficulty—work release programs for women are not adapted to their particular needs.

Education

Still another aspect of differential treatment is in the educational programs available to women. Usually these consist of classes such as remedial English and preparation for high school equivalency examinations. Men's institutions have a wider variety of academic subjects and may even have college level training. An outstanding example is New Jersey's Leesburg State Prison for men: ". . . they built an educational center and then built the prison around it. It is a college within the perimeter of a prison" (The Dome, 1973).

A former staff member commented, "Women are regarded as very selfish children with short attention spans and are treated accordingly." This attitude, which seems to permeate most of the educational and skill training programs for women in prisons, may also be reflected in the fact that law libraries are only now becoming available to women offenders, whereas many men's institutions have had them for quite a while. Even in institutions with such facilities, access is often limited by time or work restrictions for any female offenders who might wish to use them.

A frequent excuse offered for this differential treatment of women is the small number of women in institutions. Possible opportunities for program flexibility and variety afforded by this low population are rarely recognized or utilized.

While considering the meager educational opportunities available to women, we encountered a particularly blatant situation of discrimination against women whose first language was not English. All of the minority persons interviewed, as well as the Caucasians, agreed that in many instances, ". . . being Puerto Rican (with a poor facility in English) is even worse than being black." Such classes as did exist were conducted in English and we found virtually none where English was taught as a second language, or with bilingual teachers. Thus, there is a group of women who are doubly deprived. Some measure of the extent of this deprivation came from interviews with Spanish speaking ex-offenders, one of whom works extensively with offenders to help them in pre-release planning and post-release adjustment. He estimated that, "among Puerto Rican men, only one-third of the offenders I worked with could read and write English to any extent, another one-third could read it somewhat but not write and the rest could neither read nor write English. With women it's worse, many of them even have a hard time understanding spoken English." Bilingual teachers are at times available for male offenders so that they may learn English as a second language, but no such opportunity seems to exist for women.

The language problems of Spanish speaking women are further complicated since prison rules are in English and no translation is provided. This increases the likelihood of becoming involved in numerous infractions of rules which can be neither read nor understood. In addition, outgoing mail is often subjected to long delays, being held up until the visiting bilingual censor is available. Mail problems encountered by women offenders usually resulted in intensifying the feelings of separation from their families which most Puerto Rican and black women experience as a result of their incarceration. Thus, their tension and anxiety levels are significantly increased, interfering with whatever rehabilitative activity might be possible. Men do not have to function under these handicaps to the same extent as women.

Psychotherapy

Women are again neglected. We do not take issue with Conrad's (1971) statement that, ". . . our crude methods of evaluative research, when used to assess the value of psychological treatment, have produced no indications that criminals will respond favorably if treated as psychiatric patients." However, this does not in any way vitiate the use of psychotherapeutic methods in attempting to re-orient offenders in new and possibly more socially acceptable ways of responding to life situations. With the exception of some scattered programs across the country, e.g., at Vacaville, a California men's facility, there is little evidence of any statewide use of therapy programs, experimental or otherwise. Typically, when attempts have been made to introduce innovative therapeutic programs, they are first introduced into men's correctional facilities.

New therapeutic approaches are introduced into women's institutions only after demonstrable success with male prisoners.

TABLE 4

Some Aspects of Movement of Sentenced Prisoners in State and
Federal Institutions in the U.S.A., by Sex, for 1950 and 1970

Year	Unconditional releases as percent of prison population of the same sex		Conditional releases as percent of prison population of the same sex		Violators returned as a percent of those conditionally released who are	
	Women	Men	Women	Men	Women	Men
1950	29.2%	19.3%	43.5%	25.0%	20.8%	20.4%
1970	18.1%	14.6%	50.5%	31.0%	20.5%	28.2%

General Conditions

According to our interviewees, women usually experienced psychological and physical harassment rather than the physical abuse received by men. For example, women who are "on the pill" are generally taken off despite the risk of sexual encounter. Although women do not seem to have as great a problem of homosexual molestation by fellow offenders as that reported by men, they are sometimes used as sex objects by the staff. Also, men get a single physical examination on entry into an institution, while examinations for women, including internal examinations, are repeatedly given throughout their terms of residence. In some cases, such internal examinations seemed to be almost in the category of discipline for "unusual" actions or behavior which "necessitates" such searches.

Another area in which differential treatment is found is in conjugal visits. Although conjugal visiting has existed at least since World War II in Mississippi, it is only recently being introduced into other state correctional systems (Hayner, 1972, Hopper, 1969). A feature shared by all such programs, is that the privilege of conjugal visits is strictly a male prerogative and women in prisons cannot receive such visits. Furthermore, some states grant furlough privileges to men due soon to be released but such privileges are rarely extended to women.

Release

The percentage of women in state and federal correctional institutions was and is small. However, during the period 1950-1970, women constituted a disproportionately large fraction of releases. Although the difference in release rates may have been lessened over the 20-year span, it is apparent that women are being treated differentially, in this case favorably.

However, the problems of obtaining release are usually different for the two sexes. Women are usually required to have the reasonable assurance of employment and also approved living accommodations; men are released with only a reasonable assurance of the possibility of employment and with significantly less restriction as to living arrangements. This differential treatment may have some advantage since fewer women are returned from conditional release. Whereas, at the beginning of the 20-year period, 1950, the return rates were virtually equal, by 1970 the percentage of women returned from conditional release was less than three quarters that of men. These statistics do not reflect the disproportionately larger effort expended to assist male ex-offenders. Larger numbers of community volunteer groups are engaged in assisting male offenders to prepare for their release than are involved with female offenders. Also, where state or local governments have systems of halfway houses or community centers to assist ex-offenders, the focus is almost exclusively on the needs of men. There are some exceptions to this generalization. California, for example, appears to be increasing its efforts in support of female ex-offenders as well as taking the lead in other areas of institutional reforms and innovation (Spencer and Berecochea, 1971). Women prisoners, however, rarely seem to organize, participate in, and protest in response to particularly disturbing conditions (Quant-Warm, 1971) and such action is often required before any changes are initiated.

WOMEN IN MENTAL HOSPITALS

Women and men alike experience emotional and behavioral problems, but even in the contemporary literature the curious belief remains that female aberration of behavior is regarded more as an indication of need for treatment in a mental hospital than is similar activity in men (e.g., Chesler, 1972, Gove, 1972, Howard, 1966, Lindbeck, 1972, Cannon and Redick, 1973). For example, it is generally more acceptable for a man to "go on a drunk," get angry and have a fight, or leave the house for a couple of days than it is for a woman. Similar behavior exhibited by a woman is likely to result in her being questioned, harassed or sent to a psychiatrist. As with crime, the social consequences of deviant behavior are dealt with differentially in our society. Also, the likelihood of sex-differentiated behaviors under stress being socially conditioned is all too often disregarded. Many otherwise excellent research papers still do not adequately report the sex distribution of the subjects under study. Female as well as male authors are sometimes guilty of this cavalier disregard

TABLE 5

Admissions to Mental Hospitals in the U.S.A., by Sex and
Type of Facility, for 1950 and 1970

Year and type of facility	Number		Number per 100,000 of same sex in the population of the U.S.A.		Women per 100 men†
	Women	Men	Women	Men	
1950—public*	130,485	157,628	171.99	210.64	83
—private	34,834	27,411	45.91	36.62	127
Total*	165,319	185,039	217.91	247.27	89**
1970—public*	617,043	629,499	591.61	692.32	98
—private	29,354	20,326	28.14	22.35	145
Total*	646,397	649,825	619.76	714.68	99**

* Excludes admissions to Veterans Administration hospitals: 1950—43,606; 1970—97,000.
** If estimated admissions to Veterans administration hospitals are included, the rate of women per 100 men becomes: 1950—72; 1970—87.
† See footnote in text, page 359.

of what may be an important variable in this area of research (e.g., Drieman and Minard, 1971).

As far as the shielding of women is concerned, Lindbeck's (1972) statement about alcoholic females probably applies to other behavioral problem areas as long as the woman is able minimally to fulfill her societal chores. He says "The drinking woman is shielded by her physician, her husband and her family . . . the signs of her drinking although quite apparent are overlooked by husbands, family members, friends, physicians, social workers and employers."

Admissions

Women constituted 47.2% of the admissions to mental hospitals in 1950 and, by 1970, this percentage had risen to 49.9, both figures excluding V.A. admissions. However, when we included admissions to the V.A. hospitals, women were only 42.0% of the total number admitted to mental hospitals in 1950, with the corresponding statistic for 1970 being 46.6%. The disproportionate use of private mental hospitals by women is evident, with the rate of women per 100 men being one and a half times as high as in public hospitals over the 20-year period, 1950 to 1970 (Table 5).

Admission rates to psychiatric services are a result of both incidence of mental disorders and socioeconomic, attitudinal, administrative and related nosocomial factors. Here, as elsewhere in our society, sex, race

TABLE 6

Additions to General Hospitals in the U.S.A., by Sex
and Selected Diagnoses for 1950 and 1970*

Selected Diagnosis	Admissions 1950 Number/100,000 same sex in the pop. of U.S.		Women/** 100 Men	Additions 1970 Number/100,000 same sex in the pop. of U.S.		Women/** 100 Men
	Women	Men		Women	Men	
Psychotic Depr. Disorders	4.55	1.86	248	2.95	1.49	228
Manic-Depr. Disorders	3.78	2.45	156	3.99	2.13	215
Psychoneurotic (Incl. Depr.)	10.74	6.31	173	18.66	11.90	180
Other & Undiag. Psychosis	4.03	4.54	90	1.59	.81	225
Schizophrenia	15.41	13.26	118	11.15	7.87	162
Transient Sit. Disorder	.09	.40	23	1.70	1.30	151
Alcohol Addiction	2.25	8.70	26	.64	1.94	38
Alcohol Intoxication	4.86	20.15	24	1.60	4.60	40
Drug Addiction	.09	.60	68	.61	1.21	57

* Data for 1950 are listed as admissions in reference source. The 1970 term additions was used for both years herein. It corresponds closely in meaning to the 1950 term of admissions, but includes what are now called admissions as well as return from long-term leave.
** See footnote in text, page 359.

and socioeconomics play a large part in determining diagnosis and disposition. For a more detailed discussion of this complex issue see Hollingshead and Redlich (1958) and Cannon and Redick (1973). During the screening which precedes admissions, this discriminative process is already evident. Non-white females are more likely to be diagnosed as schizophrenic, treated in the emergency room and released, whereas white females are likely to be diagnosed as neurotic and referred to outpatient treatment. Also, non-white males are most likely to be admitted to the hospitals and least likely to be diagnosed as neurotic (Gross, Knatterud and Donner, 1969). The importance of diagnosis at admission cannot be overemphasized, since this labeling process usually determines the treatment procedures to be followed during any subsequent hospitalization.

The overall rate of women per 100 men admitted to general hospitals has increased by over 40% between 1950 and 1970, indicating a large shift in the proportional utilization of these facilities by the two sexes (NIMH, 1954, Cannon and Redick, 1973). This shift reflects changes in attitude toward mental illness and societal attempts to cope with the problems involved. The statement that more women admitted to general hospitals are diagnosed as depressive than are men is as valid in 1970 as it was in 1950. The next highest diagnostic rating for women is for "other neuroses," increasing only 10% over the 20-year period, 1950-1970, and the third highest rating is for schizophrenia.

TABLE 7

Additions to Inpatient Psychiatric Facilities in the U.S.A., by Sex and Selected Diagnoses, for 1970*

	Type of Facility								
	State & Co. Ment. Hosp.			General Hospital			Community Ment. Hlth. Ctr.		
	Number/100,000 same sex in the pop. of U.S.		Women/** 100 Men	Number/100,000 same sex in the pop. of U.S.		Women/ 100 Men	Number/100,000 same sex in the pop. of U.S.		Women/ 100 Men
Selected Diagnosis	Women	Men		Women	Men		Women	Men	
Psychotic Depressive Disorder	3.55	2.05	198	2.95	1.49	228	11.50	5.07	260
Manic-Depressive Disorder	10.23	5.13	229	3.99	2.13	215	2.01	9.86	233
Psychoneurotic (Incl. Depr.)	20.78	14.36	166	18.66	11.90	180	123.35	95.24	149
Other and Undiagnosed Psychosis	2.59	1.52	196	1.59	.81	225	9.36	6.59	163
Schizophrenia	66.76	72.47	106	11.15	7.87	162	43.62	31.87	157
Transient Sit. Disorder	5.08	6.58	88	1.70	1.30	151	11.30	8.31	156
Alcohol Addiction	3.34	18.00	21	.64	1.94	38	2.73	8.44	37
Alcohol Intoxication	11.54	79.06	17	1.60	4.60	40	11.76	42.45	32
Drug Addiction	4.74	15.24	36	.61	1.21	57	4.13	7.90	60

* Comparable date for 1950 were not available.
** See text footnote, page 359.

On the basis of the 1970 NIMH data, particularly information from general hospitals and community mental health centers, certain diagnostic categories seem to apply primarily to women. Statistically, when there is no breakdown by age, women constitute a disproportionately large majority of people with certain diagnoses, including schizophrenia.

Marital status and educational level both seem related to mental illness in women, at least at the statistical level. Gove (1972) noted that ". . . it is the relatively high rates of mental illness in married women that account for the higher rates of mental illness among women." If figures for men and women are added together, then married people have lower rates of mental illness than the unmarried. But, among the women, it is those who are married who are more likely to have some mental illness, whereas among the men, it is those who are unmarried who are more likely to have such problems.

Where current data on educational level are available, we noted that "almost one quarter of the male admissions had less than 8 years of schooling compared to only one sixth of female admissions, whereas 45 per cent of the female admissions had 12 or more years of schooling compared to only a third of the males" (Cannon and Redick, 1973). It seems that the *lack* of education presents difficulties in coping with society's stresses for the men; whereas for women the *possession* of such education adds to their discomfort.

According to our interview data, men complain about their loss of freedom during intake, or reception, as it is sometimes called, and women about the lack of privacy. This may be a reflection of how life appears to the two sexes on the outside and may mirror treatment patterns within institutions. MacLennan (1972) comments that "discriminatory limitations on women with their attendant effects are often not consciously felt by women, but are expressed instead in apathy, anxiety and depression and in very dependent childlike behavior." This statement somewhat parallels the attitudinal response of mental hospital and prison staff toward inmates.

Residence Conditions

The percentage of residents who are women is very similar to the percentage of new female admissions so that there does not appear to be any differential treatment in this respect (Tables 5 and 8). For both public and private mental hospitals, large fractions of resident populations are 45 and over, with the public hospitals showing the larger num-

TABLE 8

Residents in Mental Hospitals in the U.S.A., by Sex and
Type of Facility for 1950 and 1970

Year and type of facility	Number		Number per 100,000 of same sex in the population of the U.S.		Women** per 100 men†
	Women	Men	Women	Men	
1950—public*	310,818	295,254	409.69	394.55	105
—private	10,272	5,143	13.54	6.87	200
Total*	321,090	300,397	423.23	401.42	106
1970—public*	166,192	171,427	159.34	188.53	97
—private	6,444	4,233	6.18	4.66	152
Total*	172,636	175,660	165.52	193.19	98

* Excludes residents in Veterans Administration hospitals: 1950—58,547 residents. Extrapolation of available data back from 1968 indicated that less than .5% of residents were women; 1970—1,057 female and 41,660 male residents.
** See text footnote, page 359.
† If residents in Veteran Administration hospitals are included, the rates of women per 100 men become: 1950—public, 89, private 200, total 89; 1970—public 78, private 152, total 79.

ber, 74% for women and 60.6% for men. The difference between these figures is too great to be satisfactorily accounted for solely by the fact that there are more women than men over 45 in the general population, since there are only 3.4% more women than men over 45 in the general population. Several possibilities suggest themselves: e.g., that society considers women over 45 less capable of coping with their environment; that society regards the behavior of these women as less functional; or that the demands of society are such that older women are really less able to cope.

The reduction in number of residents in all mental hospitals over the 20-year span, 1950 to 1970, reflects changes in societal definitions of unusual behavior, treatment approaches, and developments in medicine and chemotherapy. Whereas in 1950 there were 423 female residents per 100,000 women in the population and 401 male residents per 100,000 men (excluding the V.A.), by 1970 the corresponding rates were only 165 for women and 193 for men. Over this same period the proportion of residents who were women remained constant so that there is no evidence that these changes resulted in any sex differentiated hospitalization pattern.

In contrast to the prison system, where the percent of women arrested for a crime was usually higher than the percent confined, in mental-hospitals there is no difference between admission and residence rates. The percent of women additions (see Table 6 for definition) to state

TABLE 9

Residents in State and County Mental Hospitals in the U.S.A., by Sex and
Selected Diagnoses for 1950 and 1970

Selected Diagnosis	1950 Number/100,000 same sex in the pop. of U.S.		Women* 100 Men	1970 Number/100,000 same sex in the pop. of U.S.		Women* 100 Men
	Women	Men		Women	Men	
Psychotic Depressive Disorder	7.25	1.99	369	1.23	.65	218
Manic-Depressive Disorder	17.20	9.34	187	9.96	4.23	270
Psychoneurotic (Including Depression)	2.19	1.57	141	3.81	2.60	168
Other and Undiagnosed Psychosis	1.94	2.06	96	2.99	1.70	201
Schizophrenia	81.46	78.69	111	79.65	87.87	104
Transient Sit. Disorder	.23	1.30	18	1.29	2.02	74
Alcohol Addiction	.56	3.07	18	.19	.40	55
Alcohol Intoxication	1.43	6.02	24	1.57	8.30	22
Drug Addiction	.13	.12	117	.56	1.50	43

* See text footnote, page 359.

and county mental hospitals in 1970 (Table 7) is virtually the same as that of women residents with similar diagnoses (Table 9).

It is again important to consider how the diagnostic label affects treatment. For example, electroshock therapy (EST) remains the "treatment of choice" for schizophrenia and depressions—particularly in the case of menopausal women—whereas the neuroses and situational disorders are customarily treated by other means.

For activities within the mental hospitals, we considered the possibility of differential treatment in much the same manner as we did in the case of prisons. Here, too, it was necessary to rely on interview data for our information. As far as such categories as education and skill training, recreation, therapy and physical treatment are concerned, women and men seem to receive similar treatment within the mental hospital systems. Where inequities do exist, these seem to be specific to a single institution or staff member rather than a reflection of general policy.

The education and skill training opportunities available to women and men are essentially the same. Although few, if any, women are assigned woodshop or similar training, this seems to be a matter of individual choice and introjection of societal attitudes rather than institutional restriction. In recreation, again, there is no apparent differential except that, in some state mental hospitals, men are permitted to go to evening recreational activities on the grounds without escorts, whereas policy requires staff escort for women.

Although some sex differences appear to exist in the choice of treatment, *per se*, there is some question as to whether this stems from sex related differences in formal diagnostic classification or from the attitudes of particular psychiatrists. Whether the difference in admitting diagnosis is itself evidence of some differential treatment has been questioned (Chesler, 1972). In our opinion the differences in behavior leading to these diagnoses are themselves socially induced as well as defined.

Many interviewers agreed that more women than men seemed to receive EST, but as already noted this is one of the treatments most often used with patients diagnosed as depressive or schizophrenic—and women tend to receive these diagnostic labels more frequently than men. Although men may require less medication than women (Taylor and Levine, 1971), there was general argument that men actually received proportionately *more* medication than women. It seemed that men who became overactive or otherwise acted-out received greater doses of medication whereas women who "misbehaved" were likely to receive additional shock treatments. Although this sort of information was not directly apparent from treatment statistics, it was noted in some of he published information (e.g., Taube, 1973a), as well as in our interviews. Furthermore, it seems that escape and acting-out behavior by men was generally punished much more severely than similar actions by women.

Virtually the only work assignment from which women are generally excluded is heavy ground maintenance labor. Women tend to be assigned to activities regarded as "women's types of work."

Women's quarters are generally more attractive than those of men. One of the reasons for this disparity seems to be that women appear to be less destructive than men and all staff interviewees agreed on this score. Also, more women had diagnoses which relate to passive, non-destructive behavior. It might also be noted that women receive more attention from volunteer groups which are largely female and that society expects women to be more interested in their surroundings than are men.

Similar differences were also noticeable in the matter of clothing, women usually being more concerned about their appearance than are men. In fact, one of the punishments applied to women in some institutions is to insist that they wear institutional clothing for violation of hospital rules.

Release

In the release phase, differential treatment again seems to be the result of societal attitudes. Men who are able to return to their families and women who have shown a willingness to assume their usual responsibilities have similar release rates. If special care or family care is indicated, men are released more slowly than women, outpatient facilities not being as readily available for them. In a study of discharges from private hospitals, Taube (1973a) noted that males received "no referral" at discharge more often than females and that women were more likely than men to be referred to private psychiatrists upon release.

CONCLUDING REMARKS

Although laws require equal treatment for women and men both in prisons and mental hospitals, there are many differences in the treatment actually received. Conditions inside institutions reflect societal conditions on the outside and there is no doubt that women are treated differentially in our society. As one consequence of this differential treatment, women sometimes exhibit behavioral and emotional repertoires which are unacceptable to society at large. As these problems become exacerbated by societal pressures, institutionalization may result.

Some of the differential treatment received by women is actually advantageous. However, such preferential treatment usually take place *before* institutionalization. Once committed, women experience many aspects of the system which are detrimental to their sense of worth and well-being as individuals. These influences persist after institutionalization is over and may lead to further difficulties (Angrist, Lefton, Dinitz and Pasamanick, 1968, Spencer and Berecochea, 1971).

In the mental hospital system, the treatment differences are more subtle than in the correctional system and stem largely from the different diagnoses for which women are labeled and possibly hospitalized. Society seems to be proclaiming that, if a woman has problems, it is all right for her to get sick as long as she is only "a little sick." She may have any set of feelings she wishes (e.g., anger, frustration, depression, etc.) so long as her house, husband and children are at least minimally cared for. However, she *must not* act-out her anger, pain or frustrations, or society will exact a price through its institutions. In the prison, she will receive second class consideration, and in the mental hospital her label will probably lead to treatment that reinforces the socially approved behavior patterns, e.g., passivity and compliance, the resistance to which may have been a factor leading to her institutionalization. In both instances, she receives treatment oriented toward producing the desired degree of social conformity.

We concluded that:

1. The reality of society's response to the differing roles fulfilled by women and men must be confronted. Concerted efforts to counteract damaging stereotyped attitudes and hence hasten change must be initiated in all areas of our social structure.

2. In our institutions, effective programs for dealing with offenders and ex-offenders, as well as with the mentally ill, may necessitate a systems approach to the problem. The full impact of such innovative programs on the families, as well as the institutionalized individual, must be considered in the treatment design.

3. To ensure a more adequate rehabilitation process for women in correctional institutions, expanded training and educational facilities must be provided. It is socially short-sighted to abandon successful facilities or programs because of administrative or minor budgetary problems.

4. Effective rehabilitative programs in both prisons and mental hospitals necessitate provision for meaningful contact with the outside environment. An effort must be made to locate institutions

within inhabited areas rather than in isolation from the rest of the world. Both the ex-offender and the ex-patient eventually have to live outside the institution's walls and therefore need to learn new ways of living in the community.

5. The terms "former inmate," "ex-patient" and "ex-offender" must be evaluated for appropriateness. Is it customary to continue to refer to a woman who has had an appendectomy as an ex-patient after her recovery? Is the person who gets speeding tickets labeled an ex-speeder after her (or his) habits have changed? How accurate is it to persist in labeling someone who no longer needs hospitalization, or who has completed her sentence and "paid the price" for her anti-social behavior? The maintenance and persistence of the modified labels "ex-" seem to perpetuate and reinforce society's negative attitudes toward individuals regardless of their sex.

While the suggestions made here are relatively direct and apparently simple, the real issues about the goals of our social institutions are subtle, complex and extensive. Final answers are elusive and must await extensive further study.

REFERENCES

ALLEN, J. Pretrial release under California penal code section 853.6: an examination of citation release. *California Law Review*, 60, 1339-1370, 1972.

ANGRIST, S., LEFTON, M., DINITZ, S., & PASAMANICK, B. *Women After Treatment*. New York: Appleton-Century-Crofts, 1968.

ATKINSON, D. *Counselieurs—An Organization of Professionals in Parole, Probation and Related Services*. Personal communication, 1973.

BROMBERG, W. *The Mold of Murder*. New York: Grune and Stratton, 1961.

The California Mental Health Services Act. *California's One Ten*, 3, (3), Sacramento: Human Relations Agency, Dept. of Mental Hygiene, 1972.

CANNON, M. & REDICK, R. *Differential Utilization of Psychiatric Facilities by Men and Women—United States*, Statistical Note 81. Washington, D.C.: Survey and Reports Section, Biometry Branch NIMH, 1973.

Characteristics of New Commitments 1970. Albany: State of New York Department of Correctional Services, 1971.

CHESLER, P. *Women and Madness*. Garden City, N. J.: Doubleday, 1972.

Conference on corrections, prison project design. *Transcript of Proceedings, U.S. Commission on Civil Rights*, Washington, D. C.: U.S. Commission on Civil Rights, 20 June 1972.

CONRAD, J. Law, order and corrections. *Public Administration Review*, 31, 562-602, 1971.

Corrections practices, their faults and shortcomings. *Hearing Before Subcommittee No. 3, Committee on the Judiciary, House of Representatives 92nd Congress*, Washington, D. C.: U.S. Government Printing Office, 1971.

Crime in New Jersey, UCR—1971. Trenton: Attorney General's Office, 1972.

Crime in New Jersey, UCR—1970. Trenton: Attorney General's Office, 1971.

Crime in the U.S., UCR for the United States—1952. Washington, D. C.: Federal Bureau of Investigation, 1953.

Crime in the U.S., UCR for the United States—1970. Washington, D. C.: Federal Bureau of Investigation, 1971.

DAVENPORT, M. The female offender. In *Proceedings of the 101st Congress of Corrections, 1971.* Washington, D. C.: American Correctional Association, 1972.

DAVIS, A. Sexual assault in the Philadelphia prisons and sheriff's van. *Transaction* 6 (2), 8-16, 1968.

Diagnostic and Statistical Manual of Mental Disorders. (2nd ed.) Washington, D. C.: American Psychiatric Association, 1968.

Directory, Correctional Institutions and Agencies, 1971. College Park, Md.: American Correctional Association, 1972.

The Dome. Rahway, N. J.: Rahway State Prison, Lock Bag R 07065, 1973.

DRIEMAN, P. & MINARD, C. Preleave planning—effect on re-hospitalization. *Archives of General Psychiatry,* 24, 87-90, 1971.

DUPUY, H. *Selected Symptoms of Psychological Disorders.* Department of Health, Education and Welfare Public Health Services Publication 1000 series 11, No. 37. Washington, D. C.: U.S. Government Printing Office, 1970.

EINSELE, H. Besonderheiten der weiblichen kriminalität und des frauen strafvollzugs. *Zeitschrift Strafvollzug,* 20, 127-140, 1971.

ELMER, F. Just like a woman. *Police Review,* 79, 1271, 1971.

EYMON, J. *Prisons for Women.* Springfield, Ill.: Charles C Thomas, 1971.

Federal Prisons—1950: Report of the Work of the Federal Bureau of Prisons. Leavenworth: U.S. Penitentiary, 1951.

Federal Prisons Statistics Report 1969-70. Washington, D. C.: U.S. Department of Justice, Bureau of Prisons, 1971.

General Information, Department of Corrections. Sacramento: California Department of Corrections, 1973.

GLASS, G., HENINGER, G., LANSKY, M., & TALON, K. Psychiatric emergency related to the menstrual cycle. *American Journal of Psychiatry,* 128, 705-711, 1971.

GLUECK, S. & GLUECK, E. *Five Hundred Delinquent Women.* New York: Knopf, 1934.

GOFFMAN, E. *Asylums: Essays on the Social Situation of Mental Patients and Other Inmates.* Chicago: Aldine-Atherton, 1961.

GOLDMAN, M. Women's crime. *Juvenile Court Journal,* 22, 33-35, 1971.

GOVE, W. The relationship between sex roles, marital status and mental illness. *Social Forces,* 51, 33-44, 1972.

GROSS, H., HERBERT, M., KNATTERUD, G., & DONNER, L. The effect of race and sex on the variation of diagnosis and disposition in psychiatric emergency rooms. *Journal of Nervous and Mental Disease,* 148, 638-642, 1969.

HAYNER, N. Attitudes toward conjugal visits for prisoners. *Federal Probation,* 36, 43-49, 1972.

HANDY, C. U.S. commission on civil rights. New York City: Personal communication, 1973.

HOLLANDER, B. *The Psychology of Misconduct, Vice and Crime.* London: Allen and Unwin, 1922.

HOLLINGSHEAD, A. & REDLICH, F. *Social Class and Mental Illness.* New York: Wiley, 1958.

HOPPER, C. *Sex in Prison: The Mississippi Experiment with Conjugal Visiting.* Baton Rouge: Louisiana State University Press, 1969.

HOWARD, J. *What, from Whom and Can I: The Influence of Parents on Teenagers.* Unpublished report, San Jose State College, 1966.

JESSE, F. *Murder and Its Motives.* London: Harrop, 1952.

KRIZINOFSKI, M. School of Nursing, State University of New York at Binghamton, personal communication, 1973.

LEKKERKERKER, E. *Reformatories for Women in the U.S.* The Hague: Walters, 1931.

LINDBECK, V. The woman alcoholic—a review of the literature. *International Journal of the Addictions*, 7, 567-580, 1972.

LOGAN, C. General deterrent effects of imprisonment. *Social Forces*, 51, 64-73, 1972.

LOMBROSO, C. & FERRERO, W. *Female Offender*. New York: Philosophical Library, 1958.

MACLENNAN, B. *Mental Health and the Status of Women*. Unpublished report for the Prince George County Task Force on the Status of Women, Oct., 1972.

MEYER, N. *Socio-economic Characteristics of Admissions to Inpatient Services of State and County Mental Hospitals—1969*. Department of Health, Education and Welfare Publication No. HSM 72-9048 (Series A No. 8). Washington, D. C.: U.S. Government Printing Office, 1971.

MEYERS, J. & BEAN, L. *A Decade Later*. New York: Wiley, 1968.

MONAHAN, F. *Women in Crime*. New York: Ives Washburn, 1941.

NIMH, *Patients in Mental Institutions 1950 and 1951*. Department of Health, Education and Welfare, Public Health Service Publication No. 356. Washington, D. C.: U.S. Government Printing Office, 1954.

NPS Bulletin: National Prisoner Statistics 1968-1970, Prisoners in State and Federal Institutions for Adult Felons. Washington, D. C.: U.S. Government Printing Office, 1971.

NPS—State Prison Admissions and Releases, 1970. Washington, D. C.: U. S. Government Printing Office, 1971.

PERSON, P., HURLEY, P., & GIESLER, R. Psychiatric patients in general hospitals. *Hospitals, Journal of the American Hospital Association*, 40, 64-68, 1966.

PERSON, P. *The Relationship between Selected Social and Demographic Characteristics of Hospitalized Mental Patients and the Outcome of Hospitalization*. Reprinted with permission by the Department of Health, Education and Welfare, Public Health Service. Washington, D. C.: U.S. Government Printing Office, 1964.

POLLACK, E., REDICK, R., & TAUBE, C. The application of census socio-economic and familial data to the study of morbidity from mental disorders. *American Journal of Public Health*, 58, 83-89, 1968.

POLLAK, O. *The Criminality of Women*. Philadelphia: University of Pennsylvania Press, 1950.

Prisoners in America, Report of the Forty-Second American Assembly, December, 1972. New York: Columbia University Press, 1972.

Proceedings of the Ninety-Eighth Congress of Correction (1968). Washington, D. C.: American Correctional Association, 1969.

Proceedings of the Ninety-Ninth Congress of Correction (1969). Washington, D. C.: American Correctional Association, 1970.

Proceedings of the One Hundredth Congress of Correction (1970). Washington, D.C.: American Correctional Association, 1971.

Proceedings of the One Hundredth and First Congress of Correction (1971). Washington, D. C.: American Correctional Association, 1972.

QUANT-WARM, P. Holloway and the Dutch women's prison. *Maanblad voor Berechting en Reclassiering*, 51, 238-240, 1971.

REDICK, R. *Referral of Discontinuations from Inpatient Services of State and County Mental Hospitals—United States 1969*. Statistical Note 57. Washington, D. C.: Survey and Reports Section, Biometry Branch NIMH 1971.

REDICK, R. *Veterans with Mental Disorders 1968-1970*. Department of Health, Education and Welfare Publication No. HSM 73-9021 (Series A, No. 12). Washington, D. C.: U.S. Government Printing Office, 1972.

Reported Offenses and Arrests—New York State—1970. Albany: State of New York Department of Correctional Services, 1972.

RYAN, M., BEER, P., & BALES, R. *California Prisoners, 1969: Summary Statistics of Felon Prisoners and Parolees.* Sacramento: Human Relations Agency, Department of Corrections, 1970.

SCHUCKIT, M. The alcoholic woman: A literature review. *Psychiatry in Medicine, 3,* 37-43, 1972.

SCIACCO, A., JR. Some observations about women and their role in the field of corrections. *American Journal of Correction, 34* (2), 10-12, 1972.

SHERMAN, J. *On the Psychology of Women.* Springfield, Ill.: Thomas, 1971.

SMITH, C., former Director of Conference on Corrections, Prisons Project, U.S. Commission on Civil Rights. Personal communication, 1973.

SPENCER, C. & BERECOCHEA, J. *Vocational Training at the California Institution for Women: An Evaluation.* Research Report No. 41. Sacramento: Department of Corrections, 1971.

A Study of Successful Treatment: California Mental Health. Sacramento: Human Relations Agency, 1972.

SUTHERLAND, E. & CRESSEY, D., *Criminology.* New York: Lippincott, 1970.

TAGGART, R. Manpower programs for criminal offenders. *Monthly Labor Review, 95* (8), 17-24, 1970.

TAUBE, C. *Admissions to Private Mental Hospitals—1970.* Statistical Note 75. Washington, D. C.: Survey and Reports Section, Biometry Branch, NIMH, 1973a.

TAUBE, C. *Referral of Persons to and from General Hospital Psychiatric Inpatient Units, United States 1970-1971.* Statistical Note 71. Washington, D. C.: Survey and Reports Section, Biometry Branch, NIMH, 1973b.

TAYLOR, M. & LEVINE, R. Influence of sex of hospitalized schizophrenics in therapeutic dosage levels of neuroleptics. *Diseases of the Nervous System, 32,* 131-134, 1971.

THOMPSON, C. Executive director of women's prison association, and home, New York City, personal communication, 1973.

TOTMAN, J. The murderess. *Police,* 15, 16-22, 1971.

U.S. Bureau of the Census, *Statistical Abstract of the United States—1950.* Washington, D. C.: U.S. Government Printing Office, 1950.

U.S. Bureau of the Census. *Statistical Abstract of the United States—1952.* Washington, D. C.: U.S. Government Printing Office, 1952.

U.S. Bureau of the Census. *Statistical Abstract of the United States—1970.* Washington, D. C.: U.S. Government Printing Office, 1970.

U.S. Bureau of the Census. *Statistical Abstract of the United States—1972.* Washington, D. C.: U.S. Government Printing Office, 1972.

U.S. Department of Justice, Law Enforcement Assistance Agency. *Statistical Center Report sci: 1970 National Jail Sentences.* Washington, D. C.: U.S. Government Printing Office, 1971.

WEIDENSALL, J. *The Mentality of the Criminal Woman.* Baltimore: Warwick and York, 1916.

The Welfare Reporter (N. J.), 21, 1-2, 1970.

WILLIAMS, K. & GOLDBERG, I. *Comparison of Psychiatric Diagnosis on Admission to and Separation from Psychiatric Facilities.* Biometry Branch NIMH Statistical Note 62. Washington, D.C.: U.S. Government Printing Office, 1972.

WITKIN, M. *Private Mental Hospitals 1969-1970.* Department of Health, Education and Welfare Publication No. HSM 72-9089 (Series A No. 10). Washington, D. C.: U.S. Government Printing Office, 1972.

WITKIN, M. *Psychiatric Services in General Hospitals 1969-1970.* Department of Health, Education and Welfare Publication No. HSM 72-9139. (Series A No. 11). Washington, D. C.: U.S. Government Printing Office, 1972.

ZOLIK, E., LANTZ, E. & SOMMERS, R. Hospital return rates and pre-release referrals. *Archives of General Psychiatry,* 18, 712-717, 1968.

17

PSYCHOTHERAPY WITH WOMEN AND MEN OF LOWER CLASSES

Before proceeding with this discussion, it would seem appropriate to state what is intended by the term "lower classes."

The lower classes do not form a homogeneous group. The aged poor, the deprived youth, the poor whites, the poor blacks, the blue collar workers, and the farmers—all have varying characteristics which may be distinguished more by their differences than by their similarities. But in the attitude of mental health professionals toward them and in the type of treatment they have received from mental health professionals, they have enough in common to be considered together.

In order to refer unexceptionably to the "lower classes" with clarity yet in a way that does no violence to ordinary usage, we can do little better than adopt Hollingshead's division of the social classes into five categories (Hollingshead, 1957). Classes IV and V of his division will, for this presentation, denote "the lower classes."

Since there are at least three broad frames of reference involved in the conceptualization of this topic, the discussion is divided into three parts. Considered first is what might be described as a research study of women and men in a specific lower class population. The need of comparative studies of mental health between the two sexes seems most pressing, in view of the great number of attempts that have recently been made to articulate the complex relationship between psychopathology and the sex roles. Second, psychotherapy is related to social class. Third, psychotherapy is considered in connection with social change.

RELATIONSHIP BETWEEN OPPRESSION OF WOMEN AND PSYCHIATRIC DISORDERS

The majority of upper and middle class psychiatric patients are seen by private practitioners; the majority of lower class patients are seen in clinics by public practitioners. It will be useful to survey the ethical implications of the differences between these two sorts of practitioners. The public practitioner is of course paid to provide certain services. He or she is therefore ethically bound to pay attention to the available data concerning problems set for him by the employing agency. Personal biases and whims must be set aside, and the limited resources of his employer must be respected. By contrast, the private practitioner is free to indulge himself in any way he chooses, provided that he does not trespass beyond professional standards. The public practitioner must be able to show that his professional activities are indeed relevant to the function to which public funds are being directed. Any deviations from specific tasks such as direct service must be justifiable in terms of such theoretically sound ideas as the prevention of mental disorders or the promotion of mental well-being; again, the practitioner's personal bias or particular socio-political orientation must be suppressed. A private practitioner can engage in any activity that in his or her personal belief might contribute towards improvement of mental health in the community or towards the prevention of mental illness. The public practitioner should not ethically feel the same prerogative during his or her working hours. Since he or she is on salary, no loss of income is suffered for indulgences, and in order for these activities to be more than indulgences there is a need to show, by some objective criteria, that they are related to the task of a mental health professional hired by an agency for the delivery of service to a population. Therefore, whenever a public practitioner feels strongly about an issue, he or she is free either to engage in supporting it during off-duty hours, or to feel obligated to inquire in most objective ways whether there is some justification for the application of professional time (beyond personal feelings and personal opinions).

Method

The Department of Psychiatry of the Johns Hopkins Hospital has been providing comprehensive psychiatric services to the families of the United Auto Workers (UAW) members employed at the General Motors plants in the Baltimore metropolitan area. The cost of these services is met through a cost-financed group practice plan mediated through Blue Cross-Blue Shield. Concomitantly, a research program was undertaken for an extensive study of the population being served. Some of the findings of that research have already been reported in the literature (Crocetti *et al.,* 1971, Spiro *et al.,* 1972a, Spiro *et al.,* 1972b, Siassi *et al.,* 1973, Crocetti *et al.,* 1973).

Here, comparisons are offered of workers (men) and their spouses (women), in two respects: concerning the prevalence of mental illness, and feelings of loneliness and dissatisfaction with life. The insured group consisted of 4,827 workers and their families. A probability sample of 1,026 was chosen. Only one adult member from each household was interviewed. In the case of married members, the spouse was the predesignated respondent in 50 per cent of the cases. The sample was representative of a population of 8,000 UAW members and their spouses. A completion rate of 87 per cent was achieved (888 subjects).

Analysis reveals the sample to be a one class population—Class IV (Hollingshead, 1957). The typical respondent is white, 40 years old, and lives in a row house. He or she is a high school dropout, has been born in Baltimore or lived there for many years, married over 17 years with two children and, in the case of the worker, has been working at the same job for over 13 years. The family income was close to $9,000. Both males and females in the sample were members of the same social class, lived in the same residential area, and did not differ significantly in any of their demographic characteristics, such as education. Both males and females were interviewed by the same set of interviewers in their home settings. The interview protocol was presented as a "general health study." The MacMillan Index used for the study of prevalence of mental disorder in this population was a modified version of the same index used in the Sterling County Study (Leighton *et al.*, 1963). It was validated for this population by including known psychiatric patients who were drawn from the same population (Spiro *et al.*, 1972a). A separate set of questions was used to elicit responses concerning loneliness and life dissatisfaction. Each of the two categories consisted of four questions with a four-fold category of answers for each question. For convenience of presentation, the responses to these questions have been dichotomized into positive and negative patterns.

Results

Table 1 summarizes the findings from the responses to the questions in the MacMillan Index. The reader interested in the details of how the scores were obtained is referred to our paper already cited (Spiro *et al.*, 1972a). It bears explaining here, however, that these results refer to *true prevalence* rather than *treated prevalence,* and furthermore the known clinic patients are omitted from the computation. As can be seen, there is no statistically significant difference between the true prevalence of mental illness in males and that of females in this population. The in-

TABLE 1

Defined "Sick" and "Well" Individuals Among a Blue Collar
Population According to MacMillan Index, By Sex

	Risk of disorder		"Sick"	"Well"
	(N)			
Male	(436)	52%	19%	81%
Female	(403)	48%	22%	78%
TOTAL	(839)*	100%	21%	79%

Source: Baltimore, Md., 1970.
* 49 former patients omitted.

TABLE 2

Response of Male Workers and Their Spouses
to Questions on Loneliness

Question	Giving Ansyers Indicative of Loneliness	Others	p Value
(Loneliness)	%	%	
How often do you feel bored?			<.50
Workers	10	90	
Wives	10	90	
How often are you alone more than you like to be?			<.01
Workers	7	93	
Wives	17	83	
How often do you feel lonely?			<.02
Workers	6	94	
Wives	11	89	
How often do you have a feeling of being apart from other people when you are at a party or social gathering?			<.50
Workers	4	96	
Wives	4	96	

significantly higher percentage of women with some mental disorder
among this unevaluated population is counterbalanced by the fact that
of the 254 patients seen over a four-year period in the clinic serving this
population, 65 per cent were male and only 35 per cent female.

Table 2 shows the responses of workers and their wives to the questions
about loneliness. As can be seen, the overwhelming majority of both
groups do not complain of loneliness, and only one question (How often

Table 3

Response of Male Workers and Their Spouses
to Questions on Life Satisfaction

Question (Life Satisfaction)	Giving Answers In- dicative of Life Dissatisfaction %	Others %	p Value
I'm generally satisfied with the way things are going for me.			
Workers	10	90	
Wives	8	92	
			<.50
I'm really very happy about the way I've been getting along lately.			
Workers	13	87	
Wives	10	90	
			<.20
Everything seems to go wrong for me nowadays.			
Workers	9	91	
Wives	11	89	
			<.20
Life is treating me pretty bad right now.			
Workers	6	94	
Wives	6	94	
			<.50

are you alone more than you would like to be?) significantly distinguishes
the worker from his spouse.

Table 3 shows the responses to the questions about life satisfaction.
As is evident, the responses do not differentiate significantly between
the workers and their spouses.

The generalizations that can be strictly drawn from this study are
naturally limited to similar populations of Class IV patients and could
only be applied inductively—with great circumspection—to lower classes
in general. However, the thesis that there is no difference in the prevalence of mental illness between men and women of the lower classes
has been strongly supported by Hollingshead and Redlick (1958), by Doh-
renwerds (Dohrenwerd and Dohrenwerd, 1969), as well as by S. Srole and
his co-workers (1962). Of all epidemiological studies of prevalence of mental disorders to date, only two have shown any difference between the
sexes that could be called significant—and that a marginal one. One

showed a higher prevalence in men (Pasamanick *et al.,* 1959) and the other in women (Leighton *et al.,* 1963).

In the present context we are interested in such sexual differences, not in the most general way, but in regard to how the pressure of contemporary social reforms and their undercurrents may distort the data available. In order to determine the direction and extent of such distortion, if it exists, we must glance at the way in which the scientific therapist proceeds in order to conduct valid research—in spite of the differences among various therapeutic schools.

The contemporary mental health professional is not simply a researcher or a practitioner; that popularly supported dichotomy is artificial and misleading. True, there are different psychotherapeutic orientations—psychoanalytic, behavioral, existential, and moral—which promulgate different images of man and mental illness. But these are all bound in a common unity by their respect for scientific research, and such research always involves the testing of hypotheses. It does not much matter how the hypothesis is conceived, i.e., to what extent "inspiration" is significant. Nor does it matter whether the hypothesis is formed by oneself or by others. The important thing is that scientific research dictates that one proceed either to gather confirming or negating data. Emotional or esthetic appeal must not count towards its validation, but only truth, i.e.., whether the hypothesis is supported by the data. Of course, one can begin with a working hypothesis and then enter the field gathering data which have a bearing on it, or one can examine the existing data in the light of a new hypothesis; the latter approach is used in this study.

Bearing the above remarks in mind, we may proceed to obtain a view of the hypotheses which are explicit or implicit in the statements of women in the mental health profession who consider themselves feminists. The first hypothesis is that oppression by a male-dominated society increases the incidence of emotional disorders in women. The second hypothesis is that women in this society are more dissatisfied with their work, more alienated, and more lonely than men of the same social class.

Since most women making such assertions belong to the middle and upper classes and also to the professions, it is interesting to examine whether or not what they present as their observations about women in other social classes in the society are true observations or essentially projections. Whether or not the mental health professional joins in his professional capacity in responding to the clarion call for changing society and social roles should depend on more than his or her personal prejudice and his or her personal preferences. The question that needs to be answered is whether we are being urged to share a particular group's biases and exhorted to join a dubious moral enterprise, or whether our attention is being drawn to a real phenomenon. If a particular social condition is shown to have a cause and effect relationship with emotional disorders, we have, as mental health professionals, an obligation to join the forces that are attempting to alleviate that condition.

What is to be said about attempts to discover in the lower classes effects of the model of male-oppressor and female oppressed? It may very well be that members of lower classes, continually engaged in the struggle to maintain a minimal standard of living, could hardly be less affected by that dichotomy between male oppressor and female oppressed which in other, higher, classes seems to be an issue today. Men and women of lower classes need whatever confraternal solidarity they have in order to bring about desirable social change. Moreover, the injustice of male oppression which receives so much careful attention today would seem to require, for its breeding, conditions which are foreign to the lower class home, which sees both mates either sharing the burden of survival or perishing. There is an obvious difference between the wife who is expected to structure her leisure time in accordance with the husband's paycheck, and the wife who must fight the structure of poverty, either with a paycheck of her own or with every minute of her time.

If the paradigm of male oppression has relevance to life in the lower classes, if male oppression has increased feelings of loneliness, frustration, or those symptoms of alienation which threaten mental health, then the data just presented do not show it. Indeed there are discriminations and burdensome inequities in this society which plague and affect the emotional stability of lower classes, but all our available knowledge is strongly suggestive of the irrelevance of the male-oppressor female-oppressed paradigm to those classes.

We may go further: In the absence of any evidence to support an oppressor, any effort by mental health professionals (however well-meaning) to portray the woman of lower class as oppressed by her male counterpart would at best appear a dubious moral enterprise. If those efforts are misguided, positive harm may be done to the well-being of the very persons whom the professionals would help; for in the name of promoting mental health we could easily become an instrument of division and confusion, thus rendering patients from lower classes even more powerless. For there is little doubt that the solidarity just referred to is one of the few positive strengths which could aid any program designed or intended to maximize mental health among the lower classes.

What is being posited is that the problem of the mentally ill from lower classes is primarily a class problem rather than a sex problem. Therefore, issues that are relevant to psychotherapy with women of lower classes will very likely apply equally to their male counterparts. Whatever can be said about the female patients will in all probability be applicable to the men of their class. This appears to me as the most logical conclusion unless tests can be devised to refute these suggestions, tests that could stringently guard against those elements of willful distortion which it would be tempting to include, especially in view of liberal and humanitarian currents which in spite of obvious goodwill are apt at times to sweep aside the dictates of truth and reason, which in this case are crucial. Therefore, rather than devote the remainder of this chapter to psychotherapy with women of lower classes, it would be more appropriate to broaden the discussions of psychotherapy to both men and women patients from lower classes.

PSYCHOTHERAPY WITH PATIENTS OF LOWER CLASSES

The purpose of this section is to relate psychotherapy to social class. This is done in the explicit context of value relevance, the primary value being equality.

The term psychotherapy is often applied indiscriminately to so many diverse activities that it would be meaningless to talk about its relevance to lower-class patients without defining to what the term used here restricts itself.

Every activity, from classical psychoanalysis at one end of the spectrum to psychosurgery at the other end, has been called psychotherapy (Mowbray and Timbury, 1966). Even when we exclude, as Wolberg has done (1954), primarily somatic interventions such as electro-convulsive treatment (ECT), psychosurgery and pharmacotherapy, the term will continue to be inclusive of so many diverse activities that it will remain meaningless. That Frank's search for commonalities among all such activities (1961) proved futile attests to the impossibility of such reductionism (Wallerstein, 1956). My definition of the term restricts itself to therapies whose primary aim is promotion of self-awareness, i.e., psychoanalytic psychotherapies. This does not imply that all other activities —educational and action therapies (the various behaviorist, learning-theory, and operant conditioning models); judgmental therapies (reality, radical, and moral models); persuasive therapies (hypnotic, counselling and directive models) and others—should not be considered psychotherapies; rather all that is implied is that they are not included in the definition of the term psychotherapy which is discussed in this presentation.

Contemporary views about mental illness are in flux, and the mental health profession as a discipline is almost formless. Its main currents are contradictory; its innovations are often bewildering. It is appropriate that claims for the relevance of one form of treatment rather than another for any individual, let alone for a whole social class, should have large elements of ambiguity, even confusion.

In addition, any generalizing statement about a class of patients, as well as its application to the individual patient, is at best a risky proposition. Stereotyping or placing low expectations on the patients from a whole social class is hardly the course of wisdom. Yet judging from the available literature and looking at the prevailing practice throughout the country it would appear that a majority of mental health professionals have a negative attitude toward psychotherapy for lower classes. Some leading mental health professionals have even gone to the extreme point of suggesting the abandonment of the service psychotherapy for patients from lower class (e.g., Riessman, 1963).

The ostensible aim of those who question the relevance of psychotherapy is the development of more effective modalities of treatment for the lower classes, but underlying this is a fundamentally negative and class-biased idea. Indeed, careful scrutiny reveals that, as a rule, the pessimism concerning psychotherapeutic services for the lower classes does not follow from therapeutic experience with the lower classes; instead, this pessimism shapes these endeavors.

When authoritative sources declare that lower classes do not benefit from psychoanalytic psychotherapy or are not candidates for such psychotherapy, it does not follow that such a claim is true. But it does follow that many people will think it is true.

The theoretical burden of this assertion is simple enough: the lower class patients are not verbally articulate; they are reluctant to postpone immediate gratification for long-range gains; they are suspicious and distrustful of intellectuals; they are unable "to share the middle-class view on which most psychotherapy is based"—that "action should be preceded by reflection and that personal problems can be solved by discussion" (Detre and Jarecki, 1971, p. 490); they only want medication, practical assistance and advice (Carlson, et al., 1965, White, Fichtenbaum and Dollard, 1964); they have difficulty with time schedules and formality of psychotherapy (Coleman, 1965, Rosenthal, Behrens and Chodoff, 1968); etc. There are two issues here, inexplicitly fused. The most obvious one is an effort to be responsive to the demands of the consumer. The second issue is less visible but far from inaccessible: It is a stereotyped view of lower classes colored by class bias.

Are these images of lower classes true? Surely, many of them are correct. But nothing will be gained by the oversimplifications which they entail.

Every clinician knows that intellectualization is often used as a defensive resistance by the articulate. The gains in self-knowledge in psychotherapy, although small at each point, are often quite immediate. A patient does not need to finish psychotherapy before he can reap some of its benefits.

The neurotic and psychotic problems of the poor cannot be dispelled by exercises in redefinition. Nor can their problems receive the attention they deserve in short-cut programs that have been shaped by the assumption that the poor cannot be benefitted by psychoanalytic psychotherapy as fully as patients in higher classes. Barten relates the widespread acceptance of brief therapies by mental health professionals in part to the "long overdue recognition of the special needs of the poor and lower socio-cultural groups, for whom traditional techniques often have been unsuitable and ineffective" (Barten, 1971, p. 3). Yamamoto and Goin (1965), Baum and Felzer (1964), Beck (1969), among many others, have proclaimed that poor and uneducated patients want support and concrete help and are not interested in the opportunity to examine their feelings. The leaden psyche of the poor depicted by these theorists is depressing. It hardly corresponds to my experience with the lower class patient: oppressed, but not resigned, tormented but strangely charged with excitement, captive, but full of glimpses of liberation.

The questions I will now try to explore are two: What is the origin of the notion that lower class patients do not want or need psychotherapy? What does such a view mean with regard to the present and future mental health services which may be provided for patients from these classes? These questions lead us directly to the following issues: What is psychoanalytic psychotherapy? Is there ideological warfare about its relevance to treatment of patients coming from lower socioeconomic classes? If so, what can we say about it that would lead to better understanding of the differing viewpoints?

Psychoanalytic psychotherapy is dedicated to making man comprehensible to himself and to helping him learn that man's self-fulfillment lies in the process of self-recognition. Freud has put the accent on the love of truth concerning one's own being (1937). Sullivan defines psychiatric cure unequivocably as a progressively expanding evolution of self and self-awareness (1947). These definitions are in line with Fromm's definition of mental health and the person who is mentally healthy ". . . who is in the process of being born as long as he is alive . . ." (1955, p. 275). The definition of psychoanalytic psychotherapy as striving by the patient and the clinician for continuous unfolding and continuous self-expansion runs like a Wagnerian leitmotiv through the writings of psychoanalytic practitioners. Psychoanalytic psychotherapists are unanimous in their belief that symptoms are concrete representations of inner states, that they express inner states, that they express inner conflicts, and that understanding these forms a basis for psychotherapy. These beliefs are shared by every school of psychodynamic psychology, be they orthodox Freudians, Adlerians, Jungians, or neo-Freudians. All psychoanalytic thinkers have expressed the belief that crucial experiences are universal and therefore, shared and understood. Their disagreements have concerned the universal nature of crucial experiences. For example, Freud (1936) suggested that the oedipus complex and its consequent castration anxiety are universal. Adler (1927) considered organ inferiority to be the universal experience. Rank (1959) thought of separation anxiety as the crucial universal experience. Sullivan (1947), however, echoes the general sentiment of all psychoanalytic thinkers that all humans are more alike than different.

It is widely held that psychoanalytic psychotherapy is (a) not relevant to the needs of the patients from lower socioeconomic classes and (b) not acceptable to these patients. Proposition (a) entails that intrapsychic and interpersonal conflicts are consequences of affluence and education. A thorough search of literature fails to produce any evidence in support of this hypothesis. Singer has addressed himself cogently to proposition (b):

> The implications of the statement that the poor and the uneducated neither desire nor are capable of benefitting from psychotherapy merely indicate the pretentiousness of he who makes the statement and his preference for the detachment of explanation over sharing of experience during therapeutic sessions. It is the height of pretentiousness to assume that members of "lower classes" are not interested in coming close to the nature of their experience or that the capacity to develop emotional insight is dependent on economic or educational status (Singer, 1970, p. xvi).

The Problematical Nature of Psychotherapy with Patients from Lower Classes

We now find ourselves confronted with two specific problems: What are the specific characteristics of the patients from lower classes that make psychotherapy difficult? What causes the specific response of the therapists to these patients?

Evidence for greater dependency of the patients from lower class has been provided by sociological research. Allison Davis, in his comparison of middle-class and lower-class practices in child-rearing, presents evidence that independence is not encouraged in lower-class children, since it is economically more feasible to treat the child as dependent than to encourage independence (Davis, 1952). Gerald Gordon has shown that in lower socioeconomic groups there is a greater tendency to treat the sick person as dependent than among the middle and upper classes, except when the illness is getting worse or is critical (Gordon, 1966).

Besides the inevitable economic pressures intrinsic to treatment programs, which cannot always respect the welfare of the patient, there are special problems of the patient-therapist relationship to consider. For many of the urban dispossessed, the aged, the non-white, the illiterate, unemployable youth, migrant tenant farm workers, etc., the shift from angry suspicion or a sense of despondency to trust in therapeutic engagement is not easy in psychotherapy. For some of the poor to become truly cooperative partners in the development of a working alliance with psychotherapists often requires a period of alternating conflict and accommodation lasting many months. The resolution sometimes never takes place, as is the case with patients from other classes. There is bound to be uneasy testing before a sense of trust can emerge. The therapist who begins with the prior assumption that the service he is rendering is not needed or wanted by such patients can easily be the beneficiary of self-fulfilling prophecy.

Problem 1: As a rule these patients come to the clinic because of some change for the worse in their life, e.g., abandonment by a boyfriend or a girlfriend, the drinking problem of a husband or the infidelity of a wife, difficulties with the children, especially when they reach adolescence, difficulty with agencies or financial catastrophes such as pressure from creditors and other conditions which on the surface appear to be primarily caused by conflict with the external world. Since resources in the real object world appear to them to be fading, their first line of defense seems to be to turn to the supportive authority figure in a psychiatric outpatient clinic. They will try to resolve their inner conflicts by help from without. The demand for medication is as much a demand for chemical control of their increased influx of aggression against their disappointing love objects as it is for oral narcissistic supplies.

Problem 2: In this situation the patient will behave in a submissive, but sado-masochistic way; he will give himself up to the therapist, but will expect the impossible in return. Much depends on the therapist's handling of the transference situation. The therapist who allows himself to be blackmailed into a continuous show of omnipotent love and power has put himself and the patient in a trap.

After having enjoyed the original status of being omnipotent benefactor the therapist finds himself in an untenable situation. The patient's symptoms refuse to disappear and the patient's demands fail to subside. The therapist now tries to prevent the patient from becoming "dependent." The patient correctly perceives this as rejection and will regress a step further. Jacobsen (1953) among others has pointed out the child's preference for an aggressive, strong love-object compared to its loss. The patient will manifest increasing masochistic provocation of the therapist's anger; the therapist will find himself no longer reacting to the patient with warmth, sympathy, and love, but in a punitive and sadistic way. Such behavior is a source of anxiety and pain for the therapist because it is in conflict with his self image. It shows him that he is not the concerned, loving, sympathetic human being that he wants to believe he is. Within the therapist this anxiety creates a dangerous schism. This schism, which is developed fairly soon when working with lower class patients, reflects the therapist's efforts to rescue his valued self image by keeping the patient at a safe distance from himself. The incessant complaints and accusations of public practitioners against the psychoanalyst in private practice or against other clinicians who engage in psychotherapy, whether it is with the poor or the non-poor, are both a denial and a confession of guilt for the crime of having abandoned their own patients. Both tell the truth: there may well be a passionate commitment to improving the condition of life for the lower classes and a devotion to the multifarious causes which plague the lower classes, but too often these are carefully conjoined to avoidance of involvement with lower class patients in psychotherapy.

In this brief introduction to the family of problems posed by psychotherapy with patients of lower classes, I have ignored difficulties that are mainly economic. No one will deny that there are grave problems of administration of resources, for example, provision of manpower and funding. Nor are these the only problems of a material or economic nature.

Even if psychotherapy on a sufficient scale could be financed for many of the lower class patients who cannot afford to pay for it themselves, we should not see the end of peripheral problems. But if provision of psychotherapy for the poor were set as the ideal to be strived for, one could at least see that the efforts could be expended in the direction of making such a service for the poor a possibility. This is not the case, however; most of the efforts being expended now in the provision of mental health services for the poor lie along other avenues of approach. Much of the practitioners' efforts can be understood as attempts to control and manipulate the lower classes chemically and behaviorally, or to avoid them altogether.

It is important to examine the values we harbor because they greatly influence the choices we make. We must continually be aware of ideologies or belief systems that are so often repeated that they appear as though they were theories based on experience. The consequences of such belief systems are far-reaching and often deleterious. For example, if one accepts the proposition that lower class patients do not need or want psychotherapy one is confronted with two difficult yet well-defined choices: 1) what, if anything, may then be deemed the relevant service— what constitutes the aggregate of what we call psychiatric service to the poor; and 2) should this activity, once determined, be the guide in shaping the training of the practitioners and determining the allocation of resources?

These considerations lead to the conclusion that the type of service rendered by a mental health professional depends more on the professional's value judgments than on scientifically determined considerations. Those professionals who see all the members of lower class as essentially incapable of making choices can have nothing but scorn for psychotherapy. It is only when the therapist believes that self-knowledge is inherently valuable to an individual, irrespective of class, that he can see psychotherapy as a worthwhile discipline. It is well to underscore the relevance of these considerations for the concern of the mental health professionals. If psychoanalytic psychotherapy is not relevant to the needs of the impoverished, but is merely a reluctantly accepted form of help, then our task becomes one of bringing to an end the wasteful expenditure of effort and funds by the public practitioners engaged in this activity. The corresponding positive aim would be to direct our energy away from psychotherapeutic work with the poor to other areas of service. If, on the other hand, the search for self knowledge is indeed the inherent tendency of being human, the unavailability of this service to the poor should be considered as undesirable. Then the mental health professional's efforts would be directed to removing financial and other obstacles which have stood in the paths of patients from lower classes receiving this service.

In the pages that follow I shall report on the research data from our work with blue collar workers and their families over a five-year period. The data will be examined to see what support it provides for either polar position outlined so far. Does our experience support the value of psychotherapy for lower class patients and their interest in utilizing such service or does it point to the irrelevance of such a service for that population and their disdain for it? It must be stressed at this time that one study does not allow one to make definite generalizations. Nevertheless, work of this type will help make discernible the outlines of some basis for rational judgment.

In a four-year study of a psychoanalytically-oriented clinic specifically designed to serve a population of blue collar workers and their families with liberal coverage for outpatient care and complete freedom of choice we found that less than 2 per cent of all patients who initiated their treatment with the clinic did not remain with the clinic for their total psychiatric experience, whereas over 12 per cent of those who had initially sought help from other sources switched to the clinic in this period (Spiro, *et al.*, 1973a, Spiro, *et al.*, 1973b, Spiro, *et al.*, 1973c). Only when patients have an option to make a free choice and are not hampered by financial barriers can one find evidence of what patients from lower class prefer to have. As to the relevance of psychoanalytic psychotherapy for patients of lower class, the evidence from this study is far more overwhelming. Though the patients who initiated their treatment with the clinic were not significantly different from those that did not, as to diagnosis, age, sex and education, less than 4 percent of the clinic patients were hospitalized in the four-year period, compared to 52 percent of the patients who did not begin with the clinic (Spiro, *et al.*, 1973c).

The data supply strong evidence for the position that these patients, far from avoiding psychotherapy and self-examination, tend to search for the opportunity to explore their mental life by preferring the service modalities that make such an opportunity available to them. Similar preferences by patients who are considered of low socioeconomic class for self-examination in psychotherapeutic work have been observed in our out-patients at Rutgers Mental Health Center.

We did not set up prospective research to prove or disprove the validity of the assumption that the members of the blue collar population or their spouses do not respond to psychoanalytically-oriented psychotherapy. The falsehood of such an assumption, however, can be inferred from our retrospective analysis of the data. Since every clinician attached to the clinic was psychoanalytically oriented; since the union members and their families apparently were satisfied with the service to the extent that at the end of each year their representatives renewed the contract with the Clinic; and since less than 4 per cent of the patients were hospitalized over a four-year period, our data suggest that the concept of working-class men and women not responding to psychoanalytically-oriented psychotherapy is difficult to substantiate. In my intensive psychotherapeutic work with women and men of Classes IV and V and in supervision of psychiatric residents and other mental health professionals and trainees, it has been impossible to substantiate the concept that such patients are not receptive to psychoanalytic psychotherapy. A preliminary examination of the data on patient dropouts of my past and present supervisees shows that the few psychiatric residents and other students of psychotherapy who had completed or were engaged in their own personal psychoanalysis and, hence, had an emotional understanding of transference-countertransference phenomena had fewer dropouts of patients from every class, and only slightly higher dropout rates from the lower classes than upper classes. However, the psychiatric residents and other mental health professionals and trainees who had not undertaken personal psychoanalysis showed significantly higher dropouts of lower class patients compared to the middle and upper-class patients they were treating. Thus the phenomenon observed, the high dropout rate of lower class patients from psychotherapy, especially of the psychoanalytic nature, may be explicable on the basis of the therapists' characteristics rather than the patients'.

The issue of dropping out versus staying in treatment is a complex one which has received attention primarily from the patient's normative and sociological characteristics. The study by Lorr, Katz, and Rubenstein (1958), the review by Fulkerson and Barry (1961) and the more extensive survey by Brandt (1965) of factors influencing the patients to drop out, point to the scant attention that has been paid the more important factor, in my view, of the therapist's sociological and normative characteristics in general as well as, again in my view, the more crucial issue of the therapist's awareness of transference and countertransference phenomena and his ability to deal with these phenomena.

PSYCHOTHERAPY AND SOCIAL CHANGE

Let us consider for a moment the fact that some of the deepest tensions are those between psychotherapy whose axial direction is individual self-expansion and individual freedom, and the antipsychotherapeutic forces. The latter include those who consider the external challenge as the only one worthy of an answer. It is this tension which is ultimately one of the most fundamental problems of the mental health profession.

The future of unity or diversity along ideological lines in the treatment of members of the lower class is problematic, but the abandonment of the role by a mental health professional in bringing to the afflicted lower class patient the benefits of his skill is quite unjustified. In the battlefront the surgeon who would leave his work-tent and rush to the lines with a rifle is clearly seen as indulging his own personal whims rather than considering his responsibilities to his comrades. Yet, when a mental health professional in a community mental health center who has the skills to treat the mentally ill, rather than seeing patients chooses to dabble in local politics, he is seen as enlightened and socially conscious. Like most analogies, this one is far from exact. But the similarities as well as the differences in the two cases are at least interesting. Creative solutions that resolve the conflicting goals of social change are needed, as well as personal service to the afflicted that permits compromise; and there is no necessary conflict between the lofty social goals which we possess who consider ourselves liberal or radical mental health professionals and the provision of psychotherapeutic service to the poor in an interdependent relationship. Furthermore, identification with a successful and capable therapist allows the patient from a lower class to visualize a future as a capable and successful person; and a few talented people in the community, long constrained by their neurotic difficulties, if freed from such difficulties, may have a much more realistic chance of creating leadership for the community and achieving greater political, economic, and social objectives than a group of mental health professionals from outside trying to organize a community.

Mental health practitioners have their own sphere of interests and duties. While they cannot be expected to confine their efforts narrowly to that sphere, it ought to be pointed out that when the energies and funds of psychiatric facilities are devoted to raising the economic status and education level of the poor, laudable as such efforts are, these are activities that fall more properly into the realm of politics, economics, education, and sociology. They often stem from withholding from the lower classes the special expertise that the mental health practitioner can bring.

Psychotherapy does not offer a panacea for poverty. It may have no direct effect on outer factors that prevent the poor from rising out of poverty. The educational system of the poor is one of the many outer factors which should act as agents of social change. The main thrust of psychotherapy for the poor can alleviate the inner sense of hopelessness, helplessness and anger. The poor will still need the help of those who are primarily concerned with the provision of opportunity and the improvement of other factors (jobs, housing, education, etc.).

Those of us who have long been engaged in psychotherapeutic work with the lower classes cannot help but be in complete accord with Fromm's position that psychological well-being of the masses will ultimately require a total economic and social reorientation and reorganization (Fromm, 1962). But we also know that psychotherapy is in no way competitive with social reform; on the contrary, it works to allow the poor to engage in meaningful participation in such reform. The problems confronting the poor are not soluble through the use of direct psychotherapeutic service alone. There is no question about the service rendered by those who are devoted to social change, and my purpose here is in no sense to be construed as an effort to detract from the service that they render and the high ideals that motivate them. Quite the contrary—psychotherapy with the poor in no way obviates the need for social action. My quarrel is with those who deny the validity of psychotherapy for the poor. They are curious sorts, who are passionately devoted to the well-being of the poor, yet avoid them at close range; who are unwittingly engaged in their display of the ludicrous pronouncement of their superiority over the poor; who would resent anything but individualized attention to their own need or those of family and friends, but would exert their countervailing forces against psychotherapy for the lower class patient. They seek to routinize and bureaucratize the public mental health professionals so that the latter's work-patterns with regard to the lower class patient will more closely approximate clerical routines.

Another facet of some social activism requires more detailed discussion. There are those among us who are at heart the apostles of the hell-fire and brimstone of the old religion, but who now have wrapped themselves in the respectable garb of social consciousness and pseudo-science spouting the same moral bonhomie, but in more fashionably acceptable forms. They are not for anything or anybody, often not even themselves, but against everything and everybody. They are not for the mentally ill, but against their own particular *bêtes noires*. The mentally ill are seen by them as troops in the battle against evil. They are not only against psychotherapy, but against every effort to help a troubled individual. They consider concern with the individual almost obscene. They care not what happens to the mentally ill, but want all of us to devote all of our time and energy to fighting their particular brand of evil. While the rest of us grope in search of the etiology of mental illnesses by studying individuals in depth in psychoanalysis, populations by surveys, brain cells under the microscope, drug actions in laboratories, they have already seen the light. They know that mental illnesses are caused by poverty, racial discrimination, the military-industrial complexes, and the conservatives—or at the other end of the spectrum by the welfare state, by forced integration, by bleeding heart liberals, and by creeping socialism. Implicit in their belief system is that by changing the social order in the direction they prescribe, all mental illnesses will automatically be eradicated overnight.

Their interest in the lower classes is not of commitment but of pseudo-commitment, for commitment clearly means a stand on behalf of somebody or something, not one against somebody or something. These people are not for the lower class patients, they are against authority or establishment or whatever particular evil they feel driven to fight. Many of these self-appointed champions of the lower class patient are shameless exploiters of these patients. They receive public funds earmarked for therapeutic work with these patients, avoid these patients like plague, and devote their time fighting their own enemies in the name of the lower class patient.

Other advocates of social change who often effect a knowledgeable stance concerning psychoanalytic psychotherapy attack it for its promotion of acceptance of the *status quo*. They pose a major threat to the future well-being of the lower class patients, not because they misunderstand, but because they are convinced by their own pretense to knowledge. They are unable or unwilling to distinguish between the liberating force that is psychotherapy, and the sedative-tranquilizing and coercive-controlling role of some other therapies. They cannot distinguish between a liberating and a repressive experience.

The goals of psychoanalytic psychotherapy could hardly be more in accord with the avowed aims of all liberal movements—to help liberate the individual from the destructive tyranny of the false values, habits and allegiances he unconsciously harbors. Psychoanalytic psychotherapy helps reduce oppressive influences on the individual so he may gain autonomy and mastery of his own life-style and social performance.

The proponents of symptom control (dispensers of tranquilizers, behavior-modifiers, hypnotists, and others) are enamored by the reductionist fallacy, i.e., seeing the patient's symptom as nothing but undersirable aberrations that need to be ameliorated or removed, so that the patient can "adjust." Adjustment to an oppressive or destructive life situation may well be tantamount to psychological death. Many who are aware of this, among them some radical feminists in our profession, have come to mistake the adaptive potential of psychoanalytic psychotherapy for just such adjustment. As Hartmann has pointed out, adaptation and adjustment not only are not synonymous, but in fact may be considered opposite. Adjustment implies passive submission to one's life situation; adaptation connotes mental equilibrium, ability to enjoy life and to achieve autonomy, to combat destructive external forces, to change social goals, and to strive for the improvement of one's social systems (Hartmann, 1958).

In the same way that concepts of social change entail both improved and detrimental consequences for different population segments, psychotherapy, then, can have both stabilizing and radical consequences, depending on the individual who is exposed.

Many have documented the evidence of substantial inequality in the distribution of incomes and of educational and occupational opportunities in the United States. Myrdal has clearly shown the disjunction between societal values and social reality in America (Myrdal, 1962). The fact is that, only in the past two decades, psychotherapy has been gradually extended to larger and larger segments of the population and has ceased to be a badge of the socially elite. Many have labored hard to bring this about.

The anti-psychoanalytic psychotherapy movement, consciously or otherwise, seeks to reverse this and will act to restore class distinctions in treatment of the mentally ill, since the affluent and educated will continue to pursue self-knowledge through psychoanalytic psychotherapy, while the poor will be steered into specific treatment programs. Proponents of social activism who are against psychotherapy do not seem to distinguish between two crucial considerations—changing society as a desirable social and political goal, in which the patient by gaining autonomy and self-understanding through psychotherapy can be an active agent, and environmental manipulation in lieu of psychotherapy. Such manipulation may of course increase the patient's opportunities, but will not help him to acquire the self-knowledge necessary for genuine participation.

The anti-psychoanalytic ideology of the so-called champions of the lower classees, combined with the strength of the reactionary right, who eschew any social responsibility, and the middle-of-the-road politicians' fear of costs, makes the betrayal of the poor seem all but inevitable. Financial considerations may indeed force most clinicians dealing with the lower classes to go the route of chemical control of symptoms, of shortcuts in therapy, etc., thus providing the poor with palliatives and gimmickry in place of genuine help for self-expansion and self-fulfillment as human beings. The exclusions and severe restrictions of coverage for psychotherapy in all the national health insurance bills now before the Congress will make it economically impossible to service the poor, even for those therapists who want to work with them. Departments of psychiatry and psychology have already less and less influence over their own curricula, as federal funding and market exigencies determine what are or are not fundable programs or salable skills.

How often have the attempts to set up special services for the lower classes, such as store fronts, paternalistic advice and counseling, unsolicited home visits, been only a thinly disguised unwillingness to see the lower classes as equal human beings? Many social activists among us have carved for themselves careers of being champions of the lower class and no doubt will continue to favor theories of mental illness that best reflect the patterns of these careers. These professionals, by moving into administrative and decision-making positions, exercise a pervasive influence; problems become defined as they see them, and are solved as they recommend that they should be solved. Not having any commitment to clinical work and propelled by a burning ambition for power, they climb the rungs of the academic or administrative ladder with breathtaking speed. Once they have obtained a prestigious position they use the position as a platform or a springboard for the espousal of their views which are then reflected in prestigious journals. The prestige of their positions, the prolific nature of their writing, their quotations of themselves and their obsequious imitators have created the impression that their belief about the lack of relevancy of psychotherapy to the needs of the lower classes has some scientific validity.

We may speculate about the possible consequences of this belief for the lower classes as it is passed from one generation of mental health practitioners to the next. The consequences can hardly be but detrimental, both because the belief may become self-fulfilling and because it shifts exploration and analysis away from the means of providing psychotherapy for the lower classes. To communicate such a message to the student of psychotherapy will not only destroy his inspiration, it will lead to the imposition of real barriers to his choosing to work with patients from lower classes.

It is unlikely that believing that the lower classes do not need or want psychotherapy will dispose the prospective mental health professional to give up his profession. A more likely outcome may be a perpetuation of a double standard of care: psychotherapy as the primary method of treatment for the middle and upper classes, and chemical control, social manipulation and hospitalization as the major methods of treatment for the patients from lower class, with each class favoring one and eschewing the other and the professionals providing what the consumer demands. The mental health professionals will then continue to believe that they are responsive to the wishes of their clients, oblivious of their role in the creation of the type of expectation. It can be safely assumed that the mental health professionals who claim that lower classes do not want and need psychotherapy are aware that their assertions will be a causal factor in the developing future, insofar as their stance influences the thinking of decision makers. But, in order to avoid inferences about ugly and subhuman motives, one must assume that they have failed to take into full account the other causality, that is, that their belief has a causal effect on the expectations of patients from the lower class. Once this is recognized, it is impossible for us to remain silent. Unless we denounce their beliefs and denounce them without equivocation, we share responsibility for the betrayal of the lower class patient.

CONCLUDING REMARKS

In a nation that produces, consumes, and disposes of myths as it does with other commodities, the myths of status are the current fashion: the status of being women related to psychopathology; the status of lower class related to psychotherapy; and the status of the lower class mentally ill related to need for social change.

With the conceptual frameworks which formed the guideposts of this chapter we have encountered many myths along the way. Chief among these have been the uniqueness of the psychopathology of lower class women; the refractoriness to psychotherapy of patients of both sexes from the lower classes; and the myth of more elementary needs. Among other myths we have encountered has been the myth of the social model of mental illness.

It is in the nature of things that in order to explode one myth one frequently creates another and to combat one stereotype one risks creating a second. To maintain that mental health professionals hold thus and such stereotypical views about lower classes is to inadvertently stereotype the mental health professionals. The heterogeneity of the lower classes referred to in the second section is more than matched by the heterogeneity of the mental health professionals.

The mental health profession nowadays is a true tower of Babel, with ideological feuds among adherents of various "models" of mental illness cutting across disciplinary lines; with rampant warfare for power and prestige among disciplines; and various schools of therapy favored by varying professionals with or without coherent theoretical underpinning. This should not be surprising in view of the American ideology of democracy and the emphasis on progress, novelty, and competition. Lust for power and prestige, envy, petty jealousy, and other follies and foibles that are our common human heritage, as well as the capacity for self-deception and self-delusions, are neither more nor less the characteristics of the mental health professional than of the rest of the populace. One often hears the term patient being vehemently denounced in favor of "client," the denouncer then proceeding to "treat" the client. That ogre of a straw man called "medical model" is frequently brought out and burnt in effigy, I presume, as a symbolic destruction of the elite role of the physician mental health practitioner, while the effigy burner proceeds to emulate the fantasied power-holder by writing behavioral "prescriptions." As long as little harm is done to the well-being of the emotionally ill, only the pedants would take issue with such foibles. But there are areas where sharp issue needs to be taken.

First, issue must be taken with the misleading notion that women of lower classes, on account of the darling model of male-oppression, present the psychotherapist with issues that are unique on the basis of sex, and therefore, in place of psychoanalytic psychotherapy we should devote our resources to formation of consciousness-raising groups, or we should convince them to reorient their role vis-à-vis their male counterparts, or should preach to them about the evils of nuclear family, etc.

Second, there is the infrequently acknowledged but obviously influential belief-system that the lower classes neither need nor (for various reasons) can profit from psychotherapy, together with the skeptical voices of many professionals who have described a refractoriness in the patients, rather than a resistance in themselves.

The difficulties inherent in psychotherapy with the lower classes point to the need for adequate training for those engaging in psychotherapy with the lower classes, rather than to the advisability of continuing to leave the lower class patients to the poorly-equipped and least trained, or depriving these patients of the service of psychotherapy altogether.

Third, the presupposition that the need for psychotherapy can be neatly subordinated to economic and sociological exigencies, with the resulting priority of the latter for the mental health professionals, must be challenged. Economic and sociological problems may well have priority for the lower classes. Real as these are, they may be conceptually distinct from the problems of self-development, which afflict the poor no less than their well-to-do brothers and sisters. The priority for the mental health professionals should remain the contribution of what they have the expertise to provide.

REFERENCES

ADLER, A. *Understanding Human Nature.* New York: Greenberg, 1927.

BARTEN, H. H. Expanding spectrum of the brief therapies. In H. H. Barten (Ed.), *Brief Therapies.* New York: Behavioral Publications, Inc., 1971.

BAUM, O. E. & FELZER, S. B. Activity in initial interview with lower-class patients. *Archives of General Psychiatry*, 10, 345-353, 1964.

BECK, J. C. Outpatient group therapy of the poor. *Current Psychiatric Therapies*, 9, 241-244, 1969.

BRANDT, L. W. Studies of "dropout" patients in psychotherapy: A review of findings. *Psychotherapy: Theory Research and Practice*, 2, 2-13, 1965.

CARLSON, D. A., ET AL. Problems in treating the lower-class psychotic." *Archives of General Psychiatry*, 13, 269-274, 1965.

COLEMAN, J. V. Therapy of the "inaccessible" mentally ill patient. *Mental Hygiene*, 49, 581-584, 1965.

CROCETTI, G., SPIRO, H. R., & SIASSI, I. "Are the ranks of society truly closed to the mentally ill? A study of attitudinal social distance. *American Journal of Psychiatry*, 127, 1121-1127, 1971.

CROCETTI, G., SPIRO, H. R., & SIASSI, I. *Contemporary Attitudes Toward Mental Illness.* Pittsburgh: University of Pittsburgh Press, 1973.

DAVIS, A. Social class and color differences in child rearing. In G. E. Swanson, T. M. Newcomb, and E. G. Hartley (Eds.), *Readings in Social Psychology.* New York: Holt, 1952, pp. 539-544.

DETRE, T. P. & JARECKI, H. G. *Modern Psychiatric Treatment.* Philadelphia: Lippincott, 1971.

DOHRENWERD, B. & DOHRENWERD, B. *Social Status and Psychological Disorders.* New York: Wiley, 1969.

FRANK, J. D. *Persuasion and Healing: Comparative Study of Psychotherapy.* Baltimore: Johns Hopkins University Press, 1961.

FREUD, S. *The Problem of Anxiety.* New York: Norton, 1936.

FREUD, S. *Analysis Terminable and Interminable.* London: The Hogarth Press, 1953, 23, pp. 216-253, 1937.

FROMM, E. *The Sane Society.* New York: Rinehart, 1955.

FROMM, E. *Beyond the Chains of Illusion.* New York: Simon and Schuster, 1962.

FULKERSON, S. C. & BARRY, J. R. Methodology and research on the prognostic use of psychological tests. *Psychological Bulletin*, 58, 177-204, 1961.

GORDON, G. *Role Theory and Illness.* New Haven, Connecticut: College and University Press, 1966.

HARTMANN, H. *Ego Psychology and the Problem of Adaptation.* New York: International Universities Press, 1958.

Hollingshead, A. B. *Two Factor Index of Social Position*. New Haven, Connecticut, 1957 (mimeographed).

Hollingshead, A. & Redlich, F. *Social Class and Mental Illness*. New York: Wiley, 1958.

Jacobson, E. Contributions to the metapsychology of cyclothymic depression. In Phyllis Greenacre (Ed.), *Affective Disorders*. New York: International Universities Press, 1953.

Leighton, D. C., Harding, J. S., Machlin, D. B., MacMillan, A. M., Leighton, A. *The Character of Danger: The Sterling County Study of Psychiatric Disorder and Sociocultural Environment*, Vol. III, New York: Basic Books, 1963.

Lorr, M., Katz, M. M., & Rubinstein, E. The prediction of length of stay in psychotherapy. *Journal of Consulting Psychology*, 22, 321-327, 1958.

McMahon, A. W. & Shore, M. F. "Some psychological reactions to working with the poor." *Archives of General Psychiatry* (Chicago), 18, 562-568, 1968.

Mowbray, R. M. & Timbury, G. C. Opinions on psychotherapy: Enquiry. *British Journal of Psychiatry*, 112, 351-361, 1966.

Myrdal, G. *An American Dilemma: The Negro Problem and Modern Democracy*. New York: Harper and Row, 1962.

Pasamanick, B., Roberts,, D. W., Lemkau, P. W., & Krueger, D. B. A survey of mental disease in an urban population: Prevalence by race and income. In Hans Nussbaum (Ed.), *Epidemiology of Mental Disorder*. Washington, D. C.: American Association for the Advancement of Science, 1959, pp. 183-196.

Rank, O. *The Myth of the Birth of the Hero and Other Writings*. New York: Vintage Books, 1959.

Riessman, F. *New Approaches to Mental Health Treatment for Labor and Lower Income Groups*. Mimeographed Report, National Institute of Labor Education, Mental Health Program, June, 1963.

Rosenthal, A. J., Behrens, M. I., & Chodoff, P. Communication in lower class families of schizophrenics: Methodological problems. *Archives of General Psychiatry* (Chicago), 18, 464-470, 1968.

Siassi, I., Spiro, H. R., & Crocetti, G. The social acceptance of the ex-mental hospital patient. *Community Mental Health Journal*, 9, 231-241, 1973.

Singer, E. *Key Concepts in Psychotherapy*. New York: Basic Books, 1970.

Spiro, H. R., Siassi, I., & Crocetti, G. What gets surveyed in a psychiatric survey? A case study of the MacMillan index. *Journal of Nervous and Mental Disease*, 154, 105-114, 1972a.

Spiro, H. R., Siassi, I., & Crocetti, G. Public contact with mental illness. *Mental Hygiene*, 56, 36-39, 1972b.

Spiro, H. R., Siassi, I., & Crocetti, G. Cost financed group practice: I. Clinical care patterns in a labor union mental health program. *Journal of Nervous and Mental Disease*, 1973a (in press).

Spiro, H. R., Siassi, I., & Crocetti, G. Cost financed group practice: II. Utilization profile of a labor union mental health facility. *Journal of Nervous and Mental Disease*, 1973b (in press).

Spiro, H. R., Siassi, I., & Crocetti, G. Cost financed group practice: III. Cost and utilization under conditions of dual option. *Journal of Nervous and Mental Disease*, 1973c (in press).

Srole, L., Langner, T. S., Michael, S. T., Opler, M. K., Rennie, T. A. C. *Mental Health in the Metropolis: Midtown Manhattan Study*. New York: McGraw-Hill, 1962.

Sullivan, H. S. *Conceptions of Modern Psychiatry*. Washington, D. C.: The William Alanson White Psychiatric Foundation, 1947.

WALLERSTEIN, R., ROBBINS, L., SARGENT, H., & LUBORSKY, L. The psychotherapy research project of the Menninger Foundation: Rationale, method, and sample use. *Bulletin of the Menninger Clinic*, 20, 221-280, 1956.

WHITE, A. M., FICHTENBAUM, L., & DOLLARD, J. A measure predicting dropping out of psychotherapy. *Journal of Consulting Psychology*, 28, 326-332, 1964.

WOLBERG, L. R. *Technique of Psychotherapy*. New York: Grune and Stratton, 1954.

YAMAMOTO, J. & GOIN, M. K. On the treatment of the poor. *American Journal of Psychiatry*, 122, 267-271, 1965.

Part VI

OVERVIEW: CONCLUSIONS AND NEW DIRECTIONS

18

THE FEMALE ROLE: CONSTANTS AND CHANGE

SUZANNE KELLER

As the person designated to assess, summarize, and evaluate the materials assembled in this volume, I have the benefits of hindsight as well as the opportunity to build on the interesting work presented in these pages.

This book is a compendium ranging over a variety of themes and topics from alcoholism and depression to consciousness-raising and new forms of therapy. Despite this topical diversity, however, a number of common conceptual and thematic threads become apparent. Chief among these are an essentially undifferentiated, hence oversimplified, conception of women and a perhaps unavoidable focus on the familiar trilogy of white, middle class, married women seeking psychotherapy.

One suspects that the images and stereotypes about women held by psychotherapists cannot help but affect their diagnoses and forms of therapy. But in order to formulate more subtle and complex concepts concerning women and their problems, psychotherapists must make explicit what is now hidden or only partially revealed, namely, their own reactions to the facts of gender. This, plus cross-cultural and subcultural information about varieties of femininity and masculinity, should greatly expand the scope of current discourse.

One striking feature of these papers is the absence of an adequate working model of sex roles. Psychotherapists do pay lip service to the existence of these roles but their notions are too global and abstract, being based on perhaps too literal a reading of the cultural script.

References to sex roles abound, notably in the important paper by Esther Menaker, but there seems to be a misunderstanding about their nature and utility. Struggling to find a bridge between psychic structure and social structure, many of the authors seem to welcome a concept

411

such as role but often reject it because it seems too contrived and theatrical. They seem to assume that sex roles are like stage roles that one acquires for a brief period, acts out for a delimited purpose, and then discards without pain. But sex roles are altogether different. Assigned at birth, they are not exterior to the self but help create its foundation. This means that they become so deeply intertwined with one's basic identity that individuals cannot wish or think them away at will. Once in place, sex roles become firmly locked into the psychic system, forming a permanent screen through which to perceive and experience the world. They are not, therefore, to use a typical, if erroneous, analogy, like a dress one puts on, but like food one ingests which then forms part of our flesh and spirit and is not extricable as a separate component of our being (Sarbin, 1954, Biddle and Thomas, 1966).

At the same time one must insist that while sex roles are fundamental to the psychic economy they are not its only props. In life, gender designations are always merged with other primary attributes operating through a variety of social and personal filters, such as age, social class, occupation, religion, and temperament. Thus a given woman patient is not simply a female but a particular kind of feminine person with a number of important, and variable, social attributes. To what extent gender affects and is affected by these other vital characteristics is not known with any exactitude but it surely does not operate outside these factors. Hence we need to build up—and clinicians could greatly contribute to such an effort—images and cases of systematic patterns of gender-based social attributes and not only, as is done haphazardly now, personal portraits by gender. As Ethel Albert (1963) has stated: "That males and females are different from each other at least physiologically is one of the few relatively clear and simple facts of life. But the male-female difference is *a* difference, not *the* difference."

The other common tendency in these papers is to stress the negative features of the female role and to ignore its positive ones. This welcome departure from an earlier tendency to idealize and accept cultural postulates about women without question may nonetheless distort the actual situation in which women experience conflict precisely because of the mix of favorable and unfavorable features built into their roles. There is furthermore no automatic carry-over between the cultural stance towards women and their own assessments of self-worth, because contrary to the assumptions made in a number of these papers, cultural directives are not simply taken over, but are transformed by individuals and groups to suit their particular reality. This then makes problematic the extent to which women accept or depart from the cultural and subcultural script according to their milieus and life-styles.

In other words there is need for greater awareness that conceptions of femininity vary not only from individual to individual but also, in structured fashion, by social class, ethnicity, region, and age, that is, according to the numerous subcultures to which individuals belong. These subcultures shape the social self, guided by the highly abstract and general sex-role constructs endorsed by the society. This is why women do not experience the female role in identical ways and harbor different self-concepts according to their desire and ability to live up to the concepts of femininity current in their milieus.

Contemporary society, in other words, projects onto its collective screen a variety of images of the sexes, a variety not easily captured by superficial generalizations and labels. The assertion that men are tough and women tender, for example, is really an expression of intent or wish and is therefore at best only partially true and always one-sided. These stereotypes may alert us to the ideal type expectations prevalent in a given setting but they will not permit us to infer how men and women actually behave. In reading these papers I found myself wondering how therapists determine the meaning of symptoms, always contextual, if they do not know the standards of normality and conventionality governing their patients' conduct. How, furthermore, do they distinguish between nonconformity and emotional illness? And when do therapists decide that a problem is individual rather than cultural, and if cultural, how much can individual therapy help?

Psychotherapists, whatever their allegiances and professional orientations, have enormous power to influence the direction of individual development and thereby to shape the future commitments of persons in their charge. This is why a knowledge of the prevalent images of women among psychotherapists is itself a datum needing to be made explicit (Bart, 1972). Fabrikant's paper is addressed to this very issue and cites findings from his own research that agree only partially with those of Broverman and Chesler who found psychotherapists as denigrating of women as the culture is presumed to be (Chapter 4, this volume).

Indeed the overemphasis on the negative and undesirable features of the female role, referred to earlier, suggests that the original Freudian notion of woman as an inadequate and incomplete version of man has not really disappeared but only changed its form. The androcentric bias persists, here as elsewhere, leading to an appraisal of women in light of male standards, as if mental health were a function of a woman's capacity to pursue and succeed in male type pursuits.

The androcentric bias was noted by several contributors, most succinctly by Gomberg who observed, in her paper on women and alcoholism, that it is not so much a matter of the double standard applied to diagnosis and therapy "but rather a problem of neglect. Virtually all psychiatric, psychological and sociological theory about alcoholism has been about men: the problem is perhaps too much of a single standard rather than a double one."

Hence treatment is less geared to challenging cultural definitions of sex roles than to improving women's capacities to live up to them.

Finally, not only is there a one-sided, negative conception of the female role, but its desirable alternative is posed in highly romanticized terms, as in the exhortation that women be free to develop their "true," spontaneous self, geared to creativity and growth. This recalls Helen Lynd's (1958) critique of the assumptions of the Sullivan-Horney school of psychoanalysis of "an already existing real or true self which can be evoked into active existence almost at will. There is a tacit assumption that somehow we know the dictates of the real self, and that we should live in terms of these rather than of a romanticized self-image or of the pseudo-self of others' expectations."

If I stress conceptualization—in this case of sex role—too much for the clinician, it is because I consider it to be of key significance for diagnosis, treatment, and, hopefully, cure. For, whether problems are considered as individual or sociological, as time-bound or universal, as amenable to treatment or not, will determine the remedies proposed (Chapter 10). And conceptualization determines the standards used to judge the nature and extent of an emotional illness. Symptoms are not self-evident but depend on systems of meaning to become intelligible. Thus two unmarried women coming for treatment, one from a milieu which takes marriage as the only desirable goal for women and one from a milieu in which this is not the case, will have to be diagnosed differently. Diagnosis is a function of the standards (all too rarely made explicit) of normality or conventionality used to evaluate presenting symptoms. Thus the yardsticks used to appraise mental health and illness are of critical importance.

In sum, the papers by and large dichotomize sex roles at a very general and abstract plane which results in highly undifferentiated conceptualizations of women. Some of the authors, notably Menaker and Fabrikant, struggle to formulate more subtle and diversified notions of role but lack the conceptual model to do so. Hence I thought it useful to sketch out a possible model of the female role and some key components usually overlooked in popular discussions as well as in much of the research literature.

The status of women is under review in many parts of the world today. Discussions about true or spurious femininity, women's duties, women's natural proclivities, their lesser sexuality, their greater sexuality, are topics that apparently command endless interest. The growing preoccupation with this question—not only among women—suggests that the traditional answers no longer ring true to a growing number of contemporary citizens.

In 1970, Benjamin Spock, a widely influential American pediatrician, saw fit to recant some of his earlier pronouncements about women by admitting that they had been less factual and more prejudiced than he had realized. His current change of heart led him to find some "of these opinions . . . embarrassing . . . to acknowledge now." "It is obvious," he confessed in belated candor, "that I, like most men and women up to a couple of years ago, harbored an underlying sexism [prejudice in favor of the dominant sex] in some matters" (Spock, 1971). This included such widespread beliefs as that "women will always play the major role in childcare," or that the mother rather than the father must give up whatever career time is necessary for the care of small children, or that the husband's work must always come first. Still going along with the conventional wisdom, Spock also warned mothers about playing a dominant role in their households. "I was right," he later reflected, "in speaking of the unhealthy effects of domineering mothers and submissive fathers, but I forgot to mention the unhealthiness of the opposite." In his current view, that is, excessive dominance and submissiveness are seen as unhealthy for both sexes.

This suggests that, as traditional assumptions about the female role are being critically reexamined, so are certain traditional beliefs about the biological determinants of sex roles.

As the evidence accumulates, it becomes clear that the biology of gender is a pretext for wide variations in cultural response, and not even that indisputable constant, the female monopoly on pregnancy and childbirth, can escape the imprint of culture and social structure. This reluctantly accepted truth precludes our predicting the personal and social traits of men and women from the sheer fact of their biological differentiation. Even in our own time we note remarkable variations in the traits attributed to women in different societies, as some cultures attribute to them what others firmly deny.

Hence one cannot generalize about women across cultures or subcultures and all such generalizations are highly selective and distort the multifaceted reality. In this discussion of the female role, therefore, I will try to confine myself to industrialized societies, especially to the contemporary United States. I will begin by sketching out the core elements of the female role and then consider the variations and departures from it.

Some Definitions

There is considerable confusion in existing discussions due to the absence of common definitions. At times, different terms refer to the same phenomenon or, conversely, the same terms are used to denote different things. To facilitate matters, I will use the following working definitions in this paper.

Following Robert Stoller, let us use gender and sex role as follows (Stoller, 1968):

Gender refers to the psychological connotations of maleness or femaleness which result in masculinity tnd femininity.

Gender identity refers to the awareness of belonging to one of the two sexes, an awareness which becomes quite complex in time. From the simple dichotomy at age two of "I am male or female," one proceeds to various qualifications such as "I am strongly or weakly feminine or masculine," or, "I like or dislike being a boy, a girl"; or "I'm not really a boy or girl, I'm only pretending." According to Stoller and others of the Johns Hopkins Group that did pioneering research on transsexualism, a core gender identity (the conviction that I am female and not male and vice versa) is established somewhere around ages two to three.

Gender role refers to the overt behavior one displays to others to indicate one's gender to them. Since others validate one's self-perception, their reactions are an important source of gender validation. If they are not reinforcing, one's gender identity may be confused or shifting.

Finally, there is *sex role*, often erroneously used to denote gender role whereas it serves as a standard for these. Sex roles are the parts society reserves for each gender. These standards will serve as guides to individuals and groups as to what is ideally desirable, not what is actually possible. If we wish to understand why Frenchmen behave differently from American men, though both are biologically male, we need to look at the standards or social expectations governing masculinity in their respective societies. At the same time, however, these general guides are no more than a rough outline of how individual men in each society will behave and react. For these will translate the cultural script to suit particular subcultural and individual circumstances.

Hence the terms masculine and feminine have a number of different connotations:

a) male and female as sexually different;
b) male and female as reproductively different;
c) masculine and feminine as subjective identity;
d) masculine and feminine as social identity or role.

Core Elements of the Female Role

In discussing contemporary problems experienced by men and women, it is not unusual to refer to sex roles as an explanatory concept for their behavior. So we are told that the differential socialization of boys and girls stems from the different role expectations entertained by parents or that the feminine self-image is shaped by contradictory role demands. However, despite these references, the concept of sex role itself is left rather vague and poorly defined, and the use of the general label obscures ignorance about significant components of gender-related expectations in different groups and settings. Hence we need a more subtle and diversified image of the female role, whose core and variable elements will now be discussed.

The core aspects of the female role in the United States currently— as gleaned from the ideals held out to women in the society at large— include the following:

1) a concentration on marriage, home, and children as the primary focus of feminine concern.
2) a reliance on a male provider for sustenance and status. This important component of the wife role is symbolized by the woman taking her husband's name and sharing her husband's income.
3) an expectation that women will emphasize nurturance and life-preserving activities, both literally as in the creation of life and symbolically, in taking care of, healing, and ministering to the helpless, the unfortunate, the ill. Preeminent qualities of character stressed for women include sympathy, care, love, and compassion, seemingly best realized in the roles of mother, teacher, and nurse.

4) an injunction that women live through and for others rather than for the self. Ideally, a woman is enjoined to lead a vicarious existence—feeling pride or dismay about her husband's achievements and failures or about her children's competitive standing.
5) a stress on beauty, personal adornment, and eroticism, which, though a general feature of the female role, is most marked for the glamour girl.
6) a ban on the expression of direct assertion, aggression, and power strivings except in areas clearly marked woman's domain—as in the defense of hearth and home. There is a similar ban on women taking the direct (but not indirect) sexual initiative.

In the three themes stressed for the female role—maternal, wifely, and erotic—primary emphasis is supposed to be given to the maternal and wifely aspects, though at certain stages of the life cycle, the erotic component may be preeminent. However, this exclusive preoccupation with maternity and wifedom is not as old as we like to pretend. As Viola Klein (1971) has repeatedly reminded us, we are victims of two serious shortcomings in reconstructing history: short memories and poor information. For, historically, women have played a great variety of significant economic and productive roles in addition to their reproductive ones. The chief dividing line seems to be the industrial revolution and the physical separation between home and workplace which gradually led to the familiar current division of work by gender.

The ensuing diminution of women's public roles coincided with an intensification of the private domestic sphere which exaggerated both the physical and the emotional isolation of women. Gradually, moreover, the very process which relieved the household of productive work and otherwise reduced its responsibilities in religion, education, and recreation also deprived of its former social significance. Hardest hit by this deflation of what had previously been an essential, indeed indispensable, contribution to human welfare were women in the middle classes who experienced these shifts and contradictions most keenly. Overeducated for domesticity yet insufficiently educated for rewarding work in the higher occupational ranks, this led to the characteristic "woman problem" among them.

Klein considers this an illustration of a cultural lag as women continue to be tied down to the household and family whereas men are already caught up in non-family institutions. Hence men are likely to feel a tug of war between family and job concerns, or between job-related travel and the domestically-based household, which women do not as yet experience. On the other hand, women are confronted by role conflict engendered by the contraction of previous responsibilities and their isolation from significant portions of public experience and participation. Nonetheless the domestic ideal persists as a cultural ideal, albeit one often bypassed or altered by structured departures from the *female core role*.

Variants of the Female Role

The female core role thus has two basic aspects—an economic-work aspect and an erotic-procreative one. Of the two major departures or variants, one challenges women's economic dependency, the other their sexual dependency on men. The self-supporting divorcée or the aspiring career girl are instances of the first category. The courtesan or prostitute are examples of the second. These modifications lead, in time, to the emergence of various hybrid or social types that combine the overarching feminine ideal with particular personal and social necessities. The working wife, the part-time mother and the successful professional woman are typical examples of how the female role may be alternatively structured.

In the following summary of sociological variants of the female role in American society we see that even in a single society one may talk of woman's role but not thereby be able to generalize to all women. The wife of the affluent executive and the wife of a modestly paid worker, for example, experience the feminine role in very different ways even though they might share certain general objectives regarding home and family life.

Affluent wives. The first example comprises women married to men in the top economic ranks, specifically, men earning at least $100,000 per year. A study of 400 such women (Wyse, 1970) showed that they can reject the more onerous routines of domesticity in favor of esthetic preoccupations. Home is not primarily perceived a shelter, this security being taken for granted, but a place of retreat, comfort, and a setting for self-expression and display. Indeed it is not always clear to which of several dwellings the term home applies, for three-fifths of the sample had at least two places they called home.

Not surprisingly, all of these women had hired help for the heavier household tasks and their domestic pursuits centered on entertaining and creating an attractive setting for themselves and their children. They are thus far less domestic than the suburban housewife but probably more so than their affluence requires.

Life consists of travel, home entertaining, charity work, and such hobbies as reading, sports, and artistic endeavors. The division of work by sex turns out to be fairly extensive in some respects and slight in others. The most striking sex differentiation concerns remunerative employment outside of the home, with the husbands clearly being worker-providers and the wives, consumer-spenders. In this sense the division of labor parallels that prevalent in the society at large but at a more affluent scale. As for the devision of labor within the home, here we find much less sex-typing and the sexes clearly socialize together.

How ready would these women be to earn their own living? Not very, judging from the fact that only ten per cent are engaged in any kind of paid employment now, although four-fifths of them had had training as teachers, nurses, and secretaries, in that order. Only one-sixth, in fact, looked favorably upon the idea of a career for themselves. Part of their reluctance is probably due to the fact that their husbands support them in such grand style. Nearly half pay their bills and debts outright and three-tenths give them an allowance with which to do so on their own. Two-thirds own wealth jointly with their husbands, and one-third have their own stocks, bonds, houses, and boats. All in all these women felt happy with their way of life and expressed no major complaints about the roles assigned them.

Workingmen's wives. By contrast, consider working class women whose worlds are bounded by family and local neighborhood and increasingly by poorly paid jobs taken out of necessity rather than desire. Whether or not they hold jobs, they must generally do all of the housework including cooking, washing, cleaning, and mending. Material survival and bringing up their children are their major preoccupations and interests. Giving top priority to the wife-mother role, they judge men by their ability to fulfill their roles as family providers. Unlike middle class wives, however, they are far less wrapped up in their husbands' jobs or their children's inner lives as long as both live up to expectations. Also, in contrast to the more affluent, home is a symbol of security and shelter, and is reserved for entertaining one's own family. There is sharp sex-typing of work and of interests, resulting in considerable role segregation between men and women.

The really interesting question is how much do these two types of women have in common? Is the biology of gender a common bond? Is their formal rank *vis-à-vis* men a common bond? Or does social class constitute a permanent wedge to any potential unity between them, therefore precluding our classifying them under a single category called women?

One shared attribute concerns consumer power. Both types of women are likely to be the spenders of the money earned by their men. Working class women, in particular, have the power of the purse and more so than middle class wives set the general pattern of family life (Komarovsky, 1964, Rainwater, 1959, Shostak, 1969). Still, despite pervasive differences in life-styles and resources by social class, one feels that the middle class ideal, extolling domesticity and maternity, exerts a strong influence on both groups of women.

A contrasting pattern exists in more rigid class systems where one often finds several cultural images, each salient for a particular class, competing for national allegiance. In Greece, for example, according to an analysis of a series of films examined by Safilios-Rothschild, we find a clear-cut distinction between two prominent feminine prototypes. One is the "good" girl—shy, sexually inexperienced, nurturant, and faithful—who is also poor and without social and family connections. Her antithesis is the emancipated, independent, and self-directing "bad" girl, who does not subscribe to the sexual double standard and who initiates and terminates her love affairs at will, expecting men to adjust to her pattern of life. Rich girls are able to pick and choose, there being "a distinct relationship between the amount of wealth and social status a girl possesses and the degree of social and sexual freedom to which she may be entitled (Safilios-Rothschild, 1968).

The rich-bad girl is very attractive to Greek men despite the fact that they are warned about her ruthlessness and her tendency to "exploit and use them as playthings" (Safilios-Rothschild, 1968). For a poor man without money or connections she is a desirable marital prospect. The poor-good girl, on the other hand, is expected to subordinate herself totally to the man's needs and interests, reassuring him by her selfless and quasi-maternal devotion. Each of these images of femininity monopolizes powerful themes in Greek life—limitless love and acceptance versus fortune and success. In recent movies, notes Safilios-Rothschild, there seems to be a fusion of previously antithetical images as class patterns converge in response to the spread of the modern ethos.

Ethnic subcultures likewise constitute points of departure from the idealized feminine prototype. In America's Black community, for example, women seem to give much greater emphasis to autonomy than is true in other subcommunities. "The strongest conception of womanhood . . . among all preadult females is that of how the woman has to take a strong role in the family" (Ladner, 1971). The symbol of the "resourceful woman" is very influential in their lives, as is the stress on self-support and hard work. Women's key duties include the conventional ones of keeping a home and caring for children, but also, if necessary, that of financially supporting a family.

The procreative powers of women are greatly and positively emphasized in this subculture and the main line of gender demarcation is not work but the female power to bear children. Along with this there is a strong accent on the erotic components of femininity—beauty, self-adornment, and sexual freedom. Thus the Black feminine ideal—to be strong, responsible, autonomous, maternal, and sensual—rewards qualities quite antithetical to the white middle class ideal.

It is evident that the three subcultural variants depart in significant ways from the cultural stereotypes of femininity. A lot seems to hinge on whether or not male providers are willing and able to assume the responsibilities of economic support. If not, women are compelled to leave their domestic havens for paid employment, thereby introducing major role modifications. And here we note an interesting division between occupations considered appropriate or inappropriate for women. Appropriate ones seem to tap some of the same qualities that adhere to the conventional image of femininity, as expressed in teaching, nursing, or the theater. Inappropriate are all the fields tagged "masculine." The distinction between the two is clearly cultural, not motivational. Dancers, singers, and entertainers, for example, are considered feminine despite their often conspicuous success and affluence gained via fierce competitiveness and ambition, whereas business and professional women are stigmatized for venturing into "masculine" territory.

The career-woman seems to be a particularly unappealing model in industrial societies, mainly it would seem because she challenges the cultural formula for the sex-typing of work and rank. Recently, of course, new avenues have opened up in previously closed spheres and the career girl as distinct from the less flattering career woman has emerged as a more acceptable type. Though women are by now engaged in virtually every occupational category, few of them manage to get into the leading ranks. Those that do form yet another social type as members of a somewhat exclusive club of queen-beedom in which they appear to have the best of both worlds. "I masquerade in vain as an old bachelor," wrote the incomparable Colette who was one of that rare hybrid, "it is still a very feminine pleasure that I enjoy in being the only woman at the Goncourt lunches, surrounded by an Areopagus of men. Five, six, eight, nine men —real men—and age has nothing to do with it—the faults and seductiveness of men . . ." (Crossland, 1953).

Erotic Variants of Femininity

There are two erotic variants from the cultural ideals of femininity. One involves the rejection of sexual fidelity as by the courtesans and the

Carmens of lore, the other, the rejection of heterosexuality as in lesbianism. Courtesans continue to be dependent on men but not on one man, whereas lesbians banish both economic and sexual dependency on men. And whereas courtesans are on the wrong side of conventional morality, lesbians are considered deviant and treated as outcasts because they challenge not only the bounds of sexual propriety but the fundamentals of the sex code. Moreover, unlike the Nun who has long existed alongside the wife-mother image as a perfectly acceptable alternative, even though she has explicitly rejected sexuality, marriage, and children, the lesbian eschews such sexual self-denial and is condemned for it.

In one sense, the courtesan is not radically at odds with the standard feminine role and its emphasis on sex appeal and erotic allure. Courtesans and other mercenaries simply carry these further and make them financially lucrative. When Gypsy Rose Lee, for example, famed artist of public undress, was only seventeen, she was earning $1000 per week while hard-working family men earned barely $5000 per year. Lesser lights naturally fare less well but still far better than women employed in "respectable" jobs.

The erotic image of woman exerts a powerful appeal from early adolescence onwards. Coleman's study of high school cliques confirmed its saliency for both sexes, leading him to wonder how girls would ever manage to reconcile this socially rewarded narcissism and self-absorption, centering on looks and sex appeal, with their later domestic destinies. (Coleman, in Farber, 1966).

But it is especially in films, that storehouse for collective erotic fantasies, that the non-domestic and non-maternal image, as the Vamp, the femme fatale, and sex symbols à la Harlow and Monroe, reigns supreme. One must wonder what they have in common with Mrs. Main Street since she flocks to see them. Surely they are tapping a fantasy image of love and glamour not easily accommodated to housebound femininity.

But just as domesticated women thrive on fantasies of eros and glamour, so women in the aforementioned nocturnal occupations are not entirely free from twinges of conventional morality. Thus strippers, prostitutes, and celebrated stars on their umpteenth marital round have been known to protest that they are just like other women and all they seek is a good man and a nest of their own.

In this brief look at variations from the contemporary female core role we note several historic themes at work. As Myrdal and Klein have observed, there are really only three main heroines in Western history: the devoted housewife-mother, the aristocratic lady of leisure, and the professional careerist (Myrdal and Klein, 1956). But whereas the housewife-mother is to devote herself to the care of children, mate, and home, the lady of leisure, exempt from menial labor, is to be pampered and indulged by obliging males. Of the three ideal types, the wife-mother is most acceptable and the careerist least desirable, while the lady of leisure enjoys perhaps the greatest appeal. As a model of luxury, beauty, and pleasure she appeals to all women who dream of being the *lady of* rather than the *servant in* their castles.

This overview also suggests that most women will be able to modify some aspects of the conventional role to suit themselves provided they abide by its two principle tenets: economic dependency on men and a heterosexual orientation. Within these limits there is some room for maneuver and escape.

Hence the female role in its general and abstract version provides a guide for expected behavior rather than a description of actual behavior. It serves as a reference point which remains at best only approximately realized. The coherence of the role construct is not likely to be matched in real life. It is a convenient fiction, a necessary myth. Thus when Arnold Bennett was asked "how he drew women so well he said he wrote the stories first and chose up the sexes afterward . . ." (Sheed, 1971).

Power of the Female Role

One point of considerable controversy regarding the female role concerns its potential for the exercise of power. For some the dependency built into the role is proof of a lack of power while for others the capacity to demand support and sustenance proves just the opposite.

Each stand has evidence in its favor. Those who see women as powerless cite their economic dependency on men, their legal subordination, their more limited opportunities for earning and learning, and their formal powerlessness. Those who see them as powerful cite various rights—to vote, to inherit property, to work divorce laws in their favor, and to obtain economic support for themselves and their children. In addition to such formal rights there are also various kinds of deference and protection, access to wealth and status without self-exertion, emotional power in the family, and erotic power over men. Not to be ignored is the well-known phenomenon of ambitious women acting as powers behind the throne, propelling men to elaborate undertakings and often reducing them to mere figureheads for their own power strivings. These indirect forms of power are often neglected or dismissed as insignificant, a neglect which may seriously distort the assessment of power by gender.

Before taking sides on the issue, it is necessary first to clarify the meaning and forms of power we are willing to acknowledge. Power may be divided into several kinds. There is institutional and personal power, for example, the first referring to the capacity to mobilize and direct social forces towards collective ends, the second devoted to dominating one's personal environment. Institutional power is vested in formal social positions in the economy, the polity, and the military sectors among others, whereas personal power is not attached to formal positions but to personal qualities. The two may interpenetrate but they do so imperfectly and unpredictably. Women who rarely possess formal institutional power in modern societies may nonetheless command a great deal of personal power.

Another distinction to keep in mind concerns the reach and scope of power. Power may be awesome in terms of the resources at its command and yet not be able to touch the inner lives of individuals, whereas it may be virtually invisible and yet work its way into the deepest levels of consciousness. Here, too, the sexes divide in predictable ways in the contemporary world: some men possess enormous institutional power that affects the fate of millions of individuals but lack the power to penetrate to the core of the self, a power that women command by virtue of their emotional centrality in the family and in the sphere of erotic intimacy.

Family power. Both as wives and mothers, women may derive a sense of power from organizing households, dominating kinship networks, disposing of family budgets, making demands on husbands, and supervising their children's lives. Of course family and wife power depend first of all on being married and having offspring and secondly on the significance of the family in the life of society. As this significance declines, the power that rests upon it does likewise, which may be one source of the current dissatisfaction with the traditional female role. However, it is the role of mother which offers women the most extensive opportunities for the exercise of direct and overt power. In their impact on their children, mothers can and have shaped history. It is interesting that Freud and Jung, two pioneers of psychoanalysis, divide sharply on where they consider the center of family power to reside. For Freud it was clearly the father and for Jung just as clearly the mother. The mother archetype is an image "sung and praised in all tongues." The memory of mother love "is among the most touching and most unforgettable memories of the adult human being: it is the secret root of all birth and of all transformation; it means for us the homecoming, and is the silent primordial source of every beginning and every end. Mother is mother-love; it is my experience and my secret" (Jacobi, 1958).

Many writers take the dependency and formal subordination of women rather too literally. They thereby miss the possibilities for women's exercise of power behind the facade of male supremacy. Thus alongside the meek and submissive wife must be placed the family despot and henpecked husband. In this light, Italy has been described as a "cryptomatriarchy" by one of its most astute observers, where men may be conspicuous but women are predominant (Barzini, 1964). And a study of American popular literature of the nineteenth century showed that the best-selling domestic novels of the day dealt frankly with the doctrine of complete female domestic domination (Peck, 1971). The plots of these novels, as indeed the lives of their authors, centered on the shared myth of the competent and resourceful heroine and the weak, sick, immoral, or missing male. In the ensuing struggle for power, the morally superior female always triumphs. "In all of these books a mature sexual relationship between a man and a woman is never really the goal or the ideal. The surface is sentiment and piety, but the subject is always power" (Peck, 1971).

Erotic Power. Quite a different form of power available to women is erotic power or the power to arouse, withhold, or gratify sexual desire and emotional longings in men. If women are made to depend on men economically and legally in patriarchal and quasi-patriarchal societies, men are made to depend on women erotically.

In most discussions of the woman question, the erotic power of women does not receive the emphasis it deserves. It is either ignored entirely or seen solely from the perspective of men's exploitation of erotic favors. This bias underestimates the equivalent exploitation of men by women. Today as throughout the patriarchal era, Eros is woman, a fact lost neither on the women who make use of it nor on the men in awe of it.

One supreme contemporary example of this kind of personal, magnetic feminine power concerns the impact of Um Khaltoum, the world famous siren of the Middle East, whose name is known to more Arabs than anyone else's. Now in her sixties, she holds her voluntary subjects enthralled by her monthly Thursday evening performance in Cairo, when public life virtually comes to a standstill. It is said that high government officials and politicians seek her advice or at least her blessings for important undertakings. "Miss Khaltoum is more popular than Nasser and Farouk together . . . No Egyptian leader could survive if she made it known that she was against him" (Tanner, 1967).

In sum, the female role does not, as is often claimed, preclude the exercise of power but its form tends to be personal, indirect, and emotionally highly penetrative. If one confines the term power only to its formal and institutional aspects, one will either ignore or underestimate other kinds without, however, diminishing their considerable importance. Which form of power one considers most impressive largely depends on one's convictions and values and perhaps opportunities for exercising one or another form. At this time I do not believe it possible to choose among different forms of power on objective grounds, though men seem to pay more attention to that reserved for their gender. There are limits to every form of power and there are special rewards associated with each. Indeed if one covets a feeling of being powerful in the lives of known individuals, personal power would seem to be both more immediate and more compelling. Hence the female role has its own special possibilities for domination. And while one can agree with John Stuart Mills in his speech to the House of Commons in 1867: "Sir, it is true that women have great power. It is part of my case that they have great power; but they have it under the worst possible conditions, because it is indirect and therefore irresponsible" (Beasley, 1968, p. 158), one should nevertheless give it its just due.

Increasingly, women are growing restive with their traditional roles and thus presumably with the power regarding family, children, and community based upon them. As a consequence of their growing contacts with the wider world of employment and enterprise, their ambitions are kindled for the exercise of institutional forms of power. This is particularly true for women in milieus where men are primed to management and leadership.

Indeed, the traditional female role appears to be less satisfactory and appealing to women who have more rather than less of the good things of life, particularly if they have either special talents or great aspirations for worldly success. Thus it is the educated, talented, middle and upper class women who are most impatient with the limits society imposes on female accomplishments. Bred in milieus where ambition, initiative, and success are most encouraged and admired, they are, by contrast with their brothers and male friends, prohibited from their realization. Thus, while absolutely better off than lower class women, they are, relative to men and to the values internalized as members of their class, worse off. This makes the conventional female role less gratifying and its rejection, in whole or in part, more tempting.

For the lower classes quite the opposite would seem to hold true. Here the men suffer both absolute deprivation in earnings and status and relative deprivation by comparison with more successful men and cultural ideals of successful masculinity. By comparison, women's work, hard though it be, centered on making a home and raising children, may seem more life-affirming and rewarding.

Self-Esteem and the Female Role

No matter what private advantage may be derived from a judicious manipulation of feminine opportunities in a culture overtly androcentric, the prevalent cultural favoritism is bound to undermine self confidence and self-esteem in women. This is not to say that most men will have self-esteem in such a culture but only that their roles provide them with a pretext for it.

In contemporary societies, despite changing priorities, most women cannot avoid realizing that they not only have a different destiny from that of men but in certain important respects a lesser one. This lesson is not always crystal clear but it is probably unavoidable in societies that seek not so much to demean women as to exalt, shore up, and elevate men.

Women come to terms with this message in a number of ways. For a few, this cultural slight is a spur to extraordinary efforts designed to prove their worthiness by conspicuous achievements. But most women, as indeed most men, will prune their ambitions to their opportunities. This leads to the familiar denial of self, of ambitions nipped in the bud, of projects abandoned, or of steps not taken. Initially the inhibition comes from a parents, teacher, or other social authority, but later one's inner arbiter takes over and what was once second nature now becomes primary impulse to self-effacement. Few find it possible to suppress ambitions at age three only to reverse this attitude at age twenty.

The conditions for low self-esteem among women are difficult to assess. In order to discover its prevalence, one needs to know how the cultural message is perceived and interpreted by particular women, and the saliency of family, love, or career in their lives.

Keeping in mind the difficulties of assessing role satisfaction and self-esteem, it is not too surprising that existing studies exhibit quite contradictory findings. One oft cited study, by Rosencrantz and his co-workers, showed that both sexes assigned less valued traits to the female than to the male role. However, these were female college students who, in light of the theory of relative deprivation referred to earlier, should react most acutely to the limitations and restrictions placed in their path. (Rosencrantz, 1968). Moreover, in this and other studies, it is not always clear whether the respondents are assessing sex roles cognitively or emotionally. Though they may know that the culture assigns a lower or more ambiguous value to the female role, they may still not value it less personally.

A more comprehensive, large-scale study of high school students, for example, found no less self-esteem among girls than among boys (Rosenberg, 1965). Indeed social class turned out to be far more important for self-esteem than sex. Moreover, both boys and girls had almost identical responses as to who had been their parents' favorite child, most naming a younger sibling of the opposite sex as their fathers' and mothers' favorite child.

Social class affected the pattern of self-esteem by sex, with upper class boys having somewhat higher self-esteem than upper class girls, with lower class girls reversing this pattern by exhibiting higher self-esteem than lower class boys.

These and other data, sporadic and incomplete though they be, suggest that women may find fault with various aspects of their roles without, however, rejecting the role itself. Femininity, though hard to define, is generally perceived as something positive and desirable (Hartley, in Seward and Williamson, 1970). It apears to involve early commitment to activities and symbols defined as feminine—beauty, grace, style, love— qualities perceived as intrinsically gratifying.

In fact, it has been shown that women are the key reference group for women and men alike. Using figure drawing tests, McAdoo found that both boys and girls drew women rather than men when asked to draw a figure, and 5th grade boys were twice as likely to draw a person of the opposite sex than were girls (McAdoo, 1971). The difference was that boys drew essentially maternal types of women, whereas girls drew glamour girls. And a study of face-saving behavior showed that, contrary to the investigator's expectations, women turned out to have a particular need to save face before a female rather than before a male audience, expecting the former to be more critical (Brown, 1971). If this is confirmed, it may help account for the so-called preference for male over female bosses, not because women do not admire other women but because they fear they will be more demanding.

Costs and Benefits of the Female Role

At this writing the liabilities of the female role are being highlighted, perhaps to make up for the long period in which its presumed benefits had been overemphasized. Since both costs and benefits are discernible, however, it might be useful to draw up a balance sheet comparing them.

Benefits. As will be evident, the advantages to be listed may be seen as disadvantages when assessed from a different perspective, which only underlines the fact that there are no absolute or objective ways to assess human values apart from the affinities and desires of the assessing person. What such a list can do, however, is to stimulate discussion and public debate. Among the benefits I have selected are:

1) Economic security—which does not necessarily mean economic well-being but rather the absence of pressures to assume onerous responsibilities and risk difficult economic decisions. Until recently, women who held jobs to help support households that lacked adequate male providers resembled men who "help" with the housework. Their efforts were commendable but not obligatory. I believe that this aspect of the female role and its converse, pressures on men to assume heavy economic obligations for their families, have not received adequate attention.

2) Emotional security: Women are permitted a wider range of emotional expression than are men and their roles accentuate the giving and receiving of love and affection—towards parents, mates, and children. Hence the sphere of intimacy is more accessible to them and they have more outlets for anxieties and tensions.

3) The cult of beauty: This, as indeed most everything, can be overdone, of course, but the accent on appearance and style may be a creative experience in a number of ways. Beauty and attractiveness arouse favorable responses in others and are thus intrinsically gratifying. Moveover, the stress on being beautiful and desirable permits, indeed encourages, women to be self-indulgent and thus promotes a socially sanctioned narcissism that feeds the ego.

4) A number of other qualities stressed for the female role, such as nurturance, warmth, and sympathy, are intrinsically pleasant both to exercise and to acquire.

5) Finally, the lack of pressure to achieve: not needing to succeed in worldly terms means that women can be more relaxed, less driven, more person-oriented, and in some ways more individualistic than men. Of course this will not be a benefit for women who do seek worldly success.

Costs of the female role. The disadvantages of the female role may be summed up as follows:

1) Lesser autonomy (by comparison with the male role): This means more restrictions and constraints on self-development which is especially difficult for independent, self-propelled, ambitious women not content with family and erotic power.

2) Ignorance and lack of training: Women acquire less formal training and know-how to cope with an increasingly technical and complicated world. As the arena of work and of public life becomes more complex

relative to the domestic household, women will find themselves increasingly at a disadvantage.

3) Categorical subordination to men: This is especially the case for the married woman for whom this subordination was in a sense designed. This affects not only the formal, legal aspects of life but one's self-conception and human relationships.

In essence it seems that the female role exchanges autonomy for security. Whether this is a good or a bad bargain depends on what sort of world one inhabits. In an age of famine, danger, and war, it may well be comforting to have someone else assume responsibility for survival. Protection from the struggle for existence in a cruel and difficult world certainly makes life easier.

These very gains, however, become obstacles and inequities for women who seek autonomy and are willing to confront the struggle for existence head-on. And even the women who welcome the protectiveness built into their role may wish to forego it if it comes to signify second class citizenship.

As women move beyond the domestic arena their dissatisfactions are likely to increase for a time because it is then that they are likely to discover the full measure of their inadequacies to cope with the world. The legal and social discrimination against women, only because they are women, may not be fully apparent to women staying close to home amidst like-minded others. Once they expand their contacts, however, they also become aware, often painfully so, of closed worlds and missed opportunitities.

Another source of contemporary dissatisfaction with the female role stems from the declining importance, hence prestige, of maternal and housekeeping duties, as a lifetime focus on maternity diminishes. This is bound to erode the sense of worth of women otherwise perfectly content with domesticity and maternity. When children were a supremely valued social resource, women felt proud about their monopoly in providing them. Today, with the advent of zero population growth the whole symbolic complex of childbirth and child-rearing is losing its central hold. Already we find it difficult to respond to Colette's memory of her pregnancy as a "long holiday of privileges and attentions."

Moreover, when motherhood was of supreme social significance, women's categorical subordination to men may well have been compensated for by their "natural" superiority. But now, as lifetime maternity is being phased out of history, women are victims of a cultural lag as well as of social inferiority.

There are, furthermore, serious discontinuities in female socialization between childhood expectations and adult realities (Hartley, 1970, p. 144 ff). One concerns their lack of preparation to earn their own living if need be or to cope with life if Prince Charming does not chance by. Expecting to find a nest with built-in male provider may set up false hopes and virtually guarantee later disappointments. The insistence, by the mass media and schools, among others, that women prefer to be safely tucked away in their suburban castles may strike some powerful sentimental chords but it is totally out of step with a reality in which some two-fifths of American women are employed full-time outside these castles.

And where women do pursue serious social or professional ambitions, they soon learn that there are quotas and exclusion devices of which they had been unaware. There is also of course the painful discovery of their lack of preparation, emotional and educational, to cope with a world geared to male patterns of achievement. In part this is linked to a discontinuity in the authority figures in women's lives and the need to replace the powerful mother of childhood with powerful males of adult life. We know all too little about how successfully they manage to do this.

There is also the discontinuity, first noticed by Freud, of erotic focus. Unlike men, women must shift their primary emotional attachment from mother to men. Men, who have serious discontinuities of their own, do not confront this particular problem since their primary caretaker and their later love-objects are both female. Some women, according to Freud, never make the transition while others only pretend to, expressing their confusion and reluctance in sexual coldness towards men or in a permanent attachment to the mothers of their childhoods.

These are among the reasons why women may be expected to suffer certain role-determined symptoms and maladjustments. Nonetheless, as was pointed out earlier, the deficiencies of the female role do not, apparently, lead to mass defections from it. Girls seem to develop positive gender identifications which give them a sense of selfhood strong and rewarding enough to withstand their later disappointments and difficulties in a remarkable way (Stoller, 1968). Also, surprisingly, in spite of male privilege, few women wish to be men. Rather they seek certain opportunities and rights as women. One psychoanalyst noted, on the basis of several decades of clinical experience, that he has never encountered a woman who would like her body to become male though he has known some who would like to add certain male features to the bodies they already possess. In other words, women may desire to be both male and female at the same time (Lederer, 1968). The various sex changes, incidentally, are, so far at least, nearly all requested by males who want to become females.

CONCLUSION

Many basic changes are under way in the areas of family, work, child-rearing, and erotic relations which will create pressures to redesign the female (as well as the male) role so as to be better suited to emerging realities. Already there is growing pressure from educated middle and upper class women for status and equality before the law, while their less educated and less skilled peers strive for more congenial conditions of employment. A labor shortage in some areas will work to the advantage of some women, while the decline of lifetime maternity will make for a large-scale exodus into new fields of interests and commitment for others. Along with occupational and economic changes, there are changes in labor laws, sex discrimination, educational opportunities, and marriage and divorce laws.

The social revolution affecting marriage, maternity, and employment cannot be ignored by those helping professionals of which psychotherapy is a part. It is clearly not realistic to perceive women in the traditional 19th century terms—themselves oversimplified and unreal—as dependent, domesticated and submissive. To still view women in this old-fashioned light attests to the power of habit and ignores the complexities introduced by the transition in which women find themselves. This raises the question of how psychotherapy, still largely guided by such traditional images of women, can help them resolve their problems.

In particular we must ask what typical problems confront women in these changing times and how different women try to cope with them. Here, too, it is important to be sensitized to women's multiple social guises. The fact that there are predictable differences by social class, educational level, age, and life style should not be irrelevant for psychotherapy. Patients from different social terrains may require quite different strategies of treatment.

In this paper I have tried to spell out the constants and variants of the female role so as to permit a more complex, and in that sense truer, grasp of the current realities affecting them. I hope that this effort to delineate a less global model of conceptions of womanhood will help those concerned with theory and practice in the healing arts.

REFERENCES

ALBERT, ETHEL M. The roles of women: Question of values. In Seymour M. Farber and Roger H. Wilson (Eds.), *The Potential of Woman*. Hightstown, N. J.: McGraw-Hill, 1963, pp. 105-115.

BART, PAULINE B. The myth of a value-free psychotherapy. In Wendell Bell and A. Mau (Eds.), *The Sociology of the Future*. New York: Russell Sage Foundation, 1972, pp. 113-159.

BARZINI, LUIGI. *The Italians*. New York: Atheneum, 1964.

BIDDLE, BRUCE J. & THOMAS, EDWIN J. (Eds). *Role Theory: Concepts and Research*. New York: Wiley, 1966.

BROWN, BERT R. Saving face. *Psychology Today*, 55-59, 86, May, 1971.

COLEMAN, JAMES S., ET AL. Leading crowds in ten Midwestern High Schools and emphasis upon personality and attractiveness. In Bernard Farber (Ed.), *Kinship and Family Organization*. New York: Wiley, 1966, pp. 378-387.

CROSLAND, MARGARET. *Madame Colette*. London: Peter Owen, 1953, p. 198.

HARTLEY, RUTH. American core culture: Changes and continuities. In G. H. Seward and R. C. Williamson (Eds.), *Sex Roles in Changing Society*. New York: Random House, 1970, pp. 126-150.

JACOBI, JOLANDE (Ed.). *Psychological Reflections*. New York: Torchbooks, 1958, p. 89.

KLEIN, VIOLA. *The Feminine Character*. Chicago: University of Illinois Press, 1971.

KOMAROVSKY, MIRRA. *Blue-collar Marriage*. New York: Random House, 1964.

LADNER, JOYCE A. *Tomorrow's Tomorrow, The Black Woman*. New York: Doubleday, 1971.

LYND, HELEN MERRELL. *On Shame and the Search for Identity*. New York: Wiley, 1958.

McADOO, B. *Self Esteem in Children's Human-Figure Drawings*. Senior Thesis, Dept. of Sociology, April, 1971.

MYRDAL, ALVA & KLEIN, VIOLA. *Women's Two Roles*. London: Routledge and Kegan Paul, 1966.

PECK, ELLEN. Review of happy endings by Helen W. Papashvily. *Central New Jersey N.O.W. Newsletter*, April, 1971, p. 12.

RAINWATER, LEE. *Working Class Wife*. Chicago: Oceana Publications, 1959.

ROSENBERG, MORRIS. *Society and the Adolescent Self-Image*. Princeton, N. J.: Princeton University Press, 1965.

ROSENKRANTZ, P. S., BEE, H., VOGEL, S. R., BROVERMAN, I. K., & BROVERMAN, D. M. Sex role stereotypes and self-concepts in college students. *Journal of Consulting and Clinical Psychology*, 32, 287-295, 1968.

SAFILIOS-ROTHSCHILD, CONSTANTINA. Good and bad girls in modern Greek movies. *The Journal of Marriage and the Family*. 1968.

SARBIN, THEODORE R. Role theory. In Gardner Lindzey (Ed.), *Handbook of Social Psychology*, Vol. I. Reading, Mass.: Addison-Wesley, 1954, p. 223.

SHEED, WILFRED. The good word: Men's women, women's men. *The New York Times Book Review*, May 2, 1971, p. 2.

SHOSTAK, ARTHUR B. *Blue-Collar Life*. New York: Random House, 1968.

SPOCK, BENJAMIN M. Male chauvinist Spock recants—Well, almost. *The New York Times Magazine*, September 12, 1971, pp. 98 ff.

STOLLER, ROBERT. *Sex and Gender*. New York: Science House, 1968.

TANNER, HENRY. An Arab singer stirs pandemonium in Paris hall. *New York Times*, November 17, 1967, p. 43.

WOLFGANG, LEDERER. *The Fear of Women*. New York: Harcourt Brace Jovanovich, 1968.

WYSE, LOIS. *Mrs. Success*. New York: World Publishing Co., 1970.

INDEX